AF754278

MISTAKES IN CONTRACT LAW

It is a matter of some difficulty for the English lawyer to predict the effect of a misapprehension upon the formation of a contract. The common law doctrine of mistake is a confused one, with contradictory theoretical underpinnings and seemingly irreconcilable cases. This book explains the common law doctrine through an examination of the historical development of the doctrine in English law. Beginning with an overview of contractual mistakes in Roman law, the book examines how theories of mistake were received at various points into English contract law from Roman and civil law sources. These transplants, made for pragmatic rather than principled reasons, combined in an uneasy manner with the pre-existing English contract law. The book also examines the substantive changes brought about in contractual mistake by the Judicature Act 1873 and the fusion of law and equity. Through its historical examination of mistake in contract law, the book provides not only insights into the nature of innovation and continuity within the common law but also the fate of legal transplants.

Mistakes in Contract Law

Catharine MacMillan

·HART·
PUBLISHING

OXFORD AND PORTLAND, OREGON
2010

Published in North America (US and Canada) by
Hart Publishing
c/o International Specialized Book Services
920 NE 58th Avenue, Suite 300
Portland, OR 97213-3786
USA
Tel: +1 503 287 3093 or toll-free: (1) 800 944 6190
Fax: +1 503 280 8832
E-mail: orders@isbs.com
Website: http://www.isbs.com

© Catharine MacMillan 2010

Catharine MacMillan has asserted her right under the Copyright, Designs and Patents Act 1988, to be identified as the author of this work.

All rights reserved. No part of this publication may be reproduced, stored in a retrieval system, or transmitted, in any form or by any means, without the prior permission of Hart Publishing, or as expressly permitted by law or under the terms agreed with the appropriate reprographic rights organisation. Enquiries concerning reproduction which may not be covered by the above should be addressed to Hart Publishing at the address below.

Hart Publishing Ltd, 16C Worcester Place, Oxford, OX1 2JW
Telephone: +44 (0)1865 517530 Fax: +44 (0)1865 510710
E-mail: mail@hartpub.co.uk
Website: http://www.hartpub.co.uk

British Library Cataloguing in Publication Data
Data Available

ISBN: 978-1-84113-507-6

Typeset by Hope Services, Abingdon
Printed and bound in Great Britain by
CPI Antony Rowe Ltd, Chippenham, Wiltshire

Dedicated to my mother, Mavis,
and in memory of my father, Ian

PREFACE

This book is a biography of an idea. It addresses the question of how English contract law came to contain the doctrine of mistake that it does. This is a matter of not only antiquarian interest but also current concern. I hope that I have addressed the question in such a way as to not only provide some insight into the development of the modern law of contract but also to provide a basis upon which others can undertake a reform of the law in this area.

How to explain mistakes in contract law? I have argued that the English doctrine of contractual mistake is itself a mistake. The doctrine arose as a result of the efforts of the scientific treatise writers of the late-nineteenth century who borrowed civilian inspired forms of mistake. They blended these theories of mistake with those cases in which courts of equity had provided relief where a mistake had occurred. As the common law slowly moved towards an unwitting acceptance of sorts of the theories of mistake proposed by the treatise writers, little concern was given as to how this new doctrine would fit within the existing structure of the common law of contract. Further mistakes were made at this point in the formation of the law. When mistake was given recognition by the House of Lords in *Bell v Lever Brothers*, it was thought of as forms of mistake which either negatived or nullified consent. The area has been one which has presented conceptual and practical problems ever since; yet another mistake. For all of these reasons, the doctrine of contractual mistake is best thought of as a series of 'mistakes in contract law'.

I have incurred many debts of gratitude in preparing this work and I am delighted to be able to thank the people and institutions who have helped me. I first discussed how best to approach the problem of mistake in contract law with my friend, the late John Yelland. His comments and insights led me to think of a project with an historical approach; I think he would have found the final result interesting. Many other colleagues gave me helpful comments and support at various points in the preparation of this work: Victor Tunkel, Stephen Waddams, Ian Yeats, Margot Horspool and Wayne Morrison. JoAnne Sweeny has helped me to tidy up certain of the chapters. Jo Murkens provided me not only with invaluable translations into English of various parts of Savigny's *System of Modern Roman Law* but also with his insights into Savigny's scholarship. Andrew Lewis kindly read a draft chapter on Roman law and gently corrected more than one error. I am particularly grateful to Michael Lobban who has not only listened to more than one tentative hypothesis but has also read several draft chapters and commented thoroughly upon them. My tutorial students have rendered invaluable assistance in commenting on various arguments. I have also benefitted from the comments given by audience members following the presentation of mistake papers at the

Current Legal Issues Session (University College London, 2002), the Society of Legal Scholars Conference (Oxford, 2003), the Second Biennial Conference on the Law of Obligations (Melbourne, 2004), and the Institute for Advanced Legal Studies (London, 2007). All remaining mistakes in this work are my responsibility alone.

A number of institutions and libraries have greatly assisted me with searches. I would like to thank Unilever for allowing me access to their historical archives and for the assistance of their staff, the staff at the Parliamentary Archives for their help and also the staff at the Beckenham Public Library and the archives at Kingston upon Thames. I am particularly grateful to the librarians at the Institute for Advanced Legal Studies library for their help and their unfailing assistance in retrieving volume after volume for me.

Last, but by no means least, I must thank my family for their patience, understanding and encouragement as this work was prepared. My family has, so to speak, had to live with the mistakes of others for some time. My initial suspicion that this research had formed a part of family life when my daughter Margaret wrote a school assignment on the topic 'what I did on my holidays' by explaining that she had spent them looking for Mr Bell was confirmed when my son Henry, having been asked to prepare a project on his local neighbourhood, explained (having spent a week in Beckenham researching war damage) where the bombs had landed in our neighbourhood during the war and the ensuing shortage of housing.

I dedicate this book to my mother and in memory of my father. Without their optimism and support none of this would have been possible.

Catharine MacMillan
London
December 2009

CONTENTS

TABLE OF CASES

TABLE OF STATUTES

1

Introduction

THIS BOOK TRACES the history of a legal idea from Rome to mid-twentieth-century England. Situated within English contract law, the idea is that when one or more parties agree to assume obligations under a misapprehension of fact their agreement is not one which the law recognises as a legally binding contract. This book attempts to address how, and why, the English common law has a doctrine of contractual mistake. While this is intended as a legal history, it informs our understanding of the modern doctrine of mistake. The work suggests that the doctrine as currently understood is dangerously unreliable.

This contractual doctrine has been chosen as the subject of this book for a number of reasons. The first is that contractual mistake is a confusing and problematic area in England and many of the common law countries which adopted the English doctrine. It is hoped that a history of this doctrine will explain the confusion surrounding its modern formation. The second is that mistake is said to be a late entrant into the common law from the theories and practices of civilian legal systems. A history of mistake, therefore, informs us of the reception and transplantation of foreign ideas into the common law.[1] Such information is important in the twenty-first century, as Europeans began to think of a common European contract law. The third reason is that mistake is said to arise in the English common law in the nineteenth century, a period of intense procedural transformation. This work examines how procedural changes combined to create an impact upon the substantive law. The fourth reason is that because mistake is said to occur both at common law and in equity, an examination of this doctrine sheds light on the process by which law and equity were 'fused' by the Judicature Act 1873. The fifth reason is that a history of the doctrine illuminates the process by which the common law develops.

[1] The literature on transplants is large. The discussion was initiated by Alan Watson, and his major arguments can be found in: *Legal Transplants: An Approach to Comparative Law*, 2nd edn (Athens, University of Georgia Press, 1993); 'Legal Transplants and Law Reform' (1976) LQR 79; 'Aspects of Reception of Law' (1996) 44 *American Journal of Comparative Law* (Am J Comp Law) 335; 'Law Out of Context' (2000) *Edinburgh Law Review* 147; and 'Legal Transplants and European Private Law', *Ius Commune Lectures on European Private Law* 2. Watson's work has been analysed by W Ewald, 'Comparative Jurisprudence (II): The Logic of Legal Transplants' (1995) 43 Am J Comp Law 489, and R Cotterrell, 'Is There a Logic of Legal Transplants?' in D Nelken and J Feest (eds), *Adapting Legal Cultures*, (Oxford, Hart, 2001). Watson's work has been criticised by Pierre Legrand in 'The Impossibility of Legal Transplants' (1997) 4 *Maastricht Journal of European and Comparative Law* 111. Also relevant is G Teubner, 'Legal Irritants: Good Faith in British Law or How Unifying Law Ends up in New Divergences' (1998) 61 *Modern Law Review* 11.

The thesis of this book can be stated briefly. It is argued that the form of the common law doctrine of mistake is itself largely a mistake. While formulations of the doctrine of mistake differ, they generally cover similar ground. A mistake of fact[2] as to a sufficiently fundamental matter will render a contract void or possibly voidable[3] if the mistake is of both parties, although in some instances the mistake of one party alone is sufficient. Some elaboration of this statement is needed. A 'sufficiently fundamental matter' is generally conceived of as consisting of a series of categories of instances of mistake: a mistake as to the identity of the other party; a mistake as to the existence of the subject matter of the contract; or a mistake as to a quality of the subject matter of the contract. Some formulations of classes can include a general class of mistake where the mistake is of some type which either removes entirely the benefit intended to be transferred in that it goes to the very root of the contract or renders performance of the contract as intended impossible. To so operate, it is said that the mistake must usually be bilateral. As a bilateral mistake, it must be common to both the parties, although in some instances where each party labours under a separate mistake it may be that this combination of different mistakes prevents a contract from arising. English contract law is reluctant to intervene in instances where only one party is mistaken, although it will do so in two circumstances. The first arises where one party is aware of the mistake of another and seeks to take advantage of this mistake in instances in which the mistake is sufficiently important to the contractual promise. The second arises where one party is mistaken as to the identity of the other party to the contract. It is important in all of these variations of mistake, except mistake of identity, that the misapprehension arise independently of the parties. Where one party induces the mistake of another, this is generally regarded as some species of misrepresentation and resolved through the application of other principles in which the focus is not the misapprehension but the fault of the party who induced it. Where a court of common law recognises a mistake as fitting within these strictures it regards the mistake as 'operative' and declares that the apparent contract is void *ab initio*. The harshness of this result, which works against both sanctity of contract and the reasonable expectations of the parties and third parties, militates against courts making many declarations of this paradox, the void contract.

Equity offers a greater number of possible results where a mistake is operative. Equity has two unique results: the refusal of specific performance and the ability to rectify a written instrument where there is a mistake in the recording of the actual agreement of the parties. Few lawyers would take issue with either of these outcomes, although they might disagree on the particular facts which would merit such a remedy. Much greater controversy surrounds the existence of another equitable remedy, the ability of equity to rescind a contract entered into

[2] And now of law: see *Brennan* v *Bolt Burdon* [2004] EWCA Civ 1017, [2005] QB 303.

[3] A matter of dispute since the decision in *Great Peace Shipping Ltd v Tsavliris Shipping (International) Ltd* [2002] EWCA Civ 1407, [2003] QB 679.

under a mistake. The effect, in such a circumstance, is to render the contract not void but voidable: the contract is a subsisting one until either a party with the right to set aside the contract does so or circumstances occur which prevent him from setting aside the contract. Equitable relief is discretionary and it is sometimes said that a contract may be rescinded on terms imposed by the court.

There can be a great difference between a void contract and a voidable contract, and the difference between the common law and equity matters here. There is little in the way of agreement by lawyers as to when a particular mistake occurs at common law and when it occurs in equity. Few guiding principles can be ascertained to determine this question. The reason given for legal or equitable intervention is that where mistake operates it operates to disrupt the consent of the contracting parties and prevents a contract from being formed. The underlying premise to this position is that contracts are based upon the consent of the parties and where this consent is removed by mistake, there is no contract. The difficulties with the doctrine are many and fundamental. Can mistakes occur outside the established categories? When is any particular form of mistake so sufficiently fundamental as to vitiate consent? How can the mistake of a party be ascertained? When does a mistake arise in equity and when at law? What is the basis of mistake? While the difficulties are numerous, the cases are rare. Very few cases have been decided on the basis of the principles set out above. The paucity of the case law prevents clear expositions of law by the courts. It is also apparent from a close examination of the cases that many of these cases were decided on grounds other than mistake, although they frequently refer to mistake.

By an examination of the history of the doctrine of mistake, from its origins in Roman law to mid-twentieth-century England, this book explains how and why this situation arose. The doctrine of mistake in contract law was a Victorian invention, the beginnings of which can be discerned in the 1860s, although it was not a doctrine which the judiciary set out to create nor was it fully accepted into the common law until the twentieth century. While the common law of contract did not recognise a doctrine of contractual mistake nor accord a legal response to a mistake as such in the middle of the nineteenth century, equity did. This equitable treatment of mistake, however, bears little resemblance to the modern doctrine. During the second half of the nineteenth century the common law moved towards the development of a doctrine of contractual mistake. This particular development occurred against a backdrop of wide, sweeping changes in English law. Most of these changes are known, and well documented: less well known and understood is their effect upon particular aspects of English law. These changes are concerned with a movement away from the narrower, procedural focus of English law towards a body of law based upon substantive principle.

The beginnings of this doctrine entered the common law in the nineteenth century during the period of immense procedural reforms to the common law which culminated in the fusion of law and equity by the Judicature Act 1873. While faint images of mistake appear in the 1850s, it was not accepted in any form until the 1870s when definite decisions were made upon this basis in relation to cases where identity was material to the formation of certain contracts. The origins of mistake in English law are partly civilian in nature. English judges and jurists borrowed ideas and examples of mistake from the civilians and merged these borrowings with their own common law conceptions of contract law. The civilian borrowings were varied in source, from Justinian to Robert Joseph Pothier to Friedrich von Savigny, and these borrowings were selective and partial. The common law is, of course, based upon cases, and the permeation of these foreign, civilian ideas into the cases came about in two ways. At times, judges, on their own initiative, relied directly upon civilian sources in reaching a decision in the case before them. This is particularly true of judges with an academic bent such as Lord Blackburn and Sir Edward Fry. More commonly, however, the civilian ideas were received into the common law through contract treatises which were based upon civilian ideas. Counsel often based arguments upon the work of the treatises. While these distillations of civilian ideas were sometimes received directly from the treatise into the case by judges, over time a more subtle and imperceptible process occurred in which many common law lawyers and judges viewed the common law differently, in a way which included the doctrine of mistake put forward by the treatise writers.

The treatise writers expressed the desire of a new generation of lawyers to conceive of their law in substantive rather than procedural terms. The extensive procedural reforms which occurred in the administration of justice in the nineteenth century, which ultimately resulted in the fusion of law and equity, simultaneously created both a desire for substantive principles and a purpose for their creation. The treatise writers, notably Sir Edward Fry, Judah Benjamin, Sir Frederick Pollock and Sir William Anson, wrote treatises in an attempt to organise English contract law or aspects of English contract law around general principles. It was intended that these principles should explain contract law in a coherent manner which allowed readers to predict the future operation of the law. In writing their treatises, the treatise writers borrowed a system of organisation from the civilians and adapted it to their purposes. There was a selective borrowing or transplant of ideas inherent in this process, and the English treatise writers sought to impose these ideas upon an existing system of contract law but they struggled to relate the borrowed ideas to this law. Sometimes this resulted in a partial borrowing, or a bending of the borrowed concept or, in other cases, the re-explanation of existing cases. The resulting body of law was often untidy, as principles were presented and expressed to have been established by cases which even a cursory examination revealed to be concerned with other matters. The process was not improved by inherent weaknesses in the borrowed theories of the civilians or by the fact that these theories were stripped from legal systems premised upon different rules and objectives than the common law.

The system that the treatise writers borrowed, primarily from Pothier and von Savigny, was based on a theory that contracts consisted of a metaphysical union of the wills of the parties. Will could be disrupted or prevented by a variety of factors for Pothier, and these included mistake; for von Savigny a mistake could disrupt the manifestation of the will and render doubtful the juridical act. Having adopted a will theory, the authors then adopted a theory of mistake which operated upon the will: contract was consensus and mistake a form of dissensus. They needed authority and force for their propositions concerning mistake and this, after some exploration, they found within the cases. Their task was rendered simpler by the fact that courts of equity clearly did accord a legal response to a mistake. The ease of the treatise writers' exercises created a problem for the development of the law as a whole because these equitable cases were not primarily concerned with consent. The treatise writers found cases which involved misapprehensions at common law and these, too, they included within their works. No doubt the treatise writers felt justified in these efforts for they sought to impose order in a chaotic system. They also sought to resolve cases upon 'principles' rather than procedure, and if some cases had to be stretched to support the principle, this was a necessary consequence of legal improvement. The problem was, however, that any dedicated reader who moved beyond the exposition of principles and into the cases found greater confusion than had existed before, as cases decided on disparate bases were united under a similar, but not common, principle.

There are, in essence, two forms of legal transplants in the treatises. The first were those external to England, those ideas which come from the civilians; the second were those which were internal to England, those ideas which came from equity into the common law. Once these new ideas and theories were employed in courts and came to be accepted into treatises, the judicial acceptance acted as further support for the doctrine espoused in the treatise and was cited as such. The common law judge, however, was concerned only with the case before him and not with the development of an entire body of law. As judges began to consider cases of factual misapprehension in terms of a substantive legal doctrine of mistake, their movement towards such a doctrine was piecemeal and fragmentary. Over time this new doctrine came to be accepted and its origins largely forgotten or misunderstood. This was a doctrine, however, which was neither well formed nor adequate to bear the practical and theoretical strains placed upon it.

This book chronicles the civilian ideas and the work of the English treatise writers who developed this doctrine. It also examines the reception of this doctrine into English law. These two strands, theory and case law, are intertwined in this reception and development. The book examines this development in a chronological fashion, although three chapters are largely concerned with theory, both in its civilian origins and its English adoption, in order to give the reader a greater understanding of the matter.

The book is developed in the following manner. Chapter two seeks to fulfil two purposes. The first is to examine Roman concepts of mistake in contract law. The chapter takes as its starting point the compilation of laws undertaken by Justinian which produced the *Corpus Iurus Civilis.* This was to form the basis of later Western legal thought and it was also to form a useful store of legal ideas into which later English lawyers would, from time to time, seek guidance and authority in the substantive development of the common law. The Romans were concerned with different forms of contract and, lacking a general law of contract, conceived of mistake not in a general form, but as separate instances of mistake. The work of the compilers preserved Roman law, but in relation to mistake their compilations were confused and contradictory since they were drawn from different sources. Chapter two also traces the post-classical development of Roman law from Justinian to the natural lawyers via the work of the sixteenth-century Spanish late scholastics. This is a subject which has been ably explored by Professors James Gordley[4] and Tony Wieacker[5] and this chapter draws upon their works in relation to the particular topic of mistake.

The focus changes in chapter three to investigate mistake within English common law in the eighteenth and early nineteenth centuries. While common law courts did not accord a legal response to misapprehensions during this time period, courts of equity did, and chapter three is concerned with the nature of this response. In the eighteenth century, equitable conceptions of mistake arose in relation to the core jurisdiction of the Court of Chancery—property management—and were developed from the ability of Chancery to admit parol evidence to establish that the written contract did not form an agreement between the parties. This was a greater procedural flexibility than that possessed by courts of common law, and the flexibility was closely allied to the forms of discretionary relief that Chancery could provide by way of rectification, specific performance and rescission. While courts of equity were cognisant of the fact that the contract arose from an agreement between the parties, they sought to give relief where a contract had been entered into under a mistake, or mistakenly recorded, for reasons beyond an attempt to give effect to this agreement. While courts of equity rarely gave an exhaustive explanation for intervention in such cases, the reasons extended beyond giving effect to an agreement and pertained also to the unconscionability and injustice which arose from allowing a party an advantage which arose from a mistake. This position was not greatly altered even as eighteenth- and early-nineteenth-century equity lawyers became aware of the ideas of the natural lawyers.

Chapter four is concerned with contractual misapprehensions before courts of common law and investigates two interrelated matters. The first is that the common law did not accord a legal response to a mistake as such, and the chapter explores some of the means by which cases of misapprehension were resolved. These means were primarily procedural and this raises the second matter of importance. The second matter is that the nineteenth century saw fundamental changes in the procedures by which the common law was administered—in pleadings, in allowing the evidence of diverse witnesses, in changes to juries and in the reforms which led to the ability of common law courts to consider equitable pleas, reforms which culminated in fusion. It is argued that as procedures became less arcane and more efficient, there was a correlative shift in emphasis from the procedures of the law to the substance of the law which was developed. This not only

[4] J Gordley, *The Philosophical Origins of Modern Contract Doctrine* (Oxford, Clarendon Press, 1991).
[5] F Wieacker, *A History of Private Law in Europe*, trs T Weir (Oxford, Clarendon Press, 1995).

set the conditions in which a mistake could be recognised and dealt with as such in a court of common law, it also led to a need for substantive principles of law upon which to decide cases. This need was to some extent intensified as England became an imperial power which sought to apply its laws within its colonial possessions.

One response to this need was in the production of treatises on contract law and, from the 1860s, these began to appear. These writers sought to organise and explain the law in what they conceived of as scientific, logical and rational principles. Rather than devise their own system to do this, they borrowed, to a greater or lesser extent, from the work of the European natural lawyers.[6] The authority of the common law, of course, derives from precedent—from case law—and the treatise writers used cases involving factual misapprehension to support their systems of contract law. While the systems devised gave lawyers a more logical and organised means of examining the common law, the cases themselves were distorted and misinterpreted in the organisation of such a system. Civilian-based conceptions of mistake entered common law legal thought largely through the treatise writers. This process, by which theory was transplanted from one legal system to another, is examined in the next two chapters. Chapter five begins with an explanation and analysis of this process as it derived from the work of Robert Joseph Pothier. Pothier's theory of mistake is examined and the impact it had upon English treatise writers analysed. Pothier's treatment of mistake was only partially adopted by the treatise writers, and the imperfections of his consideration of mistake became apparent.

Later treatise writers turned to von Savigny for guidance in constructing a doctrine of mistake. Chapter six continues the explanation and analysis of civilian theories of mistake by exploring the relevant theories of von Savigny and the use that was made of these theories by the English treatise writers, Pollock and Anson. While von Savigny's theory of mistake was superficially attractive, it was difficult to apply and only partially adopted by the English treatise writers. The theory was also largely used by Pollock as support in his process of examining English contract law as a coherent post-fusion amalgamation of legal and equitable principles. Pollock's use of von Savigny and the doctrine Pollock created for English law obscured the workings of the earlier common law and equitable cases. Pollock failed to realise his goal of ascertaining principles of mistake in such a fashion that they were rational and predictable in their application. His transplanted doctrine, which contained its own imperfections, was only partially used and resulted in a confused and cumbersome English product.

In chapter seven, the focus returns to the cases decided by common law courts. The treatise writers employed, in one form or another, a series of key cases decided between 1856 and 1871. An exploration is undertaken of these cases; *Couturier v*

[6] A process examined by AWB Simpson, 'Innovation in Nineteenth Century Contract Law' (1975) 91 *Law Quarterly Review* 247; D Ibbetson, *A Historical Introduction to the Law of Obligations* (Oxford, Oxford University Press, 1999); and Gordley (n 4 above).

Hastie (1856),[7] *Raffles v Wichelhaus* (1864),[8] *Kennedy v The Panama, New Zealand and Australian Royal Mail Company* (1867)[9] and *Smith v Hughes* (1871)[10] are set within the historical circumstances in which they occurred. None of them was decided solely on the basis of mistake nor were the judges in these cases attempting to construct a doctrine of mistake.

During the final quarter of the nineteenth century, courts of common law did construct an operative form of mistake where there was a mistake as to the identity of the other party to the contract. Chapter eight scrutinises how this doctrine was created and why it became a part of the common law. The argument is made that the theory behind this mistake came, initially, from Pothier through the work of Benjamin. The essential reason behind this transplant was to meet a need within English law. In those cases where it was said that a mistake of identity prevented a contract from being formed as a matter of contract law, it was also the case that these were instances that came within the criminal law since they generally amounted to the crime of obtaining goods by false pretences. The Larceny Act 1861 allowed title to revest in an original owner who had been the victim of such false pretences where this owner prosecuted to conviction the rogue who had duped him. A need arose to explain why as a matter of contract law the apparent contract between the original owner and the rogue was void and not voidable, as would be the case if this were resolved on the basis that it was a fraud. This was an underlying reason behind the House of Lords' decision in *Cundy v Lindsay* (1876)[11]. Once the revesting worked by the Larceny Act 1861 was curtailed by the Sale of Goods Act 1893 and ultimately abolished by the Larceny Act 1915, the common law had no need for a mistake of identity and many cases of mistake came to be dealt with as frauds. Other factors were present in the creation of a mistake of identity: courts of common law vacillated between fraud and mistake as they were concerned with whether such contracts were effected by fraud or mistake; in addition, an underlying and seldom articulated concern was whether the behaviour of the innocent parties, the original owner and the ultimate owner, should be a factor in the decision-making process. The chapter analyses how the transplanted civilian theory became rooted in the common law in an attempt to deal with common law concerns.

The final stage in the adoption of a doctrine of mistake in the common law occurred after the fusion of law and equity brought about by the Judicature Act 1873. Chapter nine observes and analyses this process. Despite the administrative fusion of the two courts, mistake cases were dealt with on much the same basis that they had been before fusion. Because of the nature of the allocation of jurisdiction by the Judicature Act 1873, most mistake cases were heard before the Chancery

[7] 8 Ex 40; 155 ER 1250 (1852, Court of Exchequer); 9 Ex 102 (1853, Exchequer Chamber); 5 HLC 673; 10 ER 1065 (1856, House of Lords).

[8] (1864) 2 H & C; 159 ER 375.

[9] (1867) LR 2 QB 580, 8 B & S 571.

[10] (1871) LR 6 QB 597, 40 LJQB 221.

[11] (1877–78) LR 3 App Cas 459; [1974–80] All ER Rep 1149, (1878) 42 JP 483; (1878) 14 Cox CC 93; (1878) 26 WR 406; (1878) 47 LJQB 481; (1878) 38 LT 573.

Division of the new Supreme Court of Judicature. Here, traditional understandings of mistake were argued by Chancery barristers and applied by Chancery judges. Changes were, however, afoot to the doctrine of mistake and these are examined. At common law, there were virtually no instances in which mistake appeared as such until *Bell v Lever Brothers*[12] in 1930. While this case was brought, and almost entirely fought, on grounds other than mistake, it became the decisive mistake case in English contract law. Lord Atkin sought to unify apparently disparate mistake cases to form a coherent doctrine, and the basis he employed for this was the treatise writings. In this process, he accepted into English law a form of civilian transplant. The transplant, however, was not admitted in a form which allowed it to function within the body of the English common law. Almost two decades later, Lord Denning, in *Solle v Butcher*,[13] recognised these difficulties and sought to give function to the doctrine by reviving the earlier equitable cases of mistake. The apparent irreconcilability of his decision with that of Lord Atkin has bedevilled the common law ever since.

The final chapter of this work examines the conclusions that can be drawn about mistake in particular and the common law in general.

[12] [1931] 1 KB 557; [1932] AC 161.
[13] [1950] 1 KB 671.

2

Contractual Mistake in Roman Law

From Justinian to the Natural Lawyers

THE STARTING POINT for any consideration of the doctrine of contractual mistake is classical Roman law. Although the English law of contract developed outside the strictures of Roman law, the influence of Roman law on modern English contract law is clearly present. This chapter has two purposes. The first is to consider how the Romans formulated mistake in contract law. This is of importance because both the common law and the civil law drew upon the Roman law in devising their own conceptions of mistake. The second purpose is to trace the post-classical development of Roman law in the Middle Ages and to outline its re-emergence in the work of the sixteenth-century Spanish late scholastics. This latter purpose is of importance because of the recent research by James Gordley[1] which illustrates the profound impact of the late scholastics upon the natural lawyers. The effect of the natural lawyers upon the Western legal systems is well known. Perhaps less well known are the conceptual difficulties inherent in their formulation of consent in contract: Gordley's work is significant in the context of mistake because it provides an explanation for these difficulties.

The Law of the Romans

Roman law itself changed over thousands of years and is best conceived as occurring within distinct epochs of Western civilisation. Wieacker noted the ambiguity of the expression 'Roman law' and divided the subject between 'ancient Roman law' and 'medieval Roman law'.[2] Only by so dividing the topic was he able to examine the primary and secondary effects of Roman law. 'Ancient Roman law' was initially one of customary and unwritten laws: the first known legislation was the Twelve Tables from the mid-fifth century BC. While not a complete code, as they presupposed a procedural and substantive knowledge, they did provide a firm basis for the growth of the *ius civile*. Three mechanisms brought about this growth:

[1] J Gordley, *The Philosophical Origins of Modern Contract Doctrine* (Oxford, Clarendon Press, 1991), and *Foundations of Private Law: Property, Tort, Contract, Unjust Enrichment* (Oxford, Oxford University Press, 2006).

[2] F Wieacker, 'The Importance of Roman Law for Western Civilization and Western Legal Thought' (1981) 4 *Boston College International and Comparative Law Review* 257, 261.

a constructive interpretation of existing rules; the recognition of usage; and later legislation.[3] It was the work of the jurists which gave Roman law its distinctive form and allowed it such great influence on the development of the law of later civilisations. The jurists undertook the interpretation of the law as a part of their public lives. These jurists created a great literature, undertook teaching of the law and were enormously influential on the practice of the law. The jurists of the later Republic often had a political life and undertook jurisprudence as a part of their public service. Later jurists were servants of the Empire, working in close connection with the Emperor.[4] The work of the jurists flourished particularly between the first century AD and the middle of the third century AD. With Ulpian's murder in 223, the era of the great jurists largely ceased and the Emperor's law formed the sole source of law. As the Roman Empire declined, so, too, did its legal structures. In the sixth century, after the collapse of the Western Empire, the Emperor Justinian sought to reverse this decline. Concerned with the confused state of the law, Justinian implemented a programme of compilation and codification of law.

The great success of Justinian's efforts is indicated by the immediate recognition given to his name by all modern Western lawyers and the legal work for which he was the impetus, the *Corpus Iuris Civilis*: the compilation of laws undertaken in Constantinople between 529 and 534. Two purposes underlay the compilation. The first was to preserve the best of the classical law; and the second, simultaneously, to reform it to suit Justinian's own era and so set out a then contemporary law.[5] However, 'in seeking to preserve the greatness of the past Justinian failed to produce a practical codification which his own subjects could use, and in seeking to present the law of his own day he distorted what he was trying to preserve'.[6] The compilation consisted of several projects: the Digest; the Institutes; and the *Codex repetitae praelectionis*; and the *novellae constitutions.*

The Digest, or Pandects, was to have a profound effect upon later legal development, and its creation was an ambitious project. Entrusted to Justinian's chief legal officer, the quaestor Tribonian, he worked with 16 men. Their task was to read the old literature, excerpt what was necessary and to collect and organise these excerpts. The provenance of each excerpt was recorded; the work of 39 authors was incorporated into the Digest. Most of these jurists had existed from the earlier, classical period between 100 and 250 AD, and half of the excerpts were by Ulpian, Paul and Gaius. The work of these commissioners was extraordinary, but 'very imperfectly done'.[7] The Digest was the centrepiece of Justinian's *Corpus Iurus*,[8] a vast

[3] H Julius, *Roman Law; An Historical Introduction* (Norman, University of Oklahoma Press, 1951) 62.

[4] W Kunkel, *An Introduction to Roman Legal and Constitutional History*, trs JM Kelly (Oxford, Clarendon Press, 1966) ch 7.

[5] It seems unlikely that Justinian envisaged substantial reform of the laws. Instead, he sought to provide clarity through compiling the law. See A Watson, *Law Out of Context* (Athens and London, University of Georgia Press, 2000) 13, 18.

[6] B Nicholas, *An Introduction to Roman Law* (Oxford, Clarendon Press, 1962) 44.

[7] ibid, 41.

[8] Scholars of the Middle Ages came to call the entirety of Justinian's compilations as the *Corpus Iurus Civilis* and it is this later title by which it is recognised in the modern world.

anthology of the law which was to have a profound influence. While it acted to preserve Roman law, this came at the cost of losing the work of earlier jurists. Recourse to other literature was not allowed and the earlier, extant writing of these jurists was lost.[9] An understanding of these jurists is further impeded by the interpolations—additions and changes—which exist within the Digest. Justinian's commissioners had been given the power to amend juristic writing to suit the then contemporary law; they used this power extensively. In some cases, the commissioners may well have worked from materials which had already received interpolations. The result is a law which can be difficult to understand: a difficulty particularly true for contractual mistake, for the nature of the sources of Roman law produce confusion in this, and other, areas.

Although the Digest was intended as the core of formal legal tuition, it was felt necessary to provide an introductory book, the Institutes. While the Code and the Digest are huge, difficult works, the Institutes provide a succinct account of private law. The Institutes were, in time, to form the basis for most modern civil codes.[10] Promulgated on the same day as the Digest, they, too, had the force of law. The irony of Justinian's creation is often noted. While the *Corpus Iuris Civilis* was to become enormously important through its influence upon the development of the Western legal tradition, it had little immediate effect in the Western Empire. In the Eastern Empire, Roman law was to fade from this Justinian glory with the fall of Constantinople to the Turks in 1453.

The unintended benefit of Justinian's *Corpus Iuris* was the preservation of these laws for future ages: it provided a storehouse for future legislators and allowed historians to find a record of the greatness of Roman law.[11] It also provided later jurists with a model of reasoning; a method by which legal problems could be identified and resolved. The Digest enabled scholars in Western Europe to revive Roman law at the end of the eleventh century as a part of a wider renaissance of learning. This revival was to mark a new epoch of Roman law.

Roman Contract Law

As Justinian ordered the destruction of earlier legal materials, most of our knowledge of Roman contract law is based upon the work of his compilers.[12] Gaius's

[9] Fragments of pre-Justinian Roman law remain; the most significant of which is the Institutes of Gaius, a copy of which was discovered in 1816 by the German scholar Niebuhr, who discovered it on the inspired suggestion of Friedrich Carl von Savigny.

[10] Watson (n 5) 22.

[11] Nicholas (n 6) 44.

[12] Although work has been conducted on earlier periods of Roman obligations; see, for example, A Watson, *The Law of Obligations in the Later Roman Republic* (Oxford, Clarendon Press, 1965). The lack of information as to the nature of contractual obligations before this time has caused enormous debates; JAC Thomas, *Textbook of Roman Law* (Amsterdam, North-Holland Publishing Company, 1976) 215–16.

classification of law was threefold: a law of persons, a law of things and a law of actions. The law of obligations was part of the law of things. Ultimately, and after Gaius, obligations themselves came to be seen in four categories: contract, quasi-contract, delict and quasi-delict.[13] Things consisted of what a man owned or what he was owed; a right *in rem* or a right *in personam.* Obligations involved on the part of one person a duty to do something which was correlative to the other person who had the right to have that duty performed. As such, obligations were rights *in personam.* While Roman lawyers came to see contracts as agreements, the concept emerged slowly. Initially, contracts were a form of debt—what one man owed another. The debt might be owed as a result of injury or wrongful act or because a formal act had been undertaken whereby one man promised another something. Gradually, lawyers differentiated the two and classified them accordingly as delict and contract.[14] It is, however, misleading to define contracts as agreements because it is indicative of a conceptual unity which Roman law lacked.[15] As has frequently been observed, the Romans had a law of contracts, rather than of contract. They recognised an agreement as contract if it fit within their classification scheme of recognised contracts. If it did not, it was not enforceable as contract—regardless of whether or not there was an agreement. The Romans were concerned with various situations in which a contract could arise rather than in devising an overarching and coherent philosophy which united contractual obligations. Attempts to devise a coherent legal system, such as that undertaken by Gaius and by Justinian's Institutes, formed exceptions to the general development of the law. Roman law recognised agreements as contracts in two ways. The first case was those obligations which were binding because they arose from a transaction, the characteristic of which was a formal feature involving the recitation of a specific formula of words or the delivery of a particular thing. The second, which evolved over time as Roman commerce increased in its development beyond a simple agrarian society, was obligations which were binding because they were based upon agreement. In both cases, the obligation was contractual because it was an agreement—but in the former case, there had to be proof of something beyond agreement.

An early example of a formal contract can be found in *stipulatio. Stipulatio* was a unilateral and *stricti iuris* contract which consisted in a formal question and a formal answer.[16] In such a formal contract, a conceptual mistake by one or both parties is irrelevant provided the proper form has been observed. The flexibility

[13] For a consideration of the English analysis placed upon this classification by the nineteenth century English legal philosopher John Austin, see P Birks, 'Obligations: One Tier or Two?' in PG Stein and ADE Lewis (eds), *Studies in Justinian's Institutes in memory of JAC Thomas* (London, Sweet & Maxwell, 1983).

[14] Nicholas (n 6) 159.

[15] ibid, 165.

[16] A stipulation is a verbal expression in which the man who is asked replies that he will give or do what he has been asked: D. 45.1.5.1. The formal requirements necessary to establish *stipulatio* were simple: one party asked the other, using precise language (*spondesne*—'do you promise?'), whether or not the other promised to do something. The other agreed, using the same formula of precise language (*spondeo*—'I do promise').

and universality of this form of contract was enormous: almost anything could be made the subject of a *stipulatio*. The *stipulatio* was of such utility and generality that it has led some commentators to observe that the early Romans may have had a general theory of contract and only later devised different types of contract.[17] Whatever the beginning point, it is clear that over time different forms of contract were devised. The Romans moved from the recognition of agreements as contract because they embodied a particular form to the recognition of certain types of agreement based on the consent of the parties.[18] These consensual contracts were binding, not because of their procedural form, but because of the substantive agreement between the parties. The acceptance of the principle that parties could be bound by a formless agreement 'was one of the most important factors in the adaptation of law to the commercial needs of a vast empire'.[19] Commercial needs demanded a bilateral form of agreement which could be promissory in nature.

Roman Contract Law and Mistake

It is beyond the scope of this work to catalogue the Roman forms of contract.[20] It must also be noted at the outset that because the Romans had a law of contracts, rather than a law of contract, it is difficult to outline with precision what the Roman law of mistake was.[21] Because the Romans had no general theory of contact, they also lacked general rules on mistake.[22] For the Roman jurists the cause of the mistake was irrelevant; what was relevant was what the mistake pertained to.[23] What is important here is the recognition that while a general feature of all Roman contracts could be described as a concurrence of the minds of the parties,[24] and in that sense, without agreement there was no contract,[25] it was only with the development of the four consensual contracts[26] that the Roman jurists had to deal substantively with mistake (*error*). The need for this treatment is obvious to the modern lawyer: if the agreement of the parties is the reason for enforcing the

[17] A Watson, *The Evolution of Law* (Oxford, Blackwell, 1985) 7.

[18] WW Buckland, *A Textbook of Roman Law from Augustus to Justinian*, 3rd edn, revd P Stein (Cambridge, Cambridge University Press, 1963) 412.

[19] Nicholas (n 6) 160.

[20] The curious reader is referred to many of the outstanding works in this field: see, eg, Thomas (n 12) chs 16–23; Nicholas (n 6) ch 4; A Borkowski and P du Plessis, *Textbook on Roman Law*, 3rd edn (Oxford, Oxford University Press, 2005) ch 9; and Buckland (n 18) chs 10–12.

[21] WW Buckland, *Elementary Principles of the Roman Private Law* (Cambridge, Cambridge University Press, 1912) 286.

[22] D Tamm, *Roman law and European legal history* (Copenhagen, DJØF Publishing, 1997) 132.

[23] ibid.

[24] Thomas (n 12) 227.

[25] D.2.14.1.3.

[26] The four consensual contracts are *emptio venditio* (sale), *locatio conductio* (hire), *societas* (partnership) and *mandatum* (mandate). It is the contract of sale which was to have the most profound effect on English contract law.

contract it is impossible to avoid those factors which disrupt or prevent agreement. Unhappily, the attempts of the Roman jurists to deal with error, or our record of those attempts, are unsatisfactory.

The consensual contracts were bilateral agreements, with duties and rights accruing to each of the contracting parties. In contrast, a formal contract such as *stipulatio* was a unilateral agreement; although it was possible to reach the same commercial end by having each party undertake separate *stipulatio*.[27] The bilateral nature of consensual contracts had two important ramifications in relation to mistaken agreements. The first is that consensual contracts rested upon a concept of good faith, of bona fides, which affected every aspect of the transaction.[28] The second is that consent involved a concurrence of two intents: there had to be real agreement between the parties. The agreement had to be a real agreement and a number of factors could work against the necessary consensus. There was the possibility of *error*—a mistake as to all or some part of the transaction. In these cases consent was defective because the parties had not actually agreed to what they had apparently agreed to. Consent might also be defective because of the manner in which the agreement was procured, through *dolus* (fraud or bad faith) or *metus* (duress). Impossibility of performance, whether for factual or legal reasons, also prevented consent.[29]

Mistake takes one of two broad forms. In the first form, the parties share a mistaken belief or intent. Thus, they may believe that the bottle contains wine when in fact it contains vinegar. In the second form, one party intends one thing and the other party another thing. This second form can be further subdivided into those instances in which the mistake of one party is known to the other. The Romans recognised both forms of mistake within their categorisation of types of mistake and found that either would invalidate a contract. A notable difference with English law exists in the case of a unilateral mistake where one party acquiesced in the mistake of the other, for the Romans conceived of this as *dolus*.[30] A party labouring under a mistake could not be held to his agreement by the party who was aware of and had acquiesced in his mistake. The Roman texts gave no example of the situation where an innocent third party's rights were at stake.[31]

As Buckland has argued, it seems likely that error in the belief as to the nature of the transaction one was entering into prevented any form of contract from arising.[32]

[27] Alan Watson has argued that the invention of consensual contracts, of which the contract for sale (*emptio vendito*) was perhaps the earliest, evolved to remedy the shortcomings inherent within the taking of stipulations. In his words, '*emptio venditio* arose to fill the interstices left by taking stipulations': 'The Origins of Consensual Sale: A Hypothesis' (1964) 32 *Tijdschrift voor rechtsgeschiedenis* 245, 248.

[28] Nicholas (n 6) 162.

[29] 'There is no obligation to the impossible': Celsus, D.50.17.185.

[30] D.44.4.4. 3; D.44.4.7.pr.

[31] WW Buckland and AD McNair, 2nd edn, revd FH Lawson, *Roman Law and Common Law* (Cambridge, Cambridge University Press, 1965) 212.

[32] Buckland (n 21) 287. This is an *error in negotio*. Buckland gives an example of a situation where one party believes he has given the thing over as a sale, while the other believes he has received it as a gift. In such a case, there is no consent to either form of transaction and there is no contract.

Error encompassed only mistakes of fact and not of law.[33] A mistake of law would not invalidate a contract. The conception of a mistake of fact is somewhat uncertain: 'error was a belief contrary to the truth whether based on a false understanding of the facts or on ignorance of the truth which prevented a person giving real consent to the agreement apparently concluded'.[34] The error had to be reasonable and it had to be made in good faith. Where error operated it removed apparent consent and the result was a void contract.[35] The Romans encountered practical difficulties in applying this doctrine. What sort of error was fundamental enough to vitiate consent? What was the nature of the agreement between the parties and what was the relation between the agreement and the reality of the situation? These questions were not easily resolved and 'on the important question when mistake did so affect the contract, it is difficult to draw any rational conclusion from the texts'.[36]

Most of the issues resolved in relation to mistake were done so in the case of the contract for sale—*emptio venditio*.[37] From this, certain generalisations about mistake can be drawn; but the picture is somewhat distorted by the fact that Roman jurists would not have seen these as broad encompassing principles applicable to all contracts. In addition, and in contrast to English law, Roman law would not have recognised the sale, in itself, as capable of transferring ownership.[38] The problem of the acquisition of title by a third party did not arise.[39] Finally, it is likely that shortcomings in *emptio venditio* could well have been remedied through use of formal contracts. *Emptio venditio* was an informal contract that rested on the agreement of the parties. To be actionable, three elements were necessary: a thing, a price and consent. Because consensus was a requisite element the Roman jurists were forced to consider the circumstances in which an absence of consensus occurred by reason of an error of the parties. English law has struggled with whether the mistake must be a subjective mistake (the situation where the parties are actually mistaken and there is no consent) or whether there must be an objective mistake (where the question is whether there is, to a reasonable bystander, an absence of consent). This latter standard is one which is easier to sustain on an evidential basis and it is also one which promotes contractual and commercial certainty. It is the standard which English law has, to a great extent, adopted for these reasons. The Romans, however, were less concerned with these evidential considerations and tended to favour the subjective standard. This general consideration needs to be applied to the way in which the Romans conceived of mistake.

[33] D.22.6.1.1, D.22.6.9 pr.

[34] Thomas (n 12) 228.

[35] D.2.14.1.3, C.1.18.9. Not all subsequent commentators have agreed with this position: see JG Wolf, *Error im römischen Vertragsrecht* (Köln-Graz, Böhlau, 1961). Wolf argued that in classical law error as such was not the basis for nullifying a contract.

[36] Buckland (n 18) 417.

[37] *Emptio venditio* arose to fill the shortcomings left by taking stipulations: A Watson, 'The origins of consensual sale: A hypothesis' (1964) 32 *Tijdschrift voor rechtsgescheidenis* 245, 248.

[38] Watson(n 27) describes the fact that the seller was under no obligation to make the buyer owner of the object as a significant defect of the contract of sale: 245. The seller only had to deliver possession of the good and was only liable for evidence if he had given a stipulation against eviction: ibid.

[39] Buckland and McNair (n 31) 197.

Because they lacked an overarching theory of contract, error was usually considered only in relation to the consensual contracts and on a categorical basis. The Romans, in other words, developed categories of mistakes which vitiated consent and rendered the contract void. As we shall see, it is one of the anomalies of modern English law, with its theory of contract, that these specific categories of mistake were largely adopted into the English law.

Roman law on mistake can be divided into three specific categories of situations where a misapprehension operated upon the consent necessary to contract: a mistake as to identity; a mistake as to price; and a mistake as to the subject matter of the contract. A brief examination of these situations is important because English judges and jurists were to draw upon them in the development of English law.

Mistake as to the Identity of a Contracting Party: *Error in persona*

Where the identity of the other party to a contract was material, an error as to the identity of this party rendered the contract void. It has been observed that Ulpian's comments on error set out all the traditional categories of error except *error in persona* but that 'such an omission is natural, because in sale such mistake rarely matters'.[40] As to what modern lawyers recognise as a mistake *inter praesentes*, a personal meeting of the parties, there is no mention. In the words of Buckland, 'strictly speaking there can be no mistake of identity where the parties are contracting face to face. There is no evidence, indeed it is hardly probable that where I had agreed to buy goods of a person called Balbus, I could back out of my bargain merely because I thought he was Titius, to whom I had been recommended'.[41]

In any contract of sale, regardless of whether it is negotiated in person or at a distance, it is rarely the sale that gives rise to concerns about identity; it is almost invariably the case that the related credit agreement is dependent upon the identity of the borrower. Where *error in persona* is discussed it is usually in connection with law other than a consensual contract.[42] Nevertheless, it is likely that in a contract of sale, an *error in persona* would avoid a contract which would not have been concluded but for the error.[43] This form of mistake was not one to which the Roman jurists gave great consideration and it is not particularly well developed.

Mistake as to the Price to be Paid: *Error in pretio*

While the ascertainment of identity is not usually cause for concern in a contract of sale, the ascertainment of price is critical. As noted above, the determination of price was a required element in the establishment of the informal contract of sale. The confluence of two of these required elements, price and consent, meant that

[40] F De Zulueta, *The Roman Law of Sale* (Oxford, Clarendon Press, 1957) 25.
[41] Buckland (n 21) 288.
[42] eg D.12.1.32; D.28.5.9 pr.
[43] ibid.

mistake as to price was something considered by the Roman jurists. Mistake as to price was an *error in pretio*, an error which was material in the formation of a contract of sale. Ulpian, in a passage[44] upon which much of the interpretation of mistake in Roman law has been based, states uncategorically that 'It is obvious that agreement is of the essence in sale and purchase; the purchase is not valid if there be disagreement over the contract itself, the price, or any other element of the sale'.[45] This passage leads one to conclude that an *error in pretio* prevented the formation of a contract of sale. An *error in pretio* appears, however, to have rendered the contract partially effective. An illustration of the principle in practice occurs in relation not to sale but to *locatio conductio*. Pomponius states that if one party leases a farm to another for ten and the lessee believes the lease to be for five, the arrangement is void. Nevertheless, while the lessor cannot lease the property at his figure, he can lease it at the lessee's figure of five. The lease can stand, but at the lower figure.[46] Zimmerman identifies this as an example of the flexible manner in which Roman lawyers applied a rule such as *utile per inutile non vitiatur.*[47]

Mistake as to the Subject Matter of the Contract

There are a range of different forms of mistake as to the subject matter of a contract. Roman lawyers recognised *error in nomine*, *error in quantitate*, *error in corpore* and *error in substantia*. We shall examine them in turn.

Error in nomine

An *error in nomine* occurred where the parties were mistaken as to the name of the object of the contract, but were agreed as to the object of the contract. 'If we are merely in disagreement over the name but at one on the actual thing, there is no doubt that the sale is good; for if the thing be identified, a mistake over its name is irrelevant'.[48] While a mistake as to the object of the sale would invalidate it, a mere mistake as to name where there exists agreement over the object will not so invalidate a contract. In this same passage, Ulpian deals with the sale of a slave and in so doing illustrates the difference between these two types of mistake. He contrasts an *error in nomine*, where the vendor and purchaser are agreed as to which slave forms the object of the sale but are mistaken as to the slave's name, with the situation where there is a sale of slave where the vendor intends to sell Stichus and

[44] D.18.1.9.pr. The passage is set out below at 21.

[45] The translation is that of Professor JAC Thomas in *The Digest of Justinian*, ed A Watson, rev English language edn,(Philadelphia, PA, University of Pennsylvania Press, 1998).

[46] D.19.2.52. There are obvious parallels here with the concept of a rescission on terms for mistake in English law in that the effect is to protect reasonable expectations and attempt to judicially strike the bargain originally achieved.

[47] R Zimmerman, *The Law of Obligations, Roman Foundations of the Civilian Tradition* (Cape Town, Juta and Co Ltd, 1990) 591.

[48] Ulpian, D.18.1.9.1.

the purchaser thought he was purchasing Pamphilus. In this latter case there is no sale because the parties are not agreed as to subject matter. An *error in nomine* was a lesser error, dealing only with name and thus did not invalidate a contract.

Error in quantitate

An *error in quantitate* occurred as a result of a divergent intent; where the parties intended different quantities of the same subject matter. In these instances, the error partially invalidated the contract. The treatment is similar to that of the *error in pretio*. Passages in the Digest indicate that a binding agreement would arise to the extent that there was consent. Such an agreement would not be one which disadvantaged the mistaken party. Ulpian observes that if one party stipulates '10' and the other '20' there is an obligation over that part of the stipulation which is shared by both parties—10.[49] Likewise, Pomponius gives the example of a lessor who leases his farm for ten to a lessee who believes he has leased it for five. The arrangement is void, but it would not be where the sum envisioned was smaller than that offered or expected: the lesser is included within the greater and there is a degree of consent, therefore, for this lesser sum. Thomas noted that these passages in the Digest have attracted suspicion as being the subject of later interpolations which confuse their meaning. He stated that while it may be that at one time the different numbers (five and ten) meant that there was a failure of correspondence which prevented a contract from arising, over time the numbers were recognised as quantities and that, as the greater included the less, an agreement for the smaller sum was found to exist.[50]

Error in corpore

An *error in corpore*, or an *error in re*, resulted where there was a divergent intent between the contracting parties, where there was a mistake as to the subject matter of the contract. Again, the principal text dealing with this form of mistake is to be found in the leading text of Ulpian.[51] He stated that where the parties had not agreed on the object of the sale there was manifestly no sale. Two examples are given to illustrate this proposition. The first is a purchaser who thought he was purchasing the Cornelian farm and the vendor thought that he was selling the Sempronian: the sale is void because the parties were not agreed on the thing sold. The second example concerns the sale of a slave. If the vendor thought he was selling Stichus and the purchaser thought that the vendor was selling Pamphilus (and where the slave is absent) then, again, the sale is void because there is no agreement

[49] D.45.1.1.4.

[50] Thomas (n 12) 230. The discrepancies in the numbers partially turns on the difference between what Ulpian says, or is recorded as saying, in the Digest and the relevant Institute of Gaius (Gaius Inst 3.102), reproduced in the Institute of Justinian (3.19.5).

[51] D.18.1.9 pr.

on the object of the sale. Had the slave been present, of course, there would have been agreement on the slave before them; the only mistake would have been as to his name and this would not have prevented contractual formation as an *error in nomine*. If there was an agreement over the principal subject matter of the contract, the contract would not be set aside for a mistake as to an accessory of the contract. Thus in the case where land was bought and was to be accompanied by the slave Stichus but it is uncertain as to which of several slaves is to be the accessory and a difference of opinion exists between the buyer and the seller as to the relevant slave, the sale of land is nonetheless valid.[52] It was irrelevant if the accessory was more valuable than the principal object of the contract; what mattered was the way in which the principal object of the contract was defined.[53]

An *error in corpore* encompassed what modern lawyers would see as several possible situations of mistakes.[54] Not only did it include those situations where, in the case of the purchase of the Cornelian/Sempronian farm, the statements of the parties were so vague as to prevent the recognition of a specific object, but also those situations where there was a unilateral mistake on the part of the buyer or a unilateral mistake on the part of the seller. In any of these situations, there was a divergent intent. As long as these intents diverged, there could be no contract. There was a lack of consensus; a situation of dissensus. For Roman lawyers, dissensus was not confined to bilateral mistakes, but also included unilateral mistakes. As long as the intent of the parties diverged, there could be no consent. Absent consent, there was no contract.

Error in substantia

An *error in substantia* differs from an *error in corpore* in that there is an agreement as to the physical identity of the subject matter of the contract, but there is a mistake as to some essential characteristic of this subject matter. Nicholas suggests that while the jurists seemed to have in mind a philosophical difference between substance and accident, the illustrations they offered make it difficult to spell out a coherent principle based upon philosophical doctrine.[55] The elusive nature of the meaning of this type of mistake has excited great debate for some time amongst scholars. The principal difficulties are that not only is the basis for *error in substantia* largely drawn from the text of Ulpian,[56] a text which many believe to have been affected by later interpolations, but the very theoretical conception of this sort of mistake is troublesome. An object has many qualities: of these, which is sufficiently fundamental to recognise that a mistake as to this quality prevents consent? To what extent is there a mistake as to quality and to what extent is there an acceptance of risk undertaken in the contract?

[52] Paul, D.18.1.34 pr.
[53] ibid.
[54] Zimmerman (n 47) 589–90.
[55] Nicholas (n 6) 178.
[56] D.18.1.11.1.

The texts in the Digest indicate a disagreement between the jurists as to whether or not an *error in substantia* avoided the contract. Marcellus believed it did not;[57] Ulpian, Julian and Paul believed that it did. It may be that Marcellus's was the older viewpoint and that the other jurists expressed a later view. It is now accepted that these principal passages had been the subject of interpolations sufficiently extensive as to render, on the face of the texts, a coherent meaning almost impossible.[58] Because these texts in the Digest were so influential on later conceptions of mistake they are worth reproducing here. The principal text, which provides *error in substantia* with its name, is that of Ulpian:

> It is obvious that agreement is of the essence in sale and purchase; the purchase is not valid if there be disagreement over the contract itself, the price, or any other element of the sale. Hence, if I thought that I was buying the Cornelian farm and you that you were selling the Sempronian, the sale is void because we were not agreed upon the thing sold. The same is true if I intended to sell Stichus and you thought that I was selling you Pamphilus, the slave himself not being there: Because there is no agreement on the object of sale, there is manifestly no sale. 1. Of course, if we are merely in disagreement over the name but at one on the actual thing, there is no doubt that the sale is good; for if the thing be identified, a mistake over its name is irrelevant. 2. The next question is whether there is a good sale when there is no mistake over the identity of the thing but there is over its substance: Suppose that vinegar is sold as wine, copper as gold or lead, something else similar to silver as silver. Marcellus, in the sixth book of his *Digest*, writes that there is a sale because there is agreement on the thing despite the mistake over its substance. I would agree in the case of wine, because the essence is much the same, that is, if the wine has gone sour; if it be not sour wine, however, but was vinegar from the beginning such as brewed vinegar, then it emerges that one thing has been sold as another. But in the other cases, I think that there is no sale by reason of the error over the material.[59]

The Digest continues to give Paul's agreement with Ulpian:

> It would be different if the thing was gold, although of a quality inferior to that supposed by the purchaser. In such case, the sale is good.[60]

To this are added the comments of Ulpian:

> Now what if the purchaser were blind or a mistake over the material were made by a purchaser unskilled in distinguishing materials? Do we say that the parties are agreed on the thing? How can a man agree who cannot see it? 1. If, however, I think that I am buying a virgin when she is, in fact, a woman, the sale being valid, there being no mistake over her sex. But if I sell you a woman and you think that you are buying a male slave, the error over sex makes the sale void.[61]

[57] Ulpian, D.18.1.9.2.

[58] JAC Thomas, 'Error in Persona and Error in Substantia', *La formazione storica, vol III*, 1213–15.

[59] D.18.1.9. The translation is that of Professor JAC Thomas in *The Digest of Justinian*, trs and ed A Watson (Philadelphia, PA, University of Pennsylvania Press, 1985). All further translations, unless specifically noted otherwise, are from the same volume.

[60] D.18.1.10.

[61] D.18.1.11.

And:

> Now what are we to say when both parties are in error over both the material and its quality? Suppose that I think that I am selling and that you are buying gold, when it is, in fact, copper, or again, that co-heirs sell to one of their number, for a substantial price, a bracelet said to be gold which proves to be largely copper? It is settled law that the sale holds good because there is some gold in it. For if a thing be gold-plated, though I think it is sold gold, the sale is good. But if copper be sold as gold, there is no contract.[62]

Julian's agreement appears in a longer passage dealing with purchases under condition in which he concluded:

> You unwittingly sold me, who did not know the facts, a silver-covered table as solid silver; the purchase is of no effect and a *condictio* will lie to recover the money paid.[63]

It will be noted that these passages provide little in the way of a comprehensive exposition of when an *error in substantia* operates. The compilers removed the jurists' passages from their context with the result that the meaning is obscure. In addition, it has long been noted that there were great interpolations to these passages. The result is that the texts do not tell a consistent story:[64] these inconsistencies meant that later jurists were unable to found a coherent, workable doctrine of mistake upon these passages. Various explanations have been put forth in an attempt to explain this result. Later commentators,[65] in the consideration of the provenance of this doctrine, have reached different conclusions. Lenel thought it possible that *error in substantia* may have existed entirely because of the efforts of Justinian.[66] Wolf asserted that, in the classical law, error was not the basis of contractual nullity.[67] Thayer advanced the possibility that while the compilers did not deliberately introduce this wider doctrine, they made it a possibility by removing the discussions of the facts upon which the jurists relied for their conclusions.[68] As will be discussed further below, different authors have put forward a variety of theories in which *error in substantia* is explained either as something else altogether or as occupying a minor role in a larger, interlocking scheme dealing with the legal consequences of factual problems such as these. What we will examine here is what *error in substantia* is likely to have meant in the Digest. An *error in substantia*

[62] D.18.1.14.

[63] D.18.1.41.1.

[64] WW Buckland (n 18) 418.

[65] See generally F de Zulueta, *The Roman Law of Sale* (Oxford, Clarendon, 1945) 28.

[66] O Lenel, 'El Error in Substantia', *Revista de Derecho privado* (Madric, E Maestre, 1924) 27. Lenel maintained that the classical law may have provided that the contract was a nullity in the cases of misdescription; the wider ground was not, however, recognised at that time. Lenel was of the view that mutual *error in substantia* was created by Justinian's compilers. The classical law allowed avoidance of the contract only in cases of misdescription.

[67] JG Wolf, *Error in römischen Vertragsrecht* (n 35). Note Watson's disagreement with this position: Alan Watson's review of Wolf, *Error in römischen Vertragsrecht* (n 35); and U Zilletti, *La dottrina dell'errore nella storia del diritto romano* (Milan, Giuffre, 1961), (1962) 28 *Studia et Documenta Historiae et Iuris* 397. Watson stated that Wolf demanded 'too much from the classical jurists both in the quality of their thought and in the exactitude of their language': ibid, 399.

[68] J Thayer, *Atti del Congresso Internationale di Diritto romana, Roma, vol ii* (1935) 411.

presents any form of contract law with a problem. The problem is this. While it is a straightforward process to determine that without a subject matter about which to contract there can be no contract (and particularly so in the Roman law of sale which did not recognise a contract of sale without a subject matter), it is much more complicated to determine the effect of an error as to a material characteristic upon a contract. The subject matter exists, but it is not as desirable or is more desirable as a result of the error as to the particular characteristic. It is often the case that in contracting, one party hopes to obtain some advantage by an assumed, possibly hidden, characteristic of the subject matter. To then avoid the contract is to disrupt an accepted calculation of risk in a manner prejudicial to the other party. A second difficulty is that of upsetting apparent contracts upon which reasonable reliance may have been made. A third difficulty is distinguishing between what is material and what is not.

Few of these difficulties are resolved in the Digest. It is generally accepted that the error could be either unilateral, the mistake of one party alone, or bilateral, a mistake made by both parties.[69] Ulpian clearly has in mind a unilateral mistake of only the purchaser when he considers the sale of the slave supposed by the purchaser to be a virgin; equally a bilateral mistake is envisioned by both Ulpian, in his consideration of the sale of the wrong slave or the wrong farm, and Julian in the unwitting sale of the table thought to be silver. Where the mistake was bilateral, an *error in substantia* could occur not only in situations where the intents of the parties diverged (divergent intent), but also in circumstances where they shared their mistake (convergent intent based on a misapprehension). Ulpian provided an example of a divergent intent when he explains that there is an error where the buyer intended to purchase one slave or one farm and the seller intended to sell another slave or another farm. Julian provided a case of convergent and mistaken intent in his consideration of the table unwittingly sold as silver. In this regard, the jurists conceived of a broad scope for an *error in substantia.* The broadness of this scope was reduced by allowing only an error which was material to avoid a contract. What was important to the Roman jurists in their conception of a material error went to the identification of the object rather than the motive for which the contract was entered into.[70] Savigny identified an error as material where the effect of it was to change the commercial category into which the object of the sale fell; the category was determined objectively.[71] The effect of the mistake is to defeat the commercial object of the transaction. Thus, the mistake concerning the sale of the slave thought to be a man but actually a woman changed the category of the good in that it changed the work that could be undertaken by the slave. A mistake as to the virginity or non-virginity of a female slave was not one which changed the commercial category of the slave. This latter

[69] Tamm (n 22) 133.

[70] FH Lawson, '*Error in Substantia*' (1936) 52 LQR 79, 80. As Buckland noted, the purchaser's motive would have been affected by an inferior quality of gold in D.18.1.10: Buckland, (n 18) 418.

[71] Savigny, *System* iii, ss 137–38. This interpretation is accepted by Lawson (n 70) 80, and Buckland, (n 18) 419.

mistake was a mistake as to a quality only and the sale was good. As de Zulueta has observed, the distinction does not provide a rational ground for mistaking the substance which an object is composed of and not accepting mistakes as to other 'essential qualities' such as the authorship of a work of art.[72] Another apparent irrationality of *error in substantia* is that although a mistake should, in conception, work in favour of both buyer and seller, it really only applies where the buyer is in error, although the seller may also be in error. Thus, *error in substantia* does not encompass those situations where the seller alone is mistaken as to the substance of his goods.

In response to these various apparent inconsistencies, commentators have devised a variety of different explanations as to what the jurists were actually concerned with. Because of the fragmented nature of the heavily interpolated passages of the jurists it seems unlikely that the correctness of any one explanation will be established. It is, however, worth considering these explanations because they shed insight into the working of the doctrine and its later role in the development of modern English and European legal systems. It has been noted that there is a difference of approach between English lawyers and continental lawyers because both groups are influenced by contemporary conceptions within their own legal systems.[73] With this caution in mind, what have commentators observed? Lawson considered that the jurists might not have been concerned with mistake but were really thinking of cases where a buyer was entitled to reject a good on the grounds that it was not what he had bargained for.[74] Another possibility advanced by Stein is that the jurists were concerned with situations where an innocent misrepresentation had occurred.[75] In the cases dealing with *error in substantia*, the buyer's mistake does not occur spontaneously but is induced, either deliberately or not, by the seller. Stein observes that while the relevant passages have been heavily interpolated, some parts are likely to be genuine. In these parts, the error is caused by misrepresentation. Thomas opined that *error in substantia* was a manifestation of a form of *error in corpore* or initial impossibility.[76]

According to his theory, the supposed *error in substantia* was a second-century development for which the earliest authority appears to have been Julian. Noting the existence of heavy interpolations and the suspicion that the content of some of the relevant passages had been altered and additions made to them, Thomas examined the language used by the jurists in the texts in an attempt to glean understanding of

[72] De Zulueta (n 65) 26.

[73] R Feenstra, 'The Dutch *Kantharos* Case and the History of *Error in Substantia*' (1973–74) 48 *Tulane Law Review* (Tul L Rev) 846, 849. The author notes the unsatisfactory nature of this 'as legal historians are supposed to go to the sources without any preconceived ideas'.

[74] Lawson (n 70) 79.

[75] P Stein, *Fault in the formation of Contract in Roman and Scots Law* (Edinburgh, University of Aberdeen, 1958) 44–53.

[76] This theory was advanced in a number of publications. See Thomas (n 58) 1203–20; JAC Thomas, *The Institutes of Justinian Text, Translation and Commentary* (Amsterdam and Oxford. North-Holland Publishing Company, 1975) 220; and Thomas (n 12) 230–32.

the doctrine. He noted that it was possible in some instances to interpret passages as pertaining to those situations in which the object is 'offered' as one thing rather than another.[77] In several of the passages, it is apparent that the sale is made in absence of the subject matter and thus by description. Thus, the sale of the slave thought to be male but who was really female must have been made by a (deficient) description. In another instance Ulpian discussed a sale that occurred before the parties but where the vendor is blind: again, the sale must have been by description.[78] Thus, 'the relevance of an *error in substantia* was to identify the thing bought and sold'.[79] The Roman law of sale required a specific object as it knew no *emptio generis*. The relevance of these cases lay in that they were cases of sale by description where the thing did not match the description. Both of the parties had to be mistaken, for bona fides were required on the part of both parties and had the vendor been aware of the true nature of the good, he would be liable for *dolus*.[80] Thomas concluded his examination of *error in substantia* as:

> So conceived, it was not a somewhat mystical addition to the principles of error but, through the dictates of *bona fides* in view of the essential finality of the contract of sale, a special manifestation of *error in corpore* or, indeed, initial impossibility: the supposed object to be sold and bought, as identified by the vendor's description of it, did not exist and the parties' apparent agreement was thereby nullified.[81]

Another theory of the relevance of *error in substantia* within Roman law is that it acted as a form of protection for buyers when the rules pertaining to the vendor's liability for defects in the object of sale were deficient. Feenstra was convinced of this theory, developed by Cornioley,[82] and added his own observations.[83] Feenstra considered the key passages of Ulpian (D.18.1.9.2; D.18.1.11.1; and D.18.1.14) as all dealing with situations where separate legal rules would otherwise have held the seller responsible for the misapprehended nature of the good: for example, a breach of warranty, or a case normally dealt with by special standard clauses in the contracts for the sale of wine. The problems dealt with were similar because they were all cases where the buyer had paid too much. *Error in substantia* was considered by the Romans because of 'the insufficience of the prevailing system of remedies for breach of warranty'.[84] Different jurists dealt with these problems with different devices. Ulpian developed an elaborate theory which distinguished between cases of *error in materia* (which lead to a nullity) and *error in qualitate*

[77] Thomas (n 58) 1212.
[78] D.18.1.11.
[79] Thomas (n 58) 1214.
[80] D.19.1.11.5.
[81] Thomas (n 12) 232. Elsewhere, Thomas explained that 'the subject matter—intended to be bought and sold—as described by the vendor in its absence does not exist, there is, therefore, no contract': Thomas (n 58) 1218.
[82] P Cornioley, 'Error in substantia, in materia, in qualitate', 2 *Studi in onore di Giuseppe Grosso* 251–95 (1968), quoted in Feenstra (n 73) 850.
[83] Feenstra (n 73) 850.
[84] ibid, 854.

(which did not). In some cases, however, an *error in materia* was also an *error in qualitate* and Ulpian was ultimately forced through expediency to create a wider category of *error in substantia.*[85]

What can be concluded from this examination of modern theories as to the nature and existence of *error in substantia* in Roman law? The most obvious conclusion is that the passages are confused and contradictory and avail themselves to multiple convincing interpretations. The importance of the overall functioning of the legal system in which these passages are found cannot be overlooked. A critical problem in understanding these passages is that they are empirical and that they have been removed from their original settings by the compilers. Devoid of this context, with subsequent additions from the compilers, they have thus become capable of multiple meanings. Error in Roman law appears virtually as confusing as mistake in English law. Seen in this light it is not surprising that later common law lawyers and judges were unable to extract a coherent form of guidance as to how to resolve the contractual problems arising from a factual misapprehension. Their difficulties were undoubtedly compounded by the erroneous belief that Roman law provided a solution to these problems.

Medieval Roman Law

Having examined the Roman approach to contractual mistake the remainder of this chapter is concerned with a second purpose. This purpose is to broadly trace the post-classical development of Roman law from Justinian to the work of the sixteenth-century Spanish late scholastics and from them to the natural lawyers.

The oddity of Justinian's compilation is that its immediate impact in Western Europe was slight and indirect. When Justinian's compilation was made, the Western Empire had already been lost. While Justinian made some gains with the recovery of Italy, Spain and north Africa, these were short-lived acquisitions. The Germanic states which succeeded the Western Empire functioned within the norms of late Roman local government. The peoples of Western Europe lived according to customary laws and, in some cases, by codifications promulgated by Germanic kings. These codifications, such as the *lex Romana Visigothorum*, *lex Romana Burgundionum* and the *Edictum Theoderici*, were based upon Justinian's codifications but lacked the complexity and depth of the Roman originals. While law did not disappear, legal science was diminished.[86] The professional jurists

[85] Ulpian was also forced to consider the problem of an error over the sex of the slave (an *error in sexu*), which fitted into neither *error in qualitate* or *error in materia*.

[86] A different view is propounded by M Lupoi, *The Origins of the European Legal Order*, trs A Belton (Cambridge, Cambridge University Press, 2000). He views the period from the fifth to the eleventh centuries not as a time in which law disappeared, but as a time in which the first system of European common law emerged. This common law was based upon vulgar Roman law and various Germanic customs: as an oral culture was moving towards writing, a written culture was moving towards orality. 'The demise of the classical jurists . . . meant not so much the disappearance of conceptual coherence

disappeared: Vinogradoff described the survival of Roman law during this period as a 'ghost story'.[87] Roman law did not entirely disappear, but it survived only as a remnant of ancient culture amongst the learned classes.

Around 1100, Roman law was revived by the (possibly chance) discovery of Justinian's Digest.[88] The 'explanation' for this discovery is a compelling one: the Investiture Contest between the Pope and the Holy Roman Emperor required legal authority.[89] This requirement drove supporters of each of these parties to search diligently through libraries for this authority: during this search, Justinian's Digest was discovered. This fortuitous discovery began a renaissance in European legal studies. Indeed, 'it is difficult to overrate the significance of the rediscovery of the Digest',[90] for while outlines of Roman law could be discerned form other sources available in the medieval world, only the Digest provided a knowledge of Roman law in its entirety to its students. The period marks the beginning of the 'medieval Roman law', the importance of which Wieacker noted was not as to the law itself but as to the tradition of Roman law and the effects this law had upon the life, society and legal systems of the medieval and modern world. There exists a critical distinction between the two objects of medieval Roman law and the preceding classical Roman law: 'On the one side, there is the reality of the ancient Roman world. On the other side, there is the conception which the jurists, historians and philologists of successive epochs had of this reality.'[91]

The conceptions and development of Roman law in the medieval and modern world can be divided into different epochs, dominated by different schools. The renaissance was marked by the work of Irnerius (*c* 1055–1130) a grammarian in Bologna. Irnerius sought to explain the Digest by way of interlinear, and later, marginal notes, 'glosses' on the Digest itself. The result of his efforts was the beginning of a school of Roman study known, from this practice, as the Glossators.[92] The Glossators had an ahistorical approach to the *Corpus Iuris Civilis* in which they viewed the texts as sacred and, despite their many contradictions and difficulties, as capable of resolving any legal problem. The Glossators sought to harmonise and systematise the Corpus through the often strenuous application of

as the predominance of rules over the principles': ibid, 37. Lupoi notes that when this European common law disappeared, from the eleventh century onwards, it remained only in England.

[87] P Vinogradoff, *Roman Law in Medieval Europe*, 2nd edn (Oxford, Clarendon Press, 1961).

[88] What follows in the discussion here is a short summary of a lengthy period of complex legal development. For an introduction to the topic, many excellent works are available. Amongst them are: Julius (n 3); F Schulz, *Classical Roman Law* (Oxford, Oxford University Press, 1954); F Wieacker, *A History of Private Law in Europe*, trs T Weir (Oxford, Clarendon Press, 1995); P Stein, *Roman Law in European History* (Cambridge, Cambridge University Press, 1999); M Bellomo, *The Common Legal Past of Europe 1000–1800*, trs LG Cochrane, (Washington DC, Catholic University Press of America, 1995); RC van Caenegem, *An Historical Introduction to Private Law*, trs DEL Johnston (Cambridge, Cambridge University Press, 1992); and OF Robinson, TD Fergus and WM Gordon, *European Legal History: Sources and Institutions*, 3rd edn (London, Butterworths, 2000).

[89] The Contest was begun during the papacy of Gregory VII (1073–95) and ultimately settled by the Concordat of Worms in 1122.

[90] Stein (n 88) 44.

[91] Wieacker (n 2) 261.

[92] See generally Robinson, Fergus and Gordon (n 88) ch 3 for a discussion of the Glossators.

reason. The work of the Glossators was significant because they created a juristic method of resolving disputes. In Wieacker's words, 'in this sense the Glossators are the fathers of European jurisprudence'.[93] Their work culminated in the *Glossa Ordinaria* of Accursius (*c* 1184–1263): the Accursian Gloss became the standard commentary and companion to the *Corpus* from the mid-thirteenth century. Accursius considered the passage in the Digest[94] regarding mistake and recognised that a mistake would render a contract void. For a mistake to have such effect, it needed to fit within a set type of mistake: an error in 'the fact of the sale'; an error in price; an *error in corpore* (as to the thing); an *error in materia* (as to the matter); an *error in substantia* (as to the substance); or an error in sex.[95] For Accursius, there was no general principle which united these errors, nor did he attempt to find a general principle based upon the passage of the Digest.[96]

Following the publication of the Accursian Gloss the school in Bologna lost its vitality, and the centre and focus of Roman studies shifted in the fourteenth century. The study of Roman law took a different turn. Two major groups of studies emerged: the *Ultramontani* and the Commentators.[97] A law faculty was established north of the Alps (*ultramontani*) at Orléans following the removal of the papal prohibition on the study of law outside Italy. The members of this school were primarily clerics, but clerics who saw the civil law as separate from the canon law. They were critical of the work of the Glossators, but also employed their work to argue independently of the texts and employed reason to discern the law. In this endeavour, they may have been influenced by the work of St Thomas Aquinas and thus somewhat anticipated the work of the late scholastics.[98] The studies at Orléans were concerned with a practical and contemporary application of Roman law. Students at Orléans took their learning into active service in the courts of princes and kings; the result was the consideration of Roman law in relation to local custom. The work and methods of the *Ultramontani* was, in turn, transmitted back to Italy. Here they were to form the impetus for the Commentators of the fourteenth and fifteenth centuries. This movement was begun by Bartolus of Sassoferrato (*c* 1313–57), who taught first at Pisa and then at Perugia. In a short yet productive life, Bartolus produced a rich and detailed commentary upon the whole of the *Corpus*. Bartolus was a significant figure because he sought to give legal solutions to practical, contemporary problems. His student, Baldus de Ubaldis, continued his work with another form of legal literature, the opinion or *consilia*. These opinions were given in response to questions concerning all areas of contemporary law—private, public, feudal and customary. A link was thus created between the practical and the academic: the Commentators were concerned with the interaction of Roman law and other sources of law. Their work left a pronounced impact on the Western legal tradition:

93 Wieacker (n 88) 45.
94 D.18.1.9.
95 Accursius, Gloss to D.18.1.9 to *aliquo alio*.
96 J Gordley, *The Philosophical Origins of Modern Contract Doctrine* (n 1) 59.
97 See, generally, Robinson, Fergus and Gordon (n 88) ch 4 for a discussion of the two groups.
98 ibid, 62. See also, Gordley *The Philosophical Origins of Modern Contract Doctrine* (n 1) 33.

> It was the work of the Commentators that produced the *ius commune*, and then enabled the reception of Roman law in the countries of western Europe during the fifteenth and sixteenth centuries although there is no doubt that the way for that reception was also paved by the canonists and the ecclesiastical courts.[99]

Baldus and Bartolus were also significant in their development of law by their ability to read into the Roman texts Aristotelian ideas in an attempt to better understand the text.[100] Gordley has indicated that there is a remarkable fit between Baldus's conception of *causa* and Aristotelian ideas of liberality and commutative justice.[101] For Baldus, the consent of the parties is binding if it is given for one of these two Aristotelian ideals—a party gives out of liberality or because he gives in exchange for something else. Where this occurred, a party would not be unjustifiably enriched. Consent could, of course, be disrupted by mistake, fraud and duress. Bartolus and Baldus gave the Roman law on mistake an Aristotelian interpretation and 'they concluded that a contract was void for an error in "substance" by which they meant . . . 'substance' or 'essence' in the Aristotelian sense'.[102] For this conclusion, these medieval scholars relied upon the key text found in the Digest[103] in which it was identified that there could be no contract where the parties were mistaken as to the substance of the subject matter of the contract, as where vinegar was sold as wine or copper as gold or lead. While the earlier Glossators had been content to consider that a mistake vitiated a contract if it fell within one of six categories of error, Baldus went further and analysed mistake in relation to an Aristotelian understanding of substance. For Baldus, the Glossators' categories of error were all assimilated into an error in substance: 'a contract was vitiated, he said, for "error in identity, substance or object" on the one hand as opposed to an error in "accidents" on the other'.[104] In considering mistake in relation to Aristotelian substances, Baldus anticipated the later work which was to have such a profound effect upon the considerations placed by later European legal systems on mistake.

As the *ius commune* developed, it created its own law and in this manner moved away from the Justinian codes. The fall of Constantinople in 1453 led many Greek scholars to take refuge in the West. With their arrival there was a renewed interest in classical, and particularly Greek, studies. The Humanists of the sixteenth century had an interest in law. The Humanists had an antiquarian and philological approach to the study of law. They were aware that the Justinian codes were the product of a particular social, cultural and historical era. The Humanists were critical of the efforts of medieval scholars who had ignored this historical context and, as they saw the matter, sought to employ Roman law to solve their particular problems. They

[99] Robinson, Fergus and Gordon (n 88) 70.
[100] Gordley, *The Philosophical Origins of Modern Contract Doctrine* (n 1) 67.
[101] ibid, 55.
[102] ibid, 57. The concept of Aristotelian essence is considered later in this chapter at pp 31–33.
[103] D.18.1.9.2, quoted above at p 21.
[104] Gordley, *The Philosophical Origins of Modern Contract Doctrine* (n 1) 61. (Gordley refers to Baldus, *Commentaria* to D.18.1I.9, no I.)

disparaged what they saw as the crude efforts of the Commentators. The importance of the Humanists in relation to Roman law was that they sought to remove from it the work of the medieval scholars and to restore it to its original meaning. While they rejected the concept that Roman law was the only authoritative law, they were amongst the first in expanding the understanding of Roman law in its classical form. Thus Politian studied the manuscript of the Digest in the Laurentian Library in Florence because he identified it as the closest possible to the original.[105] The Humanists were the first to be concerned with the Roman law which pre-dated Justinian and the first to be concerned with the problem of interpolations (the additions of the compilers and later authors).

Centred in France, the Humanists have long been acknowledged as being of central importance to the development of the seventeenth-century natural lawyers. While the influence of the Humanists upon the natural lawyers has long been noted, Gordley was amongst the first to note the influence of a group of sixteenth- and early seventeenth-century Spanish theologians and jurists known as the late scholastics.[106] While Gordley himself recognised that this explanation of legal change and continuity seems odd to those who look to external factors for legal change and continuity,[107] the seminal influence of the late scholastics upon the development of the law of reason and the natural lawyers has also been noted by Wieacker.[108] Because Gordley's thesis about the development of modern contract law is a compelling one, and critical to a proper understanding of the modern development of English contractual mistake, a summary of it will be provided here.

Gordley's work is a study of the evolution of great concepts of law in the Western world. The study is concentrated upon the intellectual history of law in which philosophers, theologians and jurists generate change or maintain continuity rather than social or economic forces brought to bear upon legal systems.[109]

[105] Politian believed it to be the actual manuscript sent by Justinian to Pope Vigilius in the 550s.

[106] The central work is J Gordley, *The Philosophical Origins of Modern Contract Doctrine* (n 1). His views are also expressed in some of his other writings: 'Natural Law Origins of the Common Law of Contract' in J Barton (ed), *Towards a General Law of Contract* (Berlin, Duncker & Humblot, 1990); 'Myths of the French Civil Code' (1994) 42 *American Journal of Comparative Law* (Am J Comp L) 459; 'Why Look Backward' (2002) 50 Am J Comp L 657; and *Foundations of Private Law: Property, Tort, Contract, Unjust Enrichment* (n 1). Gordley touches upon the previous separation of law and theory in 'Law and Religion: An Imaginary Conversation with a Medieval Jurist' (1987) 75 *California Law Review* 169.

[107] Gordley, *The Philosophical Origins of Modern Contract Doctrine* (n 1) 4.

[108] Wieacker (n 88) 208–11. Wieacker is careful to note that the work of the late scholastics permeated not only Catholic Europe but also Protestant Europe. It has also been accepted by Professor Ibbetson: see *A Historical Introduction to the Law of Obligations* (Oxford, Oxford University Press, 1999) 217–18.

[109] Gordley's thesis thus contrasts with those who argue that contract law developed in response to external factors, such as PS Atiyah, *The Rise and Fall of Freedom of Contract* (Oxford, Oxford University Press, 1979), G Gilmore, *The Death of Contract* (Columbus, Ohio State University Press, 1974), and MJ Horwitz, *The Transformation of American Law 1780–1860* (Cambridge, MA, and London, Harvard University Press, 1977). Although there is not room to explore this further, there is merit in the criticism made by one of Gordley's reviewers that it may well be impossible to separate internal and external factors: MH Ogilvie, 'The Philosophical Origins of Modern Contract Doctrine by James Gordley', (1992–93) 21 *Canadian Business Law Journal* 133, 139–40.

Internal, rather than external, forces, shape the development of legal principles. Central to this intellectual evolution is a transmission, refinement and adaptation of ideas. At its simplest, Gordley's hypothesis is that our modern law is based upon a modified version of a synthesis of Greek philosophy and Roman law achieved by a group of sixteenth-century Spanish theologians and jurists known as the late scholastics. The natural lawyers borrowed from, and thus popularised, the work of the late scholastics; and the work of the natural lawyers was, in turn, borrowed to lay the legal foundations of nineteenth-century English, French and German law. As these ideas and concepts were passed down, the law transmitted became separated from the philosophy which had embodied the law. Essentially, later jurists removed from contract theory the moral virtues which had underpinned and explained why the will of individuals should be upheld by the law in enforcing agreements entered into with the consent of these individuals: all the later jurists retained was a theory of human will and the justification that contracts should be enforced to give effect to this will. The result was a law which was adapted to serve ends which had been removed and replaced with other ends. Viewed from this perspective, it is not surprising that the resulting legal systems faced doctrinal crisis.

Gordley's account is one demarcated by the European rediscovery of the knowledge of the ancient world. The rediscovery of Roman law in the form of the *Corpus Iuris Civilis* has already been outlined. Two centuries after this rediscovery, Aristotle's works on metaphysics, physics, politics and ethics became available in the West. While Aristotelian concepts had a limited influence upon some of the medieval jurists, it was the late scholastics who sought to solve the legal problems posed by the Romans with the larger philosophical ideas of Aristotle, as interpreted by Thomas Aquinas. They believed that the inconsistencies of Roman law could be explained by Aristotelian and Thomastic doctrine. Central to the contract doctrine of the late scholastics were three Aristotelian virtues: promise-keeping, commutative justice and liberality.[110] For Aristotle, liberality is a virtue manifested in the giving and taking of wealth—particularly the giving of wealth. Wealth was given away 'to the right people, in the right amounts, and at the right time'.[111] Unlike liberality, commutative justice required equality. In this instance, the parties exchanged value in such a fashion that neither party was enriched at the expense of the other. The obligations of the parties depended upon which virtue they were attempting to exercise. The consequences of a particular contract followed from the essence of the contract, either because the consequences were included in the definition of the contract or because they were a means to the end by which the contract was defined. While Aristotle merely identified certain transactions, Aquinas defined them:

> [Aquinas] would have started from these definitions. He would have tried to show that each contract carries with it a set of obligations that follow from its definition. Either of

[110] Gordley has also explored these virtues in 'The Moral Foundations of Private Law' (2002) 47 *American Journal of Jurisprudence* 1.

[111] Gordley, *The Philosophical Origins of Modern Contract Doctrine* (n 1) 55.

> these obligations are included in the concepts used to formulate the definitions, or are means to the end in terms of which the contract has been defined.[112]

The Aristotelian and Thomastic view of the world was one made up of things referred to as substances—people, plants, animals and elements of the inorganic world they believed to be earth, air, fire and water. Each substance behaved in a definite way: this behaviour was established by what was within the substance rather than what was outside the substance. The component within the substance responsible for behaviour was described as its nature. Things with the same nature are the same kind of thing. Thus, for Aquinas, contract is defined by an end that is at once the immediate end of the parties and a means to their ultimate end. Since contract is defined by the immediate end of the parties, the definition expresses the minimum the parties must know to contract. It also identifies an end to be served through other obligations that belong to the contract although the parties may not have had them consciously in mind.[113]

The late scholastics continued the work that Aquinas had begun.[114] Their work was a part of a larger intellectual revival of Thomastic philosophy. The work of the late scholastics was begun by Francisco de Vitoria, a student of Pierre Crockaert at Paris. Vitoria returned to his native Spain, then at the height of its golden age, and taught at the University of Salamanca from 1526 until his death in 1546.[115] The late scholastics studied Thomastic philosophy because they saw it as the cure for the chief intellectual, spiritual and political evils of the age:

> Its members disliked nominalism in philosophy, Protestantism in religion, and absolutism in politics. The source of these errors, they thought, was scepticism about the existence of an order in the world that human reason could discover. Because of that scepticism, nominalist philosophers claimed that abstract concepts were creations of the mind rather than discoveries about the world. Lutherans and Calvinists claimed that the Fall had so debased man that he could neither discover nor do what is good. Princes claimed that the law depended on their will alone. The antidote was Thomism with its confidence in natural reason, and particularly Thomistic ideas of natural law.[116]

The synthesis begun by these Dominicans was completed in the late sixteenth and early seventeenth centuries by the Jesuits Francisco Suarez (1548–1617), Luis de Molina (1535–1600) and Leonard Lessius (1554–1623). The synthesis of Aristotelian

[112] ibid, 15.

[113] ibid, 23.

[114] See, generally, ibid, ch 4. Gordley's thesis is considered by Berman who observes that the Lutheran jurists Johann Oldendorp also adopted the Aristotelian concepts of liberality and commutative justice as 'causes' of law: HJ Berman, *Law and Revolution, II* (Cambridge, MA, and London, Harvard University Press, 2003) 416–17. Berman also observes Protestant influences upon the work of the late scholastics. This strengthens, in some ways, Gordley's hypothesis about the Aristotelian influence upon modern legal doctrine as Berman is of the opinion that the Lutheran Reformation had a profound impact upon the Western legal tradition. Gordley himself largely ignores the effect of the Protestant Reformation upon the process he outlines.

[115] Although he published nothing himself, he trained many highly influential pupils, notably the jurist Diego de Covarruvias (1512–77) and the theologian Domingo de Soto (1494–1560).

[116] Gordley, *The Philosophical Origins of Modern Contract Doctrine* (n 1) 70.

and Thomastic philosophy with Roman law undertaken by the late scholastics had no immediate impact upon the practice of law. What it did have an impact upon was the way in which contract law was understood. The late scholastics analysed the virtues of promise-keeping, commutative justice and liberality to discern the binding force of contract. While the Romans themselves had not so analysed contract law, the result that the late scholastics reached was that 'promises are enforceable in principle if they are made for a good *causa* and accepted by the promisee'.[117] For the late scholastics' conception of *causa* every enforceable contract had to be made for one of two *causae*, or reasons: either liberality or the receipt of a performance in return for one's own (commutative justice).[118] They expressed this idea by classifying contracts as either gratuitous or onerous. In short, *causa* was an attempt to limit the enforceability of promises because *causa* existed in two circumstances where there are good reasons for promises to be kept: by the exercise of the virtues of liberality and commutative justice.[119] The late scholastics required that the promises were binding if they were made for one of these two *causae* and were accepted. The late scholastics analysed contractual consent by applying Aristotelian and Thomastic ideas about human intellect and will. A person is responsible for his action if it proceeds from his reason and will. He must have known the essential feature of his action and chosen to perform this action. An action is not a voluntary one if the person does not know what he is doing or if he does know what he is doing but he does not choose to do so where he is moved by force.

The application of these ideas led the late scholastics to consider how duress, mistake and fraud would affect the voluntary nature of an action. In relation to mistake, Aquinas explained that an act is involuntary when a man is ignorant of some circumstance and therefore does what he would not do if he knew of the actual circumstances. A man acts to achieve an end and wants to achieve this end as a means to further ends which are meant to be his ultimate ends. A circumstance of which a person was ignorant at the moment of choice frustrates the attainment of these remote ends and thus renders the action involuntary. The required knowledge is, however, limited to the essentials of the transaction. An action is thus rendered involuntary when a man does not understand the essentials of what he is doing. Lessius and Molina cited D.18.1.9, in which it was stated that a party to a sale did not consent if he made an error in substance. For Lessius and Molina, the term 'substance' meant 'essentials'. In this way, the Roman text was given an Aristotelian theory never intended by the Romans. To recapitulate, the binding force of a promise was explained by the late scholastics in terms of the Aristotelian virtues of promise-keeping—liberality and commutative justice. These virtues formed the *causa* for a promise, and promises were binding if they were made for a good *causa* and accepted. This consent could be vitiated by the presence of a mistake—but only where the mistake was as to the essentials of what the party was undertaking.

[117] ibid, 72.
[118] ibid, 77.
[119] ibid, 79.

The curious fact for Gordley about his hypothesis as to the shape of modern law is not that it so evolved as a result of the synthesis created by the late scholastics but that when the attacks of later philosophers led to the demise of Aristotelian metaphysics and moral philosophy, the legal synthesis based upon Aristotle survived and flourished. The attacks on Aristotle began in the seventeenth century. The physical discoveries of Galileo and, later, Newton indicated that the world had a different explanation than Aristotle's metaphysics. The new science indicated that the world was not explained in terms of the substance of objects or their ends. Instead, the movement of physical objects conformed to mathematical formulae. Philosophers noticed this and also seized upon an epistemological problem noted by the medieval nominalists—that one cannot logically demonstrate that the substance of a thing exists from the fact that the accidents of it are perceived. The result was that 'one could no longer speak of activities that contribute to the end of man or the virtues that make such activities possible'.[120] Philosophers such as Descartes, Hobbes and Locke were aware that if Aristotle's metaphysical premises were false, so too was his account of morality, choice and knowledge:

> There could be no virtues in the sense of acquired faculties by which one moved towards one's end. There could be no essences in the sense of concepts through which one grasped the substantial form of a thing or an action. Choice could not depend on knowing the essence of one's action. Knowledge could not be acquired by capturing an essence in a definition and then drawing out its consequences.[121]

Ultimately Aristotelian philosophy was unable to survive an attack on such a fundamental element of its principles. How did the synthesis of the late scholastics survive this collapse?

The answer Gordley formulates is that it is possible to have intellectual continuity despite a change in philosophical principle.[122] At first instance, it was not immediately apparent that the work of these new philosophers required a response from the jurists. Grotius borrowed from the work of the late scholastics and, when he wrote, he wrote at a time when Aristotle dominated the universities of Europe.[123] It is a myth to view Grotius as rebelling against the scholastic philosophic tradition, for he was at home in an Aristotelian world.[124] Grotius reproduced the solutions of the late scholastics without reproducing their analysis: it may be that he did not understand the concepts upon which it was based.[125]

[120] ibid, 115.

[121] ibid, 112.

[122] ibid, 129. A criticism of Gordley's thesis is that the difficulties of modern contract law could be traced to a coming apart of Aristotelian and Thomastic principle and that Gordley's requirement of the ethic of virtue in contract law may be 'fundamentally incompatible with the sublimation of law inherent in natural law theory and the abstract doctrinal structures that build upon natural law': NE Simmonds, 'The Philosophical Origins of Modern Contract Doctrine. By James Gordley' (1992) *Cambridge Law Journal* 154, 155.

[123] Wieacker has also noted Grotius's intellectual debt to the late scholastics: *A History of Private Law in Europe* (n 88) 209.

[124] ibid, 123.

[125] ibid, 90.

Drawing upon the earlier work of the *Ultramontani* and the late scholastics, Grotius found that 'the treatment of agreements based on a misapprehension is perplexing enough'.[126] He noted that it was customary to distinguish errors which were of substance from those which were not, and also between errors which were caused by the fraud of one party and those which were not. He then considered, by way of analogy, that a law based on a misapprehension of fact was not a binding law once the misapprehension was discovered. Similarly, a promise based upon a misapprehension was of no force: 'For the promisor did not consent to the promise except under a certain condition which, in fact, did not exist'.[127] If the error was not the matter upon which the promise was founded, the promise is good (although if the error was brought about by fraud, the promisor would be liable for the fraud). Grotius, having separated the Aristotelian elements from the work of the late scholastics, gives no guidance on that critical issue of when an error formed the basis of an agreement and when it did not. A vague reference in his analogy to a law indicates that the matter can be inferred from substance, words and circumstances,[128] but little else is offered for guidance. Grotius's theory is impossible to apply because the reasons for the theory have been omitted. As Gordley has observed, Grotius has employed uncertain phrases to attack particular problems and no underlying theory of consent can be constructed from his work.[129]

Yet later writers such as Pufendorf and Barbeyrac removed Aristotelian elements and freely borrowed elements from new philosophies of Descartes and Locke without altering the philosophical principles upon which they based their jurisprudence. Pufendorf, in considering contracts, stated that the consent of the parties was critical because it was by this consent, freely given, that the pact or promise was enforceable against him.[130] Consent was entirely nullified by error, 'because of which it happens that the mind wanders from the true object of a promise or pact, and as a consequence the will does not in fact agree to it'.[131] Pufendorf distinguished between errors concerned with a promise or a pact. Where a promise was based on the presumption of some fact or made on the supposition of fact or quality such that the maker would not have bound themselves if the fact or quality was not there, then the promise would have no force. This was only the case where 'the very nature of the business and the circumstances clearly show' that the basis of consent was conditioned upon the fact or quality. 'The ground for this is, that the promissory did not give his absolute consent to the promise, but made as a condition the presumption of this fact or quality' and if the condition was no longer present, 'whatever had been based upon it falls to the

[126] H Grotius, *De Jure Belli Ac Pacis Libri Tres*, trs FW Kelsey (Oxford, Clarendon Press, 1925) XI, vi, 1, 333.

[127] ibid, XI, vi, 2.

[128] ibid, XI, vi, 1.

[129] Gordley, *The Philosophical Origins of Modern Contract Doctrine* (n 1) 91.

[130] S Pufendorf, *De Jure Naturae et Gentium Libri Octo*, trs CH Oldfather and WA Oldfather (Oxford, Clarendon Press, 1934) VI (402).

[131] ibid, VI, 6 (408).

ground and vanishes'.[132] Where the promise was not premised upon the presence or absence of some quality as a condition, then no matter what the quality proved to be, the promise was good.[133] Where the promise was only partly built upon an error, it would be good for the remainder of the promise unless the error was integral to the accomplishment of all of the parts of the promise or if the error was related to the performance of the condition. In these latter cases, an error in part would destroy the promise. Pufendorf further distinguished between an error which induced a man to enter into a pact and an error concerned with the subject matter of the pact. In the former case, a man induced by error to enter into a pact could 'repent' of the promise while it was still executory: once performance, even partial, had begun, 'the man who made the mistake will not be able to urge the rescinding of the contract'.[134] In the latter case, where the error concerned the thing about which the agreement is made, the pact is void, not because of the error, but because the laws of the pact have not been satisfied. 'Pacts require that the thing itself, about which the agreement is being made, and its qualities, should be understood, and unless there is this understanding no clear consent can be recognized.'[135] That to avoid the pact the error had to be one of 'essentials' rather than 'accidentals' 'is to be interpreted as meaning that by the essentials of a pact are understood not only such things as enter into the physical essence of the matter over which the pact is made, but also those qualities which the maker of the pact had especially before his eyes': a quality of the subject matter can sometimes be regarded as of the first importance, while the physical substance is regarded as a mere necessary accessory.[136] As with Grotius, there is little guidance as to when an error is of a sufficiently fundamental nature to avoid a contract and when it is not so fundamental. The ambit of the mistake is restricted, by the requirement that where a motive is based upon a mistake, the contract is good beyond the point of performance. Grotius and Pufendorf had made consent a basis for enforcing contracts in a way that the late scholastics had not. While the late scholastics had explained contracts in terms of the Aristotelian and Thomastic virtue of faith or truth, these later natural lawyers made arguments based upon such virtue without explaining its central role to the late scholastics' conception of contract.[137]

Why did these later thinkers reject Aristotle's metaphysics and yet accept the Aristotelian concepts created by the late scholastics? The reason, for Gordley, is that Grotius, Pufendorf and Barbeyrac were involved in a different sort of project than the late scholastics. Their project was not the one undertaken by the late scholastics, of tracing each legal rule back to its philosophical foundation, but of

[132] ibid.

[133] ibid (409).

[134] ibid. The same conclusion was reached several centuries later by the House of Lords in *Bell v Lever Brothers* [1932] AC 161. The process of reasoning employed by Lord Atkin was not dissimilar to that set out by Pufendorf.

[135] Pufendorf (n 130) (410).

[136] ibid.

[137] J Gordley, 'Natural Law Origins of the Common Law of Contract', in J Barton (ed), *Towards a General Law of Contract* (Berlin, Duncker u. Humblot, 1990) 425.

explaining and writing law in such a way as to place legal science within the domain of educated intelligent men. 'By making moral knowledge more accessible, they expected to raise the moral level of human conduct.'[138] Their criticism of the late scholastics was not of their philosophical foundations, but of the obscurantism present in their written style. While the natural law jurists succeeded in making moral truth accessible to mankind, it came at a cost. The cost was a loss of philosophical depth and in rigour of argument. As the link between philosophical principle and legal doctrine was obscured, the essential difficulty in preserving the late scholastic legal doctrines whilst repudiating the Aristotelian philosophy upon which it was based remained hidden. Even later, writers unfamiliar with the Aristotelian tradition abandoned those doctrines which made no sense to them and appeared to contradict what they sought to preserve of the tradition.[139] It is not intended to take the reader through the various theories of mistake devised by these later thinkers,[140] for the jurisprudence of the common law of contractual mistake was created in the nineteenth century by lawyers, judges and jurists who were greatly influenced by only two of these thinkers: the Frenchman Robert Joseph Pothier, and the German Friedrich Carl von Savigny. These jurists fit within the evolutionary pattern described by Gordley and contribute to the ultimate result in the nineteenth century, which was a legal philosophy filled with contradictions and inconsistencies. The process by which this came about is the subject of chapters five and six. We turn now to survey the state of contractual mistake in England in equity and at common law during the eighteenth and nineteenth centuries.

[138] ibid, 130.

[139] ibid, 132.

[140] For these other thinkers, see Gordley, *The Philosophical Origins of Modern Contract Doctrine* (n 1) chs 5 and 7, and also J Gordley, 'Mistake in Contract Formation' (2004) 52 Am J Comp L 433, 434–42.

3

Contractual Mistake in English Law

Mistake in Equity before 1875

WHILE CIVILIAN JURISTS were concerned with the effect of a mistake upon the formation of a contract, far less attention was paid to this subject by English lawyers. In the common law courts a mistake, as such, did not attract legal consideration and consequences until the middle of the nineteenth century. Although courts of common law would not attach legal consequences to a mistake, courts of equity, acting to complement rather than to challenge the common law, did attach legal consequences to a mistake. This chapter examines mistake in equity from the eighteenth century until the 'fusion' of law and equity in 1875. The recognition of mistake was embedded in the jurisdiction and procedures of the Court of Chancery and it is here that our examination begins.

Equitable relief for mistake was not based upon a failure of consent in the formation of the contract. While equity lawyers were clearly aware from the eighteenth century of civilian doctrines on this point, it was not the reason for equitable relief. Equity recognised mistake as a factor, like fraud, accident or surprise, which could affect the conscience of the individual. In such circumstances it was unjust for a court of equity to allow an agreement founded upon mistake to stand or to be enforced. The recognition of a mistake in equity occurred partly in response to common law rules concerned with parol evidence and the Statute of Frauds; it was also intrinsically related to the grant of equitable relief itself. Courts of equity decided whether or not to exercise their discretion to provide relief on the basis of the facts of the particular case before them and in relation to previous cases in which the discretion had been exercised. As precedents built through the nineteenth century and law reporting became more comprehensive a body of principles came to be recognised. As one mid-nineteenth-century barrister argued, equitable relief was not arbitrary, for 'it is regulated by defined rules and principles'.[1] This chapter explores the reasons why courts gave relief for mistakes, the limitations upon this relief and the forms of relief given. Equity gave relief for reasons related to conscience and not consent, and equitable relief admitted a certain flexibility not possessed by the common law. In attaching legal consequences to a mistake, equity was not in conflict with the common law. It attached legal consequence to the mistake because it had the procedures to establish with

[1] Per Mr Rolt in *Watson v Marston* (1853) 4 De G M & G 230; 43 ER 495 at 237; 498.

some certainty that a mistake had occurred and because its remedial flexibility afforded the court an opportunity to attempt to remedy the effect of the mistake. Equity provided a complement to the common law rather than a conflict.

The Jurisdiction and Procedures of Chancery

The core of the equitable jurisdiction of Chancery was property management: the court provided a forum for disputes which arose in a complicated and often arcane system of land ownership. A system which allowed contemporaneous interests of different natures coupled with the recognition, through family settlements, of the desire to control the successive interests of the land ownership in the absence of any system of registration was one bound to give rise to misapprehensions.[2] Chancery attempted to resolve these misapprehensions, and the early mistake cases are dominated by the marriage settlement which incorrectly records the intentions of the parties[3] or the distribution of an estate which the parties agreed to compromise[4] or situations where the way in which land was held and conveyed created difficulties in ascertaining the extent of the interest.[5] Mercantile cases exist, but they are not commonplace.[6] Mistake was conceived of broadly, not only with respect to mistakes in contracts, but also mistakes in wills and in powers.

While contract was a subject matter of both common law and equity, equity was able to provide relief that the law was not. In particular, with an order for specific performance, equity was able to provide the very thing which had been contracted for, whilst courts of law were confined to awarding pecuniary compensation for a breach of contract. Chancery procedures were better suited to ascertaining the existence of mistakes. While the procedures of Chancery were to cause crisis by the nineteenth century,[7] these procedures allowed parties to explicitly bring forward a misapprehension which had arisen in the contractual process. Chancery required all who had an interest in the suit to be a party, and each party could put in an answer to the bill which had initiated the suit. The Court of Chancery could also compel by oath of the defendant a discovery of the facts within his knowledge.

[2] The difficulties facing parties involved in such a system can be seen in Edward Sugden's novel volume in which he attempted to assist lay people to prevent problems arising, in part, through such misapprehensions: Sir EB Sugden, *A Series of Letters to a Man of Property on Sales, Purchases, Morgages, Leases, Settlements, and Devises of Estates* (London, J Harding, 1809) Letter I, 1.

[3] See, eg, *Uvedale v Halfpenny* (1723) 2 P Wms 151; 24 ER 677, and *Langley v Brown* (1741) 2 Atk 195; 26 ER 521.

[4] *Gee v Spencer* (1681) 1 Vern 32; 23 ER 236, and *Martin v Savage* (1740) Barn C 190; 27 ER 608.

[5] *Howland v Norris* (1784) 1 Cox 59; 29 ER 1062.

[6] See, eg, *Henkle v Royal Exchange Assurance Company* (1749) 1 Ves Sen 318; 27 ER 1055 (a policy of insurance over a vessel), *Baker v Paine* (1750) 1 Ves Sen 456; 27 ER 1140 (an agreement to sell goods), *Simpson v Vaughan* (1739) 2 Atk 31; 26 ER 415 (the bond of a tradesman). Similarly, the Court of Exchequer also considered mistake when it applied its equitable jurisdiction.

[7] M Lobban, 'Preparing for Fusion: Reforming the Nineteenth-Century Court of Chancery, Part I' (2004) 22 *Law and History Review* 389, 391–97.

Because of this ability to discover facts within the knowledge of a witness, courts of equity were said to have acquired an almost exclusive jurisdiction in mistake (along with account, fraud and accident).[8] The principle difference between courts of law and courts of equity lay not in the subject matter of the courts, but in their method of proceeding and in the relief that they could afford. In the words of one contemporary:

> The equitable jurisdiction is founded upon and follows the civil law in many of its leading doctrines, particularly of legacies and contracts; but the essential differences which distinguish the courts of equity from courts of law, seem to be rather in the mode of proceeding, than in the subjects of their jurisdiction. These differences in the mode of proceeding consist in compelling a discovery on the oath of the party; in the method of trial by depositions in writing, taken in any part of the world; and in the mode of relief, by giving a more specific and extensive remedy than can be had in the courts of law.[9]

The jurisdiction of courts of equity was defined by its relation to the jurisdiction of courts of law. A generally recognised tripartite classification divided equitable jurisdiction into an *auxiliary* or *assistant jurisdiction* in which equity assisted courts of law in their operation; a *concurrent jurisdiction* where both law and equity had jurisdiction over a matter but equity provided distinct remedies to uphold rights established by law; and an *exclusive jurisdiction* in which only equity operated, such as trusts.[10] Contract was a matter of concurrent jurisdiction, and mistake, in relation to contract, lay mostly within this concurrent jurisdiction. By the eighteenth century, equitable procedures existed to facilitate its function and this function was to remedy defects at law which courts of common law could not address. In 1737, in an early and important attempt to explain what courts of equity did, the anonymous author of *A Treatise of Equity*[11] wrote that, with regard to contracts, equity would intervene where the law was defective and fell short of natural justice because equity claimed the power to conduct and guide the rules of law according to good conscience and honesty.[12] In short:

> Equity regards not the outward Form, but the inward Substance and Essence of the Matter; which is the Agreement of the Parties, upon a good and valuable Consideration,

[8] C Barton, *An Historical Treatise of a Suit in Equity* (London, W Clarke & Son, 1796) 20–21. Henry Maddock observed that courts of equity could call or adduce evidence which could not be presented to courts of law, amongst which was evidence of mistake: H Maddock, *A Treatise on the Principles and Practice of the High Court of Chancery, vol II* (New York, Gould, Banks and Gould, 1817) 333.

[9] G Cooper, *A Treatise of Pleading on the Equity-Side of the High Court of Chancery* (London, Butterworth, 1809) xxvi. A more critical view of obtaining the evidence of the defendant is related by Augustine Birrell in 'Changes in Equity, Procedure, and Principles', in *A Century of Law Reform* (London, Macmillan and Co, 1901) 186–90.

[10] As Mike Macnair has observed, the classification was undertaken by Fonblanque and accepted with some changes by Story: M Macnair, 'Equity and Conscience' (2007) 27 *Oxford Journal of Legal Studies* 659, 665. Macnair describes Fonblanque's division as an 'error' which has, in turn, impeded understanding of equity jurisdiction.

[11] (London, Browne and Shuckburgh, 1737). The work is sometimes attributed to Henry Ballow.

[12] ibid, 5. Sixty years later, Barton wrote that the courts of equity were extraordinary tribunals established to remedy the defects which had become apparent in courts of law: Barton (n 8) 22. As to the possible meaning of conscience, see Macnair (n 10).

> and where the Persons interested fully intend to contract a perfect Obligation, tho' by Mistake or Accident, they omit the set Form of Law, so that no Remedy is to be had to compel a Performance of it in Courts of Civil Judicature; yet they are bound in natural Justice to stand to their Agreement.[13]

The author of *A Treatise of Equity* organised and explained equity jurisprudence using civilian theories, notably those of Grotius, and thus considered mistake in the context of consent. Mistake is an impediment of assent if the ignorance or error 'be the Cause and Motive of the Agreement'.[14] Where the misapprehension went to the very subject matter of the contract, it was null because there was no consent. If the mistake was discovered before performance, it was just that a party could remove himself from the agreement, where he could pay damages. Once the agreement was wholly or partly performed and no compensation could be given, the agreement remained binding. The author observed that mistake and ignorance were related to fraud[15] and to unconscionable bargains.[16] Relief for mistake often encompassed or touched upon two longstanding and constant rules by which a party to a deed could obtain relief—where there was either *suppressio veri* or *suggestio falsi* by another party. While the author accurately explained equitable practice in this area, he did so on a basis alien to the cases (consensus) and it is no coincidence that he did not directly base his theory upon the cases. The addition of cases came to the *Treatise* in John Fonblanque's later annotation.[17] Fonblanque, a barrister, resisted the attractions of civilian consensus theory and while he did not ignore these theorists,[18] his explanation of the theory in relation to English case law had the effect of limiting and qualifying the broad statements of his anonymous predecessor. From these limits, a different picture as to the nature and purpose of equitable relief for mistake emerged.[19] Interestingly, Fonblanque was also counsel in some of the leading mistake cases of his day, and he did not attempt to introduce the arguments of the civilians in these cases.[20] Equity was rarely concerned with the civilians in the formulation of equitable mistake.

The cases confirm that equity would intervene to alleviate the harshness of the common law where an agreement had been formed under a misapprehension. In

[13] A Treatise of Equity (n 11) 5.
[14] ibid, 10.
[15] ibid, 21.
[16] ibid, 23.
[17] J Fonblanque, *A Treatise of Equity, with the Addition of Marginal References and Notes* (Dublin, Byrne, Moore, Jones, Lynch and Watts, 1793). In his preface, Fonblanque explains that he has been unable to ascertain the identity of the author of the Treatise, although he attributes it to Henry Ballow. A treatise which is anonymous and without references is, he explains, 'a circumstance which of itself materially affects the authority of law publications': ibid, vii.
[18] He refers to the works of Pufendorf, Barbeyrac, Grotius, Domat and Cicero, amongst others.
[19] Fonblanque (n 17) 106–107 fn (t). The limitations he wrote of were that the relief was not available: (1) where the right was doubtful; (2) where there was acquiescence; and (3) where the agreement was to prevent family disputes or maintain family honour. If lack of consent actually rendered the contract void, none should be limitations.
[20] See, eg, *Marquis Townshend v Stangroom* (1801) 6 Ves Jun 328; 31 ER 1076, and *Rob v Butterwick* (1816) 2 Price 190; 146 ER 65.

1681, the Lord Chancellor set aside a release of arrears where the party granting the release had done so under a misapprehension.[21] Little explanation is given for why mistake has such an effect. The implication is that the mistake was something in the nature of fraud brought about by the party who procured the release. The Lord Chancellor relied upon another case decided in the same year, *Luxford's case*,[22] from which the reporter had extrapolated that the 'the principle seems to be that mistakes and misapprehensions in the drawing (and a fortiori in the executing) of deeds, form as much a head of relief in equity as fraud and imposition'.

It is clear that by the eighteenth century courts of equity granted relief to parties where a mistake had occurred in the formation of their contract or in the written expression of this contract. It is not easy to ascertain the ambit of this intervention because of the often brief nature of early law reports coupled with an apparent judicial reticence to discuss the relief in any detail. Courts of equity sought to provide a substantial justice to the parties in a way that courts of law could not. This did not mean, however, that they intervened in every case of mistake, because the courts felt themselves to be bound by administer their justice on the basis of their own previous decisions. The adherence to the precedent of early decisions was one that strengthened throughout this time period. In deciding, however, whether or not the previous decisions applied, the courts were particularly dependent upon the facts of cases. Courts insisted upon very strong evidence of the mistake, particularly as this would often take the form of parol evidence. Concerns were, nevertheless, expressed about the justice of such a system: 'This inconvenience belongs to the administration of justice; that the minds of different men will differ upon the result of the evidence; which may lead to different decisions upon the same case'.[23] The principle was, of course, one related to proof, but it indicates the basis upon which courts of equity proceeded at the beginning of the eighteenth century. Courts of equity were willing to intervene because, unlike courts of common law, they had the mechanisms to discern a misapprehension. It is the evidence of the misapprehension, provided by material witnesses and the parties themselves, which appears to compel them to act. This was, as the courts openly admitted, evidence which would be inadmissible at law.[24] As Lord Thurlow pointed out, however, where there was not distinct evidence of the mistake, equity would not intervene.[25]

While mistake in equity was to become a substantive concept, its origins lie in its relationship with what has largely become a procedural point, the admission of parol evidence. As Professor Stone observed,[26] when the use of documents as a

[21] *Gee v Spencer* 1 Vern 32; 23 ER 286; the case is also reported at 1 Eq Ca Abr 170; 21 ER 965.

[22] Cited in *Gee v Spencer* (n 21).

[23] *Marquis Townshend v Stangroom* (n 20) 334–35; 1078–79 per Lord Eldon.

[24] ibid, 333; 1078.

[25] *Burt v Barham* (1792) 3 Bro CC 451; 29 ER 638 at 454–55, 639–40. The same point is clearly enunciated by Lord Hardwicke in *Henkle v Royal Exchange Assurance Company* (n 6) and the decision in *Countess of Shelburne v Earl of Inchiquin* (1783) 1 Bro CC 338; 28 ER 1166. At other times, judges seemed to have required a somewhat lower standard of evidence (see, eg, *Simpson v Vaughan* (1739) 2 Atk 31; 26 ER 415), which lends support to Lord Eldon's concerns.

[26] J Stone, *Evidence Its History and Policies*, revd WAN Wells (Sydney, Butterworths, 1991) 24–29.

method of affecting legal rights began, this led to a 'trial by charters' in which, since the charter was the judgment and the trial merely a method of allowing this judgment to operate, it then followed that no material beyond the charter could be adduced.[27] From this developed the prohibition on the admission of parol evidence which sought to vary or add to the terms of a document embodying a legal transaction. The process by which this occurred was probably complete by the end of the seventeenth century, at which point 'the parol evidence rule then presented the appearance of an arbitrary and unqualified canon of exclusion'.[28] At around this time the Statute of Frauds 1677[29] was enacted and it provided, inter alia, that parol evidence had no effect in passing or creating a trust or estate in land, Chancery's core jurisdiction. The Statute of Frauds had its own impact upon the parol evidence rule in two principal manners: first, it authoritatively provided a rational basis of the rule (as the preamble stated, 'for prevention of many fraudulent practices, which are commonly endeavoured to be upheld by perjury and subornation of perjury'); and, second, it established that certain important classes of transactions were unenforceable unless in writing, and this acted to greatly multiply the proportion of cases before the courts in which documents were evidence.[30] Unsurprisingly, this development led to the creation of exceptions, largely designed to fulfil the purpose of the rule. Courts of equity were less constrained than courts of common law in this development. Equity soon recognised that, to prevent an injustice, evidence was admissible to show that the contract embodied in the written document was void or voidable. One of the bases upon which a contract could be avoided was mistake, and evidence could be admitted to establish this. The process was, to modern eyes, an odd amalgam of what later became distinct elements of substantive law and procedural law, a matter which can be seen in the work of Edward Sugden. Sugden, the son of a Westminster barber and wigmaker, apparently learnt most of his law himself. At 24 he wrote a major treatise, *Vendors and Purchasers of Legal Estates*, which proved enormously influential throughout the nineteenth century. Largely eschewing civilian sources,[31] Sugden turned to the cases and the statutes of the common law itself to create a coherent and rational explanation for the operation of law and equity. He considered mistake not as a substantive topic but as an integral part of the law concerned with the admission of parol evidence.[32] In Sugden's view, the rules of evidence were the same in courts of law and equity, and neither court would admit parol evidence which would substantively alter a written agreement.[33] Where,

[27] ibid, 26.

[28] ibid, 28. See also the judgment in *Clowes v Higginson* (1813) 1 V & B 524; 35 ER 204 at 526; 205, in which the process is discussed.

[29] 29 Car 2, c 3.

[30] Stone (n 26) 29.

[31] See, eg, his introduction in which he set out the positions of, inter alia, Cicero, Pufendorf and Grotius and then stated that 'our law' does not entirely coincide with their thinking: EB Sugden, *A Practical Treatise of the Law of Vendors and Purchasers of Estates*, 5th edn (London, Butterworths, 1818) 1.

[32] ibid, ch 3 'Of Parol Agreements and Parol Evidence'.

[33] ibid, 118.

however, a court of equity was called upon to exercise its unique jurisdiction, by a decree of specific performance, parol evidence would be admitted to establish that, under the circumstances, the plaintiff was not entitled to have the agreement specifically performed.[34] Similarly, equity had a jurisdiction to correct or reform a plain mistake in the writing of an agreement which went against the strong concurrent intention of the parties.[35] Sugden's analysis of mistake recognised mistake as flowing from the particular and special jurisdiction of a court of equity. Only by conceiving of mistake in this fashion—as an amalgam of procedural and substantive law merged in relation to the special jurisdiction of the court—do the judgments of the courts of equity begin to make sense. Courts of equity were as much concerned with what had to be proved in order to receive relief as they were concerned with why the relief was given.

Reasons for the Intervention of Equity

The concerns which were expressed with evidence and with the nature of the relief granted tended to diminish, sometimes entirely, the expression of reasons for why equity provided relief for mistake. This did not mean that the relief was granted in an arbitrary fashion, for courts sought to ascertain when relief had been granted in earlier cases.[36] Equity judges and lawyers conceived of mistake not as a 'doctrine' but as integrally related to the discretionary relief a court could provide to prevent an injustice in a particular case; such relief was granted where it had been in the past. Courts of equity sought to moderate 'the rigour of the law according . . . to equity and good conscience'.[37] Although rarely discussed comprehensively, a number of reasons were given for such moderation in mistake cases: agreements should conform to the intention of the parties; it was unconscientious to allow a party to obtain an advantage from a mistake; the circumstances were akin to fraud; and for the protection of a weaker party. These reasons did not include a failure of consensus. While some of the participants were clearly aware of Roman and civil law, they really did not borrow from it.[38] While there was concern as to whether

[34] ibid, 120.

[35] ibid, 141.

[36] 'Our refusal to direct a specific performance is not the exercise of an arbitrary discretion; but being satisfied that the circumstances of the case bring it within the rule to be deduced from former decisions, we think the bill must be dismissed': per Turner LJ in *Watson v Marston* (1853) 4 De G M & G 230; 43 ER 495 at 240; 499. Where no case touched the point, the bill was dismissed: see *Burt v Barham* (1792) 3 Bro CC 451; 29 ER 638. On the general development of such an equitable jurisprudence see J Getzler, 'Patterns of Fusion' in P Birks (ed), *The Classification of Obligations*, (Oxford, Clarendon Press, 1997) at 175–78.

[37] Sugden (n 2) 6. 'The principle is that it is against conscience for a man to take advantage of the plain mistake of another, or, at least, that a Court of Equity will not assist him in doing so': *Manser v Back* (1848) 6 Hare 443; 67 ER 1239 at 448; 1241 per Wigram V-C.

[38] In an interesting insight into the functioning of equity, counsel in *Okill v Whittaker* (1847) 1 De G & Sm 83; 63 ER 981 referred to the civil law, stating that where an urn was sold for silver which was

or not the reasonable expectation of the mistaken party could be protected,[39] there was no concern about a failure of the parties to bring an informed will to bear upon the contractual process. An examination of the reasons why equity intervened clearly reveals this.

An Unconscientious Advantage Obtained by Mistake

The most significant concern of courts of equity was that it offended conscience to enforce an agreement that had been procured by mistake. Most other reasons advanced for intervention are linked to this central concern. The fact of the mistake gave one party an advantage in a court of law and this attracted equitable intervention. 'The principle is that it is against conscience for a man to take advantage of the plain mistake of another, or, at least, that a Court of Equity will not assist him in so doing.'[40] As Mitford, later Lord Redesdale, explained, the fact of the advantage:

> must necessarily make that court [of ordinary jurisdiction] an instrument of injustice; and it is therefore against conscience that he should use the advantage. In such cases, to prevent a manifest wrong, courts of equity have interposed, by restraining the party whose conscience is thus bound from using the advantage he has improperly gained'[41]

By conscience courts of equity appear to refer to the conscience of the parties themselves. It might be that one party had induced the other by a non-wilful misrepresentation to enter into a contract; in those circumstances, a court of equity would not compel the innocent party to perform the contract.[42] Courts of equity were concerned about the morality of founding an agreement upon mistake rather than the mistake depriving the parties of a free will or of consent to contract.[43]

Agreement did not Conform to Parties' Intentions

Where, by a mistake, the written agreement of the parties did not conform to their intentions, equity would intervene to ensure effect was given to these intentions to

not, the sale was void: 86, 982. To this Knight Bruce V-C commented that if the civil law applied, the question was whether or not the thing differed in substance for if it was different in substance, there was no contract and he then cited part of the Digest (D. 18.1.9) concerned with *error in substantia.* While the participants in this case were clearly familiar with the Roman law of mistake, there is no mention of it in the judgment. The other existing report of the case considered this so irrelevant it was not reported: 2 Ph 338; 41 ER 973. See also the comments of Stuart V-C in *Stone v Godfrey* (1853) 1 Sm & Giff 590; 65 ER 258, aff'd (1854) 5 De G M & G 76; 43 ER 798 at 602–603; 263–64 in which he refers to the instructive and interesting translation of Pothier's *Obligations* by Evans, and the essay by Chancellor D'Aguesseau on mistakes of law contained within it. Instructive, but not determinative of the situation before him.

[39] *Howland v Norris* (1784), 1 Cox 59; 29 ER 1062.

[40] *Manser v Back* (1848) 6 Hare 443; 67 ER 1239 at 448; 1241 per Wigram V-C.

[41] J Mitford, *A Treatise on the Pleadings in Suits in the Court of Chancery by English Bill*, 2nd edn (London, W Owen, 1787) 116.

[42] *Woollam v Hearn* 2 Ves Jun Supp 24; 34 ER 981.

[43] *Marquis Townshend v Stangroom* (n 20).

protect the reasonable expectations of the parties. Of all the reasons for equitable intervention, this reason bears the greatest resemblance to the civilian theory of consent, but it existed independently of the civilians and was concerned with pragmatic matters rather than philosophical concepts of will. Courts of common law could not recognise that the deed did not conform with the parties' intentions, and courts of equity acted to remove the advantage given to one party by the mistake because it was against conscience for a party to so obtain such an advantage.[44] In these cases, the parties had reached an agreement but had then manifested this agreement in such a way as not to conform with their intentions. Thus where a deed was intended to be one thing, but on the face of it was not, the deed could be set aside.[45] Where there was a mistake in the written expression of a commercial agreement, such as a policy of insurance, equity could rectify the document to give effect to the intent and real agreement of the parties.[46] Where a party executed a bond which was intended to be joint and several, but, through their own inexperience, they executed a joint bond, equity would rectify the bond to provide that it was joint and several.[47] Equity would also intervene to a reform marriage settlement to conform with the intention of the parties,[48] although not where it was no longer possible to restore the parties to their original positions. Equity would not only rectify an agreement which failed to express the intentions of the parties but would also rescind an agreement for the same reasons.[49] Equity also refused to order the specific performance of a contract in which one party did not intend to sell what the other bought because where their intentions did not conform there was no contract between them.[50] At times, the failure to realise the intention of even one party was sufficient to grant relief.[51] Equity would not, however, reform an instrument to give it a different effect at law[52] and it would not write a new agreement for the parties.[53]

[44] Mitford (n 41) 117; *Langley v Brown* (1741) 2 Atk 195; 26 ER 521 at 203; 525. See, also, *Randal v Randal* (1728) 2 P Wms 464; 24 ER 816.

[45] Mitford (n 41) 117.

[46] *Henkle v Royal Exchange Assurance Company* (n 6); Lord Hardwicke declined to rectify the policy as there was not sufficient evidence of the intention. See also *Motteux v London Assurance Company* (1739) 1 Atk 545; 26 ER 343, where the court rectified the policy, but the jury (at law) found against the company upon it. Articles of agreement could also be rectified: *Baker v Paine* (1750) 1 Ves Sen 456; 27 ER 1140.

[47] The point is fully made in *Simpson v Vaughan* (1739) 2 Atk. 31; 26 ER 415. Other cases went to the same result: *Ex parte Symonds* (1786) 1 Cox 200; 29 ER 1128; *Thomas v Frazer* (1797) 3 Ves Jun 399; 30 ER 1074; and *Gray v Chiswell* 2 Ves Jun Supp 152; 34 ER 1035.

[48] *Uvedale v Halfpenny* (1723) 2 P Wms 15; 24 ER 677; *Doran v Ross* (1789) 1 Ves Jun 57; 30 ER 228; *Payne v Collier* (1790) 1 Ves Jun 170; 30 ER 285; *Barstow v Kilvington* (1800) 5 Ves Jun 593; 31 ER 755; *Randall v Willis* (1800) 5 Ves Jun 262; 31 ER 577; *Hope v Lord Clifden* (1801) 6 Ves Jun 499; 31 ER 1164; and *Hume v Rundell* (1824) 2 S & S 174; 57 ER 311.

[49] Mitford (n 41) 117.

[50] *Clowes v Higginson* (n 28) 535; 208. Note that in *Attorney-General v Sitwell* (1835) 1 Y & C Ex 559; 160 ER 228, Alderson B was of the view that where the parties had no intention one way or another, there could not be a mistake: at 576–77; 235–36.

[51] *Carpmael v Powis* (1846) 10 Beav 36; 50 ER 495. It was also the case that the mistaken party was a young woman who relied greatly upon the advice of her brother.

[52] *Underhill v Horwood* (1804) 10 Ves Jun 209, 32 ER 824.

[53] *Mosely v Virgin* (1794, 1796) 3 Ves Jun 184, 30 ER 959.

Instances Short of Fraud

Courts of equity often spoke of mistake together with fraud and it is clear that judges saw them as similar,[54] although the latter presented a more compelling reason for intervention. As Lord Eldon explained, a 'court will take a moral jurisdiction . . . for in a moral view there is very little difference between calling for the execution of an agreement obtained by fraud, which creates a surprise upon the other party, and desiring the execution of an agreement, which can be demonstrated to have been obtained by surprise'.[55] Equity also intervened to provide relief in cases in which, although the behaviour of a party was short of fraud, it was indicative of some form of sharp practice on his part. Examples of such instances arose where one party was led to believe some misapprehension by another party[56] or where some fact was concealed by one party from another[57] or where a party who was singularly aware of a fact upon which the other party was mistaken sent his (mistaken) agent to contract with the mistaken party.[58] Either *suppressio veri* or *suggestio falsi* were considered good reasons to set aside a release or conveyance. Imputations of wrongdoing by the defendant in procuring the agreement would allow a court of equity to provide relief on the basis of mistake.[59]

Protection of a Weaker Party

Courts of equity were also prone to intervene where an agreement had been formed under a mistake, and one of the parties to the contract was in a weaker position than the other. This appeared as a separate concern from undue influence; often the relationship was not particularly close between the parties, but one was aware of the other's weaknesses and a mistake existed. The combination of the two facts justified intervention under the head of mistake. It was, in short, unconscionable to allow the agreement to proceed. In *Cocking v Pratt*, equity intervened to assist a daughter who had been misled by her mother as to the amount of her inheritance and, upon this mistake, entered into an agreement with the mother.[60]

[54] See, eg, *Joynes v Statham* (1746) 3 Atk 388; 26 ER 1023; *Ramsbottom v Gosden* (1812) 1 Ves & B 165, 35 ER 65; and *Clifford v Brooke* (1806) 13 Ves Jun 131, 33 ER 244. Story explained that if equity did not intervene and admit parol evidence in the face of the Statute of Frauds it would be to allow a fraud: J Story, *Commentaries on Equity Jurisprudence as Administered in England and America*, 2 vols, 2nd edn (London, A Maxwell, 1839) 136, §155.

[55] *Marquis Townshend v Stangroom* (n 20) 337; 1079. A similar view was expressed in *Pitcairn v Ogbourne* (1751) 2 Ves Sen 375; 28 ER 241.

[56] *Gee v Spencer* (n 21).

[57] *Broderick v Broderick* (1713) 1 P Wms 239; 24 ER 869. See also *Gordon v Gordon* (1821) 3 Swans 400; 36 ER 910, in which a younger brother concealed from the older brother the fact of the older brother's legitimacy.

[58] *Cochrane v Willis* (1865) 34 Beav 359; 55 ER 673.

[59] *Bingham v Bingham* (1748) 1 Ves Sen 126; 27 ER 934, Ves Sen Sup 79; 28 ER 462.

[60] *Cocking v Pratt* (1749, 1750) 1 Ves Sen 400; 27 ER 1105; to the same effect is *Broderick v Broderick* (n 57).

The reason expressed for the intervention was that 'the court will always look with a jealous eye upon a transaction between a parent and a child just come of age, and interpose if any advantage is taken. The mother plainly knew more than the daughter . . . [in addition to the possible concealment], it appeared afterward that the personal estate amounted to more; and the party suffering will be permitted to come here to avail himself of that want of knowledge.'[61] Where a daughter, while still an infant, had been married off to a much older man (seemingly against her will) to assist her father with his debts, the mistake in the marriage settlement allowed intervention by a court of equity to put it right.[62] While courts were more willing to interfere in cases where there was a mistake combined with a relationship such as parent and child or husband and wife,[63] they would also intervene in transactions conducted at arm's length but where one of the parties was clearly at a disadvantage in terms of his knowledge and his ability to understand a transaction. In *Evans v Llewellyn*,[64] the Master of the Rolls, Sir Lloyd Kenyon, gave relief to the plaintiff, a tradesman, who was in 'mean circumstances', mistaken as to his rights and incapable of protecting himself from the defendant and his attorney. Sir Lloyd Kenyon equated the case to one of the expectant heir and explained that:

> if the party is in a situation, in which he is not a free agent, and is not equal to protecting himself, this Court will protect him. I do not know that the Court has drawn any line in this case, or said thus far we will go and no further; it is sufficient for me to see that the party had not the protection he ought to have had, and therefore the Court will harrow up the agreement. I am of opinion, in this case, the party was not competent to protect himself, and therefore this Court is bound to afford him such protection; and therefore these deeds ought to be set aside, as being improvidently obtained.[65]

Just as courts of equity were vague in their statements as to the reason equity intervened to grant relief in cases of mistake, they were also vague as to the exact limits of equitable intervention. We turn now to the limits that were set upon equitable intervention.

The Limits of Equitable Intervention

While Chancery would provide relief for a contractual mistake there were limitations to this relief. The relief was, of course, at the discretion of the court and the limitations were framed on the basis of when this discretion would be exercised and when it would not. For this reason, the limitations were imprecise and some-

[61] *Cocking v Pratt* (n 60) 401; 1106 per Sir John Strange.

[62] *Randall v Willis* (n 48).

[63] *Doran v Ross* (1789), Bro CC 27; 29 ER 388, and 1 Ves Jun Supp 27; 34 ER 677; *Hope v Lord Clifden* (1801) 6 Ves Jun 499; 31 ER 1164. In *Pusey v Desbouvrie* (1734) 3 P Wms 315; 24 ER 1081 the parties were siblings.

[64] (1787) 2 Bro CC 150; 29 ER 86, 1 Cox 333; 29 ER 1191, and 1 Eq Ca Abr 24; 21 ER 845.

[65] ibid, 1 Cox 333 at 340–41; 1194.

what ill defined. Fonblanque, in his annotations to *A Treatise of Equity*, added the English limitations to the anonymous author's broad civilian conception of mistake, for 'it must not be understood, that every kind of mistake is relievable in equity'.[66] The greatest limitation was that relief was not available for a mistake of law, although doubt was sometimes cast upon this limitation and there were exceptions to it. The rule was said to originate in *Bilbie v Lumley*,[67] in which the recovery of money paid under a mistake of law was refused because 'every man must be taken to be cognizant of the law; otherwise there is no saying to what extent the excuse of ignorance might not be carried'.[68] While equity accepted, in principle, this common law limitation it was difficult to reconcile with the earlier decisions in *Bingham v Bingham*,[69] in which it had been decided that equity relieved against mistakes as to misconceptions of rights, or *Lansdown v Lansdown*,[70] in which it had been stated that *ignorantia juris non excusat* applied only to criminal cases and not to civil cases. The result was that numerous exceptions to the broad bar were recognised. Where equity identified that the mistake pertained to a misconception of private rights[71], such as an ignorance of title,[72] or where the mistake of law was combined with other factors which gave rise to concerns of conscience or injustice,[73] equity would exercise its discretion and provide relief where there was what amounted to a mistake of law.[74]

A second limitation was that clear evidence of mistake was required. Because the intervention of equity for mistake formed an exception to the parol evidence rule, courts were insistent that clear evidence as to the intention of the parties and of the mistake was present.[75] It was recognised that the party who sought to undertake the task of proving a mistake undertook a task of great difficulty.[76] While the

[66] Fonblanque (n 17) 106 fn (t). Fonblanque identified six limitations: first, in cases of a mistake as to a fact which was doubtful to both parties; second, where, unknown to either party, there had been long acquiescence under the mistake; third, where the agreement had been entered into to prevent family disputes or to protect the family honour; where the mistake was of all the parties; fifth, where the parties' intention could not be adduced from the evidence; and sixth, where the mistake was one of law; ibid, 106–108.

[67] (1802) 2 East 469; 102 ER 448.

[68] ibid, 472; 449 per Lord Ellenborough CJ.

[69] n 59.

[70] (1730) Mosely 364; 25 ER 441; 2 Jac & W 205; 37 ER 605.

[71] *Ramsden v Hylton* (1751) 2 Ves Sen 304; 28 ER 196; *M'Carthy v Decaix* (1831) 2 Russ and M 614; 39 ER 528.

[72] Sugden, (n 2) 70; *Cooper v Phibbs* (1867) [LR] 2 HL 149; (1877–78) LR 3 App Cas 459; [1874–80] All ER Rep 1149; (1878) 42 JP 483; (1878) 14 Cox CC 93; (1878) 26 WR 406; (1878) 47 LJ QB 48.

[73] '[A]n admixture of other ingredients, going to establish misrepresentation, imposition, undue confidence, undue influence, mental imbecility, or that sort of surprise which Equity uniformly regards as a just foundation for relief': per Story (n 54) 106, §120. Story was critical of the exceptions to the mistake of law bar; 121–24 at §137–§138. In cases where one party was clearly weaker than other, relief would be given: *Evans v Llewellyn* (1787) 2 Bro CC 150; 29 ER 86; *Pusey v Desbeauvais* (n 63).

[74] Where the mistake was as to a plain and settled principle of law, and not a doubtful law: *Naylor v Winch* (1824) 1 Sim & St 555; 57 ER 219; *Stone v Godfrey* (1853) 1 Sm & Giff 590; 65 ER 258, aff'd (1854) 5 De G M & G 76; 43 ER 798.

[75] *Burt v Barham* (1792) 3 Bro CC 451; 29 ER 638; *Shergold v Boone* (1807) 13 Ves Jun 370; 33 ER 332; *Fowler v Fowler* (1859) 4 De G & J 250; 45 ER 97

[76] *Manser v Back* (1848) 6 Hare 443; 67 ER 1239 at 449; 1241.

evidence could take form of witness testimony, the want of credibility on the part of a party could be made up through documentary evidence.[77] Without clear evidence, however, equitable relief would be denied.

In addition, equity would not provide relief for mistake in circumstances where this would amount to writing a new agreement for the parties.[78] So, for example, where rectification was sought, Chancery would not add to an agreement.[79] Nor would it allow specific performance of an agreement with a variation, a point considered in greater detail below.[80]

With respect to some types of agreements, a court of equity would be reluctant to intervene. Thus, the compromise of a doubtful right or a contested claim where the party seeking to avoid the deed had the means to ascertain the facts was usually upheld even where there might be evidence of mistake.[81] Similarly, where the agreement was to settle disputes within the family and where the agreement was reasonable, equity would not go to the same length to deny relief upon a mistake as it would between strangers.[82] Where, however, the family agreement was made upon the mistake or ignorance of a weaker party, wanting in age, intelligence or independent advice, the combination of these factors would attract equitable relief.[83]

Regardless of the type of the agreement entered into, equity was concerned with the conduct of the party who sought relief on the basis of mistake. This party's conduct not only had not to offend conscience[84] but it also had to be such as not to amount to some sort of negligence in the conduct of his affairs. Thus, when the Duke of Beaufort signed a document exchanging land and he was mistaken as to the land he had exchanged, equity would not provide relief for this mistake. As Lord Campbell stated, there was:

> no case in which a Court of Equity had been successfully asked to interpose in favour of a man who wilfully was ignorant of that which he ought to have known—a man who without exercising that diligence which the law would expect of a reasonable and careful person, committed a mistake, in consequence of which alone the proceedings in Court have arisen. No such case is to be found; and it would be a reproach to the law if there could have been such a decision.[85]

[77] *Wood v Scarth* (1855) 2 Kay & J 33; 69 ER 682.

[78] *Mosely v Virgin* (1794, 1796) 3 Ves Jun 184; 30 ER 959.

[79] *Rich v Jackson* (1794) 4 Bro CC 514; 29 ER 1017.

[80] Considered below at 57–60 in relation to specific performance.

[81] *Rajunder Narain Rae v Bijai Govind Sing (1)* (1836, 1839) [1836–39] 2 Moo Ind App 181; 18 ER 269. See, however, *Stainton v The Carron Iron Company* (1861) 7 Jurist n.s 645, in which the compromise was embodied in a decree by the Master of the Rolls, and the Court of Appeal in Chancery considered, where prompt action was taken to set aside the decree, that what the parties intended under their agreement was more important than whether or not they knew of their rights in entering into the agreement.

[82] *Cann v Cann* (1721) 1 P Wms 567; 24 ER 586; *Stapilton v Stapilton* (1739) 1 Atk 2; 26 ER 1; *Stockley v Stockley* (1812) 1 Ves & B 23; 35 ER 9. Exceptions existed: see, eg, *Countess of Shelburn v Earl of Inchiquin* (n 25).

[83] *Dunnage v White* (1818) 1 Swan 137; 36 ER 329.

[84] *Henkle v Royal Exchange Assurance Company* (n 6).

[85] *Duke of Beaufort v Neeld* [1844–45] 12 Cl and Finn 248; 8 ER 1399 at 286; 1415.

As Story explained, equity did not provide relief in such cases because relief was provided for mistake where an unconscientious advantage was taken of the mistaken party by the other party.[86] It did not offend conscience when the mistake or ignorance arose as a result of the negligence or lack of diligence by the mistaken party. People were supposed to be vigilant in exercising their own skill, diligence and judgment in entering into agreements, and few exceptions were made to this supposition. In those instances in which the supposition was departed from there were usually other factors which affected conscience.[87] Because equitable relief was discretionary, the plaintiff had to come to equity 'with propriety of conduct . . . clear from all circumvention and deceit . . . and the agreement [had to] be certain, fair, and just in all its parts'.[88] Where the plaintiff had committed a misrepresentation, however slight, he would not be entitled to an order for specific performance.[89]

In deciding whether or not to exercise its discretion, a court of equity looked at circumstances beyond the behaviour of the individual party to see if there were factors which militated against equitable intervention. A number of such factors were recognised. Where the rights of a bona fide purchaser for value without notice of the mistake would be affected, equity would not interfere to grant relief in favour of the mistaken party.[90] Nor would relief be granted where a court of equity could not place both parties in the same position as they had been in before the execution of the deed.[91] Where there was delay and acquiescence, equity would not intervene except in extreme circumstances.[92] Any one of these occurrences would prevent equitable intervention in a case of mistake.

The mistake had to be significant to allow relief. Generally, mistakes as to quantity or quality were not considered significant because in most contracts for the sale of land, the contract provided that deficiencies were not a ground upon which performance could be refused or the contract set aside, but could be made good

[86] Story (n 54) 130–31, §147–§148.

[87] Thus in the case of *Clark v Girdwood* (1877) 25 WR 575, (1877–78) LR 7 Ch D 9, a woman was granted relief from her mistake in executing a marriage settlement because the mistake appeared to have been linked to her prospective husband, the settlement was hastily executed immediately prior to the marriage and the woman in question was a widow with seven children who was marrying in an attempt to provide for these children. Malins V-C observed that her actions were so foolish he would not have helped her but for the children who had an interest in the property that was at stake.

[88] OD Tudor, *A Selection of Leading Cases in Equity, vol II*, 2nd edn (London, William Maxwell, 1858) 423.

[89] *Cadman v Horner* (1810) 18 Ves Jun 10; 34 ER 221. *Lord Brooke v Rounthwaite* (1846) 5 Hare 298; 67 ER 926; *Brealey v Collins* (1831) Younge 317; 159 ER 1014.

[90] *Malden v Menill* (1737) 2 Atk 8; 26 ER 402; *Warrick v Warrick* (1745) 3 Atk 291; 26 ER 970. Story (n 54) 146, §165; 124–25, §139. See also, Sugden, *A Practical Treatise of the Law of Vendors and Purchasers of Estates*, 5th edn (n 31) 153; based upon the decision in *Thomas v Davis* (1757) Dick 301; 21 ER 284.

[91] *Fowler v Fowler* (1859) 4 De G & J 250; 45 ER 97; *Okill v Whitaker* (n 38).

[92] *Thomas v Frazer* (1797) 3 Ves Jun 399; 30 ER 1074. Such intervention arose in *Blachford v Kirkpatrick* (1842) 6 Beav 232; 49 ER 814 because the title was bad and equity would not compel a purchaser to take such a title. In *Langley v Brown* (1741) 2 Atk 195; 26 ER 521 at 204; 526, it was held that length of time in bringing suit was an important element because of the difficulty in gathering evidence of mistake long after the agreement had been formed.

with the payment of compensation. This would not apply, however, where the difference was so great as to make the interest conveyed something altogether different, in which case equity might provide relief.[93]

Where both parties were mistaken, or a fact was equally unknown to both parties, and it did not offend conscience to allow an agreement to stand, a court of equity would not grant relief where to do so would be to cause a party loss. To allow such a loss required justification, and the justification had to be provided by the party who sought to transfer the loss.[94]

A significant limitation in the twentieth century upon the operation of mistake was to be the almost invariable requirement that both parties be mistaken. Equity, before fusion, did not invariably insist upon a bilateral mistake, although opinions differed. The treatise writers provided contradictory views. Fonblanque opined that where the mistake was common to all the parties, the court would not provide relief, although his authority did not support this proposition.[95] Adams, writing about the correction of instruments, stated categorically that 'it must be a mistake on both sides'.[96] Story wrote that mistake of facts was only the subject of relief when it constituted the material ingredient of the contract and was a mutual mistake or where it was inconsistent with good faith and was a violation of the obligations imposed by law upon the conscience of each party.[97] Fry, accurately, recorded that specific performance would be refused where only one party was mistaken, and not only where the mistaken party was led into that mistake by the other party or where the other party had contributed to the mistake but also where the defendant had acted upon his own misapprehension.[98] Leake stated that while specific performance might be refused because of the unilateral mistake of the defendant, rectification or rescission would not be granted unless both parties were mistaken.[99]

The case law, however, demonstrated that equity did not invariably require both parties to be mistaken to provide relief. The reasons for this lack of a bilateral requirement lay both in the nature of the relief granted and the reasons for its grant. The essential basis for equitable relief was that to allow the contract affected

[93] *Ayles v Cox* (1852) 16 Beav 23; 51 ER 684; *Earl of Durham v Legard* (1865) 34 Beav 611; 55 ER 771. Similarly, a conveyance which passed more than was intended could be rectified and the excess deducted: *Beaumont v Bramley* (1822) Turn & R 41; 37 ER 1009.

[94] *Ainslie v Medlycott* (1803) 9 Ves Jun 13; 32 ER 504. Story was also of the view that there was no relief where the parties had an equal and adequate form of information or where a fact was by its nature doubtful: Story (n 54) 132–33, §150–§151.

[95] *Pullen v Ready* (1643) 2 Atk 587; 26 ER 751, where Lord Hardwicke appeared less concerned that all the parties were mistaken than as to the fact that none of the parties imposed upon the other: 592; 753.

[96] J Adams Jr, *The Doctrine of Equity; Being a Commentary on the Law as administered by the Court of Chancery* (London, William Benning and Co, 1850) 171.

[97] Story (n 54) 133, §151.

[98] E Fry, *A Treatise on Specific Performance* (London, Butterworths, 1858) 156–57, §479–§482. Fry relied upon *Mason v Armitage* (1806) 13 Ves Jun. 25; 33 ER 204; *Pym v Blackburn* (1796) 3 Ves Jun 34; 30 ER 878; *Higginson v Clowes* (n 28); *Ball v Storie* (1823) 1 Sim & St 210; 57 ER 84; and *Howell v George* (1815) 1 Madd 1; 56 ER 1.

[99] SM Leake, *The Elements of the Law of Contracts* (London, Stevens and Sons, 1867) 170.

by mistake to stand was to offend conscience; it was to cause injustice. Equitable relief was discretionary and it could be tailored, as we shall see, to suit the circumstances of the case. In addition, conscience, not consensus, was the construct by which equitable relief was conditioned. As Story explained, 'the ground of relief is, not the mistake or ignorance of material facts alone, but the unconscientious advantage taken of the party by the concealment of them'.[100] In most cases, such an advantage was likely to arise where there was a unilateral mistake, but this was not invariably the situation, and the question as to whether the mistake was shared or not was not one that courts of equity considered enormously relevant to the granting of relief. Of course, if the mistake was unilateral, it might raise concerns about fraud on the part of the non-mistaken party, but this was dealt with as such. In the case of specific performance, only a unilateral mistake on the part of the defendant was required. It offended conscience to require a party to specifically perform a contract which had been procured under or by a mistake. Equity refused its relief and left the plaintiff to his remedy at law. The situation was more complex with rectification, for the reason for the intervention was that it was unconscientious to allow an instrument to stand which did not accurately record the agreement between the parties. The relief was granted to make the instrument conform with the intention. If there was no common intention, it followed, there was no reason for relief.[101] In some cases, however, where one party protested as to the supposed common intention, the court would rectify the contract despite these protestations where to do so would be prevent the protesting party from gaining an undue advantage.[102] Again, in general terms, rescission would be granted where both parties were mistaken and the court found that the effect of the mistake was that the contract was unenforceable in equity because of the mistake.[103] Where, however, there was a strong indication that one party sought to take advantage of the mistake, a court might, exceptionally, rescind the contract.[104] Courts of equity refused to tie themselves to a rigid requirement that the mistake had to be one common to both parties. And, because equitable relief was discretionary, courts of equity had no need to adopt such a limit.

Forms of Equitable Relief for Mistake

Contract, as we have seen, was a concurrent jurisdiction shared by law and equity. In its recognition of mistake, equity presupposed that the contract was good at law—and in that sense valid—but it would provide relief of some sort on the basis of the mistake. Courts of equity would intervene only where a particular contract

[100] Fry (n 98) 130, §147.
[101] *Murray v Parker* (1854) 19 Beav 305; 52 ER 367 ; *Fowler v Fowler* (1859) 4 De G & J 250; 45 ER 97.
[102] *Garrard v Frankel* (1862) 30 Beav 445; 54 ER 961.
[103] *Cochrane v Willis* (1865) 34 Beav 359; 55 ER 673.
[104] *Hamilton v Board* 2 NR 13.

was written. The basis of equitable relief was integral to the admission of parol evidence to explain the injustice arising from the mistake. Equity allowed such evidence as a reason not to enforce the strict legal terms of the contract because to do so would be unconscientious. Courts of equity offered three forms of relief to a party where a mistake had occurred. The first two were positive: a plaintiff could seek rectification or rescission of an agreement on the ground of mistake. The third was negative: a defendant could resist specific performance on the ground of a mistake. Where equity refused to grant relief, it left the party to his remedy at law, namely damages.[105] All three remedies were available only in courts of equity up to the middle of the nineteenth-century. Rectification and specific performance were utterly beyond any similar powers of the common law courts. Rescission, however, was similar to the ability of a court of law to decide that, depending upon the facts of a particular case, no contract had arisen. This was a similarity which would lead to later confusion. It is important to remember that before fusion, if equity refused to provide relief for a mistake, it left the parties to their remedy at common law.[106]

I turn now to examine these forms of relief.

Rectification[107]

In his *Commentaries on Equity Jurisprudence*,[108] Story described rectification as one of the most common forms of equitable relief in cases of mistake.[109] The most common instance in which such relief was sought was in relation to the articles of agreement in anticipation of marriage where equity would reform marriage settlements not founded on the earlier written agreements.[110] While a court of law would not allow an obvious mistake of a word to defeat the intentions of the parties, a court of equity could go further.[111] Equity would reform a contract, whether executed or executory, to make it conform to the precise intentions of the parties: (1) where by mistake the written contract contained less than the parties intended;

[105] A point discussed in numerous cases: *Twining v Morrice*; *Taggart v Twining* (1788) 2 Bro CC 326; 29 ER 182; *Howell v George* (1815) 1 Macc 1; 56 ER 1; *Myers v Watson* (1851) 1 Sim NS 523; 61 ER 202; *Wood v Scarth* (1855) 2 K & J 33; 69 ER 682.

[106] A situation explicitly recognised in *Joynes v Statham* (n 54); *Twining v Morrice* (1788) 2 Bro CC 326, 29 ER 182 *Marquis Townshend v Stangroom* (n 20), *Howell v George* (1815) 1 Madd 1; 56 ER 1; *Cochrane v Willis* (n 103) at 368; 676; *Myers v Watson* (1851) 1 Sims NS 523; 61 ER 202.

[107] I have described this relief by its modern term; contemporaries would have referred to 'reforming' the contract.

[108] Story (n 54).

[109] ibid, vol I, 133, §152.

[110] G Jeremy, *A Treatise on the Equity Jurisdiction of the High Court of Chancery* (London, J & WTClarke, 1828) 378. As a general rule, a court of equity would rectify settlements made after marriage to conform with the articles drafted prior to the marriage where the later settlement did not record the earlier articles, although if both articles and settlement occurred prior to marriage, equity would only allow rectification in the settlement where the settlement stated that it was made in pursuance of the articles: ibid, 378–82.

[111] Sugden (n 31) 140 fn (i).

or (2) where it contained more than was intended; or (3) where it varied their intent by expressing something different in substance from what was intended.[112] It was recognised in these instances that the parties had formed an agreement but that the written document did not conform to the intentions of the parties when they had made their agreement.[113] While courts of law were incapable of reforming an agreement, equity would admit parol evidence to reform the written agreement where the evidence established beyond any reasonable controversy that by a mistake, the written agreement did not record the agreement between the parties.[114] This could occur even after the contract was executed,[115] although a deed would not be rectified for mistake where to do so would be to prejudice a bona fide purchaser without notice.[116] A court of equity allowed the admission of parol evidence not to circumvent or undermine the Statute of Frauds, but to uphold its central purpose: the prevention of frauds by creating this exception. To do otherwise, wrote Story, would be to allow 'the guilty party . . . to avail himself of such a triumph over innocence and credulity, to accomplish his own base designs'.[117] Equally, where the parties mistakenly omitted or inserted a stipulation into a written agreement, contrary to their intention, a court of equity would also intervene to rectify the agreement.[118] Rectification was provided to prevent an injustice. As Story explained:

> A Court of Equity would be of little value, if it could suppress only positive frauds, and leave mutual mistakes, innocently made to work intolerable mischiefs, contrary to the intention of parties. It would be to allow an act, originating in innocence, to operate ultimately as a fraud, by enabling the party who receives the benefit of the mistake, to resist the claims of justice, under the shelter of a rule framed to promote it.[119]

Most courts insisted that there had to be proof of a concurrent intention of all the parties, although this was not a rigid requirement. Lord Eldon appeared to state that Lord Thurlow had required the mistake to be of all the parties and on this basis to doubt whether it could be given on the mistake of one party alone. Lord Thurlow himself had observed that he could not find instances where a mistake

[112] Story (n 54) 133–34, §152.

[113] *Henkle v Royal Exchange Assurance Company* (n 6) 318; 1055.

[114] *Uvedale v Halfpenny* (1723) 2 PW 151; 24 ER 677; *Simpson v Vaughan* (1739) 2 Atk 31; 26 ER 415; *Langley v Brown* (1741) 2 Atk 195; 26 ER 521; *Heneage v Hunloke* (1742) 2 Atk 456; 26 ER 676; *Henkle v Royal Exchange Assurance Company* (n 6) 318; 1055; *Jalabert v Duke of Chandos* (1759) 1 Eden 372, 28 ER 729; *Countess of Shelburne v Earl of Inchiquin* (n 25); *Thomas v Frazer* (1797) 3 Ves Jun 399; 30 ER 1074 and 1 Ves Jun Sup 392, 34 ER 842; *Burn v Burn* (1797) 3 Ves Jun 573, 30 ER 1162 (where a bond was reformed in the face of creditors); *Marquis Townshend v Stangroom* (n 6); *Beaumont v Bramley* (1822) Turn & R 41; 37 ER 1009; *Wheelton v Hardisty* (1857) 8 El & Bl, El 232; 120 ER 86.

[115] *Motteux v London Assurance Company* (1739) 1 Atk 545; 26 ER 343; *Henkle v Royal Exchange Assurance Company* (n 6) 318; 1055: in this case, Lord Hardwicke described the rectification of an executed contract as 'the harshest case that can happen'.

[116] *Thomas v Davis* (1757) Dick 301; 21 ER 284.

[117] Story (n 54) 135, §154.

[118] *Joynes v Statham* (n 54); *Woollam v Hearn* (1802) 7 Ves Jun 211; 32 ER 86, *Ramsbottom v Gosden* (n 54).

[119] Story (n 54) 136, §155.

prevailed against a party who had insisted that there was no mistake.[120] By the middle of the nineteenth century the dominant approach to this question was to require that to rectify an instrument it had to be established that to so reform it would conform with the intention of all the parties at the time of its execution.[121] At times, however, courts granted rectification in the case of marriage settlements where it appeared that only one party was mistaken, but that the mistake was attributable to the other party.[122] Related to the relief provided by way of rectification, courts of equity would also provide relief and supply defects where the parties had mistakenly omitted acts or circumstances necessary to give validity and effect to written instruments.[123] In providing such relief, the court was able to supply defects in the circumstances of conveyances which had been caused by mistake. Similarly, where a deed had been mistakenly delivered up or cancelled, equity could grant relief 'upon the ground that the party is conscientiously entitled to enforce such rights; and that he ought to have the same benefit, as if the instrument were in his possession with its entire original validity'.[124]

A limitation on the remedy of rectification lay in the inability of a plaintiff to seek both to reform a document and to obtain an order for specific performance upon the reformed document. Equity refused to allow parol evidence to amend an agreement and then to execute it, on the basis that to do so would be to erode entirely the force of the Statute of Frauds.[125] This limitation was the subject of criticism by later treatise writers[126] and was an area of significant change following the Judicature Act 1873. Contemporaries viewed the issue as one more concerned with the specific performance of contracts rather than their rectification and it is to this subject that we now turn.

Specific Performance

At law, the remedy for a breach of contract lay in an action for covenant or assumpsit for which damages could be awarded. Such a remedy might be inadequate and Chancery, by its control over the parties, could, uniquely, compel the execution of a contract with an order for specific performance. Chancery came to recognise that it would be inequitable to make such an order where the contract was affected by extrinsic circumstances such as fraud, mistake or accident, and

[120] Sugden (n 31) 141–42. Sugden relied upon Lord Eldon's decision in *Marquis of Townshend v Stangroom* (n 20), and Lord Thurlow's observations in *Irnham v Child* (1781) 1 Bro CC 92; 28 ER 1006.

[121] *Fowler v Fowler* (1859) 4 De G & J 250; 45 ER 97 per Lord Chelmsford LC at 264–65; 103; *Murray v Parker* (1854) 19 Beav 305; 52 ER 367 per Romilly MR at 309–10; 369.

[122] See, eg, *Clark v Girdwood* (n 87); *Maunsell v Maunsell* (1879) 1 LR Ir 529; and *Cordeaux v Fullerton* (1880) 41 LT 651.

[123] Story (n 54) 147, §166.

[124] ibid, 147–48, §167.

[125] See, eg, *Woollam v Hearn* (1802) 7 Ves Jun 211; 32 ER 86; *Clarke v Grant* (1807) 14 Ves Jun 519; 33 ER 620.

[126] Story(n 54) 141, §161; Fry (n 98) 164–69; and Sir E Fry, *A Treatise on the Specific Performance of Contracts*, 2nd edn (London, Stevens and Sons, 1881) 346–56. .

thus where a contract had been affected by a mistake, a court of equity could refuse to exercise its discretion to order the specific performance because of the mistake.[127] Such a mistake might be common to both parties or only that of the defendant. To act as a defence the mistake had to extend beyond the mere value or quality of the subject matter of the contract, for these were matters remediable by an order for specific performance with compensation for the deficiency.[128] The refusal of equitable relief was not seen as an injury to the plaintiff, for it left him to his remedy at law, namely damages.[129] For the most part specific performance occurred in relation to contracts concerned with realty rather than personalty.[130] The Statute of Frauds required a contract to convey land or an interest in land to be evidenced in writing and signed by the party to be bound in order for an action to be brought upon the contract.[131] In refusing to grant specific performance on the basis of mistake a court of equity was necessarily admitting parol evidence of the mistake. Such an admission was justified on the basis that the statute could not be allowed to work an inequity. This exception to the parol evidence rule was jealously guarded. It was sometimes the case that the admission of the parol evidence established that, by mistake, a term of the agreement had been omitted from the written contract or, more severely, that there was a mistake such that the parties had never agreed with each other. In these cases, a court of equity was thus asked to vary a contract and order its execution. In a number of cases, equity declined to do this. In 1801, Eldon LC refused on the facts to vary and enforce an agreement affected by mistake, although his reasons for refusal in law were not clear.[132] In *Woollam v Hearn*, brought the following year, in which the plaintiff sought specific performance of a contract with a variation as to the terms of the written contract, Grant MR clearly stated why this would not be granted. Independently of the Statute of Frauds, the rule of law was that parol evidence would not be admitted to contradict a written agreement because the writing was a better form of evidence. To admit parol evidence to establish that a different agreement was intended, for the purpose of enforcing this different agreement, would be to

[127] See, eg, *Joynes v Statham* (n 54); *Marquis Townshend v Stangroom* (n 20); *Mason v Armitage* (1806) 13 Ves Jun 25, 33 ER 204; *Garrard v Grinling* (1818) 1 Wil Ch 460; 37 ER 196; *Neap v Abbott* (1838) CP Cooper 333; 47 ER 531; *Wood v Scarth* (1855) 2 K & J 33; 69 ER 682; and *Denny v Hancock* (1870–71) LR 6 Ch App 1.

[128] Jeremy (n 110) 460; FT White and OD Tudor, *A Selection of Leading Cases in Equity*, vol II, 3rd Am edn, ed JI Clark Hare and JB Wallace (Philadelphia, PA, T & JW Johnson & Co, 1859) 698; and Fry (n 98) 225, §510.

[129] Jeremy (n 110) 425. See, also, *Joynes v Statham* (n 54), *Lord Gordon v Marquis of Hertford* (1817) 2 Madd 106; 56 ER 274 at 122; 280, and *Howell v George* (1815) 1 Madd 1; 56 ER 1. Following the enactment of the Chancery Regulation Act 1862 (25 & 26 Vict c 42), it was thought prudent to preserve the right of the party to seek damages lest a court of law find that Chancery's refusal to grant specific performance 'was tantamount to a decision of the whole case': *The Wycombe Railway Company v The Minister and Poor Men of Donnington Hospital* (1866) 14 LT ns 179, 182 per Turner LJ. The award of damages would, however, necessarily be small in most cases: *Flureau v Thornhill* (1776) 2 Bl W 1078; 96 ER 635, accepted in *Bain v Fothergill* (1874) 31 LT 387.

[130] Jeremy (n 110) 424.

[131] s 4.

[132] *Marquis Townshend v Stangroom* (n 20) 342; 1081. The point had been adverted to in *Rich v Jackson* (1794) 4 Br Ch C 514; 29 ER 1017.

remove the rule. While equity would allow a defendant the use of parol evidence to resist an order for specific performance, it would go too far to allow the admission of the same parol evidence for the purpose of varying the written agreement and obtaining a decree for specific performance with the variation. 'Thinking, as I do, that the Statute has been already too much broken in upon by supposed equitable exceptions, I shall not go farther in receiving and giving effect to parol evidence, than I am forced by precedent. There is no case, in which the Court has gone the length now desired.'[133] The effect of the decision was to establish that while equity would receive parol evidence to resist specific performance it would not admit it to vary a contract: in this sense, parol evidence could not be admitted as the foundation for a decree enforcing specific performance although the same evidence would be admitted to rebut the equity of a plaintiff seeking specific performance.[134]

Certain erosions were made to this general principle. One occurred in circumstances in which the plaintiff brought a bill for specific performance which the defendant resisted with parol evidence which established a mistake. Equity would allow the plaintiff to have specific performance of the agreement on the terms advanced by the defendant.[135] In these instances, the plaintiff was given an election: to either have his bill dismissed or to have the agreement executed with the parol variation.[136] The plaintiff, it was said, accepted the defendant's variation to obtain his order for specific performance 'on the ground that he who seeks equity must do it'.[137] A second instance occurred where there had been part performance of the agreement. Following the enactment of the Statute of Frauds, courts of equity had

[133] *Woollam v Hearn* (n 118) 219; 89.

[134] Sugden (n 31) 123. See, also, Jeremy (n 110) 433–34, H Maddock, *A Treatise on the Principles and Practice of the High Court of Chancery*, 3rd Am edn (Hartford, Oliver D Cooke, 1827) 383, OD Tudor, *A Selection of Leading Cases in Equity, vol II*, 2nd edn (London, William Maxwell, 1858) 413–414, and FT White and OD Tudor (n 128) 686–88. The point was forcefully made in *Okill v Whitaker* (n 38). Nor would a court of equity rescind the contract on the same evidence: *Davis v Symonds* (1787) 1 Cs Ch C 402; 29 ER 1221.

[135] Initially the plaintiff's bill was dismissed but without prejudice to a bill for performance of the admitted agreement because of the dangerous consequences of having the plaintiff swear witnesses to support his agreement and then, should he fail, of taking the defendant's agreement: Maddock (n 8) 383; ER Daniell, *A Treatise on the Practice of the High Court of Chancery, vol I* (Harrisburg, PA, M'Kinley & Lescure, 1845) 303. In time, however, courts of equity dispensed with the need for a second bill and allowed the agreement in the same action if the plaintiff agreed to accept it: see J Story, *Commentaries on Equity Pleadings*, 3rd edn (Boston, NJ, Charles C Little & James Brown/London, A Maxwell & Son, 1844) 415–16, §394.

[136] See, eg, *Higginson v Clowes* (1808) 15 Ves Jun 516; 33 ER 850 at 524–25, 853, where the plaintiff refused to accept specific performance with this variation and his bill was dismissed. The bill was a part of a long-running dispute between two parties: the defendant then brought his own suit to take the property on his terms. This suit was dismissed at which point the first plaintiff then offered to take the property on the terms proposed in the first suit but this was rejected. In short, 'at different periods of a long litigation, each party strenuously contended for terms which, when they were offered to him, he rejected': *Higginson v Clowes* 2 Ves Jun Sup 421; 34 ER 1161. Other cases in which the election was offered were *Fife v Clayton* (1807) 13 Ves Jun 546; 33 ER 398; *Ramsbottom v Gosden* (1812) 1 V& B 165; 35 ER 65; *Winch v Winchester* (1812) 1 V& B 375; 35 ER 146; and *Lord Gordon v Marquis of Hertford* (1817) 2 Madd 106; 56 ER 274.

[137] White and Tudor (n 128) 694.

been quick to create rule that part performance of an agreement took it outside the statute.[138] 'Where, however, a parol variation has been in part performed, a specific performance of the written agreement with the variation will be decreed.'[139] A third instance appears to have been recognised in those limited number of cases in Chancery in which the agreement was not within the Statute of Frauds. Finally, if a party to a contract prevented it from being in writing by a fraud, it would be enforced against him notwithstanding that it was within the statute.[140]

There was obvious merit in dismissing those cases in which each party was mistaken and the mistake or mistakes effectively prevented any agreement from arising.[141] The anomaly of admitting parol evidence to resist specific performance but not admitting the very same evidence to reform an agreement in accordance with the intention of the parties for the purpose of ordering performance lacked the same merit and attracted the criticism of later writers on the subject, principally Joseph Story and Edward Fry. While writers such as Sugden, Jeremy, Maddock and Tudor sought to give an account of the law as it was, Story and Fry sought to go further than a simple account and to state what they thought the law should be.

The author of the leading treatise on the subject, *The Specific Performance of Contracts*,[142] Edward Fry was a man with extraordinary gifts.[143] A devout Quaker, Fry was a member of the cocoa-manufacturing family. A noted zoologist who turned down the first directorship of the Natural History Museum, Fry finally settled upon law rather than science as a career. Fry sought to organise his subject according to scientific principles spanning different types of contract and, fluent in French and German, he derived many of his principles from the work of the French theorist Robert Joseph Pothier. Pothier wrote of mistake as a defect of consent[144] and Fry adopted this conception and tied it to the traditional equitable concerns in his description of mistake:

> The principle upon which equity proceeds in those cases where mistake is the ground of defence is this: that there must be an agreement binding at law, but that this is not enough, that to entitle the plaintiff to more than his legal remedy, the contract must be more than merely legal. It must not be hard or unconscionable; it must be free from fraud, from surprise, and from mistake: for where there is mistake, there is not that consent which is essential to a contract in equity: *non videntur qui errant consentire*.[145]

[138] AWB Simpson, *A History of the Common Law of Contract* (Oxford, Clarendon Press, 1975) 614–16. Professor Simpson opines that the likely reason for this exception was the recognition that the statute could work an injustice and protect frauds where the agreement had been acted upon.

[139] Tudor (n 88) 415. The point is established by *Legal v Miller* (1750) 2 Ves Sen 299; 28 ER 193, and *Pitcairn v Ogbourne* (1751) 2 Ves Sen 375; 28 ER 241. Sugden explained that such part performance was tantamount in the eyes of equity to a written agreement: Sugden (n 31) 133.

[140] White and Tudor (n 128) 704.

[141] As occurred in the case of the agreement litigated in *Higginson v Clowes* (n 137) and *Clowes v Higginson* (n 28).

[142] Fry (n 98).

[143] The extent of his gifts can be seen in the fact that he was a Fellow of both the British Academy and the Royal Society.

[144] For Pothier's analysis of mistake, see ch 5.

[145] Fry (n 98) 155, §475. Fry was amongst the first to attempt to so organise and explain English contract law; others followed this course as the century unfolded. See ch 5.

While Fry imposed upon equity an element of consent which was not always found in the case law of the day, his organisation of the topic was a successful and ultimately influential one. One of Fry's concerns was the specific performance of a contract with a variation. Fry considered that a parol variation in a suit for specific performance might fall within one of three forms. In the first instance the mistake occurred in reducing the agreement to writing, and where the defendant's parol variation represented the true contract between the parties, 'the court will, it seems, enforce specific performance of the contract so varied'.[146] The second instance was where each party was mistaken in the formation of the agreement; one party understood one thing and the other another. In this instance, there was no contract such as the court would enforce.[147] In the third instance, the parol variation did not fall clearly within either of the first instances and the court put the plaintiff to his election to either have his bill dismissed or to have the contract executed with the parol variation.[148] Fry was troubled, however, with what occurred when a party sought to enforce a contract with a parol variation. While the authorities were not clear, the prevailing view was that 'under no circumstances can a plaintiff sue for the specific performance of a contract with a parol variation'.[149] Fry regarded it as an injustice to allow such an action where the mistake was of one party alone. However, where both parties were mistaken in the reduction of the agreement to writing, equity should allow specific performance with such a variation. He was of the opinion that 'it seems that by two bills, one for reform and the other for specific performance, the plaintiff's end may now be attained'.[150] He gave no authority for this proposition. The confusion in the case law Fry attributed to a failure to distinguish between when the mistake was that of the plaintiff only and when it was of both parties in the reduction into writing of the contract. In the latter case, it was totally unjust to exclude the plaintiff from the right of proving a parol variation in suits for specific performance.[151] Fry surveyed the authorities with the argument that they did not uniformly establish the position said to be the rule and then went on to examine the criticism of the position by the Americans and noted that there were cases in English law in which a plaintiff, in the same suit, had an instrument rectified and obtained consequential relief upon it. Fry's argument was sound in principle but short on authority. Ultimately, however, it was to be accepted into English law and with it an important distinction between unilateral and bilateral mistakes.

146 Fry (n 98) 216, §484. Fry based his opinion on *Howell v George* (1815) 1 Madd 1; 56 ER 1, and *Joynes v Statham* (1746) 3 Atk 388; 26 ER 1023.

147 ibid, 217, §486. Fry relied upon *Clowes v Higginson* (n 28).

148 ibid, 218, §489.

149 ibid, 227, §514.

150 ibid, 227, §517.

151 ibid, 228, §518–§519.

Rescission

The third form of equitable relief was to rescind the contract, although this power was used sparingly. A court of equity had the power to order up the delivery, cancellation or rescission of agreements, deeds and other instruments on the basis of a protective or preventative justice (*quia timet*) in cases where there was concern that the instrument could be vexatiously or injuriously used against a party in law when there was a good defence against it in equity (although not in law).[152] It was against conscience to allow the party holding such an instrument to retain it since it could only be retained for some sinister purpose.[153] Equity required a stronger case to set aside an agreement than it would to refuse specific performance of an agreement.[154] Rescission was a more drastic remedy than a refusal of specific performance because rescission prevented a party from any remedy at common law, as well as in equity. Rescission was primarily directed to the situation where there was fraud and an inaccurate consideration,[155] and Jeremy opined that where both parties were mistaken the remedy was not rescission but rectification.[156] Story explained that rescission was not generally an appropriate, adequate or equitable relief because in most cases:

> the accident or mistake may be of a nature, which does not go to the very foundation and merits of the agreement; but may only require that some amendment, addition, qualification, or variation should take place, to make it at once just, and reasonable, and fit to be enforced.[157]

Story, writing with an eye to Pothier, was of the view that a court of equity would rescind a contract only where the mistake was 'essential to its character, and an efficient cause of its concoction'.[158] That equity would only exceptionally rescind a contract for mistake is borne out by the fact that the early preponderance of mistakes were dealt with either through rectification or a refusal of specific performance. Nevertheless, despite the early infrequency of the use of rescission, Story's opinion is borne out by the authorities.[159] In early cases of rescission, courts of equity tended to intervene in circumstances in which the behaviour of

[152] Story (n 54), vol II, 5, §694. *Martin v Savage* (1740) Barn C 190; 27 ER 608; *Lansdowen v Lansdowne* (1730) 2 Jac & W 205; 37 ER 605.

[153] J Story, *Commentaries on Equity Jurisprudence, vol I*, 9th edn, ed IF Redfield (Boston, NJ, Little, Brown and Company, 1866) 663, §700.

[154] Jeremy (n 110) 482.

[155] ibid, 484.

[156] ibid, 490–91.

[157] Story (n 54), vol II, 4, § 693.

[158] Story (n 54), vol I, 126, §141. Story's classification of mistakes that went to the essence of the contract depends upon the civilian law rather than the decisions of courts of equity. The cases he cited for this proposition indicate other concerns: that the court would not force a party into a contract he did not intend: *Calverley v Williams* (1790) 1 Ves Jun 210, 30 ER 306; or that the court would construe an instrument in accordance with the intention of the parties: *Farewell v Coker* (1726) 2 Jac & W; 37 ER 599.

[159] *Lansdowne v Lansdowne* (n 152); *Martin v Savage* (n 152); *Bingham v Bingham* (n 59); and *Hitchcock v Giddings* (1817) 4 Price 135; 146 ER 418.

one of the parties was close to fraud[160] or where the court intervened to protect a weaker party[161] or to remedy unconscionable conduct.[162] Rescission is granted because to allow an agreement to stand when it was formed under a mistake would be 'manifestly unjust'.[163] Examples of such injustice occurred where a party mistakenly purchased his own estate[164] or where the vendor had no interest in the estate to be sold.[165] Agreements were rescinded in cases of both unilateral and bilateral mistakes. Story considered a bilateral mistake to be grounds for relief where the mistake pertained to a material ingredient in their contract and disappointed the parties' intentions and a unilateral mistake to be grounds for relief where the effect of the mistake was to offend the conscience of either party.[166]

Where rescission was granted, the court ordered the repayment of any sums paid pursuant to the contract because equity insisted that the parties be returned to the status quo. For:

> the equity is to have the entire transaction rescinded; and if the obligor will have equity, he must also do equity. The Court will remit both parties to their original positions, and will not relieve the obligor form his liability, leaving him the fruits of the transaction of which he complains.[167]

Cooper v Phibbs[168] was one of the mistake cases to reach the House of Lords. The case is important not only because it illustrates the circumstances in which equitable intervention occurred but also for their Lordships' considerations of law. As a House of Lords' decision, the case was to acquire later importance although the effect of the relief was frequently mis-stated. The later importance of the case justifies some discussion of it.[169] The case was viewed as unexceptional in its day and provoked little contemporary discussion. The facts typify those cases before nineteenth-century courts of equity, involving complex proprietary interests, intestacy and a lunatic. As Matthews has observed, it is important to understand the context in which the case arose in order to understand what the House of Lords did.[170] The case concerned an extensive estate in Ireland which contained a fishery. The dispute was between Cooper and his five female cousins. Their fathers had been brothers; the female cousins were the daughters of the older brother but because the marriage settlement of their father preferred male heirs to female ones,

160 *Gee v Spencer* (n 21); *Bingham v Bingham* (n 59); *Ramsden v Hylton* (n 71); *Smyth v Smyth* (1817) 2 Madd 75, 56 ER 263; *Gordon v Gordon* (1818–1821) 3 Swanston 400, 36 ER 910.

161 See, eg, *Cocking v Pratt* (n 60) and the explanation of this case tendered in *Carpenter v Heriot* 1 Eden 338, 28 ER 715—that *Cocking* was an example of an undue exercise of parental authority in circumstances where the parent was not mistaken.

162 *Broderick v Broderick* (n 57).

163 Per Lord Langdale MR in *Colyer v Clay* (1843) 7 Beav 188; 49 ER 1036 at 193; 1038.

164 *Bingham v Bingham* (n 59).

165 *Hitchcock v Giddings* (n 159).

166 Story (n 54), vol I, 133, §151.

167 Adams (n 96) 191.

168 (1867) [LR] 2 HL 149.

169 An excellent discussion and analysis of the case has already been undertaken. See P Matthews, 'A Note on *Cooper v Phibbs*' (1989) 105 LQR 599.

170 ibid. The facts are simplified here; Matthews, ibid, provides a more detailed version.

the Irish estate descended as a remainder to their male cousin. The father of the Cooper sisters had considerably improved the fishery on the estate, apparently in the mistaken belief that he owned it outright rather than having an equitable life interest in it as a part of the larger estate. His daughters and their cousin shared this misapprehension and believed that the fishery was owned by the five sisters who had inherited it as a part of their father's personal estate. It was on this basis that Cooper entered into an agreement with his cousins' agent and trustee, Phibbs, to lease from them the fishery and an adjacent house. Shortly before the first half-yearly rent was due, Cooper discovered information which led him to believe that the fishery was a part of the settlement to which he held the life interest. He then brought a petition in the Irish Court of Chancery to have the agreement rescinded and delivered up and a perpetual injunction granted to restrain Phibbs from suing upon it.[171] Cooper had to take this course of action because at law there was either an agreement for a lease or a lease which was binding at law.[172] It was only in equity that he was entitled to be relieved of this agreement because he had entered into it 'by mistake in ignorance of his title to the property . . . agreed to be demised to him'.[173] Two issues were presented: first, was Cooper the owner of the fishery?; and, second, if he was, could the agreement be set aside because it had been entered into under a mistake? The Lord Chancellor of Ireland dismissed the petition with costs.[174] Cooper brought an appeal to the House of Lords. The Cases for the Appellant and Respondents[175] indicate Cooper's appeal faced a number of problems. The first was the ownership of the fishery; the second, as the Respondents' Case stated, was that if Cooper had acted under a mistake, this was a mistake in law[176] and not a mistake for which a court of equity should give relief and that in the circumstances it would be against good conscience to give such relief.[177] The Respondents' Case also stated that the agreement between the parties also comprised of property (the house) to which good title was held by the respondents and that it would be impossible to impose terms upon the relief

[171] Nothing turns on the fact that the estate was in Ireland rather than England. Had the estate been in England, Cooper would have been entitled to bring a bill in the Court of Chancery on the same grounds and seeking the same relief.

[172] As Matthews (n 169) at 603–604 has observed, it may have been that the lease was void at law; however, if neither party had the legal estate, which was vested in a third person, the doctrine of tenancy by estoppel would prevent Cooper from denying that Phibbs had the legal estate. Cooper was thus forced to bring his petition in equity before he paid the rent or he was sued in a court of law for arrears of rent, because in a court of law, his equitable life estate would not assist him and he would lose an action brought at law. It was for this reason that he had to seek the assistance of equity.

[173] *Cooper v Phibbs*, Appellant's Case, 17 (Parliamentary Archives, Appeal Cases 1867, vol 231).

[174] (1865) 17 Ir Ch Rep 73. The Irish Lord Chancellor recognised that while relief could be given where a party had acted under a mistake, and even a mistake of law, such relief would not be given unless equity and good conscience required it, and these elements did not so require relief in this instance. The dismissal was without prejudice to the question of the ultimate right of the fishery.

[175] Both are to be found in the Parliamentary Archives (n 173).

[176] Case for the Respondents (n 173) 2; (1867) [LR] 2 HL 149, 156. Counsel for the respondents questioned whether there was any mistake and, if there was, this was a mistake in a matter of law brought about by Cooper's own neglect and this was no ground upon which a court of equity would interfere with the agreement.

[177] ibid, 27.

sought which would make the relief equitable.[178] Cooper had asserted that this was a mistake of fact and not of law,[179] and he offered to submit to such terms as would be necessary to do justice. These positions are important because they indicate what the perceptions were of the participants as to the nature of the law involved. It is significant that all of the parties began from the premise that equity could rescind a contract which had been entered into under a mistake. It is also significant that neither side viewed it as essential that the mistake was a shared mistake; both sides appear to have accepted that it was sufficient if Cooper had entered into the agreement under a mistake. What concerned the participants was whether it was contrary to justice and good conscience to bind him to the agreement.

The House of Lords reversed the order and declared that Cooper had an equitable life interest in the fishery. The agreement was not binding in equity upon the parties 'but ought to be set aside' because it 'was made and entered into by the parties to the same under mistake, and in ignorance of the actually existing rights and interests of such parties to the said fishery'.[180] The concerns often expressed about relieving for a mistake of law received little consideration. Lord Cranworth thought Cooper entitled to relief because the case was within the decision in *Bingham v Bingham*, where the relief was granted upon a 'perfectly correct doctrine'.[181] And even if it were not, Cooper was entitled to relief because he had been led into his mistake by the misrepresentations of his uncle, who was now represented by the respondents.[182] Lord Westbury dealt expressly with the mistake of law bar and stated that it did not apply to those cases concerned with a mistake as to a private right for 'private right of ownership is a matter of fact'.[183] Lord Westbury continued and in doing so appeared to add a qualification to the availability of relief for such a mistake: 'if parties contract under a mutual mistake and misapprehension as to their relative and respective rights, the result is, that that agreement is liable to be set aside as having proceeded upon a common mistake'.[184] This requirement of mutuality appears to have originated with Lord Westbury for it does not appear in the Cases nor in the reported arguments of counsel. What Lord Westbury may have intended by this was to indicate that such relief extended beyond cases where there was a fraud or suspicions of fraud by the other party. At times, the decisions in *Bingham v Bingham* and *Lansdowne v Lansdowne* had been explained on the basis that these were really causes of fraud or misrepresentation.[185] The respondents' counsel in *Cooper v Phibbs* had argued that relief was not available in equity for a mistake of law unless 'the mistake was occasioned by fraud and misrepresentation'.[186] In this

[178] ibid, 27–28.
[179] Appellant's Case (n 173) 17; (1867) [LR] 2 HL 149, 154.
[180] (1867) [LR] 2 HL 149, 173.
[181] ibid, 164.
[182] ibid.
[183] ibid, 170.
[184] ibid.
[185] See, eg, the discussion in Anon, 'Mistake of Law' (1869) 13 *The Solicitors' Journal & Reporter* 809 (31 July 1869).
[186] (1867) [LR] 2 HL 149, 156.

context, Lord Westbury did not impose a new requirement of 'mutuality' of mistake in relation to rescission but simply stated that the relief sought was available in absence of fraud or misrepresentation by the other party. One contemporary account of his decision rejected Lord Westbury's observations as enunciating a general rule that a mistake as to private rights would always be treated as a mistake of facts.[187]

Terms were imposed upon this rescission, although the terms are not as radical as they might appear to modern eyes. Because equity would only rescind a contract where it would not cause an injustice to the other party, the House of Lords made its order for rescission subject to terms: Cooper would reimburse the respondents for the expenses their father had incurred in relation to establishing the fishery and he would pay a proper rent for the occupation of that property which was owned by the respondents. As Matthews has observed, [188], the expenditures of the respondents' father had been incurred as a trustee and he had a trustee's lien as a matter of right for these expenditures; in addition, Cooper was liable at law for an occupation rent of the respondents' cottage. By making the fulfillment of these two rights conditions of the rescission, their Lordships also saved the respondents from separate proceedings.

The importance of *Cooper v Phibbs* was that the House of Lords accepted that a mistake as to fact included a mistake as to private rights and that where a contract was entered into under such a mistake (even absent fraud) equity would rescind the contract and could rescind it on terms. Lord Westbury's decision may have contributed to what was to become a growing acceptance by lawyers that mistake, to attract relief, had to be a common mistake.

Sir John Romilly MR, during the same time period, also appeared to believe that a common mistake was required to grant relief. Like their Lordships, he was prepared to grant relief on terms. However, in the decade before the fusion of law and equity, Romilly MR began to increase the flexibility of the relief Chancery would provide in cases of mistake. In particular, by stretching the remedial powers of equity farther than they had been stretched before, he effectively rescinded contracts on terms. Equitable relief for mistake had always been premised on being able to restore the parties to their original positions and such relief was not granted where innocent third parties had become involved in the matter. *Garrard v Frankel*[189] concerned a lease between Garrard, the owner of a house on Oxford Street which was the subject matter of the lease, and Frankel, who sought a central London location for her wool business. Garrard had intended to let the house to Frankel at £230 per annum and the two had discussed that sum and recorded it in their memorandum of agreement. The agreement referred to a lease of the premises; Garrard accidentally inserted the figure of £130 in the draft lease. The lease was executed with this error; Garrard only realised the error when he sought to collect the rent and Frankel replied that the lease provided for a rent of £130.

[187] 'Mistake of Law' (n 185) 810.
[188] Matthews (n 169) 605.
[189] (1862) 30 Beav 445; 54 ER 961; 31 Law Jo Eq 604; 8 Juris ns 985.

Garrard was unable to sue at law to recover the rent and filed a bill praying that either the lease should be rectified to state the higher sum or that the lease be delivered up and cancelled and a new lease at the higher sum executed. When the matter came before the court further complications were discovered. Frankel, within a month of executing the lease, had assigned it by way of mortgage to a third party who had in turn sold it to one of Frankel's creditors, a Dr Brünn. Brünn was then added as a party to the suit.

Frankel argued that there was no mistake or, if there was, that she was unaware that a mistaken sum had been inserted in the lease, never having previously realised that a higher sum was discussed. Romilly MR preferred to attribute her curious state of knowledge to forgetfulness although such forgetfulness meant that Garrard's evidence was to be preferred. Romilly MR rejected Frankel's counsel's further argument that it was now settled that rectification would only be granted where the mistake was mutual. Romilly MR stated that:

> though, as a general rule, this is correct, it does not apply to every case. The Court will, I apprehend, interfere in cases of mistake, where one party to the transaction, being at the time cognizant of the fact of the error, seeks to take advantage of it.[190]

He found that Frankel must have been cognisant of Garrard's error and sought to take advantage of it. In the circumstances she could not be allowed to derive any advantage from this mistake nor could the plaintiff be bound by the terms of the lease as it stood. The plaintiff was entitled to relief, and the 'correct' form of relief was to give the defendant an election. She could either take the lease with the mistake rectified or she could give up the lease and pay a use and occupation charge with a deduction for any improvements made. This was effectively a rescission on terms. Romilly MR cited no case for this relief, but it is remarkably similar to the cases of specific performance, where the non-mistaken plaintiff was put to the election of having their bill dismissed or having the contract enforced on the terms put forward by the defendant. This practice may have provided a model for Romilly MR in circumstances where he was concerned with the undue advantage that would accrue to the defendant and was also concerned with the rights of a third party, Brünn.[191]

While Romilly MR's decision was somewhat different than previous relief granted in equity, it attracted little contemporary notice or criticism.[192] Five years later he explained *Garrard v Frankel* in *Harris v Pepperell*.[193] While equity was

[190] (1862) 30 Beav 445; 54 ER 961 at 451; 964.

[191] Brünn was found to be a purchaser for value without notice and it was ordered that the amount due on his mortgage and his costs in the suit were a charge against the plaintiff's house. The Jurist's case digest noted that Brünn's claim in respect of the mortgage and the sums advanced thus had priority over the plaintiff's equity to reform the lease: (1864) 9 Jurist ns 157.

[192] Writing in the twentieth century, Palmer explained that Romilly MR encountered serious problems in this case, all of his own making, when he assumed that rectification was only available if the mistake were mutual: GE Palmer, *Mistake and Unjust Enrichment* (Columbus, OH, Ohio State University Press, 1962) 19–20. Certainly Romilly MR in the earlier case of *Murray v Parker* (1854) 19 Beav 305; 52 ER 367 at 308–309; 368 stated that rectification required a common error of the parties, and in the later case of *Bentley v Mackay* (1862) 31 Beav 146; 54 ER 1092 at 151–52; 1096.

[193] (1867) LR 5 Eq 1; 17 TLR 191; 16 WR 68.

reluctant to reform marriage settlements where the marriage had taken place and children born because it was impossible for the court to put the parties back into their original position, cases involving vendors and purchasers (in their widest sense) were different, for here 'it is in the power of the Court to put the parties in the same position as if the contract had not been executed'.[194] The exercise of this power lay in offering the non-mistaken defendant the option of having the whole contract annulled or taking it in the form which the mistaken plaintiff intended it. Again, Romilly MR cited no precedent, beyond *Garrard v Frankel.* This he described as acquiesced in by the parties, not appealed from and 'correct'. While the lack of precedent was not unusual at the beginning of the nineteenth century, it was increasingly unusual after the mid-century. While Romilly MR's relief was analogous to those situations where the non-mistaken party was offered an election between a specific performance of the agreement as it was understood by the mistaken party or a refusal of specific performance altogether,[195] contemporaries were critical of his decision in *Harris v Pepperell* because it could not be easily explained and went far beyond *Garrard v Frankel.* Relief would be granted in equity when the party taking the benefit knew the other was labouring under a mistake and that the written agreement did not express his real intention. Where, however, there was no such personal equity, the agreement between the parties was judged by the expressions of intention that they had communicated and would not allow one party to state that his expression did not convey his intention. To allow a party to state this would be to allow the dangerous consequences that the parol evidence rule was intended to avoid.[196] *Garrard v Frankel* was consistent with this rule because Frankel must have known that there was a mistake: the only oddity of the case was the option of allowing Frankel to give up the lease. In the later case, however, there was no evidence that the Reverend Pepperell was in any way aware of Harris's error and, for that reason, Harris's suit should have been dismissed.[197]

The final case in which Romilly MR applied the same form of relief was *Bloomer v Spittle.*[198] As we shall see, this line of authority was not to survive long into the twentieth century. Fusion, combined with changing attitudes as to when contracts could be rescinded, acted to stymie development of this form of relief, namely rescission on terms.

[194] ibid, 5.

[195] The case is not dissimilar to *Earl of Durham v Legard* (1865) 34 Beav 611; 55 ER 771, in which Romilly MR gave a purchaser seeking specific performance of a contract to sell land based upon a mistake an option. In *Baskcomb v Beckwith* (1869) LR 8 Eq 100, 105, Lord Romilly expressly referred to *Harris v Pepperell* during arguments concerned with a unilateral mistake.

[196] Anon, 'Rectification of Conveyance *Harris v Pepperell*, MR, 16 WR 68' (1867) 12

[197] ibid. Romilly MR also applied *Garrard v Frankel* in *Bloomer v Spittle* (1872) LR 13 Eq 427 in which he ordered that a sale of land be rectified or set aside on terms. In *Bloomer v Spittle* the defendant had apparently not realised that the mineral rights were mistakenly reserved to him at the time of sale but when he subsequently realised this he attempted to sell them, conduct of which Romilly MR disapproved.

[198] n 197.

Conclusions

The body of case law established prior to 1875 demonstrates that courts of equity recognised mistake as a ground upon which equity would intervene and provide relief. While equity treatise writers and judges were aware of the civilian conceptions of mistake, that mistake was relevant because it disrupted the necessary consent to contract, this was not of great significance in equity. Equitable relief for mistake was premised upon the principle that conscience would not allow an advantage obtained by mistake to prevail in the way that it would not allow an advantage obtained by fraud. Equity intervened to remove this advantage with three forms of relief: rectification, the denial of specific performance, and rescission. This relief was provided to remove an advantage which would otherwise occur at common law in circumstances where the advantage was inappropriate. In particular, courts of equity would admit evidence contrary to a written agreement to establish that a mistake existed with respect to the agreement. In granting relief where a mistake had occurred, courts of equity were concerned with a variety of factors which related to conscience: that the agreement should conform to the intentions of the parties; that mistake could create the same disadvantages as fraud or that mistake was sometimes a form of fraud which could not be proved; and that mistake or surprise upon a weaker party deserved relief. Courts of equity acted with reference to earlier cases in which relief had been granted. While they would not create a contract between parties, they would not enforce one where a mistake made it unconscientious to do so. Limits were recognised by courts of equity and set upon the granting of equitable relief. One of the most significant of the twentieth-century limitations, that the mistake be common to the parties, was not entirely present in courts of equity before fusion.

During the first half of the nineteenth century, courts of law did not recognise mistake as attracting legal consequences in its own right, and mistake was thus entirely confined to courts of equity. There could be no doctrinal conflict as to what effect mistake, as such, had upon contractual formation nor was there any reason for misperceptions to arise at common law as to what should be done in equitable mistakes because common law courts were not concerned to resolve such problems. The capacity for doctrinal conflicts and misperceptions arose from the middle of the nineteenth century as procedural reforms[199] moved the two courts closer together. When this procedural process began, common law courts began to receive arguments on mistake. These arguments, however, were often premised upon a new basis for mistake, that of consent. In this sense, mistake is a substantive area of law affected by the procedural fusion of law and equity. The fusion created the conditions for doctrinal and remedial conflict and misperceptions to exist and for differences to be perceived between mistake at common law and mistake in equity. The piecemeal nature of reform, culminating in the Judicature Act 1873, the scarceness of mistake cases and the transplantation of civilian conceptions disguised this process.

[199] An example is the Common Law Procedure Act 1854, which allowed equitable defences to be pleaded in common law actions.

4

The Lack of Contractual Mistake at Common Law and the Nineteenth-century Transformation of Procedure

MISTAKE WAS NOT a doctrine recognised by the courts of common law before the nineteenth century. By the middle of the century arguments based on mistake, often made by desperate counsel, began to appear before courts of common law.[1] By the 1870s a limited form of mistake, as to the identity of the other party, was recognised.[2] If factual misapprehensions have always dogged human transactions, why has the common law been so slow to recognise a doctrine of mistake in contract law? The answer to this question is difficult to establish with certainty because the question of why something does not happen is necessarily a difficult inquiry. Some reasons can be discerned. One reason was that the availability of relief for a mistake in courts of equity would have diverted litigants away from courts of common law. Other reasons exist which arose from the procedures of the common law courts. These procedures both operated to provide an alternate means of resolving cases of misapprehension but also worked in ways that obscured the fact that a mistake had occurred. The ongoing programme of procedural and administrative reforms conducted during the nineteenth century created the conditions by which a contractual mistake could be recognised and dealt with as such. Until that time, the fact that a mistake had occurred in the formation of a contract was largely irrelevant at common law and often indiscernible. The preoccupation of legal thought, at the commencement of the nineteenth century, was still upon administrative, procedural matters rather than jurisprudential, theoretical matters. The most commonly known manifestation of this was the forms of action: from medieval times, English law was concerned with the mechanism by which legal proceedings were commenced. The writ which originated the legal proceedings determined their course from beginning to end. English lawyers conceived of their legal system on the basis of these writs.[3]

[1] C MacMillan, 'Mistaken Arguments: The role of argument in the development of a doctrine of contractual mistake in nineteenth century England' in A Lewis and M Lobban (eds) *Law and History: Current Legal Issues 2003* (Oxford, Oxford University Press, 2004).

[2] *Cundy v Lindsay* (1877–78) LR 3 App Cas 459.

[3] As Professor Baker has written, the earliest treatises on the common law, Glanvill and Bracton, 'were essentially books about writs and the procedures generated by them': JH Baker, *An Introduction to English Legal History*, 4th edn (London, Butterworths, 2002) 56.

While the writs had been designed to regulate justice rather than to limit it,[4] the effect by the late eighteenth century was to limit the conceptions of law. As Lord Lindley wrote towards the end of his life, 'with us the tendency was to study remedies and learn principles from procedure, which is less scientific and satisfactory in dealing with new and difficult questions'.[5] The nineteenth century saw sweeping changes in the administration of justice, and the forms of action were abolished.[6] The removal of the forms of action left 'conceptual problems'[7] and, as Maitland observed, 'the forms of action we have buried but they still rule us from their graves'.[8] The abolition of the forms of action was only a highly visible act in a much larger process of piecemeal procedural transformation which began in 1829 and was largely completed by 1875. The question of how this procedural transformation affected the development of substantive law has received little attention.[9] What will be considered here is how procedural transformations created an opportunity for mistake in contract to emerge as a legal doctrine. It is argued that these nineteenth-century procedural changes had two effects: first, they created an opportunity for the consideration of mistake as a matter of law rather than simply a factual occurrence; and, second, the disappearance of older procedural rules obscured the meaning of the earlier cases from later eyes.[10]

The principal forms of action at law in which contracts were litigated were *indebitatus assumpsit*, special assumpsit (including the important count for money had and received), covenant, debt on obligation, and debt on simple contract. The procedure surrounding the way in which these actions were brought was such that a misapprehension in the formation of a contract was not a concern of the litigants in a legal sense. In other words, while a factual misapprehension might have occurred in the formation of the contract, as a matter of legal substance in the litigation of the dispute arising from the contract, it was not of interest. There was no need within the procedure of the early nineteenth century to have a concern about a mistake as a matter of law. While the misapprehension would undoubtedly be apparent to litigants, there was no need for it to be raised a s a matter of law. Legal procedure, in this sense, determined the shape of substantive law regarding factual misapprehensions. The transformation of common law civil procedure during Victoria's long reign thus acted to create the conditions necessary for the development of a substantive doctrine of mistake.

[4] ibid, 55.

[5] The excerpt is from an unpublished autobiography quoted by Martin Dockray in 'Lord Lindley's Autobiography' (1986) 7 *Journal of Legal History* 102, 103. Lord Lindley contrasted this unfavourably with French and German law, which looked to the legal principles before giving effect to them.

[6] Uniformity of Process Act 1832, 2 & 3 Will IV, c 39; Real Property Limitation Act 1833, 3 & 4 Will IV, c 27, s 36; Common Law Procedure Act 1852, 15 & 16 Vict, c 76, ss 2–3.

[7] Baker (n 3) 68.

[8] FW Maitland, *The Forms of Action at Common Law* (Cambridge, Cambridge University Press, 1948) 2.

[9] See, however, chs 3 and 4 of M Lobban, *The Common Law and English Jurisprudence 1760–1850* (Oxford, Clarendon Press, 1991).

[10] A point made in general terms in R Sutton, *Personal Actions at Common Law* (London, Butterworth & Co, 1929).

Mistake, as a matter of law, generally operates as a defence to a contractual claim. At the outset of Victoria's reign, cases of misapprehension could be defeated by other devices. It is argued that four principal changes brought about by these reforms are significant in the development of mistake in common law. The first was in the changes which occurred from the 1830s to the 1860s in the manner in which cases were pleaded. These changes acted to focus thought and argument away from procedural technicalities and towards the legal substance of a case. The second was in the changing procedure which allowed equitable defences to be raised in common law courts by mid-century. The third lay in the increasing body of evidence, both oral and documentary, which could be considered in common law courts. These courts, increasingly, were able to accurately ascertain the facts upon which the case had arisen and that a mistake had occurred in the formation of a contract. The fourth change was brought about by the changes in the administration of justice: the changes in courts and in the way in which justice was administered acted to bring a greater consideration to bear upon substantive law. The diminishing number of civil jury trials and the development of an appeal process acted to transform the responses of the common law away from a resolution based on fact and towards one based on law.

Pleading

To understand why a factual misapprehension was not, in itself, a matter of substantive legal concern, one must understand how such misapprehensions might well be dealt with under the procedures employed immediately before the reign of Victoria. The first point of significance lay in the pleadings. As Victorian observers noted, English law employed a unique practice to settle the legal issue between litigants. The litigants themselves determined, before the matter was tried, the nature of their dispute. The plaintiff made a declaration as to the nature of his claim against the defendant; the declaration might contain several counts. To this declaration, the defendant provided a defence by way of a plea. The defendant was required to make a plea to each count of the declaration. To these pleas, the plaintiff could proceed to make an answer, and the process continued until the issue was clear between the parties. The object was to settle the nature of the problem and present it before the relevant form of trial for resolution. This process had evolved over several centuries. By the beginning of the nineteenth century, however, the process was becoming cumbersome and it was clear that it no longer served the objective of providing a clearly defined issue for resolution. To investigate the situation and to propose possible reforms, a Royal Commission was struck in 1829 to enquire into the practice and proceedings of the superior courts of common law.[11]

[11] The Commissioners produced two reports: (1829) (46) Royal Com on Practice and Proceedings of Superior Courts of Common Law, First Report; and (1830) (123) Royal Com on Practice and

The Second Report of the Commissioners provides a description of the practices of the day. The system of pleadings was one of great formality and full of technicalities; the Commissioners themselves acknowledged that it was possible for a litigant to succeed on technicalities rather than merit and, indeed, even where his case had no substantive merit.[12] Lord Bowen, writing extrajudicially, recognised that 'frivolous and vexatious defences upon paper delayed the trial of a litigant's cause. Merchants were hindered for months and years from recovering their just dues.'[13] At the heart of this system lay the doctrine of variance. The plaintiff had to ensure that the counts of his declaration accurately set out the nature of his claim. If they did not so accurately set it out, a defendant could plead that there was a variance. If, at the trial, a variance was established between the allegations and the state of the proven facts, the effect upon the plaintiff's claim was fatal. Even if the variance was wholly immaterial to the substantive merits of the case, the effect was still fatal.[14] There was a very real incentive for the party whose case had no real foundation to look for a variance, and it was recognised by contemporaries that in some circumstances no amount of diligence on the part of his opponent could prevent this.[15] The doctrine of variance was compounded by the problem that pre-trial methods of discovery at common law were primitive and it was hard to establish a case in advance.

Variance occurred in different forms: since a variance might well arise in cases of factual misapprehension, it is worth considering them. One form of variance existed where there was a variation between the facts as alleged and those proved: the Commissioners considered the situation where the plaintiff declared a contract to deliver certain goods upon the ship *Juno*, and the proof established a contract to deliver the goods upon the ship *Thetis*.[16] It is not hard to see how such a variation might also amount to what modern eyes would view as an operative mistake. A second was where the discrepancies were such as to remove the claim or defence as a matter of law. A third was where the precise terms of the arrangement were not pleaded. A fourth occurred where there was a misdescription of an element of the facts.

The variance defence acted to create a situation which impeded the ability of common law courts to determine cases. The possibility of a variance led to

Proceedings of Superior Courts of Common Law, Second Report. The reforms and their effect on contract law are discussed in Lobban (n 9) 211–22, and ch 9.

[12] Royal Com on Practice and Proceedings, Second Report (n 11) 35–36.

[13] Lord Bowen, 'Progress in the Administration of Justice During the Victorian Period', in E Freund, WE Mikell and JH Wigmore (eds) *Select Essays in Anglo-American Legal History, vol I* (Boston, NJ, Little, Brown and Company, 1907) 520.

[14] Royal Com on Practice and Proceedings, Second Report (n 11) 36. Thus, in the case of *Walters v Mace* (1819) 2 Barn & Ald 756; 106 ER 541, the declaration declared that the defendant went before a justice by the name of Richard Cavendish, Baron Waterpark of Waterfork when his name was in actuality Richard Cavendish, Baron Waterpark of Water*park*. The variance was fatal and resulted in a non-suit.

[15] Royal Com on Practice and Proceedings, Second Report (n 11) 36. See also, Lord Bowen's comments on the subject (n 13) 521.

[16] The example is that given by the Commissioners: Royal Com on Practice and Proceedings, Second Report (n 11) 39.

pleaders setting out multiple, often contradictory, counts in their declaration. The pleader, desperate to prevent a variance, set the claim out in multiple counts and pleas to attempt to ensure that some version of the pleading would accord with the facts proved at trial. The result was that pleaders were less concerned with defining their facts and more with drafting their declarations and pleas. The effect was to make the ascertainment of the issue, in advance of the trial, difficult; it also made the proceedings far more expensive and complex. As the Commissioners reported: 'it often leads to such bulky and intricate combinations of statement, as to present the case to the Judge and jury in a form of considerable complexity; and is apt, therefore, to embarrass and protract the trial, and occasionally leads to ultimate confusion and mistake in the administration of justice'.[17] While there is merit in the argument that the variance defence diverted attention from a substantive legal doctrine of mistake,[18] the reality is probably more subtle. The existence of a variance could be easily made out in circumstances where there was a factual misapprehension and, in these circumstances, there was little incentive to borrow or create a legal doctrine of mistake at law. Common law lawyers and judges had little incentive to create a more difficult concept to cover a matter adequately dealt with at a simpler procedural level. It must have been the case that lawyers throughout the nineteenth century recognised that a variance was based upon a factual misapprehension[19] but the misapprehension was one which was dealt with at a procedural level rather than a substantive level.

A second popular form of defence before 1834 was that it was also open to a defendant to plead the general issue by way of defence. Thus, if the claim was in *assumpsit*, it was open to the defendant to plead *non assumpsit*. The plea was a summary form of denial of all the allegations made by the plaintiff's count; the effect was to put the plaintiff to the strict proof of every element of his count or counts. The defendant himself was entitled to prove in his own defence almost any kind of matter in confession and avoidance. By this was meant that the defendant could admit the truth of the plaintiff's allegations but seek to avoid their legal effect. The advantage to the defendant of such a tactic was that he was not compelled to disclose to the plaintiff his possible defence[20] and he had the advantage of forcing the plaintiff to prove all his allegations. The result was that issues of fact were determined at trial, often by a jury. It was recognised by contemporaries that

[17] ibid, 34–35.

[18] PA Hamburger, 'The Development of the Nineteenth-Century Consensus Theory of Contract' (1989) 7 *Law and History Review* 241, 244, 280.

[19] Frederick Pollock in the first edition of his influential treatise on contract law wrote of a variance between the terms of an offer and its acceptance which prevented the creation of a contract: F Pollock, *Principles of Contract At Law and in Equity: Being a Treatise on the General Principles Concerning the Validity of Agreements* (London, Stevens and Sons, 1876) 372. Pollock also employed the decision in *Thornton v Kempster* to support the proposition that the parties must be agreed as to the subject matter; simultaneously noting that this was really a case of variance: ibid, 397.

[20] 'It not unfrequently, therefore, happens, that the parties are taken by surprise, and find themselves opposed by some unexpected matter of defence or reply, which from the want of timely notice, they are not in due condition to resist': Royal Com on Practice and Proceedings, Second Report (n 11) 45.

the determination of matters of law also suffered under such a procedure. Rather than being dealt with on a demurrer by a court *en banc*, the matter was considered by one judge alone, who was unable to anticipate the argument and had to decide it without reference to any books. The situation was recognised as unsatisfactory and inconclusive.[21] 'The consequence is, that the trial often fails to accomplish the purposes of justice', a consequence which led to difficulty and expense.[22] It was entirely possible that the reason for the *non assumpsit* was a misapprehension; in such circumstances, however, it would be dealt with as a matter of fact rather than as legal doctrine. Indeed, the possibility of legal doctrine would have been irrelevant because the common law already provided a different method by which the problem could be resolved.

The Royal Commission of 1829, in deciding how to deal with the problems presented by pleading practices, was greatly influenced by one of its members, Mr Serjeant Stephen. Under his influence, the Commission concluded that the means of remedying the defects caused by pleadings to the administration of justice lay in largely eliminating the general issue and returning to the stricter forms of special pleading employed by an earlier generation. In other words, 'special pleading [was] rendered still more *special*.'[23] Acting upon the Commission's recommendations, Parliament empowered[24] the judges to make rules of court implementing the Commission's recommendations. The result was the *Regulae Generales of Hilary Term* 1834. Taken as a whole, the Hilary Term Rules were meant to simplify the trial process by drastically reducing the availability of the general issue. To achieve these ends, they implemented the Commission's specific recommendations,[25] a number of which pertained to agreements. The first was that the plea of *non assumpsit* was not available where the promise could be implied from the facts; it was only to be available elsewhere where there was a denial in fact that the promise was made. In other instances, where confession and avoidance applied, the defendant was to specially plead the element which made the promise void or voidable in point of law. These grounds of defence, which could show the transaction to be void or voidable in point of law, were expressly enumerated in the Hilary Term Rules of 1834: they did not include mistake or error.[26] The second recommendation was that in actions in *debt* on *specialty* and *covenant*, where *non est factum* was pleaded, no defence would be admissible but the denial of the

[21] ibid, 45–46.

[22] GTC, 'Special Pleading' (1836–37) 16 *American Jurist & Law Magazine* 324, 330.

[23] ibid, 324. The author noted the oddity that as England moved towards special pleading, Massachusetts had moved to abolish it. On the whole, the author thought the English approach the better one, and one which had benefited 'with the light and aid of whatever of wisdom and experience the country could furnish': ibid, 325.

[24] Civil Procedure Act 1833, 3 & 4 Will IV, c 42, s 1.

[25] Royal Com on Practice and Proceedings, Second Report (n 11) 48.

[26] *Regulae Generales (Common Law) Hilary Term, 4th Wm IV 1834*, 'Pleadings in particular actions, I Assumpsit, 3d', printed in (1834) 11 *Law Magazine, or Quarterly Review of Jurisprudence* (Law Mag Quart Rev Juris) 259, 267. Equally, Lord Brougham in his great speech on the state of the common law in 1828 enumerated eight pleas behind the general issue of *non assumpsit* given in the action of *assumpsit*: none was of mistake: *Hansard* xviii, 201.

execution of such a deed in point of fact. All other defences were to be specially pleaded, including matters which made the deed void or voidable. The third was that in debt on a simple contract, the general plea of *nil debet* was not to be employed. In such cases, the defence in confession and avoidance was to be specifically pleaded according to the principles set out for *assumpsit.*

While the purpose of the Hilary Term Rules of 1834 was to remove the defence of the general issue and to compel pleaders to focus on the substance of their case in an attempt to define the issue, the desired effect was not achieved. Rather than plead the defence of a general issue, pleaders settled into a practice of traversing every single averment in the declaration. In exasperation, Lord Campbell CJ declared:

> it grieves me to observe how the system of pleading several pleas has grown into a perversion of justice. Since the new rules have abolished the general issue, it has become the practice to Multiply pleas by traversing every averment in the declaration. It is of the greatest importance that this should be checked. The common law allowed only one plea; that strictness is properly relaxed for the promotion, but not for the perversion, of justice.[27]

While Lord Campbell was regarded as a man who was 'not wedded to the narrow technicalities'[28] he struggled with his brother judges on the virtue of procedural technicality. Coleridge LJ was to write that: 'for some time he [Campbell] struggled in vain against the idolatory of Baron Parke to which the whole of the Common Law at that time was devoted'.[29] In the words of one vociferous critic:

> That special pleading is the great and prominent evil of our present system, that it makes the clearest right precarious, and the most dishonest pretension plausible, that so far from bringing the facts really in dispute of the parties to a clear, short, intelligible, and satisfactory issue . . . it is obvious that the purpose of its inventors was to involve the simplest and easiest subjects in the thickest obscurity and confusion the most hopeless; these are facts which any one who will take the trouble of turning over a volume of our Reports may satisfy himself are incontrovertible.[30]

While the object of special pleading had been to eliminate surprises at trial, the real effect was that it prevented the jury, and in some cases the judges, from having any idea of the real point in dispute and it provided triumph to those who lacked merit.[31] So intricate and arcane had this system become that even the best special pleaders were unable to force the case to be heard on the merits and were liable to be defeated on technicalities which they could not meet.[32] The Commissioners

[27] *Cooling v Great Northern Railway Co* (1850) 15 QB 486; 117 ER 544 at 496–97; 548.

[28] Coleridge LJ, 'The Law in 1847 and the Law in 1889' (1890) 57 *Contemporary Review* 797, 801.

[29] ibid. Coleridge LJ also recalled a statement of Sir William Maule: '[well] that seems a horror in morals and a monster in reasoning. Now, give us the judgment of Baron Parke which lays it down as law': ibid 800.

[30] JG Phillimore, *Thoughts on Law Reform and the Law Review* (London, William Benning and Co, 1847) 3. More conventional authors shared these views: see, eg, the later comments in JC Day, *The Common Law Procedure Acts*, 4th edn (London, Henry Sweet, 1872) 1.

[31] ibid, 7.

[32] ibid, 21, 55.

appointed to inquire into the practice and procedures of the common law explained that:

> The rules which govern the form and application of the special traverse are so technical and artificial as to perplex the practitioner; for instance, the inducement must not be a direct denial, but it must be a sufficiently indirect one, and it must not be in confession or avoidance. The rules also as to when an inducement may or may not be traversed, and how the pleading may be answered by the opposite party, are extremely difficult and abstruse.[33]

While parties could, after a non-suit, bring their action again, the cost of so doing was prohibitive; for those who were not wealthy, legal procedure was a 'tremendous instrument of torture' in which the poor litigant could be 'reduced to beggary by success itself'.[34] It is no surprise that, in a system in which the focus was invariably formal and technical, that there was little scope for the consideration of a substantive legal doctrine.[35] The Hilary Term Rules of 1834 were not to produce conditions conducive for the introduction of a doctrine of mistake at common law. There was, once again, no reason to so introduce a new substantive legal doctrine when time-tried procedural techniques could reach the same end.

The return to medieval special pleading was not to last. Holdsworth described the result as a 'disastrous mistake',[36] and it is estimated that under the Hilary Rules one case in four was decided on the pleadings.[37] The 'agitation' against special pleading came from within and without the legal profession.[38] The reduction of the scope of the general issue was to affect actions of *assumpsit*: the plea of '*non asssumpsit*' now operated only to deny the promise.[39] All other matters had to be specifically pleaded: in order to show that a contract had been discharged or was void or voidable, there had to be a special plea of fraud, infancy, coverture, release, payment, performance or illegality.[40] To correct the effects of this disastrous mistake, a Royal Commission was established in 1850 to inquire into the process, practice and system of pleading in the superior courts of common law. The

[33] 1851 [1389] Royal Com to inquire into Process, Practice and System of Pleading in Superior Courts of Common Law, First Report, 26.

[34] Phillimore (n 30) 23.

[35] One of the problems that arose from the Hilary Term Rules of 1834 was that a plaintiff could raise multiple counts in his declaration, to which a defendant could raise multiple defences. The plaintiff, however, was then restricted to a single reply, even if, on the merits of the case, multiple replies were possible. The system encouraged a multiplicity of spurious defences, a problem noted by the Commissioners in their first report (n 33) 19, and Phillimore (n 30). Another vexatious problem was the creation of special demurrers which were addressed at a lack of form or a technical objection: the result of such demurrers was to facilitate the success of the unmeritorious. See first report (n 33) 19, and Phillimore (n 30).

[36] WS Holdsworth, *A History of English Law, vol IX* (London, Methuen & Co. Ltd, 1926) 325.

[37] CB Whittier, 'Notice Pleading', HLR xxxi, 507, quoted in ibid.

[38] JP, 'Pleadings at Common Law Must they be Good in Substance?' (1855) 22 Law Mag Quart Rev Juris ns 201, 202.

[39] In actions on bills of exchange and promissory notes, it was wholly excluded.

[40] Interestingly, the treatises on pleading do not list mistake as a matter which had to be pleaded to render the contract void or voidable. The most likely reason for such an omission was that mistake was not something which defendants pleaded because it did not exist in law as a doctrine.

Commissioners[41] discovered that the problems were so great as to require three reports. The first report, given in 1851, was concerned with the proceedings attendant upon an action at law;[42] the second report, given in 1853, considered the proceedings applicable at trials of fact, the evidence receivable at these trials and the ability of common law courts to administer certain procedures previously only administered by courts of equity.[43] The third report, given in 1860, considered amendments to certain types of actions and to the role of juries, and a renewed consideration of the ability of common law courts to deal with those auxiliary matters dealt with by Chancery.[44] The Common Law Commissioners' work resulted in the Common Law Procedure Acts of 1852, 1854 and 1860: these three pieces of legislation changed enormously the procedures which determined the practice of the common law in the lead-up to the fusion of law and equity effected by the Judicature Act 1873. It is interesting to note that the Commissioners looked entirely inward for solutions to the problems concerned with practice and procedure: there were few gazes at the practice of civil jurisdictions.[45] Instead, there was an analysis of the problems faced by the common law courts and an examination of the procedures of the new county courts and the Court of Chancery. The Commissioners affirmed the importance of common pleading for its simplicity and utility. While recognising the system as sound in principle, they noted that it had been considerably abused and many mischiefs had grown up. While the Commission formed in 1829 had framed rules to curb these abuses, 'unhappily the rules framed to prevent these mischiefs have been abused, and they and certain arbitrary regulations and forms have caused the existence of those objections to the practice of special pleading, the justice of which we thoroughly feel'.[46] The Commissioners agreed with their predecessors as to the merits of special pleading, but having noted the strong dissatisfaction within the profession as to the results of special pleading, agreed with this dissatisfaction and thus decided that the 'defects by which the system is vitiated must be cut away with an unsparing hand'.[47]

[41] The Commissioners chosen were men who would dominate the administration of the common law in the nineteenth century: Sir John Jervis, Samuel Martin, William Henry Watson, George William Bramwell and James Shaw Willes. When Sir John Jervis became Lord Chief Justice of the Court of Common Pleas, Sir Alexander Cockburn was added to the Commission.

[42] n 33. The Report was followed by the Common Law Procedure Act 1852.

[43] 1852–53 [1626] Royal Com to inquire into Process, Practice and System of Pleading in Superior Courts of Common Law, Second Report. The Report was followed by the Common Law Procedure Act 1854.

[44] 1860 [2614] Royal Com to inquire into Process, Practice and System of Pleading in Superior Courts of Common Law, Third Report.

[45] That this inward focus was not atypical of lawyers of the day can be seen in *The Law Times*' comments on the examination of Miss Wagner (in the case of *Lumley v Wagner* (1852) 1 De Gex M & G 604; 42 ER 687) by a Prussian judge. The author commented with surprise that the Prussian judge had first read the document to Miss Wagner before asking if the signature it bore was hers. On balance, the author approved of the system as 'a much more rational one than ours': *The Law Times*, 3 December 1853, 101.

[46] First Report (n 33) 12.

[47] ibid, 13.

The Commissioners examined the principal objections to the system of pleading then in place. Three are of relevance to our examination. The first was the undue length and prolixity of proceedings; the second was the requirement of unnecessary precision accompanied by certain technical rules, excessive rigour of which often led to a defeat of justice; and third, the power which a party now had of passing by an objection to his antagonist's pleading when fault first occurred and taking advantage of it afterwards when all expense of suit had occurred and the defect could not be remedied. In each of these areas, the recommendations of the Commissioners was to shift the focus on to the substance of the cause. A problem that they noted in relation to personal actions, including *assumpsit*, was that the effect of the special pleading was to introduce

> the technical and formal defects of the system, which had previously existed in some actions only, became extended to all, and the inconvenience was increased in proportion. Special demurrers for want of form, and for objections of a technical nature, were much increased. From the necessity of specially pleading all defences to actions in most general use, new pleas were introduced; and defendants who had no real defence availed themselves of the chance of a temporary success by pleading subtle and tricky pleas to invite special demurrers for the mere purpose of delay.[48]

The recommendations of the Commissioners was to focus the attention of litigation upon the 'right of the cause' rather than the technicalities of the pleadings. Contemporaries greeted with delight the abolition of the trickeries of special pleading, which could work a substantive injustice upon procedural form.[49] Judges were to be given the discretion of allowing amendments or not, dependent upon whether the right of the particular cause justified the exercise of their discretion. A number of recommendations, and their implementation in the subsequent Common Law Procedure Act 1852,[50] have a bearing upon the later development of a doctrine of mistake in contract law. The first was that the Commissioners recommended that it would be desirable to allow the joinder or removal of parties to an action.[51] No longer would the non-joinder of a person as plaintiff act as a fatal variance to an action on contract, for an amendment would be allowed.[52] Second, the form of the pleadings was to emphasise those facts necessary to sustain the action or defence, and 'it shall not be necessary that such matters should be stated in any technical or formal language or manner'.[53] Unnecessary fictions were to be removed from pleadings.[54] Where issue was joined on a demurrer, the Court was to give judgment 'according as the very right of the cause', 'without regarding any imperfection, omission, defect in or lack of form'.[55] The Commissioners were

[48] ibid, 19.
[49] 'The Common Law Procedure Act' (1852) 17 Law Mag Quart Rev Juris ns 290, 294.
[50] 15 & 16 Vict, c 76.
[51] Implemented in the Common Law Procedure Act 1852, ss 34–40.
[52] First Report (n 33) 71.
[53] ibid, 72.
[54] ibid. The recommendation was implemented as s 50 of the Common Law Procedure Act 1852.
[55] ibid.

adamant that the technical hurdles presented in pleadings were to be abandoned and asserted 'that duplicity, argumentativeness, and uncertainty shall no longer be grounds of objection to a pleading' unless the pleading had been so designed to mislead the other party.[56] Judges were to possess the power to set aside frivolous or vexatious pleadings. Third, the manner in which the issue was determined was altered. The special traverse was abolished to avoid prolixity.[57] Henceforth, parties were to be allowed to raise as many counts in their claim or pleas in their defence as they wished, subject to a judicial discretion to strike down such counts or pleas: 'we would allow the utmost latitude to the parties in placing upon the record all the grounds upon which they can fairly rest their claim or defence'.[58] The purpose of such an amendment was to avoid the harshness of the sixth and seventh rules of the Hilary Rules, which restricted parties to one statement.[59] The recommendations were intended to shift the emphasis of adjudication from procedural technicality to substantive law.

Parliament accepted these recommendations in enacting section 81 of the Common Law Procedure Act 1852, which allowed parties to plead several matters at any stage in the pleadings; it went even further in section 84 and allowed as a matter of course for a defendant to raise multiple pleas.[60] It was not an objection that the pleas were inconsistent.[61] Where the 'real justice of the case' required several pleas to be pleaded, the practice was legitimate, although not where several pleas were founded upon the same ground of defence.[62] The results were adjudged far from perfect by contemporaries, who noted that it was sometimes the case that more than one defence was mixed in a single plea or a defence uncovered on the record which clearly amounted to, and could have been given in evidence, under a general issue or a simple traverse.[63] The change had a significant effect for mistake because it cleared the path for later defendants to raise mistake as a plea where

[56] ibid, 73.

[57] ibid, 26.

[58] ibid, 30.

[59] ibid, 30.

[60] A defendant could now raise a plea denying any contract or debt as alleged and plead that the claim was statute barred, or affected by infancy or coveture. The *Regulae Generales as to Pleading*, made by judges pursuant to s 223 of the Common Law Procedure Act 1852, known as the Trinity Term Rules 1853, provided in r 2 that several pleas would be allowed where 'the court or the judge may allow such counts on the same cause of action, or such pleas, replications, or subsequent pleadings . . . founded on the same ground of answer or defence, as may appear to such court or judge to be proper for the determining of the real controversy between the parties on its merits, subject to such terms . . . as the court or judge may think fit'. If there was no ruling as to costs and the party who maintained the count or plea was unable to establish a distinct cause of action or distinct ground of answer or defence, that party was liable to the other party for all the costs occasioned by the plea or count: r 3. Such a rule would encourage those who raised defences to attempt to sustain them.

[61] *Tribnerr v Duerr* (1834) 1 Bing NC 266; 131 ER 1119. This was a marked departure from the previous practice, a fact acknowledged by writers of the day: see S Prentice, *Chitty's Archbold's Practice of the Court of Queen's Bench*, 12th edn (London, H Sweet and Stevens & Sons, 1866) 281–82.

[62] Prentice (n 61) 282. See, also, E Bullen and SM Leake, *Precedents of Pleadings in Actions in The Superior Courts of Common Law* (London, VR Stevens and Sons, 1860) 254–57.

[63] Anon, 'Results of the Common Law Procedure Acts, 1852 and 1854' (1858–59) 6 *Law Magazine & Law Review, or Quarterly Journal of Jurisprudence* (Law Mag & L Rev Quart J Juris), 3d ser, 248, 251.

they would not have risked doing so prior to the enactment. The enactment, in other words, allowed defendants the opportunity to attempt to develop new substantive defences in ways that the older common law system had not. Defendants confined to a single plea would only reluctantly have tried a new legal argument. An examination of nineteenth-century mistake cases indicates that the defence was often raised by counsel who appeared likely to fail but for the acceptance of the defence.[64]

A fourth change in moving pleading from the technical to the substantive was found in the recommendation, subsequently embodied in section 80 of the Common Law Procedure Act 1852, to allow a party to both plead and demur to pleadings at the same time with the leave of the court or judge.[65] The section thus gave the ability for a defendant to raise objections to the cause of action on the grounds both of law and of fact, and he was not required to elect between the two. The effect was that the pleader's 'position was considerably eased by the provisions . . . which permitted both a demurrer and a plea to the same pleading . . . before that act [of 1852] this was not permissible, for the effect of both demurring and pleading was to raise two issues, one of law and one of fact, which had to be decided in different ways, and . . . originally only one issue of any kind was allowed'.[66] This liberality further facilitated more adventurous pleadings, which could include matters such as mistake. A fifth change, oft noted by historians, was the abolition of the forms of action. What they meant by forms of action was that 'it may be said to be the peculiar technical mode of framing the writ and pleadings appropriate to the particular injury which the action is intended to redress. By the established practice of pleading, peculiar forms of expression characteristic of each action have been appropriated thereto, many of which are of a purely formal nature, and are wholly independent of the merits of the cause of action.'[67] The difficulty presented by the forms of action was that if a plaintiff did not frame his action correctly, he was at risk of having his declaration found to be bad. Another problem was mistaking the form of action applicable to his facts. The abolition was a further factor in allowing the development of a substantive doctrine of mistake, for it further removed the incentive for defendants to look for success in narrow technicalities.

That the Common Law Procedure Act 1852 was designed to put an end to the ability of the unmeritorious litigant to succeed on technicalities can be seen in the enactment of section 222. This provision, which substantially changed the powers of judges, gave them the power to amend 'all defects and errors in any proceeding in civil causes, whether there is anything in writing to amend by or not, and whether the defect or error be that of the party applying to amend or not'. It was expressly enacted that 'all such amendments as may be necessary for the purpose

[64] MacMillan (n 1).

[65] The granting of the leave was entirely within the discretion of the court or judge: *Thompson v Knowles* (1855) LJ 24 Ex 43. Where the demurrer went to the whole of the cause of action, the demurrer should first be argued, although this required the consent of the plaintiff or the leave of the judge: JC Day, *The Common Law Procedure Acts*, 4th edn (London, Henry Sweet, 1872) 114.

[66] Sutton (n 10) 121.

[67] ibid, 32.

of determining in the existing suit the *real question in controversy between the parties* shall be so made' (emphasis added). As one treatise writer stated, 'it is difficult to exaggerate the importance of this section'.[68] The allowance of amendments was made at the discretion of the judges with regard to the particular case before them. The purpose, as contemporaries recognised, was to prevent any suit from going off on a technicality, for the incentive to raise such technicalities had been removed by the legislation which allowed an amendment: 'it will be almost impossible for any suit to go off upon any question of form—all will be decided upon their merits'.[69] So radical a change would be presented by this that it was feared that 'the changes in Procedure have almost ousted the Bar from employment'.[70] Special pleaders would no longer be employed to draft the much-shortened pleadings.[71] The overall effect of the Act was to simplify the process of the common law and to remove the subtleties of pleading.[72] Contemporaries acknowledged that the Act effected 'a more important revolution in the complicated, costly jurisprudence of this country than it has yet witnessed'.[73] Reforms such as this contributed to create an environment in which a misapprehension would be dealt with as a matter of substantive law rather than as a procedural technicality.

The reforms to pleadings obtained the desired result, for litigation over procedural matters diminished greatly. *The Law Times* reported that 'in procedure, indeed, questions are now so rare, that the reports of an entire term do not produce half a dozen'.[74] The Commissioners, in their Third Report, in 1860, noted with satisfaction a considerable diminution in the number of cases concerned with procedural difficulties: from 38,009 to 3,081.[75] What had been questions of procedure had been transformed into questions of law, 'which come chiefly in the shape of motions for new trials'.[76] While the hand was not entirely unsparing, the effect of the Commissioners' recommendations as embodied in the ensuing Common Law Procedure Acts, was to remove objections and delays based upon technical matters and shift the focus of litigation more clearly onto the merits of

[68] Day (n 65) 216. Judges were quick to exercise the powers of amendment granted by the section 'freely and liberally': 'Common Law Procedure Act' (1853) 18 Law Mag Quart Rev Juris ns 311, 314.

[69] *The Law Times*, 25 September 1852, 3.

[70] *The Law Times*, 2 October 1852, 14. Great concern was expressed in the pages of *The Law Times* in the immediate aftermath of the passing of the Common Law Procedure Act 1852 that the Bar would be greatly diminished; see, for example *The Law Times*, 18 March 1854 in which the author opined that the Bar would be reduced to one-fiftieth of its current size, a problem not only for the Bar but for the Bench as well for 'where are our Judges to be found?' from such a diminished Bar: at 246.

[71] *The Law Times*, 30 October 57.

[72] *The Law Times*, 4 November 1854, 75.

[73] 'The Common Law Procedure Act' (1852) 17 Law Mag Quart. Rev Juris n.s 290.

[74] *The Law Times*, 28 October 1854, 57.

[75] Third Report (n 44) 6. The comparison was between the first nine months of the new system in 1852–53 and the same nine months in the preceding year, before the reforms. The diminution had occurred despite the increased number of writs. The Commissioners explained that the effect of the reforms had 'rendered Procedure simple, economical, and speedy, and have had the effect of limiting the costs to the expenses of the necessary and essential steps in a cause': ibid. Day (n 65) observed that the litigation over technicalities had become a thing of the past: 8.

[76] Day (n 65) 8. Parties were more willing, given the simplicity of the new procedure, to take a matter to trial.

the case. In short, archaic procedural rules were removed. Although the Commissioners may not have foreseen this, the ultimate result of their unsparing hand was shift the focus of practitioners from procedural technicalities to substantive law. There was no longer any incentive for pleaders to seek out narrow technical devices to defeat an action and the preoccupation with procedure greatly diminished. The changed focus, in turn, was to give rise to new concerns about the body of the substantive law which could be argued. The treatise writers of the second half of the nineteenth century both arose to meet this need for substance and, in so meeting it, facilitated the development of the substantive law. It was not immediately apparent that some of this substantive law merely replicated in the substantive law a form of trickery previously practised in procedure.

Equitable Defences

The second principal change, the introduction of equitable defences, was enacted by the Common Law Procedure Act 1854.[77] As we have seen, mistake as a ground of defence existed in equity. The 1854 Act allowed a defendant the opportunity to raise in common law courts any defence that he would have been able to raise in equity.[78] The provision had been passed to remove a glaring procedural problem which arose in those instances where 'Courts of Law and Courts of Equity apply different rules of right and wrong to the same subject-matter',[79] a problem of particular significance when a court of law was obliged to hold as untenable a defence a court of equity considered valid. The result in such circumstances was that the court of law gave a judgment in favour of the plaintiff, which the court of equity immediately restrained him from enforcing by way of an injunction.[80] To resolve this problem, the Common Law Commissioners recommended that courts of law should be able to receive pleas of equitable defences and that where such relief would be conditional or discretionary in a court of equity, that the courts of law should have the power to give the same relief. In the words of Cockburn CJ, 'The object of these provisions is, to enable a court of law to do substantial justice between the parties, by doing that at once which might be done by having recourse to a court of equity'.[81] While the object of the reform was to speed up the admin-

[77] The jurisdiction conferred upon courts of common law was increased to include other equitable jurisdictions: the power to compel the discovery and production of documents (s 50), the power of compelling the discovery of facts (s 51); the power to grant specific performance (s 68); and the power of granting injunctions (s 79).

[78] Common Law Procedure Act 1854, 17 & 18 Vict, c 124, s 83. The significance of this defence in relation to contract law was noted by Leake in his contract treatise: SM Leake, *The Elements of the Law of Contracts* (London, Stevens and Sons, 1867) 179–81.

[79] RM Kerr, *The Common Law Procedure Act 1854* (London, Butterworths, 1854) xxiv.

[80] The practice is explained by William Williamson Kerr in *A Treatise on the Law and Practice of Injunctions*, 2nd edn (London, William Maxwell & Son, 1878) 9.

[81] *Flight v Gray* (1857) 3 CB 320, 321; 140 ER 763, 764.

istration of justice by ensuring that parties did not have to go back and forth between different courts, and in so doing to reduce the costs and difficulties of litigation, it was immediately recognised that this had substantive legal ramifications. As a writer in the *Law Magazine*, calling this 'the great feature of this sweeping Act', noted, 'it introduces more than the thin edge of a fusion of Law and Equity'.[82] The 1854 Act only partly implemented this proposal; it gave the power to plead an equitable defence[83] but only where that defence was an unconditional one. In cases where the equitable defence would involve the substantive powers of equity, where relief was given on conditions, the court or judge was empowered by the Act to strike out the equitable plea.[84] Only where a court of equity would have granted an unconditional and perpetual injunction would the equitable plea be good in courts of common law.[85] Courts of law were concerned not to extend the equitable jurisdiction conferred upon them[86], and were quick to decide after the enactment that the statute did not give them power to allow an equitable defence where a court of equity would also have compelled one or both of the parties to perform other acts. In the words of Parke B:

> the equitable defence allowed to be pleaded by this statute means such a defence as would in a Court of Equity be a complete answer to the plaintiffs' claim, and would, as such, afford sufficient ground for a perpetual injunction, granted absolutely and without any conditions. But, according to the statement in the plea, a Court of Equity would not interfere, except upon the condition of the execution of a valid surrender by the defendant. We have no machinery by which we can compel the execution of a surrender. The statute does not say that the Courts of Common Law may give relief on equitable conditions, but that a plea shall be allowed which discloses a defence upon equitable grounds.[87]

Courts of common law refused to accede to later arguments that the jurisdiction conferred upon them was any greater.[88] While the 1854 Act only partly implemented this proposal (it did not give courts of law the ability to grant an injunction upon terms),[89] it was enough to change the substantive law in mistake in contract

[82] Anon, 'The New Procedure Act' (1854) 21 Law Mag Quart Rev Juris ns 121, 126.

[83] s 83.

[84] s 86. See, generally, FF Pinder, *A Treatise on the Principles of Pleading in Civil Actions* 7th edn (London, Stevens & Sons, H Sweet & W Maxwell, 1866) 210–11.

[85] *Davis v Nisbett* (1861) 10 CB NS 752; 142 ER 649.

[86] *Wakley v Froggatt* (1863) 2 H & C 669; 159 ER 277, per Pollock CB, at 673–74; 279.

[87] *Mines Royal Societies v Magnay* (1854) 10 Ex 489; 156 ER 531 at 493–94; 533. The court decided that s 86 of the Act allowed a court of law to strike out an equitable plea where it could not do justice between the parties and determined that since the equitable relief would have been conditional (something they thought beyond their legal powers) the court struck out the equitable defence. Interestingly, the limit upon relief where a perpetual injunction only could be granted by a court of equity had been raised in anticipation of the section by Charles Edward Pollock in *A Treatise on the Power of the Courts of Common Law to compel The Production of Documents for Inspection* (London, S Sweet, 1851) 61.

[88] See, for example, the argument made by counsel in *Wodehouse v Farebrother* (1855) 5 E & B 277; 119 ER 485 that s 83 of the 1854 Act empowered the court to grant any relief, and not simply unconditional and perpetual relief and that Parliament had never intended to so confine the relief: 285; 488. The argument was rejected by Lord Campbell CJ: 289; 489.

[89] A court of law still did not have the power to effectively rescind a contract on terms by granting an injunction on terms. In regard to mistakes, equitable defences operated as all-or-nothing propositions: the contract was either enforceable or not enforceable but its terms could not be changed.

law. It was recognised by writers at the outset of the enactment that one of the grounds upon which equity would give relief was on the ground of a mistake of fact.[90] Unsurprisingly, defendants were soon keen to raise such defences in courts of law[91] and, for the first time, mistake entered into the forms of defence considered in treatises on pleadings.[92] Here, however, the abilities of common law pleaders, lawyers and judges seem to have encountered initial difficulties in understanding the intricacies of equitable defences.[93] Many of the common law judges, suspicious and wary of a move towards fusing law and equity, refrained from exercising their new equitable powers.[94] Coleridge LJ later wrote extrajudicially that Baron Parke had taken a particular delight in defeating the success of equitable defences:

> He bent the whole powers of his great intellect to defeat the Act of Parliament which had allowed of equitable defences in a Common Law action. He laid down all but impossible conditions, and said, with an air of intense satisfaction, in my hearing, 'I think we settled the new Act to-day, we shall hear no more of Equitable defences!' And as Baron Parke piped, the Court of Exchequer followed, and dragged after it, with more or less reluctance, the other common Law Courts of Westminster Hall.[95]

The result was that when equitable defences were raised, they could only be raised on an all-or-nothing basis: the contract was either enforced or it was not enforced.[96] What could not occur in courts of law, even after the 1854 Act, was the reform of a contract upon terms because it was held that the statute did not give this power.[97] Any such relief was, still, only available from a court of equity.[98] In

[90] Kerr (n 79) 54.

[91] *Scott v Littledale* (1858) 8 El & Bl 815; 120 ER 304. In *Lyall v Edwards* (1861) 6 H & N 337; 158 ER 139, Wilde B, giving judgment, went so far as to say that 'The doctrine of a Court of equity is, that a release shall not be construed as applying to something of which the party executing it was ignorant, and we have now to act on that doctrine in a Court of law. I think it will be found that a Court of law would correct a mistake of fact; but it is not necessary to decide that point': 348; 144.

[92] See, eg, Bullen and Leake (n 62); T Chitty, *Forms of Practical Proceedings in the Courts of Queen's Bench, Common Pleas, and Exchequer Pleas*, 10th edn (London, Henry Sweet & Stevens and Sons, 1866); and S Prentice, *Chitty's Archbold's Practice of the Court of Queen's Bench, vol 1*, 12th edn (London, H Sweet and Stevens & Sons, 1866) 253–54.

[93] The contemporary observation that counsel 'must lose no time in reading up two branches of equity law now introduced into the practice of the common law': *The Law Times*, 'Some Hints on the New Procedure Act', 4 November 1854, 74.

[94] For the larger political context in which this arose, see P Polden, 'Mingling the Waters: Personalities, Politics and the Making of the Supreme Court of Judicature' (2002) 61 *Cambridge Law Journal* 575, especially 579–81.

[95] Coleridge (n 28) 800. Coleridge observed that although Lord Campbell, once Chief Justice, struggled to overcome the narrow technicalities that prevailed, 'he struggled in vain against the idolatry of Baron Parke to which the whole of the common Law at that time was devoted': 801.

[96] As the Judicature Commission noted in 1869, the result was that the equitable remedies provided to the common law were not of much use and that much 'of the old mischief still remains' of requiring parties to resort to Chancery: 1868–69 [4130] Royal Com to inquire into Operation and Constitution of High Court of Chancery, Superior Courts of Common Law, Central Criminal Court, High Court of Admiralty, and other Courts in England, and into Operation and Effect of Present Separation and Division of Jurisdiction between Courts. First Report, 7

[97] *Teede v Johnson* (1856) 11 Ex 840; 156 ER 1073.

[98] *Flight v Gray* (n 81) established that for a defendant to successfully raise a defence under s 83 of the 1854 Act the equitable defence had to be absolute and unconditional.

addition, a mistake in a written contract would require rectification and this was not something that a court of law could do under the 1854 Act because it required the determination of an equitable issue.[99] The only equitable relief available under the 1854 Act was that which was unconditional; and this was not the case with either a rectification or a rescission on terms. Mistake could only operate as an equitable defence in situations where it could be raised without a claim to rectify the contract.[100] If, for example, the contract containing a mistake in terms had been executed according to the terms intended by the parties, the mistake could be relied upon as a matter for an equitable plea or replication because no object would be served in reforming the contract.[101] Courts did go so far as to say that where a document was held out as the contract between the parties, and this was not the case, by reason of mistake or fraud, the court would admit parol evidence to establish what the real contract was: this was done grudgingly and not without doubt on the part of the judges.[102] Thus, when mistake entered into the common law courts from equity, it entered in a fashion which encouraged judges to see it as a defence which rendered the contract utterly unenforceable, or, in other words, void. The common law judges were recognised as being excessively cautious in their limitation of equitable defences to those instances in which the plea showed that an injunction would be absolute and unqualified, because the legislation was intended to give them broader powers.[103] In so doing, one critic noted that they 'have either stultified the meaning of those who designed the provision for equitable jurisdiction, or have evaded a duty'.[104] It may be that the common law judges were so cautious in their application of equitable defences because of the initial

[99] *Perez v Oleaga* (1856) 11 Exch 506; 156 ER 930. The court refused to rectify a contract which, in the translation into Spanish, had failed to record the agreement between the parties. In reaching this decision, Alderson B left open the possibility that, in such circumstances, the subject matter of the proposed plea could be given in evidence as a denial of the contract. The case is an early illustration of the cross-over of mistake from courts of equity into courts of law. See also *Teede v Johnson* (n 97); *Drain v Harvey* (1855) 17 CB 257; 139 ER 1069; and *Official Manager of Solvency Mutual Guarantee Company v Freeman* (1861) 7 H & N 17; 158 ER 374.

[100] *Wake v Harrop* (1861), 6 H & N 768; 158 ER 317, affirmed, 1 H & C 202; 158 ER 859; *Steele v Haddock* (1855) 10 Exch 643; 156 ER 597; *Vorley v Barrett* (1856), CB NS 225; 140 ER 94 (in which Crowder J pointed out that there was only purpose in reforming an agreement in equity when it was executory, and not once it had been executed and performed); *Borrowman v Rossel* (1864) 16 CB NS 58; 143 ER 1045; and *Wood v Dwarris* (1856) 11 Exch 493; 156 ER 925. As one of the leading pleading treatises of the day explained, a court of law could allow pleadings upon equitable grounds 'only where by the judgment at law they can do complete and final justice and settle all the equities between the parties': Bullen and Leake (n 62) 330 fn (a).

[101] Bullen and Leake (n 62) 331 fn (a).

[102] *Rogers v Hadley* (1863) 2 H & C 227; 159 ER 94.

[103] Anon, 'The Results of the Common Law Procedure Acts, 1852 and 1854' (1858–1859) 6 Law Mag & L Rev Quart J Juris, 3d ser, 248, 253.

[104] ibid. The complaint was repeated in 1860: 'Jurisdiction and Procedure of Courts of Law and Equity' (1860) 9 Law Mag & L Rev Quart J Juris, 3d ser, 147, 154; and by the Commissioners in their Third Report (n 44). *The Law Times* described the early cases as follows: 'the tendency has been not to give a wide or even liberal interpretation to the sections of the Act affecting the equitable jurisdicition': 3 March 1855, 231.

criticisms that they were not up to the task of applying equitable defences.[105] At this time, of course, it was possible for the disappointed party who needed equitable relief upon terms or conditions to proceed to the Court of Chancery. Relief, although more expensive, was still available in the traditional manner granted by equity. Strikingly, these early 'cross-over' cases between equity and law, facilitated by the new jurisdiction given to courts of law to receive equitable defences, do not consider mistake as vitiating consent, or even as factors preventing consensus from being formed. The concerns of the courts of law were those of the courts of equity: the unconscionability of allowing one party to benefit by a mistake.[106]

Evidence and the Pre-trial Discovery of Facts

We turn now to the third major procedural change effected in the nineteenth century which was significant in establishing the conditions in which a doctrine of mistake could be created. This change was concerned with the pre-trial discovery of facts and the admissibility of evidence in a court of law. Over the course of the century, there was a relaxation of the rules of evidence, which increased both the oral and documentary evidence available to a court in order to establish the facts of a particular case. The effect of these procedural changes was to facilitate the ability to isolate and identify the relevant problem as one attributable to a mistake in the formation of the contract.

Pre-trial Discovery

Courts of common law were traditionally limited in the extent to which a pre-trial discovery of witnesses and documents was allowed. At common law, one party was greatly restricted in his ability to inspect the documents of the other: where one party set forth and relied upon a deed in his pleadings, he was said to make *profert* and his opponent was entitled to demand *oyer*, to have the deed read and in that way to have a copy of it. Courts of common law extended this over time to a form of *quasi oyer* which encompassed documents relied upon in pleadings which were not deeds; there was also a power by which a party could compel inspection where

[105] As one author noted in 1854, 'it needs but to reflect on the total inexperience of most of our Common Law Judges in the practice of equity, to be assured of the extreme hazard of such a step': Anon, 'The New Procedure Act' (1854) 21 Law Mag Quart Rev Juris ns 121, 127. The author's fear was that the choice of equitable defences, and their applicability 'will be at the will and pleasure of each judge, and the practice on this most vital point is henceforth at the mercy of judicial idiosyncrasies': ibid, 129.

[106] See, eg, the argument of Montague Smith in *Lyall v Edwards* (1861) 6 H & N 337; 158 ER 139 at 346; 143, in which he raised the point that the ground for relief was not the mistake but the unconscientious advantage taken of it.

he, or a person he claimed directly through, was a party to the document.[107] There was no ability at common law to obtain the evidence of the other party by way of interrogatory at all. To obtain the inspection of documents and an indication of what facts might be established at trial, a party was obliged to go to a court of equity and bring a bill of discovery. The bill was brought not seeking relief, but seeking facts within the knowledge of the other party. Courts of equity were able to compel the discovery of facts in the knowledge of one of the parties in aid of civil rights: documents and interrogatories could be ordered by the court.[108] The system of prosecuting a claim in one court and obtaining discovery from another was laborious, expensive and prone to excessive delay. The Common Law Commissioners despaired over the inadequacy of the procedures of the common law courts:

> That the powers and machinery of the courts of common law are insufficient, even within the scope of their own jurisdiction, is clear from the fact that, for the very purposes of an action, parties are frequently under the necessity of resorting to a court of equity to compel the discovery either of facts exclusively within the knowledge of an opposite party, or of documents, as to which they may be ignorant in whose custody or power they are.[109]

While the inadequacies of the common law procedure to compel pre-trial discoveries had long been apparent,[110] little was done to change the situation until Lord Brougham's Evidence Act in 1851.[111] The Act enabled courts of law upon the application of a litigant to compel the opposite party to allow the applicant to inspect all documents which would, in equity, have answered his bill of discovery. The section did not provide the courts of common law with the larger powers possessed by a court of equity[112] and probably did not confer the broad powers intended by the legislature[113] but it was a start. If the documents came within the ambit of the section, the party was compelled to allow inspection of them.[114] A shortcoming of the legislation was that an applicant was to establish whether or not the documents were within the possession of his opponent, and the difficulty of establishing this meant that recourse still had to be made to equity because the

[107] 'Common Law: Inspection of Documents, 14 & 15 Vict, c 99 s 6' (1854) 20 Law Mag Quart Rev Juris ns 133, 134; the common law position was considered by the court in *Price v Harrison* (1860) 8 CB NS 617; 141 ER 1308.

[108] The process is outlined in JA Wigram, *Points in The Law of Discovery* (Philadelphia, PA, John S Littell, 1836) 1–10.

[109] Royal Com to inquire into Process, Practice and System of Pleading, Second Report (n 43).

[110] It had attracted the criticism of the Common Law Commissioners of 1830: ibid, 20.

[111] 14 & Vict c 99; the relevant section was s 6. The section was the subject of a treatise by Charles Edward Pollock (n 87). The 1851 Act became the means by which documents were inspected when s 55 of the Common Law Procedure Act 1852 abolished *profert.*

[112] Pollock (n 87) 9–10. An applicant, for example, had to supply the information as to the existence and description of the documents sought rather than requiring the other party to declare the relevant documents, and the applicant had to establish that the document was within the possession of his opponent.

[113] Royal Com to inquire into Process, Practice and System of Pleading, Second Report (n 43) 35.

[114] ibid, 21.

common law courts had the power to compel inspection, but not discovery.[115] The Common Law Commissioners, critical of this deficiency, recommended that the common law courts not only have the power to compel discovery of documents but also the power to examine the parties upon all matters pertaining to the dispute.[116] As the Commissioners recognised, such a discovery would not only spare time and expense, it would also 'tend to make more clearly manifest the matters which are alone in contest between the parties'.[117]

While the Common Law Procedure Act 1854 did not go as far as the Law Commissioners' recommendations, it made provisions which corrected the weakness in Lord Brougham's Evidence Act of 1851 and in so doing further extended the ambit of pre-trial discovery. The Common Law Procedure Act 1854 provided that a party to an action could apply to the common law court for the discovery of documents in the possession or power of his opponent.[118] Courts read this provision together with the earlier 1851 Act to create a procedure whereby parties applied under the 1854 Act for the discovery of the documents which they then, under the earlier Act, had the right to inspect.[119] The purpose of these sections was not only to remove the difficulty of turning to equity for information, but in so doing to allow parties to learn the truth of the matter in litigation.[120] Courts of common law turned to the practice of the courts of equity in applying the procedures in these sections.[121]

A further change effected by the Common Law Procedure Act 1854 related to evidence was the power to deliver written interrogatories to the opposite party.[122] The change was associated with the elimination of the procedural delays which occurred in a system in which common law litigants were compelled to resort to courts of equity for assistance with interrogatories in the furtherance of their legal case. The enactment allowed one party to seek to interrogate another as to information about the matter in litigation and provided that a court could compel an oral examination of the interrogated party.[123] While it appears that the procedure was not viewed as an immediate success,[124] it did provide at the outset the ability to establish, at common law, that a factual misapprehension existed. In the event that there was an omission without just cause to answer the interrogatories, a court

[115] ibid, 35.
[116] ibid, 36.
[117] ibid.
[118] s 50.
[119] *Herschfeld v Clarke* (1856) 11 Ex 712; 156 ER 1017.
[120] *White v Watts* (1862) 12 CB NS 267; 142 ER 1146, per Erle CJ, at 272; 1148.
[121] *Lacharme v Quartz Rock Mariposa Gold Mining Company* (1862) 1 H & C 134; 158 ER 832 per Martin B, at 138; 833.
[122] By s 51.
[123] By s 53.
[124] The *Law Magazine* observed that 'at present we cannot declare interrogatories to be a complete success', a situation they attributed in large part to the inability of 'every one in an attorney's office' to undertake a skill equity barristers considered one of the most difficult tasks they faced: 'Results of the Common Law Procedure Acts, 1852 and 1854' (1859) 6 Law Mag & L Rev Quart J Juris. 3d ser, 248, 257–58.

could direct an oral examination of the party before a judge or master.[125] Greater powers of pre-trial discovery created the opportunity to discover if the agreement necessary to form a contract was present in a given case.[126] These greater powers of pre-trial discovery also allowed the truth of the matter to be exposed and indicated plainly where the problem in the contract cases was one of a misapprehension. Once it was so indicated the need arose to deal with it in legal terms as a mistake.

Witnesses

Related to the greatly increased ability to make a pre-trial discovery was the increased range of evidence that could be considered by courts of common law. At the beginning of the nineteenth century, courts of law faced severe restrictions upon what could be considered as evidence.[127] In relation to oral testimony, certain persons were excluded from testifying. Some of these restrictions probably had a limited impact in contract-based claims, notably the exclusion of persons with a criminal conviction or those who, for reasons of conscience, could not take an oath.[128] Other restrictions would have had a significant impact in contract cases, notably the inability of not only parties and their spouses to testify in an action but also all those parties who had any pecuniary interest in the suit. Without the testimony of such individuals, it is difficult to see how many factual misapprehensions could be established. The injustice of such a disbarment was apparent to contemporaries. The Common Law Commissioners noted in their Second Report that:

> It is painful to contemplate the amount of injustice which must have taken place under the exclusive system of the English law, not only in cases actually brought into Court and there wrongly decided in consequence of the exclusion of evidence, but in numberless cases in which parties silently submitted to wrongs from inability to avail themselves of proof, which, though morally conclusive, was in law inadmissible.[129]

The justification for such an exclusionary rule was the twin concerns that those with an interest in a suit, no matter how minute, would succumb to the temptation to perjure themselves and that jurors would be unable to discern such perjury. It has been convincingly argued that the exclusionary rule existed originally to deal with the possible dangers of social destabilisation which could be brought about if

[125] Common Law Procedure Act 1854, s 53. *Smith v Great Western Railway Company* (1856) 6 E & Bl 405; 119 ER 916.

[126] See *Meyer v Barnett* (1863) 3 F & Fin 696; 176 ER 319 as to s 58 of the Common Law Procedure Act 1854, concerned with the inspection of property.

[127] The topic is thoroughly dealt with by Christopher Allen in *The Law of Evidence in Victorian England* (Cambridge, Cambridge University Press, 1997).

[128] This limitation must have caused some problems to Non-Conformists who ran businesses due to the difficulty of entering into professions which required certain religious adherences.

[129] Royal Com to inquire into Process, Practice and System of Pleading, Second Report (n 43) 11.

members of the gentry perjured themselves.[130] Whatever the origin or purpose of the rule, it was subject to increasing criticism, primarily on the grounds that it was ill conceived, irrational, tended to prolong proceedings in evidentiary arguments and led to unjust results.[131] Writing towards the end of the century, Lord Bowen described the bar as 'the most serious blemish of all . . . [of common law procedure] the established law of evidence, which excluded from giving testimony all witnesses who had even the minutest interest in the result, and, as a crowning paradox, even the parties to the suit themselves'.[132] Contemporary critics did not, however, consider the possibility that procedural changes to the rules of evidence could lead to substantive legal changes.

The first major change was brought about in 1843 by Lord Denman's Act, which allowed persons with either an interest in the suit or a criminal conviction to give evidence in an action.[133] In 1846, the county courts were established and in these courts not only were persons with an interest competent to give evidence, the parties themselves were competent to give evidence,[134] a development described by one county court judge as 'courageous'.[135] The success of this procedure led to changes in the superior courts of common law. In 1851, Lord Brougham's long campaign to allow the competence of parties to an action to give evidence was given legislative force,[136] and 'this final absurdity, which closed in court the mouths of those who knew the most about the matter'[137] was removed. The change, greeted with initial scepticism, soon came to be viewed as one of great significance in establishing the facts of any case:

> Although at the time when these sections first came into operation, learned judges might have been found, who, taking a cautious view of the subject, were inclined to regard the examination of parties as a questionable, if not a very dangerous experiment; it is believed, that, at present, every eminent lawyer in Westminster Hall will most readily admit, that this change in the law has been productive of highly beneficial results. In courts of law, it has not only enabled very many honest persons to establish just claims, which, under the old system of exclusion could never have been brought to trial with any hope of success; but it has deterred at least an equal number of dishonest men.[138]

By the Evidence Amendment Act 1853 spouses of parties to an action were made competent and compellable witnesses. The Common Law Procedure Act 1854[139]

[130] Allen (n 127) 97.

[131] See, eg, the comments of the Common Law Commissioners, (n 43) 11–22, and those of 'B', 'Of the Disqualification of Parties as Witnesses' (1857) 5 *American Law Register* 257, 264.

[132] Bowen (n 13) 521.

[133] 6 & 7 Vict c 85.

[134] 9 & 10 Vict c 95, s 83. Religious principles were also overcome by allowing witnesses to either swear an oath or make a solemn affirmation.

[135] JP Taylor, *A Treatise on the Law of Evidence as Administered in England and Ireland vol II* (London, William Maxwell and Son, 1872) 1171. Taylor was also the draftsman of Lord Brougham's Evidence Act 1851.

[136] Lord Brougham's Evidence Act, 14 & 15 Vict c 99.

[137] Bowen (n 13) 521.

[138] Taylor (n 135) 1172.

[139] s 20.

completed the process and allowed witnesses previously excluded by reason of religious principle to testify by allowing them to make a solemn affirmation or declaration.[140] The 1854 Act gave the common law courts the ability to get at the truth of the matter before them.[141] In addition to these legislative changes, it appears that common law courts were themselves increasing the range of evidence relevant to contracts which could be admitted.[142] The result of these changes was to greatly expand the ability of courts of law to ascertain how a particular problem arose and conceive of its resolution in substantive legal terms rather than through procedural devices. In relation to cases of contracts formed under a misapprehension, the misapprehension could be seen for what it was. 'Where juries are now in the dark, and grope blindly after truth, they will be enabled to see the truth face to face; and where justice was once dimly *guessed at*, it will be grasped with certainty, and brought palpably into view'.[143] The change had an enormous impact upon the law of evidence.[144] There was no longer a need to resort to procedural devices or to assumptions as to trade custom to resolve the difficulty caused by the misapprehension, for the mistake was now identifiable as such. The most obvious example of this is the case of *Smith v Hughes*,[145] in which the Court of Queen's Bench considered the legal effect of the oats' purchaser's misapprehension as to the age of the oats upon the contract alleged to have been formed. The court was able to examine the case in this light because the parties had testified as to their statements and their state of knowledge at the time of the transaction: testimony exposed the buyer's misapprehension as to the age of the oats he was purchasing and the seller's knowledge of the buyer's beliefs.

Matters of Law rather than Fact

Over the course of the century, matters that had been dealt with on the basis of fact came to be dealt with as matters of law. No longer was a judge suddenly posed with a legal question (without the benefit of his books) and possibly without the benefit of detailed argument by counsel. Following the Common Law Procedure Act

[140] It had been established that depositions of witnesses professing non-Christian religions were admissible provided that the oath had been taken according to the particular ceremonies of their religion: *Omychund v Barker* (1744) 1 Atk 21, 40. By legislation, Quakers had already been permitted to make a solemn affirmation in civil actions: Allen (n 127) 52. The author considers the topic in ch 3 of his work.

[141] *The Law Times*, 4 November 1854, 75.

[142] Allen (n 127) 42 concludes that by the 1840s the laws relating to the admissibility of declarations made in the course of business were allowed by courts. The admission of such evidence would illuminate the contractual matters.

[143] 'B' (n 131) 267. The author noted that contracts would be particularly affected as each party would know that the other could testify as to the nature of the contract.

[144] Sir J Fitzjames Stephen, *A Digest of the Law of Evidence*, 3rd edn (London, Macmillan and Co, 1977) 177.

[145] (1871) [LR] 6 QB 597.

1854, it was noted that most questions of law were usually dealt with not at a trial at Nisi Prius but 'usually reserved for the opinion of the Court above'.[146] Matters of law require doctrine. It is one of the reasons that the treatise writers wrote their treatises; and, in so doing, contributed further to the process of change.

The nineteenth century saw a further procedural change of significance: the reduction of the use of the civil jury. While it is difficult to gauge the extent to which questions of fact, determined by a jury,[147] were converted to questions of law, determined by a judge, the changes were sufficiently extensive that some impact must have occurred.[148] It seems likely that some cases of factual misapprehension could be resolved by juries on their determination of facts. At the beginning of the nineteenth century, juries were able to determine matters such as the intentions of the parties, the construction of a document, and the understanding and custom of merchants.[149] An example of the last situation can be seen in the decision in the case of *Taylor v Briggs*[150] in which the question of what was meant by a 'bale' in the context of a sale of cotton (in which one party intended one commodity and the other another) was determined by the jury according to the custom and usage of the trade and without any discussion of 'mistake' in a legal sense.[151] Diminishing jury trials meant that cases of factual misapprehension could not be so determined. The changes were brought about by mid-nineteenth-century reformers who looked to the experience of the newly formed county courts, in which the use of a jury was at the parties' option, to limit the use of juries

[146] *The Law Times*, 'Some Hints on the New Procedure Act', 4 November 1854, 74.

[147] The intention of the parties was considered a matter of fact to be determined by the jury: *Powis v Smith* (1822) 2 B & A 850; 106 ER 1402.

[148] The boundaries between law and fact were often difficult to demarcate with precision, however: Anon, 'Of the Functions of the Judge as Distinguished from the Jury' (1845) 2 *Law Review* 27, 28.

[149] A further change in the division of matters to be determined by juries as fact and matters to be determined by judges as law occurred through the decisions of the judges themselves, as they increased the number of matters said to be of law, a point noted in ibid, 41. The author noted that the effect of Baron Parke's decision in *Neilson v Harford* (1841) 8 M & W 806, 151 ER 1266, in which he stated that the construction of a document (including agreements) was a matter for the court rather than the jury, effectively overturned the earlier authority of *Hill v Thompson* (1817) 3 Mer 622; 36 ER 622. When Willes J followed *Neilson v Harford* in *Berwick v Horsfall* 4 CB NS 450; 140 ER 1160, he effectively overturned the earlier decision of *Macbeath v Haldimand* (1786) 1 TR 172; 99 ER 1036. The later cases indicate a judicial suspicion of the abilities of jurors. Thayer, however, noted that judges, particularly at the outset of the century, seemed keener to know the 'custom of merchants' in an attempt to better understand the implications of the law they were going to lay down: JB Thayer, ' "Law and Fact" in Jury Trials' (1890) 4 *Harvard Law Review* 147, 174–75.

[150] (1827) 2 C & P 525; 172 ER 238.

[151] Cases abound of instances in which ambiguities were resolved, even in the case of written contracts, by allowing the matter to be determined according to the custom and usage employed by the particular merchants. See, eg, *Baker v Paine* (1750) 1 Ves 456; 27 ER 1140; *Jolly v Young* (1794) 1 Esp 186; 170 ER 323; *Cochran v Retberg* (1800) 3 Esp 121; 170 ER 560; *Smith v Wilson* (1832) 3 B & A 728; 110 ER 266; *Grant v Maddox* (1846) 15 M & W 737; 153 ER 1048. In *Couturier v Hastie* (1856) 5 HLC 673, 10 ER 1065, the Lord Chancellor intimated that he would have been prepared to decide the case on the basis of evidence as to the mercantile usage in interpreting the relevant contract. In *Raffles v Wichelhaus* (1864) 2 H & C 906; 159 ER 375 itself, Pollock CB considered it possible that which ship *Peerless* was meant was a question for the jury.

in civil trials. Despite the calls for reform,[152] the Common Law Commissioners, in their Second Report, defended the use of the civil jury in superior courts[153] and recommended that trial by jury continue to be the rule, although the parties could dispense with juries where the parties sought to do so in certain circumstances. This recommendation became law in the Common Law Procedure Act 1854, which allowed parties, where the court agreed, to have the court try an issue of fact. The new Rules of the Supreme Court 1883 again made the use of juries permissive rather than dispensing with them. The apparent effect of these changes was to diminish the proportion of jury trials. Jackson noted that jury trials in the Queen's Bench Division entered into a period of decline throughout the 1870s, followed by a period of steep decline between 1883 and 1887.[154] On this evidence, it can be argued that judges were deciding issues of fact previously decided by juries and bringing legal considerations to bear upon them in a way that juries had not. The qualitative impact of Jackson's quantitative study has been questioned by Lobban who has examined the question of when civil jury trials were used and for what purpose.[155] Lobban suggests that while the use of civil juries did decline, the trend appeared to be the strongest in contractual cases which were increasingly determined by a judge alone.[156] This is significant because judges determine issues on the basis of law and with the knowledge that their decision forms a precedent. As one nineteenth-century supporter of the civil jury noted, 'hard cases tried with a jury do not make bad law, for they make no law at all . . . the principle is kept intact while the jury do justice in the particular case by not applying it'.[157] This is particularly applicable in cases of factual misapprehensions: to determine them on the basis of the facts requires no unsettling of contract doctrine. To decide them on the basis of law is to attempt to rationalise them on legal grounds establishing precedent. In short, a need emerged for a basis upon which to resolve these cases of misapprehension on grounds of principle.

A final related point concerns the development of the appeal process during the nineteenth century, for such a process increases the importance of the legal basis for a decision. At common law, the nisi prius system operated by allowing the jury verdicts taken by assize judges to be entered in the office the following term. A full court meeting in Westminster could, however, stay the process if cause were

[152] The nineteenth-century debate over the use of civil juries is considered in M Lobban, 'The Strange Life of the English Civil Jury, 1837–1914', in JW Cairns and G McLeod (eds), *The Dearest Birth Right of the People of England—The Jury in the History of the Common Law* (Oxford, Hart Publishing, 2002) 176–86.

[153] Royal Com to inquire into Process, Practice and System of Pleading, Second Report (n 43). The Commissioners defended the practice on the basis that 'the jury also bring with them a varied stock of information which the judge cannot be expected to possess, and which is of the most essential advantage in the administration of justice': ibid, 4. They also stated that jurors, acting on a temporary basis, performed their duties with a freshness and interest a professional judge could not be expected to feel.

[154] RM Jackson, 'The Incidence of Jury Trial During the Past Century' (1937) 1 *Modern Law Review* 132, 142.

[155] Lobban (n 152).

[156] ibid, 191.

[157] M Chalmers, 'Trial by Jury in Civil Cases' (1891) 7 *Law Quarterly Review* 15, 21.

shown but these powers were exercised before judgment and not as an appeal.[158] In 1854, legislation allowed an 'appeal' to be taken from a court in banc to a court in error; courts of error became courts of appeal.[159] When the Exchequer Chamber, and thus proceedings in error, ended in 1875, a 'Court of Appeal' was created which heard appeals from both the common law side of the High Court and equitable appeals from the Chancery Division. In turn, an appeal from the decisions of the Court of Appeal lay to the House of Lords.[160] A process of appeals, brought almost exclusively upon an error in law, increased the importance for the legal basis of the trial decision. Appeal judgments based on law both created a need for substantive legal principles and acted to reinforce legal principles. Such a situation is conducive to the development of legal doctrines, of which mistake in contract law was one.

Conclusions

The Victorians revolutionised the process by which their law was administered: civil procedure and practice was changed enormously between the beginning of Victoria's reign and the end of it. While this process of procedural change has long been noted and many of its more significant aspects have been studied closely, the substantive changes brought about by such procedural changes have not been studied. The doctrine of mistake in contract law is a substantive change brought about, in part, as a result of the changes in common law practice and procedure. The changes both explain in part why mistake was not accorded a legal consequence at common law. Not only did the existence of a bifurcated administration of justice mean that relief was available for a mistake in equity but it also meant that the common law provided different resolutions for mistake cases. The changes facilitated the development of the doctrine of mistake at common law. The allure of technical devices, such as variances, disappeared, as did the possibility of referring the mistake to the jury for determination as a matter of fact rather than grappling with the mistake as a matter of law. An emphasis upon substantive justice meant that courts had an increasing tendency to resolve matters on the basis of substantive legal principles rather than factual ones. To some extent, substantive legal principles had to be developed; a process largely undertaken by the treatise writers rather than by judges or law reformers. The changes in pleading allowed counsel the latitude to try out new arguments at comparatively lower risk than would have been presented in the past. This spurred a process of innovation which interacted with the work of the treatise writers. The slow 'fusion' with equity begun in the 1850s and completed 20 years later with the Judicature Acts allowed

158 Baker (n 3) 139.

159 Common Law Procedure Act 1854, s 36.

160 Appellate Jurisdiction Act 1876, 39 & 40 Vict, c 59.

equitable mistake cases to cross over into the common law courts. It was clear that mistake, as a matter of law, was present in the courts from that point. Finally, changes in the admissibility of evidence and the competence of witnesses meant that courts could obtain the vital material necessary to address squarely the fact that the entire problem was brought about by a factual misapprehension. These procedural changes set the necessary conditions for the development of a substantive doctrine of mistake. The development of this doctrine was to emanate from the contract treatise writers of the nineteenth century.

5

Pothier and the Development of Mistake in English Contract Law

AN IMPORTANT INFLUENCE upon the development of mistake in English contract law was the work of Pothier. While this influence has long been recognised, it is rarely examined closely. This chapter examines the influence of Pothier upon the common law contract treatise writers of the nineteenth century. The chapter is developed as follows. First, the mistake theories of Pothier are examined in the context in which he developed them. The chapter then discusses the impact Pothier had upon early attempts to write English contract law as a series of general principles. The earliest efforts came about by those who were attempting to implement English contract law in an alien environment: British India. The chapter looks at the use made of Pothier by Colebrooke and Macpherson. The chapter then examines the use of Pothier made by the important works of Leake and Benjamin. The focus of this examination is concerned with the process by which English authors 'received' the theories of Pothier by 'integrating' them with the existing English cases. This, it is argued, is the beginning of the process of transplantation, which was concluded once English judges began to adopt, consciously or unconsciously, the work of these treatise writers. The principal importance of Pothier for these English writers was that he provided a structure into which to fit mistake and he stipulated an effect for mistake: that the apparent contract was void. This consideration is completed in the next chapter, in which a similar examination is undertaken with regard to the work of Friedrich Carl von Savigny and his impact upon the work of Anson and Pollock.

Pothier and the *Traité des Obligations*

Robert Joseph Pothier was born in Orléans in 1699 and died there in 1772. Engaged almost entirely and single-mindedly in legal practice and study, his life's achievements were such as to establish him as a jurist of great influence not only in his own country but also in his European neighbours, England included. Pothier's gifts lay not in the originality of his thought but in his knowledge of Roman law and in his organisational abilities. An intelligent youth, although of 'feeble temperament',[1] Pothier studied law at the University of Orléans, an institution which at that time had descended from the high reputation it had held as the home of the *Ultramontani* to a 'state of languor and apathy'.[2] After some indecision between choosing a profession as a cleric or a lawyer, he was persuaded by his mother to enter the legal profession. At the age of 21, he was nominated to the magisterial position previously occupied by his father and grandfather, Conseiller au Présidial d'Orléans.[3] Although he chose law as his profession, Pothier maintained a lifelong interest in theology and his legal writings combine a study of positive law with moral law. Involved in the practice of law (then French customary law, which had itself been greatly influenced by Roman law), Pothier undertook a prolonged study of Roman law. A quarter of a century later, in 1748, the results of his labours to give order to the disorder of the pandects was published as the *Pandectae Justininae in novum Ordinem digestae.* Having completed his attempt at ordering the Roman texts, and now the Professor of French Law at the University of Orléans, Pothier set about ordering and writing up the laws of France. The first of these efforts was the *Traité des Obligations*, published in 1761. In this work, Pothier undertook to explain the substance of obligations in general (as distinct from the particular characteristics of particular Roman contracts), the effect of obligations, the divisions and kinds of obligations and the manner in which obligations were extinguished and discharged. He based his treatise upon the principles he had gathered from Roman law and the laws of France.

Obligations, for Pothier, had two significations: the first, and more extensive, was synonymous with duties (such as duties of charity and gratitude); the second, and more confined, were 'personal engagements', which gave the person with whom they were contracted a right to demand their performance.[4] This second signification was divided into four categories of which contract was one.[5] Pothier defined contract as 'a particular kind of agreement', and 'an agreement is the consent of two or more persons to form some engagement, or to rescind or modify an engagement already made'.[6] The consent, or will, of the parties to engage in a contract was at the centre of Pothier's conception of contract.[7] If consent was the basis

[1] 'Eloge de Pothier', in RJ Pothier, *A Treatise on the Law of Obligations or Contracts*, trs WD Evans (London, A Strahan, 1806; reprinted Clark, NJ, The Law Book Exchange Ltd, 2003) 12 (all subsequent references are to this edition and to the Evans translation).

[2] Anon, 'Life and Writings of Pothier' (1834) 12 *American Jurist & Law Magazine* 341, 345. The author explains that 'the professors, who then filled the chairs of the University, were absolutely indifferent to the progress of their pupils, and contented themselves with oral instructions, which were unintelligible and which they did not deign to accommodate to the capacity of their hearers.': ibid, 342–43.

[3] 'Pothier', in Sir J Macdonnell and E Manson (eds) *Great Jurists of the World* (Boston, Little, Brown and Company, 1914) 448–49.

[4] Pothier (n 1) preliminary article, 2.

[5] The others were: quasi-contracts ('engagements in the nature of contracts'); *delits* ('injuries'); and *quasi-delits* ('acts in the nature of injuries'): Pothier (n 1) pt I, ch I, p 3. These were the divisions of Roman law.

[6] Pothier (n 1) pt I, ch I, s I, Art I, §1, p 3.

[7] Having defined a contract, he immediately distinguished it from what he called a 'pollicitation' or a mere promise as something which the parties had not concurred upon: ibid, §2.

of the contract, then those matters which disrupted or prevented consent were of particular importance. For this reason, Pothier dealt with these matters at the outset of his treatise. He termed these disruptive matters 'defects which may occur in contracts' and enumerated 'error, force, fraud, inequality, want of consideration, and want of obligation'.[8] He dealt with what he considered to be the most important of these first: error. For Pothier, 'error is the greatest defect that can occur in a contract, for agreements can only be formed by the consent of the parties, and there can be no consent when the parties are in error'.[9] He then explored the ambit of this principle and referred directly to the Roman law of sale, most notably to the confusing passage of Ulpian.[10] In this endeavour Pothier, following the Glossators and the Post Glossators, employed an aspect of a form of Roman contract, but elevated it to a central element of his theory of contract. In so doing, he ran into conceptual and practical difficulties. Unsurprisingly given the resort to the Roman law on the subject, Pothier conceived of error in a variety of forms or types of error. Three forms are recognised. First were errors as to the identity of a transaction, which could take two forms. One was an error as to the nature of the transaction: where one party intends one form of transaction and the other party another, there is no contract. The other was where there was an error as to the price for which a good would be sold.[11] A second form of error was an error as to a quality of the subject matter of the contract: 'error annuls the agreement . . . when it affects that quality of the subject which the parties have principally in contemplation, and which makes it the substance of it'.[12] Unfortunately, Pothier did not provide any mechanism by which one could determine when a quality would define the substance of the subject. Instead, he provided the example of a buyer who sought to buy silver candlesticks and was sold, unwittingly on the seller's part, silver-plated candlesticks. The contract would be void because the buyer's error destroyed his consent; his intention was to buy silver candlesticks. Pothier then fell back on the examples given in the Digest by Julian and Ulpian.[13] While this was not unusual, what was unusual was that the passages he chose were contradictory, and one passage refutes Pothier's example. Julian pointed out that a sale of a silver-covered table sold as solid silver was no sale and that a *condictio* lay to recover the money paid. He says this, however, in a passage dealing with purchases made under a condition; the implication is that the seller has sold the table on the condition (which is a misapprehension to the seller) that the table is solid silver. Ulpian, in contrast, dealt with parties who are both in error over a material and its quality. If the parties contract to sell gold and the item is copper, then there is no

[8] Pothier (n 1) pt I, ch.I, s I, Art III, p 12. Evans translated Pothier's *causa* ('*le defaut de cause dans l'engagement*') as 'consideration' in English.

[9] ibid, pt I, ch I, s I, Art III, §1. The particular sentence was directed towards an error as to the object of the agreement, but it is clear from the following passages that Pothier envisioned the same outcome with regard to other forms of error.

[10] Discussed earlier: see ch 2.

[11] Pothier (n 1) pt I, ch I, .s I, Art III, §1, p 12. He relied upon Ulpian, D.18.1.9, discussed in ch 2.

[12] ibid.

[13] D.18.1.41.1 and D.18.1.14, discussed earlier, in ch 2.

contract. If, however, the parties contract to sell gold and the item is gold-plated, then the sale is good, despite the mistake of both parties and a sale price suitably enhanced because of the gold. The sale is good because there is some gold in the item. Pothier's problem with a mistake as to substance was not only that he had failed to provide any definitions or guidance as to the matter of when a substance is essential, he had also based his argument on apparently contradictory passages that, once resolved, work against his own example. Pothier's predicament arose because he preserved the doctrines of the late scholastics but did not explain them by Aristotelian or Thomastic principles.[14] In the Aristotelian and Thomastic traditions, the essence of a contract was its end, which gave the contract and the object contracted for its identity.[15] Without this essence, a mistake as to substance became difficult to define. Pothier completed his discussion of essential qualities by contrasting them with accidental qualities of a subject matter. Again, an example is given. If a buyer purchases a book thinking it to be a work of excellence when, in fact, it is not, the error does not destroy consent. The reason is that the buyer has purchased what he intended to purchase: the book before him. His motive for buying the book was that he believed it to be a work of excellence but this does not in any way interfere with it being the book before the buyer, the one he intended to buy. And thus, Pothier deduced, 'an error in motive does not destroy the agreement. It is sufficient that the parties have not erred respecting the *object* of the agreement'.[16] Absent a formula by which the purpose of the contract is ascertained, it is impossible to establish precisely when a quality is accidental and when it is essential. The difficulty was not resolved by use of the example.

The third type of error Pothier considered is the one with which his name is most closely associated in English law, despite Lord Denning's assertions to the contrary[17]: a mistake as to identity. Pothier asserted that where the identity of the person was essential to the other party, then a mistake as to identity annulled agreement: 'wherever the consideration of the person with whom I contract is an ingredient of the contract which I intend to make, an error respecting the person destroys my consent, and consequently annuls the agreement'.[18] Two examples are given. In the first, if one intended to give or loan a thing to Peter and it is given or lent to Paul, who is mistaken for Peter, the gift or loan is void for want of consent. In the second, where a party intended their portrait to be painted by a particular artist and mistook another for that artist and engaged the other, the contract was void for want of the sitter's consent because: 'a consideration of the person and reputation of the artist whom I had in view was an ingredient in the bargain which I intended to make'.[19] Pothier noted, however, that if the painter engaged was ignorant of the sitter's mistake and produced a painting, then

[14] J Gordley, *The Philosophical Origins of Modern Contract Law* (Oxford, Clarendon Press, 1991) 71.
[15] ibid, 187.
[16] Pothier (n 1) pt I, ch I, s I, Art III, §1, p 13.
[17] *Lewis v Avery* [1972] 1 QB 198, 206.
[18] Pothier (n 1) pt I, ch I, s I, Art III, §1, p 13.
[19] ibid.

the sitter was 'obliged to take it and pay him a proper compensation' on the basis, not of the agreement, which was void, but because of 'the principle of equity which obliges me to indemnify the person whom I have imprudently led into an error'.[20] The Romans, Pothier asserted, knew of such an obligation as an *actio in factum*. Where identity played no part in the decision to contract, and a party was willing to contract with anyone, then the contract was good.[21]

Having established these three forms of error, Pothier returned to the question of whether an error in motive annulled an agreement. In doing so, he engaged Pufendorf's assertion that where one party communicates his motive for entering into a transaction with the other party and the motive turns out to be mistaken, the first party can rescind the agreement provided that he provides an indemnification to the other party for any loss he has suffered from the non-execution of the agreement. Pothier, however, disagreed with Pufendorf for the reasons asserted by Barbeyrac. Barbeyrac had argued that such an error in motive did not produce a defect in the agreement because if the agreement depended upon the truth of the intelligence, it would be void as soon as the intelligence proved false and the seller would have no claim to damages for the non-execution of the gift. Pothier further supported his position that an error in motive did not avoid a contract by comparing it to the case of a testator influenced by a false motive to leave a legacy to a beneficiary. The false motive does not interfere with the validity of the legacy. So, too, should a false motive not affect the validity of the contract for 'there is much less reason to presume that the parties intended their agreement to depend upon that motive as a condition'.[22]

After *Traité des Obligations*, Pothier published *Traité du Contrat de Vente* the following year, in 1762. The contract of sale was a consensual contract, dependent upon the consent of the contracting parties.[23] This consent, which was the very essence of the contract of sale, consisted 'in a concurrence of the will of the seller to sell a particular thing to the buyer, for a particular price, and of the buyer, to buy of him the same thing for the same price'.[24] Since consent was again at the centre of this contract, Pothier dealt with those circumstances which would prevent a true consent. Once again error was considered as a circumstance which could prevent consent. Error was, again, conceived of as a series of different types of error, a conception which arose, again, from Pothier's reliance upon Roman law. Three further forms of mistake were considered. The first was a mistake concerning the subject matter of the contract. Where one party intended to sell one thing and the other to purchase another, no contract arose. Again, Pothier relied upon Ulpian[25] and gave examples of this form of error: a sack of barley which the

[20] ibid, 13–14.
[21] ibid, L 3, ch 6, n 7 [OK - doesn't follow style of other Pothier refs?].
[22] ibid, pt I, ch I, s I, Art III, §1, p 15.
[23] RJ Pothier, *Treatise on the Contract of Sale*, LS Cushing (trs) (Boston, MA, Charles C Little and James Brown, 1839; reprinted Union, NJ, Lawbook Exchange Ltd, 1999) pt I, ss I and II, p 3.
[24] ibid, pt I, s II, Art III, p 17.
[25] D.18.1.9.

buyer purchased on the assumption it was corn, or a snuff box of pinchbeck which the buyer purchased on the assumption it was gold. In these cases, there was no contract because there was no agreement concerning the matter of the substance of the contract, and the essential element of the contract of sale, an agreement in relation to the thing sold, is not made out. Pothier repeated a form of error considered in his *Traité des Obligations*: if the mistake pertained 'only to some accidental quality of the thing'[26] this does not prevent the parties from being agreed and in such a case there is a sale. Pothier gave, as an example, cloth sold for good which was in fact bad: he relied for authority upon Paul's statement following Ulpian's.[27] Where the error related only to the name of the thing, this was not an error which prevented the necessary consent.[28] Similarly, a contract of sale required the existence of a thing to be sold 'and which may make the object of the contract'[29] and if there was no such thing, there was no contract of sale. Thus, if a vendor, unaware that his horse was dead, purported to sell him, there was no contract. Likewise, if the parties agreed to the sale of a house which had, unbeknownst to them, burnt down, then the contract was void. If the greater part of the house existed, however, the sale would be good subject to a diminution in the price.[30]

A second form of error was as to price, but only when the buyer intended to pay less than the seller had intended to sell the good for. In such an instance, there was no consent. There was consent, however, when the buyer intended to pay more than the seller had intended to sell for, for there was an agreement at the lower price.[31]

A third form of error was as to the consent to sell. One party had to be willing to sell and the other to buy; if the parties each intended a different type of contract, there was no consent to sell. Thus, if one party intended to sell a certain house at a certain price and the other intended to hire the house, then there was neither a contract of sale nor a contract of hire.[32]

Three important general observations can be made about Pothier's conception of error. The first observation is the extent to which Pothier has removed himself from the late scholastics' concern about the essence of an agreement. He writes, in both *Traité des Obligations* and *Traité du Contrat de Vente*, of the essential and accidental qualities of the subject matter of a contract, but he does so in an unsatisfactory fashion. There is no workable formula as to how to discern one from the other, with the result that it is almost impossible to predict accurately when an error affects consent so as to annul agreement and where it does not. He acknowledged in *Traité des Obligations* that the purpose of some contracts is 'mutual interest' in which the parties have a reciprocal interest and that the purpose of

[26] Pothier, *Treatise on the Contract of Sale* (n 23) pt I, s II, §II, p 20.
[27] D.19.1.10.
[28] Again, with reference to Ulpian's statement at D.18.1.9.
[29] Pothier (n 23) pt I, s II, Art I, p 3.
[30] ibid, pt I, s II, Art I, p 4. Pothier relied upon Ulpian for this proposition: D.18.1.57.
[31] Pothier (n 23) pt I, s II, Art II, p 21.
[32] ibid.

other contracts is of 'beneficence' in which one party alone is benefited.[33] The discussion is confused and he makes no attempt to link the purpose of these contracts to the essence of the subject matter of the contract.[34] Equally, in his later discussion of the necessity that each contract have a just cause, he stated that every engagement had to have a cause in order to form a contract. The nature of the cause was dependent upon whether the contract was one of beneficence or mutual interest. The break with the late scholastics and the lack of an alternate mechanism to ascertain the purpose of a given contract, produced the difficulty that one cannot determine when a characteristic is essential and when it accidental. This created an inherent instability in any attempt to consider the effect of an error upon a contract.

The second observation is that Pothier's conception of error is a subjective one; indeed, probably a unilateral error was sufficient to avoid a contract.[35] Although both parties might be in error, what caused error to operate as a matter of law was that one of the parties was in error and this error did not have to be an error which would affect the consent of the 'reasonable man' but simply an error which had operated upon the particular party in forming his agreement. In the case of a mistake of identity, Pothier clearly regarded a unilateral error as sufficient. It would appear that he also viewed a unilateral error as to the subject matter or a quality of the subject matter as sufficient to avoid the contract ('my error destroys my consent'). Theoretically elegant, a subjective error creates practical problems. It is elegant in theory because once the basic principle of contract is established as consensus, the logical deduction, as Pothier himself noted, is that where there is no consensus, there is no contract; if even one of the parties labours under a mistake he does not consent and no contract can arise. The practical difficulty with such a set of principles is that the other party is not mistaken and must have properly given consent: to hold that the agreement is not a binding contract upsets his reasonable expectations and, possibly, those of third parties who have placed reliance upon the apparent contract. As we shall see, these practical problems were to lead English courts away from the subjectivity of Pothier's formulation. Modern French law has adopted a subjective approach to error, but it is an approach which French courts have applied in a manner verging upon the objective.[36]

[33] Pothier (n 1) Art II, p 10. A third category of 'mixed contracts' consisting of those in which one party confers a benefit and receives something of inferior value is also considered.

[34] The same problem crops up in his later discussion of the requirement of a just cause: an engagement could only be a contract where there was a cause in order to form the contract. The nature of the cause was dependent upon whether the contract was one of mutual interest or beneficence. ibid, pt I, ch I, s I, Art III, §6, p 24.

[35] His formulations are rather imprecise on this point and while some of his examples are clearly unilateral errors, in other cases both parties are in error.

[36] B Nicholas, *The French Law of Contract*, 2nd edn (Oxford, Clarendon Press, 1992) 84–85, 92–95. The same point is advanced by Catherine Valcke in 'Comparative History and the Internal View of French, German and English Private Law' (2006) 19 *Canadian Journal of Law &and Jurisprudence* 133, 142–43. Valcke explains the subjective approach of French jurists with regard to contractual mistake as a logical extension of will theory. Contract is presented as a logical implication of the ideal of human liberty, an 'autonomy of the will'. For a contract to be formed, there must be 'subjectively formed

The third is Pothier's view that the effect of error was to annul the agreement; indeed, he goes further and states that no contract has arisen. Once English law came under the influence of Pothier, this effect was to create enormous practical problems. The problem is that English law relies upon the contract to effect the conveyance of a proprietary interest. If the contract is void, there is no conveyance despite the putative buyer's possession or occupation of the subject matter of the void contract. The problem that arose was that a third party, or parties, might well have relied upon the void contract in circumstances where they could not possibly have known of the invalidity of the original 'contract'. Ironically, by the time English treatise writers utilised Pothier in their writings on mistake, the drafters of the Code Civil had provided that a contract induced by error was not void but gave rise to an exception. A party could bring an action to set aside the contract, but it was not a nullity.[37] Error produced a relative nullity rather than an absolute nullity. The result is that modern French law recognises *erreur,* with *dol* and *violence,* as *vices du consentement* which can prevent the contract from being freely made.[38] The effect of a contract vitiated by *erreur* is to create a relative nullity: the contract can be set aside by the party protected by the law, but by no one else. The most significant consequence which arises is as to who may bring the action.[39] In contrast, an absolute nullity (which would arise if, for example, the contract had an absence of *cause* or *objet*) may be asserted by anyone who has an interest directly connected with the nullity.[40] The distinction between absolute nullity and relative nullity is

congruent intentions to contract'; a mistake in the mind of either party as to an essential aspect of the contractual relationship is sufficient to remove the existence or validity of the contract. French judicial practice differs and 'French courts have gone to great length to restore some measure of equality between mistaken and non-mistaken parties'.

[37] Gordley (n 14) 188.

[38] Nicholas (n 36) 76–8; Art 1109 *Code civile.* The position of modern French law has led some commentators to suggest that Pothier intended error to produce a relative nullity and that nineteenth-century common law lawyers erred in their conclusion that Pothier had conceived of this as an absolute nullity rather than a relative nullity and in so doing created a doctrine of mistake based upon their error: a conclusion also reached by JM Perillo, 'Robert J Pothier's Influence on the Common Law of Contract' (2004–05) 11 *Texas Wesleyan Law Review* 267, 280, relying upon HF Fuller, 'Mistake and Error in the Law of Contracts' (1984) 33 *Emory Law Journal* 41, 50. Such an interpretation ignores the text of Pothier which was used by the common law lawyers. He is categorical in his assertion that 'error annuls the agreement' and that there is, eg, no sale where the mistake effects a contract of sale. His discussion of the other 'defects which may occur in contracts' supports this position. These defects were a want of liberty (duress), *dolus* (fraud), *lesion* (inequality) and the want of a just cause. Each of these, except the last, results in a relative nullity because, as Pothier explains, there is a consent, but the consent is defective or improper: Pothier (n 23) pt I, ch I, s II, Art III, §2 as to duress; pt I, ch I, s 1, Art III, §3 as to fraud ('when a party has been induced to contract by the fraud of another, the contract is not absolutely and essentially void, because a consent, though obtained by surprise, is still a consent; but the contract is vicious, and the party surprised may institute a process for its rescission'); pt I, ch I, s I, Art III, § 4 as to inequality' and pt I, ch I, s I, Art III, §5 as to the want of a just cause. Pothier deliberately contrasted the effect of duress upon a contract with mistake, and stated that in the latter case, 'there is no contract': ibid, pt I, ch I, s II Art III, §2.

[39] Nicholas (n 36) 77. Two other important consequences exist. The first is that a relative nullity may be subsequently confirmed by the protected party where an absolute nullity never can; the second pertains to the limitation period during which action can be brought (a much longer period is provided for an absolute nullity).

[40] ibid.

not dissimilar to the English distinction between a void and a voidable contract. While this result in French law appears to have been brought about accidentally by the drafters of the Code,[41] it has meant that French contract law does not suffer from one of the harsh result present in modern English law.

Pothier and English Contract Law

Despite the inherent weaknesses of Pothier's conception of mistake, his work was considered useful by nineteenth-century English lawyers. English lawyers struggled with internal problems in the common law of contract. Substantive and adjective law were combined in ways that meant that disputes were sometimes resolved in fashions that were less than satisfactory. Procedural reforms throughout the nineteenth century removed a system approached through forms of action, pleading and remedies. Pothier presented an apparently rational and principled theory of contract, organised around will theory. English law was not oblivious to the fact that contracts were about agreement, and an organisation around will was not an enormous leap. Once will theory was accepted, defects of the will were as well. The principal defects of fraud, duress and mistake, had counterparts within the common law (and equity). Pothier's explanation of the relationship between these defects and contract as a whole must have been useful. The uses to which Pothier was put indicate that practising lawyers and judges employed him in areas where English law lacked clarity or had little answer. Treatise writers employed him for structure and organisation. The difficulties that could arise in attempting to apply his theories to practical problems would not have been apparent. The acceptance of Pothier into the common law was also assisted by a coincidence, namely the arrival in England of a lawyer well versed in French civil law, Judah Benjamin. Pothier was also useful in developing a principled system of contract within the Empire, notably British India. Something of the state of English contract law at the outset of the nineteenth century can be deduced from William Evans' notes to his translation of Pothier. Evans explained in his introduction that he had originally intended to write a treatise on English law, using Pothier as a guide. After a lapse of time, he was induced to commence his work as an entire translation.[42] Evans explained that he really had only two propositions to advance in his translation. Both related to improving the state of the common law: the first was that substantial justice shall not be sacrificed to the 'subtleties of artificial reasoning'; the second was that courts of justice should act to correct erroneous precedents where to correct them would be to act in the general good.[43] Evans

[41] Gordley (n 14) 188.

[42] WD Evans, 'Introduction' in Pothier (n 1) 98. It is claimed that it was Lord Mansfield who prevailed upon him to translate the treatise.

[43] ibid.

annotated his translation by means of a series of footnotes to the principal text. Most of these footnotes explain the position taken by English law on the matter discussed in Pothier: Evans indicated an agreement or a disagreement with the English law and frequently provided English cases which contrast or support the French position. The notes concerned with vitiating elements, Pothier's 'defects', are interesting. Evans made no annotations concerned with mistake, although he made plenty of annotations concerned with the treatment of fraud in English law.[44] It may be that he regarded English law as roughly similar to Pothier's statement[45]: more likely is the fact that English law had not really considered the problem from the perspective advanced.

Pothier's writings on contracts had a profound effect upon the development of law not only in France, where they were to form the basis of the treatment of the law of contracts in the *Code civil*,[46] but also in England where judges and jurists alike had frequent recourse to Pothier.[47] While the question of the extent and the determination of his influence upon English contract law is a complex one, there can be little doubt that his writings exerted an influence upon the process by which the English common law acquired a doctrine of contractual mistake. The process is, in many ways, more complex than that which occurred within civil law countries. The leading protagonists of will theories of contract, with the concurrent doctrine of mistake, were treatise writers: but the common law is created by judges who decide cases on the basis of the legal arguments before them.[48] It is clear that even before Evans' translation of Pothier, English barristers were familiar with Pothier's work and willing to cite it in argument where there was a disputed point about principle within English law.[49] The resort to Pothier, a systematic writer of great clarity, occured because his treatise achieved a feat that English treatises did

[44] ibid, pt I, ch I, s I, Art III, §3.

[45] He wrote in a footnote to the heading of inequality that 'in the preceding parts of this article the law of England very nearly accords with the civil law in its exposition of the general principles of justice': ibid, §4.

[46] It has been argued that the *Code civil*, far from enshrining the new individualistic principles of the French Revolution, was based upon the principles advanced by eighteenth-century jurists (which were themselves borrowed from the late scholastics) and that two thirds of the texts of the Code have close parallels with the work of Domat and Pothier: J Gordley, 'Myths of the French Civil Code' (1994) 42 *American Journal of Comparative Law* 459, 460.

[47] JH Baker, *An Introduction to English Legal History*, 4th edn (London, Butterworths Lexis Nexis, 2002) 352–53; DJ Ibbetson, *A Historical Introduction to the Law of Obligations* (Oxford, Oxford University Press, 1999) 153–54; AWB Simpson 'The Rise and Fall of the Legal Treatise: Legal Principles and the Forms of Legal Literature' (1981) 48 *University of Chicago Law Review* 632; J Cartwright, 'The rise and fall of mistake in the English law of contract', in R Sefton-Green (ed), *Mistake, Fraud and Duties to Inform in European Contract Law* (Cambridge, Cambridge University Press, 2005) 68–69; and JM Perillo (n 38).

[48] I have discussed the process by which mistake entered the common law through these arguments in 'Mistaken arguments: The role of argument in the development of a doctrine of contractual mistake in nineteenth century England' in A Lewis and M Lobban (eds), *Law and History: Current Legal Issues 2003*, (Oxford, Oxford University Press, 2004).

[49] *Cooth v Jackson* (1801) 6 Ves Jun 12; 31 ER 913, at 23; 919. Romilly and Hart relied upon 'a very high authority, Pothier, in his Treatise upon Obligations' to argue a point based upon 'principle and general reasoning'. The impact of the argument was not convincing: Lord Eldon dismissed the bill and did so on another ground.

not: it provided an apparently coherent, organised and lucid exposition of the underlying principles of contract law based upon Roman law, a body of jurisprudence which contemporaries across Europe valued. It is not surprising that English lawyers were attracted to the potential utility of such a volume: judges and barristers could 'dip' into it for points of principle; legislators could use it as a basis for organising such contract legislation as was produced in Victorian England; and, significantly, jurists could use it as a source by which to organise their own English treatises of contract law when these came to be written later in the century. It was to prove useful in the development of a body of contract law to be administered in many British colonies. It is also important to note that these various actors interacted with each other and that their efforts were not isolated and discrete, but cumulative.

Early Contract Treatise Writers

The utility of Pothier was not admitted by all common law lawyers. Writing in 1824,[50] Joseph Chitty (the father of the famous contract treatise writer) observed that England's victory in the Napoleonic wars had occurred, in large part, as a result of the inherent and paramount advantages to be derived from her legal system. Foremost amongst these advantages were those laws governing the regulation of a profitable commerce, without which England would never have had the reserves of wealth necessary to triumph.[51] The lawyers of the victor, however, had already set about borrowing from the jurists of the vanquished. As English treatises upon contract law came to be written, their authors turned to Pothier for guidance. While the early treatise writers did so in a piecemeal fashion, later writers did so to provide a conceptual structure for their work and a principled explanation of why English law operated as it did. The challenge facing these writers was that while it was clear England had a substantive body of law, this body of law was organised around procedural devices, and whilst this did not preclude substantive law, it disguised it. The treatise writers both revealed and invented a body of substantive contract law around which they organised the English case law. Pothier was a useful guide: the clarity of his written style, the highly organised structure of his treatises and the fact that most educated Englishmen had sufficient French to read him in the original, made his work ideal as a structure.

It is argued that while early treatise writers 'dipped' into Pothier and borrowed useful points, later treatise writers were to employ a structure of will theory derived, in large part, from Pothier. Integral to this will theory was a doctrine of mistake concerned with the issue of what happened when there was no consensus.

[50] J Chitty, *A Treatise on The Laws of Commerce and Manufactures, and The Contracts relating Thereto* (London, Henry Butterworth, 1824).

[51] ibid, vi.

One of the matters which complicates a study of mistake prior to the late nineteenth century is the division of jurisdiction between courts of common law and equity. It is important, in examining treatises, to examine both those concerned with the law administered by the common law courts and those administered by courts of equity. Only by so doing can an accurate picture of the role of mistake in English contract law be discerned. As a general observation, the writers of common law treatises on contract law made only passing use of Pothier before the middle of the nineteenth century. It is only after the mid-century reforms of common law procedure and practice that more ambitious treatise writers set out to structure treatises about a theory or set of principles of contract law. Previous writers were content to organise their treatises around types of contracts or forms of proceedings rather than theories based upon general principles. Exceptions, however, exist in both time periods.

Colebrooke and Contract Law

An early attempt, in law, of organising English contract law around natural law principles, with copious references to Pothier and Pufendorf, was undertaken by Henry Colebrooke in 1818 in his *Treatise on Obligations and Contracts*.[52] Colebrooke was a man of many gifts: a polyglot engaged in administration in India, he wrote a treatise on contract law based on natural law principles. True to the underlying conception of natural law, he sought common principles from English, Scotch, Roman and Hindu law. His work appears incomplete,[53] and while it is an ambitious work, it takes its position on English law from the work of jurists, principally Powell, Newland, Blackstone and Comyn, rather than from the case law. Colebrooke organised his conception of contract around six concurrent elements: a person able to contract; a person capable of contracting; a thing to be contracted for; a good and sufficient cause or consideration; the assent of the contracting parties; and clear and explicit words to express agreement.[54] Having borrowed the elements necessary for a contract from Pothier and Comyn, Colebrooke then borrowed those elements which were defects which could vitiate a contract.[55] Following Pothier, Colebrooke dealt with error first. He conceived of error in a voidable sense—a contract can be set aside for an error, because error,

[52] HT Colebrooke, *Treatise on Obligations and Contracts* (London, HT Colebrooke, 1818).

[53] Only the first volume of his work was completed. It is thought that a second volume was nearly complete or complete at the time of his death: AWB Simpson, 'Innovation in Nineteenth Century Contract Law' (1975) 91 *Law Quarterly Review* 247 (reprinted in *Legal Theory and Legal History* (London and Ronceverte, 1987)) 179.

[54] Colebrooke, *Treatise on Obligations and Contracts*, Book II, ch I, §39, p 20. Colebrooke arrived at these elements by a marriage of factors stipulated by Pothier and Comyn.

[55] ibid, Book II, ch VII, s I, §96, p 46. To Pothier's list of error, force, fraud and lesion, he added the cause and object of the obligation, the capacity of the parties and the ties that bind them.

of either fact or law, vitiates a promise or agreement.[56] Borrowing principally from Pothier, Colebrooke pointed out that the error had to be one which concerned the substance of the matter—something that was of the absolute essence, rather than some accidental quality. Again, analysis of the means by which this essence can be determined is weak, and Colebrook fell back upon examples—something which affects the object of the engagement, the identity of the subject, or that particular quality the parties have in mind when contracting. The error had to pertain to the reason for the contract—it could not be a mere happenstance, or a concomitant error.[57] Colebrooke then referred to Powell, pointing out that the error had to pertain to the very circumstances of the contract. Anything less than this was not operative. Confusingly, he then added that the contract was void (rather than voidable). Error as to the person is recognised, on Pothier's grounds, where the personality of the other party is the reason for the contract. An error in motive, however, is not a ground for avoiding a contract. Colebrooke concluded that while contracts affected by mistake are strictly void because the consent necessary to form a contract is missing, they are in fact voidable because they may be ratified and affirmed by a subsequent assent once the error is discovered.[58]

Macpherson and the Indian Contract Act 1872

Although Colebrooke's attempt to organise English contract law around will theory was not influential, this was not true of the next treatise with an Indian connection. The common law of England never did receive a codified law of contract. English lawyers were, however, engaged in the exercise of working out how to codify law. If the challenge facing France and Germany in the nineteenth century was the role of law in a unified nation state, the challenge facing England was the role of law in running an increasingly vast and multi-ethnic empire, filled with different customs and legal systems. Macpherson wrote to solve one small section of these problems and, in so doing, effectively produced legislation which gives us a good indication of the sort of codification English contract law would have taken at the time. Macpherson's work gives us an idea of English thinking on mistake immediately prior to the rise of the major English treatises on the subject, and a decade and a half before the fusion of law and equity occurred. Remarkably, Macpherson produced a model which would arguably have been more successful than that which several generations of common law lawyers have managed to produce.

William Macpherson, an Aberdonian who attended Trinity College, Cambridge, was called to the English bar in 1837. After almost a decade of practice in London, Macpherson went to India to practise law. Within a short period of time he was

[56] ibid, s III, §98, p 47.
[57] ibid.
[58] ibid, §102, p 48.

appointed the master of equity in the Supreme Court in Calcutta in 1848. He returned to England in 1859, and in 1860 he published *Outlines of the Law of Contracts as Administered in the Courts of British India.*[59] Macpherson's declared purpose behind the publication was to provide an outline of the general principles of contract law which would 'form a guide to the rules which the courts of the Bengal Presidency, and also the courts of Madras and Bombay . . . to apply to the cases that may arise'.[60] There was a need for such a work in India because the existence of different forms of courts and two indigenous legal systems, Hindu and Muslim, meant that, in practice, 'cases arising out of contract are left to be determined in general by applying to each the principles of "Justice, Equity, and Good Conscience" '.[61] Not only did these words form 'an indefinite foundation for a judicial system' but the difficulties were compounded by the fact that the judges were not trained lawyers and 'the native officers . . . are timid where they have no Regulations to guide them'.[62] Macpherson, accordingly, set out to ascertain how principles of contract were to be applied in individual cases and what decisions these principles would produce in individual cases. Macpherson took as the basis of his work the applicable English law of the day, and arranged under appropriate heads such decisions of Indian courts as appeared to recognise and illustrate the principles of 'Justice, Equity, and Good Conscience'. For his exposition of English law, Macpherson turned principally to Addison's treatise on contract, but to avoid 'as much as possible all technical phrases and distinctions' he had utilised the Code Napoleon for its order and arrangement, and the work of Pothier, upon which the Code had been based.

Unsurprisingly, given these foundations, Macpherson began by defining a contract around the requirement of consent: a contract is a binding agreement which 'requires a concurrence of intention' in at least two parties.[63] Following Pothier's structure, Macpherson found that where the consent of a party had been given 'through mistake, or has been extorted through violence, or surreptitiously obtained by fraud, such consent confers no validity upon the contract'.[64] Macpherson added to Pothier's structure the particular concerns of the common law and he gave the defect 'error' its English name of 'mistake'. He followed Pothier in finding that only a mistake as to the very substance of the object of the agreement is cause for annulling an agreement: it has to be a mistake 'in the very substance of the thing which is the object of the agreement'.[65] There was no guidance as to what is the 'very substance' and what is not: equally, it was unclear as to whether the effect of the mistake is to render a contract void or voidable. The language used was imprecise: on the one hand, the overall tenor indicated that there

[59] W Macpherson, *Outlines of the Law of Contracts as Administered in the Courts of British India* (London and Calcutta, RC Lepage and Co., 1860).
[60] ibid, ix.
[61] ibid, vii.
[62] ibid.
[63] ibid, 1.
[64] ibid, 2.
[65] ibid, 2.

was no agreement; on the other hand he wrote of 'annulling the agreement' or that the consent so obtained 'confers no validity upon the contract'.[66] He proceeded to outline instances of types of substantial mistakes. The first was a mistake as to essentials: a coin sold as genuine which turned out to be counterfeit: 'there was a mistake as to the very substance of the thing which was the object of the contract'.[67] If, however, a purchaser got what he wanted, although it was not as good as he thought (a horse, thought sound, later discovered to be blind) then the contract was good. The distinction is an odd one: in neither case does the purchaser obtain an object which is fit for the purpose for which he presumably would have intended it. The second type of mistake was one which Pothier had dealt with in *Contrat du Vente* although not as a mistake but as a situation in which the contract had no subject matter.[68] The example Macpherson gave was the then recent decision in *Couturier v Hastie*: the sale of the non-existent cargo of wheat. This would apply equally where the parties had not really agreed as to the subject matter of the contract, as when they were unsure as to how much land was within a certain estate which was the subject of a sale. This would occur only when there was real doubt as to what had been bought and sold and would not apply where there was a mistake as to the quantity of land within an estate or where the vendor was ignorant of the value of the estate. The third type of mistake that Macpherson dealt with is a mistake as to the person. Mistake was a cause for a nullity when the principal cause of the contract was 'a feeling in favour of a particular person' and where the contractor believed that the person with whom he was contracting was that particular person. Tellingly, there were no examples in the English or Indian case law upon which Macpherson could draw upon to illustrate the type.

Macpherson, having written his *Outline*, became the Indian Law Commission secretary, based in England. Here his work included an attempt to codify Indian Contract Law. The result was a report of the Indian Law Commissioners on the subject of contracts[69]: the report was largely enacted as the Indian Contract Act 1872.[70] The Commissioners' result was clearly based upon Pothier and with an eye to Macpherson's outline. The report was clear that the result of a contract formed under a mistake is a void contract. The mistake, however, has to be 'as to a matter of fact essential to the engagement',[71] a formulation very close to Pothier's quality of the subject that the parties had principally in their contemplation when they made their agreement.[72] The Act contained various illustrations after each section,

[66] ibid.

[67] ibid, 3.

[68] Pothier (n 23) pt I, s II.

[69] *Papers showing present Position of Question of Contract Law for India; Reports of Indian Law Coms on Contracts* (1867–68) 239. The Commission was composed of both common law and equity lawyers.

[70] The Act formed the basis for contract law in British India. Roscoe Pound used it as an example of the fact that the 'English race is not instincitively averse to codification . . . where there was no developed system of courts at hand to receive the law gradually and work out its application to Indian conditions by a process of judicial empiricism. . . . Englishmen were quite willing to codify': RPound, *Interpretations of Legal History* (Gloucester, MA, Peter Smith, 1967) 81.

[71] ibid, 8, §7.

[72] Pothier (n 1) pt I, ch I, s I, Art III, §1.

a form of legislative interpretation of the text intended to make the application of the laws easier.[73] The illustrations in relation to mistake were few: *Couturier v Hastie* and the non-existent cargo is again referred to (although never by name); the purchase of a horse which was dead at the time of the sale (from Pothier[74]); or the sale of a life interest in property in a case in which, unknowingly the life has been extinguished.[75] The mistake had to be a mistake of fact: a mistake of law would not affect the validity of a contract.[76] Where the mistake was occasioned by the other party to a contract, it had the same effect as a false representation, and the contract was voidable at the option of the injured party.[77] The Act did not deal separately with law and equity as the two were administered together in British India. The Act also dealt with one of the most pressing problems that has bedevilled the application of mistake in English law. The longstanding problem associated with mistake has always been that if the mistake operates, it is not certain whether in any particular case, it renders the contract voidable or void. At law, it is said to render the contract void. This creates a harsh result for a third party who purports to acquire an interest in the subject matter of the contract (usually goods) but has acquired nothing. The Law Commissioners recommended that the ownership of goods be transferred where the seller was in possession of the goods and the purchaser acted in good faith and the circumstances were such as not to raise a reasonable presumption that the person in possession had no right to sell them.[78] The Law Commissioners made their recommendation knowing that this was contrary to the position in England and admitted that 'the subject is difficult'.[79] In considering which of two innocent parties should suffer, the Commissioners thought it a greater hardship to impose the burden upon a bona fide purchaser who would suffer where his conduct was blameless. In contrast, the original owner was 'very often justly chargeable with remissness or negligence in the custody of the property'.[80] It is interesting to speculate how the course of the English law of contractual mistake would have been decided if this provision had been adopted into English law: not only would the mistake of identity cases have been decided more justly and consistently, but it is also likely that courts would have been more willing to find mistakes, secure in the knowledge that there would have been a consistent rule as to the ownership of the subject matter. The legislation was delayed

[73] TL Murray Browne, 'Notes on the Codes of India' (1870) 29 *Law Magazine & Law Review, or Quarterly Journal of Jurisprudence* (Law Mag & L Rev Quart J Juris), 3d ser, 197, 203–204.

[74] Misleadingly given as a distinct second illustration; it is actually employed by Pothier in his *Contrat du Vente* to illustrate the need for a subject matter to a contract for sale (Pothier (n 23) pt I, s II, pp 3–4) and in this capacity had been argued in *Couturier v Hastie* itself.

[75] It is difficult to ascertain if this is an actual case. Two possible cases are: *Strickland v Turner* (1852) 7 Exchequer 208; 155 ER 919 (an action at law decided on the ground that the money was paid without consideration) or *Cochrane v Willis* (1865) 34 Beav 359, 55 ER 673 (an action in equity decided on the ground that there was no consideration and thus a *nudum pactum*).

[76] *Papers showing present Position of Question of contract Law for India* (n 71) p 8, §8.

[77] ibid, pp 7–8, §6.

[78] ibid, p 23, §81.

[79] ibid, p 4 ('Second Report').

[80] ibid.

in its implementation due to a dispute between the Law Commissioners and Sir Henry Maine, the legal member of the Viceroy's Council, and was not enacted in India until 1872. The result was adjudged a considerable success[81]: a decade and a half later, one English commentator wrote that it was important for the Indian law student to have modern British–Indian legislation brought to his attention as illustrating points of law.[82] The codification of Indian contract law was watched by these English lawyers with an academic interest in the law and with a concern for codification: it was not something that attracted the attention of practitioners. It was, however, to assume a role in the mistake theories of Sir Frederick Pollock.

Leake: The First Scientific Treatise Writer of Contract Law

The first author to compose a treatise on the common law of contract following the procedural reforms of the mid-nineteenth century was Stephen Martin Leake. Leake had practised as a barrister, but retired to the country and turned to treatise writing when he became increasingly deaf. He produced two significant treatises: *Precedents of Pleadings in Actions in The Superior Courts of Common Law*[83] and *The Elements of the Law of Contracts*,[84] the first English work to contain a significant consideration of mistake as a topic in its own right. The other two major treatises of the day, by Addison and Chitty, did not consider mistake as an isolated subject.[85] Leake presented contract law, as Macpherson and Colebrooke had, in a general and abstract form. Leake's treatise differed from the then contemporary considerations because he attempted to consider 'the elementary rules and principles of contract law' rather than 'detailed applications of that law to specific matters'[86] and specific contracts, a course of development adopted by contemporary contract writers. In the exposition of these principles, Leake was guided not only by the cases of the common law,[87] but also by English jurists (principally Austin

[81] See JF Stephens, 'Codification in India and England' (1872) 1 *Law Magazine and Review*, 4th ser, 963—although Stephens, a great proponent of codification, is not an objective voice. WH Rattigan, *The Science of Jurisprudence; chiefly intended for Indian Students* (London, Wildy and Sons, 1892) 26, was of the view that the treatment of mistake could hardly be improved upon.

[82] Anon, 'Rattigan's Jurisprudence' (1887–88) 13 *Law Magazine and Law Review*, 5th ser, 382, 384.

[83] SM Leake and E Bullen *Precedents of Pleadings in Actions in The Superior Courts of Common Law* (London, VR Stevens and Sons, 1860); this treatise was written with Edward Bullen, whose student he had been.

[84] SM Leake, *The Elements of the Law of Contracts* (London, Stevens and Sons, 1867).

[85] Indeed, Chitty would not include a chapter on mistake until almost halfway through the twentieth century: *Chitty's Treatise on the Law of Contracts*, 20th edn, H Potter (ed) (London, Sweet & Maxwell, 1947).

[86] ibid, v.

[87] As he explained in the introduction to his second edition, it was 'the prevailing habit of regarding the decisions of judges as constituting the body of law to which the practitioner must refer for

and Maine). He was also influenced by the civil law through Pothier and certain of the German pandectists. He wrote for a readership who had tired of digests of authorities on various points and who sought a 'modern' approach in which system was brought out of chaos through the application of reason to analyse the authorities and elucidate the relevant principles.[88] Leake is an important figure in the development of the common law of contract because he forms a bridge between the earlier approach of the common law in which issues were often resolved by methods which combined procedural and substantive law and the later approach of resolving these issues on the basis of substantive principles of law. Leake borrowed from the civilians, notably Pothier, the concept of unifying principles and, in the course of this, was amongst the first in the common law[89] to structure English law using Pothier. Leake sought, however, to write a treatise of English contract law, and his primary concern was to state English principles, rather than to introduce civilian principles supported by English cases. As a former barrister and a pre-eminent author in that most technical of common law subjects, pleading, Leake had a detailed understanding of English contract law.

Leake divided his subject between 'Rights to Things' and 'Rights against Persons'.[90] Contracts were within a *jus in personam*, a 'legal obligation between two persons . . . found in some act of the persons, or in some act or transaction affecting both, upon which the law operates by attaching the right on the one side and the correlative duty on the other'.[91] Contracts were divided into three kinds, dependent for categorisation upon their mode of formation: simple contracts, contracts under seal and contracts of record. He divided simple contracts into two classes: those formed by agreement and those implied by law. An agreement consisted of two people being of the same mind concerning the matter agreed upon: since the individual's intention was 'impalpable to the senses'[92] it could only be ascertained by means of outward expression such as words and acts. Agreement also required a mutual communication between the parties as to their intentions to agree. With regard to these communications, the law determined their agreement from the outward communications and the intentions were gleaned from a person's words and acts. Where the words were inconsistent with the conduct, conduct was considered a more reliable guide to intention. Leake also noted the peculiarity of English law in that to create a binding contract, it also required consideration. Without *consensus ad idem*, there could be no contract. A variance

authority': SM Leake, *An elementary Digest of the Law of Contracts*, 2nd edn (London, Stevens and Sons, 1878) viii–ix.

[88] See, for example, the review published of Benjamin's treatise in the *Solicitors Journal* in 1868: 13 *Solicitors' Journal and Reporter* 14 November 1868, 28. Leake's own work was praised for its 'scientific form', by which the reviewer meant the methodical and logical arrangement of the subject around general rules and principles: 42 *The Law Times*, 30 March 1867, 430.

[89] A notable predecessor in the attempt to explain elements of the common law of contract by reference to Pothier was E Fry, *A Treatise on the Specific Performance of Contracts Including Those of Public Companies* (London, T & JW Johnson, 1858).

[90] ibid, 1.

[91] ibid, 3.

[92] ibid, 8.

between the terms offered and the terms accepted prevented the necessary *consensus ad idem.* Although Leake conceived of an agreement between the parties as being an observable fact rather than a metaphysical correspondence of wills, once he accepted that contract could be formed by agreement, he also had to consider matters which disrupted agreement. Leake dealt with mistake as a matter relevant to the formation of contracts and placed it together with succeeding sections on fraud and duress. In employing this basic structure Leake was clearly influenced by civilian theorists, notably Pothier, but he also did not work as hard as others later would to bend the English cases around the civilian theories. Throughout the various editions of his work, Leake was conscious that the common law had a different basis than the civil law and did not slavishly adhere to the latter. The result was that his treatises attempted to set out the English case law but through the prism of a civilian theory. Leake wrote after the mid-century procedural reforms which allowed equitable defences to be pleaded at law with the effect that the common law could generate a legal response to cases of factual misapprehension. Leake acknowledged this and gathered these cases together under a broad principle of mistake which produced a lack of agreement. This was not unlike the common law query as to what the parties had intended by their agreement. This was generally followed by a corollary query as to the extent to which English law would, as a matter of procedure and evidence, consider this first query relevant or provable.

Mistake, Leake wrote, was occasioned 'by the ignorance or misconception of some matter' by which either the agreement intended to be made was not the agreement apparently made or the agreement was one which would not have been made but for the mistake.[93] Having borrowed a conceptual structure which saw mistake as vitiating agreement, Leake did not slavishly adhere to Pothier's ideas of mistake, large portions of which he ignored when he introduced his own ideas. For Leake, as for Pothier, mistake was a cause, along with duress and fraud, which could influence a contract founded on agreement such that under certain conditions the contract may be rendered 'void of legal effect'.[94] Leake came close to accepting Pothier's position that the effect of a mistake upon a contract was to render it an absolute nullity, or, in English parlance, void. He did not entirely accept the French proposition, probably because it was clear that courts of equity would act upon a mistake and recognise that a contract might be binding at law. Leake then examined the question of the effect of a mistake upon an agreement. He divided mistake into two forms: the unilateral mistake of one party and the bilateral mistake shared by both. 'Considerations of a different character'[95] attended each of these forms. In the first instance, where a party entered into a contract in which he was mistaken in his intention or in his motives, but the other party was unaware of this mistake, the mistaken party could not avoid the mistake by seeking to assert his mistake. The formation of agreements in English law was an objective matter and the law was concerned with expressions of intention actually

[93] ibid.
[94] ibid.
[95] ibid.

communicated. Leake relied upon common law cases for this proposition but acknowledged that the courts had been concerned with matters other than mistake.[96] Leake agreed with Pothier that a mistake in motive did not affect the resulting contract; again he supported this with English cases, in which the courts had been concerned with the question of what a seller had warranted to a purchaser.[97] Where the mistake was known to the non-mistaken party, the resulting contract could be effected. Where the non-mistaken party had induced the mistake, his conduct might be dealt with as fraud. Where the non-mistaken party was not responsible for inducing the mistake, the situation turned on what sort of mistake it was. If the mistake was in the expression of the agreement, the non-mistaken party could not hold the other party to an expression of intention he knew did not accord with the real intention, and a court of equity would find the agreement void. Leake was forced, here, to rely upon the equitable principles as courts of law had not considered the point as such.[98] Where the unilateral mistake was in the formation of the agreement, the effect of the mistake turned on the type of contract. In a contract in which one party was bound to inform the other of all he knew (such as insurance) a unilateral mistake would likely avoid the contract. If, however, there was no such obligation attached to the type of contract, a unilateral mistake without fraud would not avoid the contract. Leake also observed, in relation to a case of unilateral mistake, that a court of equity could refuse to grant the specific performance of a contract entered into under the mistake of one party, even where the other party was unaware of the mistake or implicated in the cause of the mistake. A court of equity would not rectify or rescind a contract simply on the ground of a unilateral mistake.[99] Leake overstated this latter qualification, for equity had never closed the possibility of relief upon a unilateral mistake.[100]

Leake then considered the effect if both parties were mistaken and subdivided his considerations into three instances: mistake in the expression of the agreement; mistake in some matter inducing the agreement; and mistake in some matter to which the agreement was to be applied. All three formulations were made with reference to existing common law practices.

The first formulation, a mistake in the expression of the agreement, is conceived on the basis of the equitable remedy of rectification. Leake approached the issue

[96] *Scott v Littledale* 8 E & B 815, 27 LJ, QB 201, 120 ER 304, and *Phillips v Bistolli* (1824) 2 B & C 511, 107 ER 474.

[97] *Chanter v Hopkins* (1838) 4 M & W 399, 150 ER 1484, and *Ollivant v Bayley* (1843) 5 QB 288, 114 ER 1257. Leake also relied upon *Cumberlege v Lawson* (1857) 1 CBNS 709, 140 ER 292, another case decided for reasons other than mistake.

[98] *Garrard v Frankel* (1862) 30 Beav 445, 54 ER 961. In this case, the Master of the Rolls, Sir John Romilly, refused to find the agreement void but gave the non-mistaken party the option of either taking the agreement as it was obviously intended or leaving altogether.

[99] Leake relied upon the decisions in *Alvanley v Kinnaird* (1849) 2 Mac & G 1, 42 ER 1 (the court itself considers it a situation where it 'might' refuse specific performance); *Sells v Sells* (1860) 1 Drew & Sm 42, 62 ER 294 (the reasoning of the court is confined to marriage settlements); and *Swaisland v Dearsley* (1861) 29 Beav 430, 54 ER 694 (a case really concerned with the difference between a subjective and objective standard of mistake—where the mistake is not patent on the face of the documents and is of one party alone, courts of equity will not grant relief).

[100] See ch 3.

from a practical perspective. Where the mistake in the document was so obvious as not to require external assistance, the contract would be construed consistently with the intention of the parties.[101] The usual problem, however, was the parole evidence rule: once the parties had agreed upon certain terms and agreed to write these down, it was the general rule of English law that a written contract could not be varied by the admission of extrinsic evidence to establish that the contract was other than that which was written and the parties were bound by the contract as written.[102] Leake observed that the common law was able to maintain such strictness in the interpretation of written agreements because courts of equity provided relief according to their own doctrines. While Leake accurately observed that the equitable relief available was to refuse specific performance, rectify or set aside a mistaken agreement, he avoided discussion of the doctrines upon which courts of equity provided relief. The likely reason is that equity acted upon a misapprehension to realise the intention of the parties or to prevent one party from taking an unconscionable advantage of another and not on the basis that mistake had influenced the parties' agreement. Leake also failed to mention that where equity provided relief because of a mistake, the effect was one akin to voidability rather than voidness. If, for example, a court of equity refused to grant an order for specific performance, it left the injured party to his remedy in damages at law.

The second formulation concerned a contract induced by a mistake. Leake encountered, here, the familiar problem of ascertaining which mistakes were serious enough to prevent a contract from arising and which were not sufficiently serious. He solved this problem using a common law analogy and distinguished between absolute and conditional contracts: 'the question arises whether the agreement is made absolutely, or only conditionally upon and with reference to the state of circumstances supposed by the mistake'.[103] Where it is a condition of the contract that the subject matter of the contract is in existence and it is erroneously supposed by the parties to be so in existence when it is not, the contract is void.[104] The question turned on the construction of the terms, for if the contract was expressly or impliedly conditional upon the supposed state of facts it was not applicable if the facts were not as supposed. Equally, if one party had undertaken 'the responsibility of performance at all risks and in all events',[105] a misapprehension would not vitiate the agreement. Intriguingly, Leake draws no parallels or

[101] Leake (n 84) 173–74, relying upon *Wilson v Wilson* (1854) 5 H of L Ca 40, 10 ER 811; *Coles v Hulme* (1828) 8 B & C 568, 108 ER 1153; *Lang v Gale* (1813) 1 M & S 111, 105 ER 42; and *Way v Hearn* (1862) 13 CBNS, 142 ER 1000.

[102] Leake relied upon the decisions of *Hitchin v Groom* (1848) 5 C B 515, 136 ER 979 and *Halhead v Young* (1856) 6 E & B 312, 119 ER 880. Where there was ambiguity on the face of the document, evidence could be admitted to ascertain the intention of the parties.

[103] Leake (n 84) 176.

[104] Leake relied upon *Couturier v Hastie* (1852) 8 Ex 40 (Court of Exchequer); (1853) 9 Ex 102 (Exchequer Chamber); (1856) HLC 673 (House of Lords); *Strickland v Turner* (n 77) and *Pritchard v Merchants' Life Insurance Soc* (1858) 3 CBNS 622, 140 ER 885, 27 LJCP 169. For good measure, he also combined equitable cases to the same effect in which relief was given for the mistake: *Hitchcock v Giddings* (1817) 4 Price 134; 146 ER 418 and *Cochrane v Willis* (n 77).

[105] Leake (n 84) 360.

comparisons between these cases and an *error in substantia*. This is all the more interesting given that none of the cases he relied upon was decided on the basis of mistake or even with reference to mistake as a failure of consent.

The third formulation concerned an agreement capable of being applied to different things or in different ways and was accepted by each party with a different application. In such circumstances 'there is no real agreement between them and consequently no contract',[106] for the contract was affected by a latent ambiguity. Where there was a patent ambiguity, 'a doubt or uncertainty appearing in the terms of the agreement as expressed by the parties themselves' which could not be altered or explained by extrinsic evidence, then the contract was void. Leake supported this proposition with the ubiquitous case of *Raffles v Wichelhaus.*[107] Having used the only legal case which might, doubtfully, support such a proposition, he then set out the equitable cases which asserted that where each party intended different terms, there was no real agreement. Leake then concluded his chapter by examining the new availability of equitable defences in common law courts, but noting the limitations placed upon this relief.[108]

Leake's detailed consideration of the effect of a mistake upon the formation of a contract was a new beginning in the common law of contract, for it introduced, as a coherent whole, a new means of vitiating a contract. While Leake's contractual mistake was undoubtedly conceived of with civilian will theories in mind, the detailing of the circumstances in which it operated was related in common law terms. It may have been that Leake, as a practising barrister of some experience, just could not bend the cases entirely around the civilian theories. The importance of Leake's new topic was that it marked a clear enunciation of a different way of looking at contract as a body of law with coherent, underlying principles and not a collection of remedies and rights organised around procedures. In this regard, Leake was a part of an evolutionary process of introducing civilian theories into the common law. Later authors not only followed Leake's work but also took this evolutionary process further. Leake's work is also interesting for what it does not contain. A comparatively weak conception of mistake in English law appears. As we have noted, Leake ignored the Roman *error in substantia* in defining a sufficiently serious mistake. He also ignored entirely Pothier's mistake as to the person. He considered the cases upon which later treatise writers were to 'found' such a doctrine in English contract law, but he considered them in a different context altogether. Leake wrote of the decisions in *Boulton v Jones*[109] and *Hardman v Booth*[110] as instances of the general rule where a party could not sue in his own name and claim to be the principal in a contract in which he had expressly contracted as the

[106] ibid, 178.

[107] (1864) 2 H & C 906; 159 ER 375; 160 LJ Exch 160.

[108] The relief was available only where a court of equity would decree an absolute, unconditional and perpetual injunction in the circumstances. See ch 4.

[109] (1857) 2 H & N 564; 27 LJ Ex 117; 21 Jur 1156; 6 WR 107.

[110] 1 H & C 803, 158 ER 1107.

agent of another person.[111] He also considered that these were instances where no contract arose with the plaintiff because the defendant had never intended to contract with him.[112] That an experienced barrister with a knowledge of English contract law and of Pothier would ignore such a form of mistake is highly indicative that English law did not recognise such a doctrine at that time.

Leake wrote two further editions of his treatise on contract. The second appeared just over a decade later. Significant changes in the law and the way in which the law was perceived by jurists had occurred during that time period: the reforms of common law procedure were completed with the Judicature Acts and the publication of treatises by Benjamin and Pollock. Leake changed the design of his own work, a change reflected in his new title, *An elementary Digest of the Law of Contracts*[113] and in the stated reasons for the treatise. Leake's major purpose in writing had 'been to treat the exposition of law upon a general scientific method, and to develope [sic] the use of such a method in dealing with law for practical purposes'.[114] Leake also wrote in the hope that the law would be advanced by a public code or digest, and that such an effort would only be realised after there had been the 'attainment of a correct scientific basis of order, and the habit of regarding and treating legal subjects in an orderly and connected form'.[115] Leake also hoped that his contract digest would, with his more recent publication of *An elementary Digest of the Law of Property in Land*, form two titles in a comprehensive digest of the common law as a whole. Leake's *Digest of the Law of Contract* was written not only as an exhaustive digest of the decisions of the courts (a form of digest Leake identified as the type a practitioner was in the habit of referring to with confidence), but also as a digest of general principles and doctrines of contract law. Leake's treatment of mistake in the second edition[116] was subtly different in conception and he took into consideration the newer decisions in *Smith v Hughes*,[117] *Cundy v Lindsay*[118] and *Kennedy v Panama Mail Co.*[119] Leake still saw mistake as a factor, with duress and fraud, which could affect the agreement between the parties. Mistake, for Leake, was brought about by the ignorance or misconception of some matter under which influence an act is done which, with a full and accurate knowledge of the matter, might not have been done 'so that the intention of the act and its consequences can not be fully imputed except under the condition of the mistake'.[120] While Leake had previously considered the major division in mistake to be whether the mistake was unilateral or bilateral, he later

[111] ibid, 306. Leake also cited the earlier decisions in *Bickerton v Burrell* (1816) 5 M & S 383, 105 ER 1091 and *Rayner v Grote* (1846) 15 M & W 359, 153 ER 888.

[112] Leake (n 84) 16.

[113] SM Leake, *An elementary Digest of the Law of Contracts* (London, Stevens and Sons, 1878).

[114] ibid, vii.

[115] ibid, viii.

[116] (n 113).

[117] (1871) LR 6 QB 597; 40 LJQB 221; 19 WR 1059.

[118] (1877–78) LR 3 App Cas 459; [1974–80] All ER Rep 1149, (1878) 42 JP 483; (1878) 14 Cox CC 93; (1878) 26 WR 406; (1878) 47 LJQB 481; (1878) 38 LT 573.

[119] (1867) LR 2 QB 580.

[120] SM Leake (n 113), 311.

considered the major divisions to be into different instances of mistake, the consequences of which varied according to whether the mistake was shared or not. As he wrote 'the question of the effect of a mistake is complicated . . . [by the] variations in its elements'.[121]

The incidence in which mistake could occur were fourfold: in the act of the agreement; in the expression of the agreement; in the application of the agreement; and in a collateral matter inducing the agreement. Again, Leake did not attempt to bend the cases around a civilian doctrine; instead, he has taken a civilian idea and re-conceived of it in light of the English cases. The second and third instances were largely similar to what he had presented in his first edition; the first and fourth were new. The first instance was the effect of a mistake upon the making of the agreement. While the general rule of English law was that a party 'cannot contradict or vary the written terms of an agreement',[122] it was the case that a party could contradict the fact that he had agreed to the terms of a contract when he had apparently assented to them. Leake considered here those situations in which a party executed a document when he was illiterate or where the effect of the instrument was different than that which was explained to him.[123] Such an act was a mere accident and not binding unless the mistaken party was negligent. In these cases, the mistake affected the mere signing; it did not go to consensus per se.[124] Leake's second instance was in the expression of the agreement; he expanded somewhat on his treatment in the first edition. A mistake in the expression of an agreement could be rectified only where the mistake was common to the other party as well.[125] The importance in a unilateral mistake in the expression of the agreement lay in its use as a defence to a suit for specific performance, for courts of equity would not generally order specific performance where one party was mistaken but would, instead, leave the other party to his remedy in damages at common law.[126] Leake observed that the effect of the recent decision in *Smith v Hughes* was that in some circumstances of unilateral mistake, if the other party was aware of the mistake, this party could not hold the first party to the mistaken expression of the terms because he was aware that the agreement did not accord with the real intention of the first party. In equity, such a circumstance might be a ground upon which the contract could be set aside altogether.

In the second incidence of mistake, where the mistake occurred in the expression of the agreement, Leake discussed the relief available at common law and in equity. He began with the 'elementary principle' that the law judged the intentions of a party by their objective actions and where the other party had no knowledge of the mistake in the expression, nothing would be done about such a mistake. Generally, at common law, while evidence would not be admitted to contradict

[121] ibid.
[122] ibid.
[123] *Foster v Mackinnon* (1869) LR 4 CP 704 (Common Pleas); the case was, itself based upon the earlier decision in *Thoroughgood's case* (1582) 2 Coke Rep 9b, 76 ER 408.
[124] Leake (n 113) 318.
[125] ibid, 314.
[126] ibid, 316.

the terms of a written agreement, where the mistake in the expression of the written agreement is obvious upon its face, a court of law would correct the mistake as a matter of construction.[127] In equity, however, a mistake of one party known to the other might not only preclude the grant of specific performance, but might also be a ground for setting aside the contract altogether.[128] Where the written contract made a common mistake in the expression of the terms of the parties' agreement, then a court of common law could not vary the agreement by extrinsic evidence of intention. It was left to the Court of Chancery to administer relief in such cases 'by restraining proceedings at law, or by rectifying the writing, or by setting it aside, upon equitable terms, according to the [equitable] principles'.[129] Following the fusion brought about by the Judicature Act 1873, the parties to proceedings in any courts were entitled to the administration of the equitable relief which would have been granted by a Court of Chancery.

Leake's third instance was a mistake as to the application of the contract; an instance he had previously considered as a category in which an agreement was capable of being applied to different things or in different ways such that there was no real agreement. The fourth instance of mistake was as to some fact or circumstance collateral to the contract. Where the mistake was a unilateral mistake in which the other party was not implicated in any way and it did not enter the agreement as a matter of stipulation or warranty, the mistake was of no effect and the contract was binding.[130] The mistaken party had bought the article upon his own suppositions as to its suitability, and the mistaken party alone bore the risk of any unsuitability. This, for Leake, was confirmed in the recent decision of *Smith v Hughes*. Interestingly, Leake also placed *Cundy v Lindsay* within this category.[131] Separate consideration was accorded to the rules of equity regarding a unilateral mistake as to a material collateral fact. Courts of equity would not rescind or rectify a contract for such a mistake, although they would refuse specific performance, even where the non-mistaken party was not implicated in the mistake. By refusing specific performance, they left the non-mistaken party to his remedy at law, namely, damages.[132]

In examining his fourth instance of mistake, Leake returned to the analysis he had employed in his first edition, namely, that the determination of which mistakes were effective to avoid a contract could be resolved by ascertaining the behaviour of the parties and the nature of the terms of the contract. He employed

[127] ibid, 327.

[128] ibid, 318. Leake based this argument on the decisions in *Garrard v Frankel* (n 97) (which he accepts, without criticism, as good law), *Harris v Pepperell* (1867) LR 5 Eq 1 and *Calverley v Williams* (1790) 1 Ves Jun 210, 30 ER 306.

[129] Leake (n 113) 319.

[130] ibid, 333. He relied upon *Scott v Littledale* (n 96) and *Scrivener v Pask* (1866) LR 1 CP 715 for this proposition.

[131] Leake pointed out that liability for a unilateral mistake had to rest with the non-mistaken party in order to affect the contract. Following this reasoning, *Cundy v Lindsay* established that the buyer of the goods had, by fraud or misrepresentation, induced the mistake as he knew that the seller did not intend to sell to him.

[132] Leake (n 113) 335.

the recent decisions in *Smith v Hughes* and *Kennedy v Panama Canal Co* in this position. The behaviour of the parties determined whether the concern was one of mistake or misrepresentation: if the mistake was created by deliberate misrepresentation of a party, this was fraud, and both law and equity would avoid the contract on that ground.[133] If a party created a mistake negligently, equity would refuse specific performance and might rescind the contract altogether. *Smith v Hughes* decided that where the mistake was as to a collateral fact inducing the contract and known to the other party (although not caused by him or attributable to him), mistake avoided the contract. Leake considered the case analogous to fraud: if the non-mistaken party proceeded to contract knowing that the other party was under a mistake or in ignorance of a fact which induced him to contract, and if both sides understood this matter to be the basis upon which the contract was made, this was equivalent to a fraudulent inducement. The mistaken party could then seek to avoid[134] the contract. If, however, the mistaken party acted entirely upon his own judgement, then the mistake was not a sufficient ground to avoid the contract unless the contract was a contract *uberrimae fidei.*[135] The terms of the contract also acted to determine whether the mistake was operative: if the terms expressly or impliedly made a conditional agreement, dependent upon the supposed state of affairs, the agreement was void if the state of affairs was not as supposed. If the agreement was absolute, a misapprehension could not vitiate the contract. Thus, where the parties made their agreement conditional upon some supposed state of affairs, if those affairs proved not to exist, the contract was void. If, however, the agreement was made unconditional and absolute, in the sense that the parties had made their intention unconditional and independent of the real state of facts, misapprehension could not vitiate the contract.[136] Leake considered that *Kennedy v Panama Mail Co* decided that where there was a sale of a specific article, if it was accurately identified in substance, the contract was absolute and independent of any mistake or erroneous supposition respecting the qualities and accidents of the article. Intriguingly, Leake's treatment of the case indicated an awareness of the civilian theory of *error in substantia*, but also, and importantly, that English lawyers dealt with the question on a different basis as one of ascertaining what was warranted.[137] It was for later generations to blend these two approaches together.

[133] ibid.

[134] There is no indication that the contract was void *ab initio*, merely that it could be rescinded by the other party. Leake applied this principle to the newer cases concerned with company shares: if it was believed a certain state of affairs existed in relation to a company when it did not, then equity would not enforce the agreement but leave the party to his legal remedy: Leake (n 113) 343.

[135] In which case, the party had the duty to communicate all material facts as a condition of the validity of the contract: ibid, 338–39.

[136] ibid, relying upon *Barr v Gibson* (1838) 3 M & W 390, 150 ER 1196 and *Barker v Janson* (1868) LR 3 CP 303.

[137] Leake cited the portion of the judgment based upon *Street v Blay* (1831) 2 B & A 456; 109 ER 1212 in his text and confined that portion of Blackburn J's decision concerned with the Roman doctrine of *error in substantia* to his footnotes: Leake (n 113) 344–45.

Leake concluded his examination of mistake with the rule that the mistake, if it were to be effective, must be one of fact and not of law.[138] This general rule was subject to certain qualifications: if the written document did not produce the intended effect by reason of a common mistake as to the legal meaning or construction of the terms; if the parties mistakenly omitted a term in their agreement; or if the parties were mistaken as to the private rights of property dependent upon the general law (*Cooper v Phibbs*[139]).

Leake published a third edition of his treatise in 1892, a year before his death.[140] His approach to mistake remained largely unchanged as he updated his text with recent decisions. One change that he did make was that in his consideration of what was essentially a mistake as to a quality, he removed his discussion of conditions precedent and warranties, although they clearly formed an unenunciated basis for his considerations. Equally significant was what Leake did not change: his examination of the relationship between law and equity as regards mistake. Leake observed that equity might recognise the effectiveness of a mistake in a way in which law would not: where, for example, a court of equity refused an order for specific performance on the basis of mistake, the disappointed party could still seek damages at law for any loss he had sustained by reason of the mistake.[141] Leake also viewed as good law those cases in which a court of equity effectively offered rescission on terms.[142]

What conclusions can be drawn from Leake's efforts? His work clearly shows a Pothieresque influence: mistake is a factor which, like duress or fraud, can upset an agreement, or in Leake's words, 'influence' it. His fundamental idea of mistake—an element which disrupts consent—is borrowed from Pothier. After that point, the similarities begin to fade. Leake grafted to this fundamental idea the methods by which both law and equity dealt with cases of misapprehension. The common law was concerned less with the consensus between the parties and more with facilitating the intention of the parties. Equity, as we have seen, was also concerned with unconscionable advantages. Leake's categories of mistake were of his own devising and he conceived of them in relation to the procedural mechanisms by which common law actions could be brought. This is no surprise given that he was also the co-author of a highly successful treatise on civil procedure.[143] Leake's

[138] ibid, 345–49.

[139] (1867) [LR] 2 HL 149; (1877–78) LR 3 App Cas 459; [1874–80] All ER Rep 1149; (1878) 42 JP 483; (1878) 14 Cox CC 93; (1878) 26 WR 406; (1878) 47 LJQB 481; (1878) 38 LT 573.

[140] SM Leake, *A Digest of Principles of the Law of Contracts* (London, Stevens and Sons, 1892). While Leake retained his digest system, he intriguingly removed the 'elementary' portion of his title and now, like Anson and Pollock, concentrated on 'principles' of contract law.

[141] Leake gave as an authoritative example the decision in *Tamplin v James* (1880) LR 15 CD 215.

[142] *Paget v Marshall* (1884) LR 28 CD 255 was a recent example of such an authority for him: a case in which one party appeared to take advantage of the mistake of the other party, where equity would either allow the contract on the original terms or not at all. Leake discusses the case at 267–68 (n 140). He continued to refer approvingly to the authorities of *Garrard v Frankel* (n 98); *Woollam v Hearn* (1802) 7 Ves 211, 32 ER 86, and *Harris v Pepperell* (1867) LR 5 Eq 1; 17 TLR 191; 16 WR 68.

[143] E Bullen and SM Leake, *Precedents of Pleadings in Actions in The Superior Courts of Common Law* (London, VR Stevens and Sons, 1860).

conceptions of the instances of mistake also display a concern for the commercial consequences of mistake. This is particularly true in his consideration of a fact collateral to the agreement—a mistake as to quality—he restricted the operation of such a mistake to circumstances where the terms of the agreement made it clear that the very agreement was premised upon what was later revealed as a misapprehension. This reliance upon contractual terms operated to put final control with the contracting parties.

At the end of the day, Leake was not a particularly vehement will theorist. He sought to explain the operation of the common law according to the procedures it had adopted and he attempted to explain this in the language of the common law. The civilian theories helped to establish a framework, but not much beyond this framework. Leake's work was important because it was the first successful attempt to organise English contract law on the basis of principles and because of the influence it had not only upon judges but also upon later English common law writers who recognised 'the great learning, the clear intellect, the patient unselfish industry of Mr. Leake'.[144] Leake's work is best viewed as part of an evolutionary process in which contract law came to be recognised as a coherent body of law administered in both courts of law and courts of equity, unified through principles and not as a collection of different procedures and types of contracts. Leake borrowed from Pothier a general structure which involved mistake as a vitiating element but Leake went his own way in developing what constituted a mistake. Leake was a transitional figure upon whom the authors who followed him, notably Benjamin, were to borrow more than simply structure but also a greater amount of Pothier's more detailed conceptions of mistake and its effect upon contractual formation. What Leake began, others completed.

Judah Benjamin—The Living Transplant

While Leake's attachment to will theory was not substantial, the same cannot be said of Judah Benjamin. Benjamin's *A Treatise on the Law of Sale of Personal Property: with References to the American Decisions and to the French Code and Civil Law*[145] referred extensively to Pothier. This is not surprising given Benjamin's background, for Benjamin was himself a form of living transplant. Benjamin had begun his legal career in the United States, where his contemporaries considered him to be one of America's greatest litigators.[146] Significantly, for English law, he

[144] WRA, 'Stephen Martin Leake' (1894) 37 LQR 2, 4. 'WRA' (in all likelihood William Reynell Anson) applauded Leake's selection and arrangement of contract material.

[145] JP Benjamin, *A Treatise on the Law of Sale of Personal Property: with References to the American Decisions and to the French Code and Civil Law* (London, Henry Sweet, 1868).

[146] Benjamin has been the subject of a number of biographies. See, in particular, P Butler, *Judah P Benjamin* (Philadelphia, PA, George W Jacobs & Co, 1907); RD Meade, *Judah P Benjamin, Confederate Statesman* (New York, Oxford University Press, 1943; reprinted Baton Rouge, LA, Louisiana State University Press, 2001); and EN Evans, *Judah P. Benjamin, The Jewish Confederate* (New York, Free

had extensive knowledge of French civil law: he had, since the 1840s, made frequent trips to Paris for personal reasons[147] and, even more importantly, because he had been called to the Louisiana Bar in 1832. Louisiana then, as now, had a unique legal heritage because of its colonisation by both France and Spain prior to entry into the United States. Its legal system was a mixture of French and Spanish law.[148] Benjamin was fluent in both languages, well versed in both civil and common law, and the author of a Digest of Louisiana law. He combined a legal career with a political one and became the United States' senator for Louisiana; when his state seceded from the Union, Benjamin left the Senate and joined the Confederate cabinet at the invitation of Jefferson Davis. Holding successive cabinet posts, Benjamin was considered one of its most able members. When the Confederacy fell, he feared for his life and fled, arriving in England in 1865. In an attempt to indicate his abilities, he wrote a treatise on the English law of the sale of goods. He followed the design of Pothier's *Contrat du Vente* in beginning his own treatise, although he combined with this structure considerations that Pothier had undertaken in *Traité des Obligations.* As a general observation, the influence of Pothier upon Benjamin's writing was structural and general rather than detailed and specific. Benjamin used Pothier as a means of ordering and unifying English cases decided upon apparently disparate, and often procedural, grounds. Pothier is used as a part of a process by which substantive principles of contract could be discussed. Benjamin was conscious of this process; as he wrote after outlining *Couturier v Hastie*,[149] 'perhaps the true ground' for the decision was a mutual mistake of fact which prevented assent.[150] Many of Benjamin's readers understood the processes he applied.[151] Benjamin was aware of differences between the civil law and within civilian systems[152] but he nevertheless maintained that the principles of the civil regarding mutual assent did not in general differ from those recognised in America and civil law countries.[153] Benjamin was a proponent of the will theory of contract and regarded the mutual assent of the parties to contract as one of the general principles which governed all contracts.[154] He had maintained in his

Press, 1989). Benjamin's life at the English Bar has also been considered: AL Goodhart, 'Judah Philip Benjamin, 1811–84' in *Five Jewish Lawyers of the Common Lawyers* (London, Oxford University Press, 1949).

[147] Benjamin's wife, Natalie, was a French Creole who had moved to Paris in the 1840s and Benjamin, upon his retirement, joined her there briefly before his death.

[148] An appreciation of the situation can be seen in R Batiza, 'The Louisiana Civil Code of 1808: Its Actual Sources and Present Relevance' (1971) 46 *Tulane Law Review* (Tul L Rev) 4, and 'The actual sources of the Louisiana *Projet* of 1823: A general analytical survey' (1972) 47 Tul L Rev 1; and VV Palmer, 'The French Connection and the Spanish Perception: Historical Debates and Contemporary Evaluation of French Influence on Louisiana Civil Law' (2002) 63 *Louisiana Law Review* (La L Rev) 1067.

[149] (1856) 5 HLC 673; 10 ER 1065.

[150] Benjamin (n 145) 58.

[151] See, eg, the review in 13 *Solicitors' Journal and Reporter*, 14 November 1868, 28.

[152] Benjamin (n 145) 290.

[153] ibid, 43.

[154] Sale was only a form of contract, which Benjamin defined as 'a transfer of the absolute or general property in a thing for a price in money': ibid, 1.

earlier Louisiana Digest that consent was necessary to form a contract[155] and he retained this requirement. Although Benjamin's treatment of mistake is clearly influenced by Pothier, Benjamin does not depend upon Pothier here and he departed from Pothier in various ways. This may, in part, be attributable to his experience with the Louisiana Civil Code of 1825, which replaced a single article dealing with contractual mistake with a more complex system involving 26 articles.[156] The Louisiana Civil Code with which Benjamin was familiar thus possessed a more complex treatment of the subject of contractual mistake than the French Civil Code. The Louisiana Civil Code has been described as the code which most thoroughly reflects Pothier's treatment of contractual mistake.[157] One departure Benjamin made was that while Pothier considered the effect of mistake only upon the formation of a contract, Benjamin considered this and also the effect mistake had as an element upon which one party could rely to rescind or avoid a contract which had been performed or executed. In doing this, Benjamin appears to have been following the Louisianan approach of absolute and relative nullity.[158] Benjamin dealt with these two effects in different chapters, and the treatment was not entirely satisfactory. The importance, however, of Benjamin's writings upon mistake cannot be underestimated. Hailed as 'one of the most important contributions to legal literature which has appeared for many years',[159] his treatise on sale was greatly relied upon by members of the bench and bar alike. It was reported that Baron Martin advised his chief clerk that he was never to take his seat in court again without 'that book by my side',[160] and Willes J described it as 'a work from which I have derived great advantage and which is remarkable for the acumen and accuracy of the writer, who possesses not only a knowledge of English law but of jurisprudence in general'.[161] Benjamin's treatise formed the impetus behind the decisions in two prominent mistake cases: *Cundy v Lindsay*[162] and *Smith v Hughes.*[163]

[155] JP Benjamin and T Slidell, *Digest of the Reported Decisions of the Superior Court of the Late Territory of Orleans, and of the Supreme Court of the State of Louisiana* (New Orleans, LA, John F Carter, 1834) 98.

[156] Louisiana's codification of error in 1825 was clearly derived from Pothier. The Revision of 1825, with which Benjamin would have been familiar, replaced this general provision with a careful enumeration of different categories of error, based on both the Roman categories and with additions by Pothier. See S Litvinoff, 'Vices of Consent, Error, Fraud, Duress and an Epilogue on Lesion' (1989–1990) 50 La L Rev 1, 10, 46; and '"Error" in the Civil Law' in J Dainow (ed), *Essays on the Civil Law of Obligations* (Baton Rouge, LA, Louisiana State University Press, 1969) 259–69. The development of a doctrine of mistake is also discussed in DP Doughty, 'Error Revisited: The Louisiana Revision of Error as a Vice of Consent in Contracting' (1987–1988) 62 Tul L Rev 717.

[157] T Hoff, 'Error in the Formation of Contracts in Louisiana: A Comparative Analysis' (1978–1979) 53 Tul L Rev 329, 331.

[158] These concepts are discussed by Hoff: ibid, 341–42.

[159] *Solicitors' Journal and Reporter* (n 151). The anonymous reviewer did, however, advise readers that some parts of the treatise needed to be used 'with some degree of caution' because it appeared that Benjamin had been hasty in some of his conclusions.

[160] *Daily Telegraph* (London, 10 February 1883).

[161] *Seymour v The London and Provincial Marine Ins Co* (1872) 41 LJNS CP 198.

[162] (n 118).

[163] (n 117).

Pothier, in *Contrat du Vente*, followed Roman law and stipulated that the three elements necessary for a contract of sale were a thing, a price and the consent of the contracting parties. Like Pothier, Benjamin worked from the general principle that contracts were formed by the mutual assent of the parties; a corollary to this general principle was that where mistake prevented agreement, there was no contract. Benjamin, like Pothier, wrote that where, through a mistake of fact, each party was assenting to a different contract, there was no valid agreement. What Benjamin meant, however, when he wrote of a different contract was not Pothier's example of different kinds of contract, where, for example, one party intends to make a loan and the other a gift. What Benjamin intended by this was the situation in which the parties had not agreed to the very subject matter of the contract, or the price or quantity of the subject matter, situations specified by Pothier as particular forms of error.[164] Benjamin was not concerned that the English cases[165] he provided were not decided on the basis of mistake[166] and that one, at most, was concerned with the absence of consensus.[167] Benjamin seemed untroubled by the inconsistencies between his statements and the actual bases of the decisions.[168]

While Leake had ignored mistake of identity, Benjamin adopted this concept from Pothier and stated that a mistake as to the identity of the other party could render a contract void. While Pothier stipulated in *Contrat du Vente* that the consent of the parties, the concurrence of the will, was a necessary element in the contract of sale, he considered mistake of identity within his *Traité des Obligations*. Benjamin placed the specific considerations of the latter within the structure of the former. Benjamin recognised, as Pothier had, that a mistake as to the identity of the other party could render a contract void only where the identity of the other person was an important element of the sale. Identity was important where it influenced the assent of the vendor. Benjamin refrained from adopting the specific illustrations of Pothier, and Benjamin's illustrative examples were drawn from familiar common law cases concerned with the payment of goods where either the solvency of the purchaser was an issue for a vendor who extended credit or where

[164] Pothier (n 1) pt I, ch I, s I, Art III, §1, p 12.

[165] *Thornton v Kempster* (1814) 5 Taunt 786, 128 ER 901; *Raffles v Wichelhaus* (1864) 2 H & C 906, 33 LJ Ex 160, 159 ER 375; and *Phillips v Bistolli* (n 95).

[166] *Thornton v Kempster* (n 165) was concerned with the sale of hemp. In *Raffles v Wichelhaus* (n 165) the judges famously gave no reasons for their judgment, which was given after counsel argued that as the parties each meant a different ship *Peerless* there was no *consensus ad idem* and therefore no contract. *Phillips v Bistolli* was argued on the basis of the Statute of Frauds and whether or not possession had passed to the putative buyer. The matter was left to the jury to decide, without any mention of mistake.

[167] *Raffles v Wichelhaus* (n 165).

[168] In the later decision of *Henkel v Pape* (1870) LR 6 Ex 7, the purchaser sought to purchase three rifles, and due to the telegraphist's error, 150 were sent. The Court of Exchequer found that the purchaser was not bound to take more than three rifles. The Court did not decide the case on the basis of a mistake rendering the contract void, and Benjamin included the case in his third edition to illustrate an instance where a mistake as to quantity rendered the contract void; yet this was clearly not what the Court had done: AB Pearson and HF Boyd, *Benjamin's Treatise on the Law of Sale of Personal Property*, 3rd edn (London, Henry Sweet, 1883) 56–57. Although written by Pearson and Boyd, this portion was approved by Benjamin before his death: ibid, v.

the purchaser had a right of set-off against a particular vendor.[169] In the usual case of a sale for cash, it made no difference who the purchaser was and a mistake of identity did not prevent the contract's formation. Benjamin grafted his theory onto two English cases,[170] neither one of which was decided on the basis of mistake or even with reference to a doctrine of mistake. In both cases there was a factual misapprehension but this had limited significance in legal terms.[171] Benjamin went further, however, and stated that cases of mistake as to the person which had been occasioned by fraud were also cases in which the contract had never come into existence: 'the whole contract is void'.[172] This extended English law farther than had previously been the case. He provided two cases[173] to support this position, neither one of which was concerned with a 'doctrine' of mistake as to identity. Benjamin's statement was, however, to be relied upon by the House of Lords in deciding *Cundy v Lindsay*.[174] By the third edition of his treatise, Benjamin had, in *Cundy v Lindsay*, an impressive House of Lords' authority for the proposition he had first asserted in 1868.[175] What Benjamin had posited as law had become law.

Benjamin also borrowed from Pothier the idea that a mistake in motive did not vitiate an agreement. He rationalised this, however, on a different basis by distinguishing a bilateral mistake from a unilateral mistake. This distinction was logically consistent with the view he expressed later as to the objectivity of the common law of contract. The mistaken motive of one party alone would not vitiate consent. Consequently, it was important to distinguish between a 'mutual mistake', as to the subject matter of the sale, or the price, or the terms, from a mistake made by only one party as to a collateral fact 'or what may be termed a mistake in motive'.[176] The former prevented a contract from coming into existence because there was no *consensus ad idem*: in the latter case, there was a contract of sale. A mistake by one party in his motive to contract (the supposition that the object bought was suitable for one purpose when it fact it was not) was only a mistake as to a 'collateral fact' and 'affords no ground for pretending that he [the buyer] did

[169] Benjamin (n 145) 40.

[170] *Mitchell v Lapage* (1816) Holt NP 253, and *Boulton v Jones* (1857) 2 H & N 564; 27 LJ Ex 117; 21 Jur 1156, 157 ER 232.

[171] In *Mitchell v Lapage* the court attached no significance to the misapprehension. In the later case of *Boulton v Jones*, Bramwell B indicates a cognisance of Pothier's mistake as to identity, but this was not the basis of the decision. The case was decided with reference to the will of an individual to decide with whom he wishes to contract but the court was clearly not applying a doctrine of mistake.

[172] Benjamin (n 145) 42.

[173] *Hardman v Booth* (1863) 1 H & C 803, 158 ER 1107, and *Higgons v Burton* (1857) 26 LJ Ex 342. The former had been decided on the latter, a point Benjamin did not appear to realise. Benjamin also ignored the fact that in the former case the court was struggling to reconcile the civil and criminal law applicable to the case.

[174] (n 118).

[175] Pearson and Boyd (n 168) 63. The third edition was published after Benjamin's death, having been completed by Pearson and Boyd once Benjamin's health failed 'and he was interdicted by his physicians from any further work, and ordered absolute repose and cessation from all intellectual fatigue': ibid, v. Benjamin, however, had already written the mistake sections before his health failed.

[176] Benjamin (n 145) 38–39.

not assent to the bargain'.[177] In Benjamin's view, if a party sought to purchase an article which was suitable for a particular purpose, he should seek a warranty for this from the vendor.

Benjamin found that his treatment of mistake had to depart from Pothier's in order to attempt to explain the legal and equitable cases of the common law. Like Leake, Benjamin considered the legal response to a mistake in the written expression of an agreement. Benjamin also wrote that if an agreement was expressed by the parties in an unintelligible language, then there was no contract. However, the agreement would not be unintelligible 'because of some error, omission, or mistake in drawing it up, if the real nature of the mistake can be shown, so as to make the bargain intelligible'.[178] As Benjamin accurately stated, courts of both law and equity would correct an error which was obvious on the face of an instrument. The correction would be made simply from the construction of the document itself.

Benjamin conceived of mistake in an objective sense: the law gave effect to the intention manifested to the other party, not the actual intention of the party. Where a party had one intention, but manifested a different intention to another party to induce the latter to act upon it in contracting, the first party was 'estopped from denying that the intention as manifested was his real intention'.[179] In this, Benjamin departed from Pothier, who clearly envisioned a subjective mistake. It may be that he did this in accordance with the established practice in Louisiana, although it is definitely the case that Benjamin needed to accommodate the objective basis upon which the English common law was clearly constituted. Benjamin needed to accommodate this objective basis for three reasons. The first was that it was too deeply ingrained within the common law to be extracted. The second was that Benjamin sought to write a practical treatise upon sale rather than a theoretical work. Borrowing the structure of Pothier gave an appealing framework to his treatise and presented a form of intellectual coherence to readers; trying to adopt pre-codified French law would not have created a practical treatise. The third reason was the interaction of commercial and legal practicalities. English law favoured an objective basis, in part, because the lack of quasi-contractual rights meant that to rescind a contract for a unilateral mistake left the non-mistaken party in a perilous state. Within France itself the practical application of mistake had moved towards a more objective basis. In establishing an objective basis

[177] ibid, 39. Benjamin relied upon the decisions in *Chanter v Hopkins* (n 97) and *Ollivant v Bayley* (n 97) (a decision which applied *Chanter v Hopkins*) to establish this. The former decision was clearly based on the ground that, when a purchaser ordered a good by a general description, whether or not it suited the particular purpose he had in mind for the good was his concern and not the vendor's. The vendor discharged his liability when he supplied the good according to the general description. The case is not, however, one concerned with a mistake in motive at all, but in allocating liability according to the interpretation of the terms of the contract.

[178] Benjamin (n 145) 38. Benjamin relied upon *Coles v Hulme* (n 100) (bond omitted that the sum owed was in pounds, court supplied the species where the intent was clear from the bond itself that the species was pounds sterling), and *Wilson v Wilson* (n 100) (deed following upon the separation of a married couple reformed to accord with what, on the face of the deed, must have been the intention of the parties).

[179] Benjamin (n 145) 39.

Benjamin used cases as authorities which were not cases of mistake, but were ones in which the court held that when one party had conducted himself in such a fashion that the other party was reasonably induced to contract on that basis, the party could not then assert that no contract had been made.[180]

Benjamin did not address the question of what was an essential element of the contract of sale and what was not. This was also a weakness inherent in Pothier's analysis. This was a significant omission for only a mistake as to an essential element (generally mutual) was sufficient to render the contract void. As Pothier had written, an essential element was the subject matter of the sale or the price or the terms: but not just any mistake as to these elements would suffice. What Benjamin did consider in connection with an essential mistake was that a mistake, to be effective, generally had to be mutual. He used the decision in *Scott v Littledale*[181] to establish that a unilateral mistake as to quality was not operative. He also observed that the real mistake in the case was that the vendor had given the warranty under a mistake which might be a ground upon which a purchaser could seek relief but it was not a ground which prevented the sale. Benjamin ignored the procedural concerns upon which the case had actually been decided.[182]

While Pothier conceived of the efficacy of mistake in relation to the formation of a contract, Benjamin went beyond this and considered mistake to be a ground upon which to avoid an executed contract. He thought of mistake in this sense as akin to a failure of consideration and, in that sense, similar to fraud or illegality. The contract was thus voidable for mistake. To so operate, the mistake had to be a mutual mistake and it had to be as to some essential fact 'forming an inducement to the sale'.[183] Benjamin's distinction between a mistake which rendered the contract void and a mistake which rendered the contract voidable rested upon whether or not the contract had been performed by either party 'during the continuance of the mistake'. Once the mistake was discovered, the party could set aside the contract provided that *restitutio in integrum* was possible. If the parties could not, however, be restored to their original pre-contract position, the remedy of the deceived party lay solely in damages. Benjamin tied mistake together neatly

[180] The principal case was *Freeman v Cooke* (1848) 2 Ex 654, 154 ER 62. The other cases cited were: *Cornish v Abington* (1859) 4 H & N 549, 157 ER 956; *Alexander v Worman* (1860) 6 H & N 100, 158 ER 42; and *Van Toll v South Eastern Railway Company* (1862) 12 CB NS 75, 142 ER 1071. None is concerned with a doctrine of mistake, although, arguably, modern eyes could recognise a mistake of identity in *Cornish v Abington.*

[181] See n 95.

[182] The court refused relief on an essentially procedural ground: the plea could not be admitted because it was not a case that a court of equity would have provided simple relief for and the court did not have the ability to provide a partial or conditional relief. On the procedural aspects of this point, see ch 4 at pp 82–86. Although the case was essentially decided upon a procedural point, the court was clearly hostile to a claim of mistake. In the questioning of counsel for the vendor it is pointed out that he could have bought tea equal to the sample to fulfil the contract and that the purchaser had been willing to take the tea on the specified ship. As Crompton J indicated in his questions, it was a case in which the vendor, in seeking to rescind the contract, sought 'too large a relief': 820, 306. Crompton J. also hinted at the fact that the problem lay around what was warranted and that a court of equity would only have provided relief with regard to the term: 820–21, 306.

[183] Benjamin (n 145) 303. As to the requirement of a mutual mistake, see also 306.

with fraud here by stating that even where the mistake was caused by the fraud of the other party it was operable. It does not appear that a mistake which rendered the contract voidable was in some way qualitatively different from a mistake that prevented a contract from being formed. Benjamin considered that a number of mutual mistakes of fact could render an executed contract voidable. One was the sale of an annuity on the misapprehension that the life in question was in existence;[184] the second was a silver bar sold on the assumption it contained a smaller amount of silver;[185] and another was a mistake as to the mode of payment.[186] Benjamin appeared to have considered that the setting aside of such an executed contract occurred in equity rather than at law although the point is not clearly made.

To allow an executed contract to be set aside, the mistake generally had to be a mutual mistake. Benjamin considered that in limited circumstances, the mistake could be of one party if the other party was aware of the mistake.[187] If the other party was not aware of the mistake, then the mistaken party must bear the consequences of this mistake, absent any fraud or warranty. This follows from Benjamin's proposition that the law was concerned with objective assent in the formation of contracts rather than subjective:

> For the rule of law is general, that whatever a man's *real* intention may be, if he *manifests* an intention to another party, so as to induce that other party to act upon it, he will be estopped from denying that the intention as *manifested* was his *real* intention.[188]

Men can only bargain by mutual communication, and if the proposal of A is made in unmistakeable terms, and B's acceptance is 'unequivocal and unconditional', then B is bound, however clearly he might later make out that he was thinking of something else.[189] Although Leake's influence can be seen here, Benjamin appears to have been the first to so formulate this proposition and it was one which came to have an influence upon the decision of *Smith v Hughes*.[190] In most situations where only one party is mistaken the other party will have caused the mistake and this is a matter of fraud. Where, however, the first party is aware that the second party has a different essential element in mind than the first party, there is no contract because the first party is in no position to show that he was induced to act by a manifestation of the second party's intention which was different from his real intention. And if he had caused the second party's mistake, his conduct would be

[184] *Strickland v Turner* (n 77).

[185] *Cox v Prentice* (1815) 3 M & S 344; 105 ER 641.

[186] *Boulton v Jones* (n 170). Benjamin ignored completely his earlier use of the case as one which supported the proposition that a mistake as to identity could render a contract void.

[187] ibid, 306.

[188] ibid. The cases Benjamin relied upon are those cited earlier, at 39 (n 180), in asserting the same proposition in relation to a mistake affecting the formation of a contract.

[189] ibid.

[190] (1871) LR 6 QB 597. Benjamin wrote three years before the case came before the court, but his example of a merchant selling cotton goods by sample to a purchaser who mistakes them for linen, is strikingly similar. Benjamin thought there would be a contract in such a case because the transaction was one at arm's length and each party took their own risks.

fraudulent.[191] Benjamin formulated this on the basis that the contract of sale is generally between parties who deal at arm's length 'each relying on his own skill and knowledge' and each able 'to impose conditions or exact warranties before giving assent' and thus taking upon himself all risks other than those arising from the fraud of, or breach of warranty or condition by, the other party.[192] In addition to this estoppel-based reasoning, another possible basis may be found in the Louisiana Civil Code of 1825. The Code, in dealing with motive, posited that no error of motive on the part of one party would invalidate a contract unless the other party was apprised that it was the principal cause of the agreement or unless from the nature of the transaction it is presumed that the non-mistaken party was aware of this.[193] The second edition of Benjamin's treatise was published two years after the decision in *Smith v Hughes*.[194] Intriguingly, Benjamin asserts his basic proposition of objective assent, and thus of mistake, but does not deal with it in his chapter on mistake. Instead, he directs readers to his chapter on fraud, and it is there that he discusses the case. His account of the case, which is largely descriptive, claims no personal credit for the influence of his treatise.[195]

By his second edition, Benjamin also considered the possibility that the mistake could have been brought about by the innocent misrepresentation of a party. In such a circumstance, the party deceived by the innocent misrepresentation was entitled to avoid the contract on that ground.[196] To establish this, he relied upon another recent decision, the one curiously overlooked in his first edition, of *Kennedy v The Panama, New Zealand, and Australian Royal Mail Company*.[197] Benjamin developed the civil law influence exhibited by Blackburn J in that case. Benjamin was concerned to develop the consideration of a mistake as to a quality in the civil law and link it to the approach taken by the common law. What had to be determined was whether 'the mistake or misapprehension is *as to the substance of the whole consideration*, going as it were, to the root of the matter, or only to some point, even though a material point, an error as to which does not affect the whole consideration'.[198] He continued to further expand the argument made in his first edition, in which he had written that a misrepresentation of law could result in a failure of consideration and, as such, was a valid ground for avoiding a

[191] Benjamin (n 145) 306–307. Benjamin makes the point by altering the facts of *Raffles v Wichelhaus* (n 165) as follows. If the vendor knew that the purchaser had a different ship *Peerless* in mind from that intended by the vendor, there would be no contract because the vendor could not say he had been induced to act by a manifestation of the buyer's intention different from his real intention.

[192] Benjamin (n 145) 307.

[193] Litvinoff, 'Vices of Consent, Error, Fraud, Duress and an Epilogue on Lesion' (n 156) 47. As Litvinoff points out, the application of this provision in Louisiana was not without problem. In particular, it was unclear as to whether the other party had to know of the motive *and* the mistake or only one of these elements.

[194] JP Benjamin, *A Treatise on the Law of Sale of Personal Property*, 2nd edn (London, Henry Sweet, 1873).

[195] ibid, 388–89.

[196] ibid, 328.

[197] (1867) LR 2, QB 580, [1861–73] All ER Rep Ext 2094.

[198] ibid, per Blackburn J, quoted by Benjamin (n 194) 329.

contract. In doing so, he relied upon cases concerned with misrepresentations and linked them implicitly with mistake, which he regards in this context as synonymous with a failure of consideration.

A mistake of law would not entitle a party to avoid a contract. Benjamin relied on the 'universal rule' of *ignorantia juris neminem excusat* and stated that the cases illustrating the maxim were too numerous to cite fully, giving only a small selection of them.[199] While the law accorded no efficacy to a mistake of law, it would give relief for a misrepresentation of law where it could be shown that a failure of consideration occurred. In his second edition, Benjamin dealt with *Cooper v Phibbs*[200] as a new precedent for an exception to the general rule barring avoidance of a contract based on a mistake of law. The exception was that when the mistake of law in question was in the nature of a mistake as to a private right, then such a mistake could be a ground to avoid a contract. Benjamin devoted little space to discussing the decision and did not consider the equitable aspects of the case at all.[201] While Benjamin had an eye to the equitable treatment of mistake, he was concerned with a contractual subject matter, goods, which had not traditionally appeared in courts of equity, and he may well have thought it unnecessary to repeat at length the equitable treatment of mistake.[202]

While Benjamin wrote about the contract of sale in particular, his work as it pertained to mistake had a general effect in contract. The first edition of Benjamin's treatise set out to resolve some of the ambiguities in the common law and Benjamin's resolution of these points was accepted into the common law by judges who sought the resolution of a particular problem. Two such instances occur in mistake: the first is *Smith v Hughes*,[203] and the second is *Cundy v Lindsay*. Benjamin was also the first author to advance *Kennedy v The Panama Canal Co* to prominence. In addition to the importance these particular cases came to play in the development of a doctrine of mistake, Benjamin's authoritative treatment of the subject worked to position it firmly within English contract law. The deficiencies in his treatment of the subject do not seem to have been apparent to his contemporaries.

[199] ibid.

[200] (1867) LR 2 Eng & Ir App 148.

[201] Benjamin (n 194) 328. That he did not consider the matter in detail is unsurprising, for Benjamin was writing on sale and *Cooper v Phibbs* was a case concerned with the sale of a proprietary interest in real property.

[202] In his third edition, he did briefly consider the effect of the Judicature Act 1873 in relation to mistake, noting where certain claims or defences should be brought and also that the cases in which equity granted relief for a mistake of law in circumstances in which it was inequitable for a party to profit by their mistake should prevail over the more rigid common law rule: Beilby and Boyd (n 157). For the basis of his equitable rule, Benjamin relied upon *Stone v Godfrey* (1854) 5 D M & G, 43 ER 798, *Ex parte James* (1874) LR 9 CA 609, *Rogers v Ingham* (1876) 3 CD 357, and *Daniell v Sinclair* (1881) 6 AC 190. On this basis, Benjamin would have viewed the 1949 decision in *Solle v Butcher* [1950] 1 KB 671, [1949] 2 All ER 1107, 66 TLR (Pt. 1) 448, [1949] EGD 346, as correctly decided.

[203] Benjamin's reliance upon Leake's resolution of this point makes it possible to attribute the decision in this case to Leake.

Conclusions

The common law treatise writers set out to organise contract law on a scientific, systematic and rational basis. Their focus was on the substance of the law rather than procedure, upon the general, rather than the particular. Their organisation was, they believed, necessary to facilitate the proper development of the law. Some, such as Leake and Macpherson, saw their writing as a necessary pre-condition to codification. In their efforts, these common law authors sought guidance as to a substantively based structure for their thoughts. Pothier's writings were clear, systematic and analytical: it is hard to deny their apparent desirability and it is easy to see why the common law writers turned to them.

Several observations can be made about the adoption of Pothier's theories into English contract law. The first is that the direct extent of the influence was limited. Pothier is used to provide a general structure: contracts are based on consensus, on the will of the parties, and various factors, one of which is mistake, can disrupt this consensus. The treatise writers borrowed this general structure and referred to Pothier in the process. They also borrowed, although not unanimously and not without some ambiguity, the idea that the effect of mistake was to render a contract void. English treatise writers did not accept Pothier's work on mistake in its entirety: they were selective in their borrowing and they merged this with common law concerns, such as objectivity. The second relates to Pothier's work itself. Pothier himself had relied upon Roman sources and later works based upon these sources for his conception of mistake. This was undoubtedly attractive to common law lawyers possessed of a classical education and able to access these texts in their original. However, the state of knowledge with regard to Roman law was not sufficiently well advanced to see the dangers in relying upon Roman law. The problem, as we have seen earlier, was that the Roman law of mistake was not developed as a coherent body. In particular, the Romans did not see the principles pertaining to mistake as broad principles applying to all contracts, but as specific considerations pertaining to specific contracts. The Romans did not regard consent as necessary to the formation of all types of contracts. The Roman treatment was inconsistent and contradictory, despite its superficial coherence. Any detailed consideration of the Roman law found it wanting and challenging to apply to particular situations. Pothier, and through him the English lawyers, thought they were applying a coherent and principled body of law when they were not. In short, Pothier's Roman-based considerations of mistake proved troublesome to apply in practice. This difficulty was compounded by the fact, particularly apparent in relation to a mistake as to a quality of the subject matter, that when Pothier relied upon earlier natural law theorists he was not true to the late scholastic tradition. The result was that while essence had been crucial to the late scholastics, quality proved impossible to define with precision in Pothier's theory. A central problem encountered by the English writers was that it was difficult to establish a mechanism to apply with certainty to resolve a particular problem. The authors struggled, and ultimately failed, to establish when a particular mistake as to quality operated and when it did not. Because mistake, when operative, upsets the commercial allocation of risk between the parties and disrupts their reasonable expectations, defining with precision when mistake has this effect is critical. The failure to do so meant that the doctrine was unlikely to be applied by courts from the outset.

Over time, and throughout the nineteenth century, French jurists came to realise the deficiencies of Pothier's work. Many set out about resolving these deficiencies and improving his theories. Rather surprisingly, English lawyers did not refer to these later writings; indeed, they seemed almost oblivious to them. The English lawyers were also seemingly unconcerned with the application of the Civil Code in French courts. They extracted from Pothier and the Civil Code (which, in its contract sections, was largely derived almost directly from Pothier) a will theory and the necessary analytical framework around which to organise English case law. That concluded their interest in French jurisprudence and they admitted no need to examine it further. The effect was that having allowed a certain infection into their thoughts, they cut themselves off from the course of treatment developed at the source of this infection: by greatly restricting their interest in French jurisprudence to finding practical solutions to English problems, they greatly limited their ability to solve the problems that they had transplanted.

A problem common to all of the English writers in adopting aspects of Pothier and his will theory was that they were not creating a legal system where none had existed before. Where they were, such as in India to some extent, it was possible to resolve some of the particular problems that arose from welding a case-based structure upon a new theory. Within England, these problems could not be avoided. English law had had existing methods for dealing with cases of factual misapprehensions. The treatise writers largely ignored these methods, but relied upon the cases of factual misapprehension to illustrate a very different theory. The result was confusing, for the statements of principle were not borne out of the determination of the cases. As Professor Ibbetson has observed, 'the result was a mess'.[204] By not admitting the change that they were effecting, the writers served to create confusion rather than dispel it.

Similarly, the treatment of the equitable cases presented great problems to these authors. Equity had something approaching a doctrine of mistake, but, despite the attempts of authors such as Edward Fry and Henry Ballow, it was not one based upon consensus. Equity was concerned with the intentions of the parties, unconscionable advantages and the problems which a severely procedure-based system of common law presented where misapprehensions occurred. To counter these, courts of equity had devised specific remedies. Unsurprisingly, these were not dealt with by Pothier, and the treatise writers struggled to fit them into their treatment of mistake. In many cases, it proved impossible to reconcile the two: hence their creation of mistakes in the writing of agreements or the points observed by Benjamin that an executed agreement could be set aside for mistake.

[204] DJ Ibbetson (n 47) 221

Two particular problems that arose from the adoption of Pothier lay first in the nature of the mistake necessary to disrupt a contract and, second, in the result of so disrupting the contract. Pothier, as we have seen, wrote of mistake in a subjective sense. The mistake of one party alone, without awareness of the other party, prevented consensus. There could be no agreement where one party laboured under a mistake. Logically correct, this presented the common law writers with a difficulty, for the common law was wedded to a much more objective conception of contract law.[205] The writers struggled to adopt Pothier's theory of mistake and apply it in such an objective setting. The way in which they resolved this struggle was to require that the mistake be a common one, a mistake shared by both parties, or that both parties were mistaken although they did not share their mistake. Where only one party was mistaken, the writers decided that the mistake would only operate to prevent a contract from coming into force where the non-mistaken party was aware of the mistake and that the mistake was such as to raise an estoppel preventing him from relying upon the contract. All of these devices operated to ensure that a void contract arose only where there were no reasonable expectations to protect on the part of any of the parties to a contract. This proved to be a great departure from Pothier's theory. In this area, the treatise writers presided over a renewed commitment to objectivity in the common law. This commitment came at the cost of sacrificing Pothier's theory. A similar problem presented itself with the effect of the mistake. Equity, where it had recognised a mistake, settled upon a solution akin to voidable contract, through rescission, or non-enforceability by way of specific performance. Pothier wrote of a contract being void for mistake. The problem was that when English writers settled upon a void contract as a result of mistake, this had the effect of unsettling conveyances in a way that would not have been the case for Pothier or, indeed, for the Romans. The weak state of English restitution in the nineteenth century acted to further exacerbate cases of apparent injustice. There was no recourse for the non-mistaken party for some form of compensatory damages. In short, the severity of the consequences of a void contract in English law would make judges reluctant to recognise that it existed in a particular case.

In conclusion, the English writers were required to adopt a theory of mistake, of dissensus, as soon as they had adopted a will theory of consensus. The problems inherent in their reliance upon Pothier were probably not immediately apparent. It was not just that they often ignored the common law methods of resolving factual misapprehensions, nor even that the cases they supported their new theory with were inconsistent with the theory itself; the very theory they adopted was flawed. It was partly to overcome some of these flaws that later treatise writers, particularly Pollock and Anson, turned to the German jurist, von Savigny.

[205] The presence of a jury undoubtedly made possible such a wedding.

6

Von Savigny and the Development of Mistake in English Contract Law

THIS CHAPTER IS concerned with the influence that the nineteenth-century German legal theorist Friedrich Carl von Savigny had on the development of the English doctrine of contractual mistake. The chapter begins with a consideration of Savigny's work, with a particular focus on his theory of obligations and how mistake fits within this theory. It then proceeds to examine how and why these theories were utilised by the later treatise writers of the nineteenth century, Anson and Pollock. Both authors also employed some of Pothier's conceptions of mistake and both authors attempted to support their civilian theories with English legal and equitable cases. Interestingly, and perhaps critically for the development of the English doctrine, both authors were to turn away from Savigny in their theories of contract, but not in mistake. The result was that in these treatises English contract law received a doctrine which came to be partially severed from the body of legal theory which had sustained it. The doctrine, as it remained, made little sense, both within itself and in relation to other areas of contract law. It was difficult to work out when mistake vitiated a contract and it was also hard to ascertain why a misapprehension sounded in mistake rather than in fraud, misrepresentation or even a failure of consideration. The doctrine of mistake constructed by the treatise writers was not only alien to the law, but it worked from a very different premise than mistake in equity. The treatise writers began their structures utilising a will theory; equity had very different concerns. The result was a bending, or outright avoidance, of the equitable mistake cases. Such treatment only operated to obscure the workings of the common law rather than to illuminate them.

Von Savigny and German Legal Development

While the influence of French civil law, through Pothier, upon English contract law has long been recognised, the influence of German civil law has received little scrutiny. Post-Napoleonic Germany thus seems an odd place to examine the mystery of contractual mistake in English law.[1] It is, however, an accurate place. The

[1] The European legal background to this time period is outlined by R Zimmermann in 'Savigny's Legacy: Legal History, Comparative Law and the Emergence of a European Legal Science' (1996) 112

defeat of Napoleon left European states with many problems. The Congress of Vienna was convened in 1814 to establish a new political order following the collapse of the last vestiges of the Holy Roman Empire. The concerns of the new order went beyond the political and encompassed the legal. The French Revolution had noticeably swept away the old legal order in France; the Revolution and the Napoleonic Wars had damaged and impaired the operation of the same legal order in the German states. It is no coincidence that it was in the same year as the Congress of Vienna that a professor of Roman law at Heidelberg, Anton Friedrich Justus Thibaut, published a booklet entitled 'On the Necessity of a General Civil Law for Germany'. Thibaut argued that a German civil code, modelled upon the French Civil Code, would enable the emergence of an undivided German state. The law would be rendered accessible in such a code and provide stability against the forces of political reaction. In making such proposals, Thibaut was also attacking the concept of a law created by a learned professoriate. Thibaut's proposal met a response from another German professor, Friedrich Carl von Savigny, in his essay 'Of the Vocation of our Time for Legislation and Legal Science'.[2] Although the essay is a refutation of Thibaut's programme of codification, it contained ideas already devised by Savigny as a part of his own legal programme which opposed an immediate codification of German law. Savigny's programme was more than a simple opposition to immediate codification because it set out his own programme for legal reform in Germany. Savigny opposed immediate codification because he was unimpressed by the three legal codes of his day: the Napoleonic Code, the Prussian Landrecht and the Austrian Gesetzbuch. He believed that none of these were successful. Although Savigny regarded codification as inorganic and arbitrary, he did not oppose it absolutely. His opposition was to timing: an immediate codification was inappropriate for Germany because of a paucity of German jurists. In short, his Germany contained no one capable of codifying German law. Before a code could be written, preparation was necessary. Savigny took it upon himself to begin this preparation. In doing so he revolutionised German legal science and engendered a debate amongst legal scholars and jurists which would eventually produce the *Bürgerliches Gesetzbuch* in 1900. Savigny's work established a methodology, thought-patterns and concepts that have now become common place.[3]

Savigny has traditionally been depicted as a conservative, a member of the land-owning aristocracy who sought to prevent the liberal and egalitarian forces which had swept over France from sweeping over Germany.[4] New research has questioned this depiction and portrayed Savigny as an advocate of legal reform

Law Quarterly Review (LQR) 576. Savigny and his work is discussed in H Kantorowicz, 'Savigny and the Historical School of Law' (1937) 53 LQR 326.

[2] *Vom Beruf unserer Zeit für Gesetzgebung und Rechtswissenschaft* (1814), reprinted in in H Hattenhauer, *Thibaut und Savbigny, Ihre programmatischen Schriften* (Munich, Vahlen, 1973).

[3] S Riesenfeld, 'The Influence of German Legal Theory on American Law: The Heritage of Savigny and His Disciples' (1989) 37 *American Journal of Comparative Law* (Am J Comp Law) 1, 3.

[4] See, eg, F Wieacker, *A History of Private Law in Europe*, trs F Wieacker (Oxford, Clarendon Press, 1995) 314.

without revolutionary change.[5] Savigny sought to understand the law within a given period: this understanding necessitated an historical study of the nature of law. Legal science had to be of a historical nature: 'its main task is the intellectual penetration, adaptation and rejuvenation of the legal material as it has come down to us'.[6] Because Roman law had provided the historical foundation for the *ius commune*, it constituted the starting point in the attempt to comprehend and then refine contemporary private law. The purpose of this study was to produce a law which was a consistent and logical system of concepts, rules and principles. Savigny was a part of a broader movement of Roman law professors who sought to revive Roman civilisations as a part of German modernisation. They believed that the Roman law tradition could both infuse political life with the strength and free sensibility of an older Germanic society and also lend a sense of moral mission to the Germans, a sense drawn from the grandeur of the classical tradition.[7] In this sense the Romanist lawyers were a part of the political life of the day, a romantic era which revolved around the ideological revival of the Middle Ages and the Reformation. The Romanist lawyers sought to spare Germany the angst of a revolution by creating a new Roman law which facilitated change:

> German liberalism was 'fundamental law' liberalism, comparable to the 'fundamental law' politics of the previous century elsewhere in Europe. It was backward- not forward-looking, and was characterized not by a struggle for principled freedom but by a struggle for Germanic freedom that was the German analogue of the gothic freedom that formed the (perceived) basis of English and American political life . . . 'backward looking' was by no means necessarily an equivalent of 'reactionary' in the Germany that emerged after 1815.[8]

Savigny established his views early in his professorial career and then devoted the rest of his life to advancing them. In establishing the German Historical School, he was also the founder of the modern German *Rechtswissenschaft*, a legal science in the Kantian sense of a science of positive law.[9] This new legal science, which emerged towards the end of the eighteenth century, had to meet two criteria: first, it had to be empirical so that it avoided speculation; and second, it had to develop an inherent structure of its subject, and its goal was a scientific system. It was Savigny who best dealt with these two, somewhat contradictory, concepts of empiricism and system. He did so by advocating historical studies to ascertain the leading principles to which the system then gave a scientific form. In other words, Savigny combined the concepts of *Geschichte* (history) with *System*: 'the two methods actually pursued the same goal, albeit in different dimensions'.[10] Savigny's study of the past was only a tool; he

[5] JQ Whitman, *The Legacy of Roman Law in the German Romantic Era, Historical Vision and Legal Change* (Princeton, Princeton University Press, 1990).

[6] Zimmermann (n 1) 579.

[7] ibid, 99.

[8] ibid, 97–99.

[9] M Reimann, 'Nineteenth Century German Legal Science' (1989–1990) 31 *Boston College Law Review* 837, 845. The article provides an excellent discussion of, among other matters, Savigny's contribution to legal science.

[10] ibid, 855.

envisaged not *Rechtsgeschichte* (legal history) but *geschichtliche Rechtswissenschaft* (historical legal science). Once a study of the past had revealed the leading principles, the historical work was completed. Legal science would then turn from these sources and leave them safely in the hands of archivists and antiquarians.[11]

Savigny undertook extensive Roman law research and his published results gave credence to his conceptual approach. He established his reputation in 1803 with *Das Recht des Besitzes* (*The Law of Possession*): 'the book at once established Savigny as one of the leading Roman law scholars and was admired by jurists all over the world'.[12] He continued two equally impressive multi-volume works on Roman law: *Geschichte des römischen Rechts im Mittelalter* (*History of Roman Law in the Middle Ages*), published between 1815 and 1831; and *System des Heutigen römischen Rechts* (*System of Modern Roman Law*), published between 1840 and 1849. The latter work remained incomplete. Savigny completed the study of the general principles but only managed to deal with the law of obligations in 1851 and 1853 in *Das Obligationrecht* before his death. Even incomplete, the effect of *System of Modern Roman Law* was profound. Two forms of scholarship arose: the conceptual jurisprudence, *Begriffsjurisprudenz*, of men such as Puchta and von Jhering; and also the practical application of Roman law material by the pandectists, the *Pandektenwissenschaft*, which many outside Germany associated with German legal scholarship as a whole. The work of the pandectists had a particular significance in Britain, which awaited Buckland and the British Roman law scholars who followed in his footsteps. Adherence to Savigny's work began to wane by the mid-nineteenth century,[13] it was at this point, however, that many English scholars became aware of the significance of his work. Translations of many of his important works were made.[14] The works translated into English indicate a desire for a practical system of law rather than an understanding of conceptual jurisprudence. While Savigny had an impact upon English jurisprudence, the man himself was somewhat removed from English lawyers. In an unusual twist of fate,[15]

[11] ibid, 854.

[12] ibid, 856.

[13] For the causes of this decline, see Reimann, (n 9) 864 and Whitman (n 5) 200.

[14] The translations into English were: E Cathcart (trs), *The History of Roman Law in the Middle Ages, vol 1* (Edinburgh, A Black, 1829); A Hayward (trs), *Vom Beruf unserer Zeit fur Rechtsgeschichte and Gestzgebung* (London, Littlewood, 1831); Sir E Perry (trs), *Savigny's Treatise on Possession* (London, S Sweet, 1848); F von Savigny, *System of the Modern Roman Law, vol 1*, W Holloway (trs) (Madras, J Higginbotham, 1867); W Guthrie (trs), *Private International Law* (Edinburgh, T & T Clark, 1869, translation of vol 7 of *System of Modern Roman Law*); A Brown, *An Epitome and Analysis of Savigny's Treatise on Obligations* (London, Stevens & Haynes,1872); F von Savigny, *Jural Relations; or the Roman Law of Persons*, WH Rattigan (trs) (London, Wildy and Sons, 1884, vol 2 of *System of Modern Roman Law*); and F von Savigny, *Possession in the Civil Law*, JF Kelleher (trs) (Calcutta, Thacker & Co, 1888, volume of *System* on possession).

[15] William Wetmore Story was the son of Joseph Story, the prolific treatise writer and US Supreme Court Justice. Story, *fils*, greatly admired his father and his early life was taken up with the law, writing a treatise on contract (which he dedicated to his father) and another on the sale of goods. After his father's death, the son, to his mother's dismay, resolved to become an artist and left Boston for Europe. Although he settled principally in Rome, becoming a sculptor of sufficient ability to undertake the bust of his father at Harvard, he spent a winter in Berlin where he improved his German and attended law lectures at the university. It was during this period that he met von Savigny and his family.

William Wetmore Story, the author of *Story on Contracts*, became acquainted with Savigny and attended his lectures in Berlin. His observations are intriguing:

> Von Savigny, the celebrated jurist, I have seen repeatedly, and I can assure you that he is of all petrifications the most remarkable I have seen. He is as dry as dust. Very courteous and affable and complimentary I found him, but living wholly in a book-world, and that book-world a law-book-world.[16]

Von Savigny and Contract

Savigny wrote under the influence of the philosophy of German idealism, notably Kant.[17] Kant, convinced of the freedom of the individual, wrote that individuals formed a state by means of a social contract. In a construct not dissimilar from Rousseau's, Kant conceived of a social contract in which individuals, by an act of will, surrendered their external freedom to acquire it again as a member of the state. Kant's conception of contract was profoundly influenced by the freedom and moral autonomy of the individual: a contract (*Vertrag*) was a meeting of wills. Savigny built upon this; contract became a 'union of wills with the object of determining legal relations'.[18] The will theory was the basis of all juristic acts (*Rechtsgeschäfte*) of which contract was only one form of legal transaction. For Savigny, the unity of the legal order was brought about not by legal rules but by legal relationships.[19] Private autonomy and freedom of contract are counterparts of the will theory. The legal system was based upon the moral freedom of the individual with a right to self-determination. Within this system, the ability of parties to contract did not mean that they were creating all law, but that they had an ability to create obligations within the law-making authority delegated to them by the state's legal system.[20] Based on these ideals, Savigny developed Roman law to produce a legal science which combined the systematic with the historical. He had employed Roman law as a means to counter Thibaut's call for codification, and to employ Roman law, he needed to systematise it. In Wieacker's words 'the work [*System des heutigen römischen Rechts*] really promotes with marvellous clarity the construction of a general theory of law which could take the place of natural law, and even amounts to a "philosophy of positive law"'.[21] The result was a Kantian concept of law: 'law as an "independent entity" which empowers the individual to

[16] H James, *William Wetmore Story and His Friends* (reprinted London, Thames & Hudson, 1953) 215–16.

[17] F Kessler, 'Some Thoughts on the Evolution of the German Law of Contracts—A Comparative Study: Part I' (1974–75) 22 *University of California at Los Angeles Law Review* 1066, 1068; and Wieacker (n 4) 297–98, 314–16.

[18] FC von Savigny, *System des heutigen römischen Rechts* (Berlin, Veit und Comp, 1840–1849) vol 3, §140–§141; the quote is taken from Kessler (n 17) 1068.

[19] Wieacker (n 4) 315.

[20] Kessler (n 17) 1069.

[21] Wieacker (n 4) 315.

be independently ethical, but does not force him to be so; the individual's rights as the space in which he is free to act consistently with the freedom of others; legal transaction and contractual intention as the action-space of the autonomous personality'.[22]

Savigny regarded the modern Roman law employed in the German states as a product of the people, the *Volk*. His conception of the people was not one of a commonwealth of adult citizens or nation, but as a cultural concept.[23] The law was a part of a general culture and the history of law was a part of civilisation as a whole.[24] Law was a manifestation of *Volksgeist*.[25] Because it was intrinsically and organically linked to the *Volk*, a law could not be imposed by codification. While Savigny wrote *System* to support this theory, the work was simultaneously a brilliant exposition of contemporary Roman law. Because of the profound and widespread impact of Roman law upon the legal systems of Europe, Savigny's work received considerable attention outside Germany.

Von Savigny and Mistake

In an exposition based upon Kantian ideals, legal transactions such as contract received a new logic. Savigny proceeded on a jurisprudence of conceptions. By employing historical and analytical conceptions of a contract, he was then able to deduce particular rules to govern the conditions of the contract.[26] As a will theorist, Savigny defined contract as a union of several people who concurrently declare their will (*übereinstimmende Willenserklärung*) which determines their legal relations. The contract arose from a manifestation of the will regarded as a juridical act. The particular elements of this juridical act were threefold: the will itself; the manifestation of the will; and the concordance between the will and the manifestation of it. The key characteristic of a contract was the union of plural wills to a single, whole, indivisible will. The existence of duress, mistake or fraud or surprise could render doubtful the existence of the juridical act, for they disrupted the manifestation of the will.[27] In so developing his theory, Savigny thought that he was expressing Roman law; in fact, in so developing the Roman texts to bring out these theoretical implications, Savigny (and his successors) imputed to the Romans new ways of thinking. They thus gave to the Romans preconceived theories and doctrinal logic where the Romans had only dealt with

[22] ibid.
[23] ibid, 311.
[24] ibid, 305.
[25] Andreas Rahmatian has recently outlined the principal ideas addressed in *Beruf* and the Volksgeist doctrine it espoused: 'Friedrich Carl von Savigny's *Beruf* and *Volksgeistlehre*' (2007) 28 *Journal of Legal History* 1.
[26] R Pound, 'Mechanical Jurisprudence' (1908) 8 *Columbia Law Review* 610.
[27] A Brown, *An Epitome and Analysis of Savigny's Treatise on Obligations in Roman Law* (London, Stevens and Haynes, 1872) 111. The volume is a summary of Savigny's *Obligationrecht*.

practical necessities.[28] In dealing with mistake as a force which could prevent consent, Savigny needed not only to reconcile the Roman authorities but also to preserve the stability and security of transactions.[29] In reconciling the apparent conflict between the Roman authorities, Savigny was impeded by his blindness to the interpolations: 'the most sophisticated solution seemed preferable to assuming an interpolation'.[30] Savigny's genius can be seen in his ability to reconcile the authorities and to provide protection to the security of transactions. He began by examining the concept of will. The expression of the will was distinguished from the formation of the will which preceded it: 'The correct approach to the problem thus rests upon a sharp distinction between the will itself and that which precedes it in the soul of the person exercising the will (*Wollenden*); the will is a self-sufficient event, which alone is significant for the development of legal relations, and it is wholly arbitrary and unreasonable if we united this preparatory process with the will as if it were an ingredient of its essence'.[31] The existence of the will could be nullified by coercion and mistake. If mistake motivated the will, the person who wanted the thing had no true awareness of the matter: he was just as incapable of a declaration of the will as though he were a minor.[32] It was deceptive to understand mistake as nullifying awareness and hence the will: the real reason behind the legal response was the immorality (*Unsittlichkeit*), which necessitated a positive counteraction. Savigny then examined mistake as a possible obstacle for the existence of a true and effective declaration of the will. What was important about mistake was the absence of the true image of the object in question.[33] Savigny drew a fundamental distinction between mistake in motive (*echter Irrtum*) and mistake in expression (*unechter Irrtum*).[34] Mistake in and of itself had no effect.[35] It was only relevant when it was a mistake in expression. Logically, any error would prevent the will from arising and the law ought to respect and preserve the contractor's freedom of will because the error prevented the free exercise of will. Pothier, as we have seen, relied on such logic. Savigny postulated that an error in motive was insufficient to determine the will of the contractor because it was the contractor himself who gave this determining character to the will. The contractor's freedom of choice was unrestricted and thus the mistake in motive did not impair the validity of the transaction.[36] 'If we say that the erroneous impression (*Vorstellung*) has determined the will, this statement is true only in a very improper sense. It was always the transactor himself who gave the error this

[28] HJ Wolff, *Roman Law: An historical introduction* (Norman, University of Oklahoma Press, 1951) 218.

[29] EW Patterson, 'Equitable Relief for Unilateral Mistake' (1928) *Columbia Law Review* (Colum L Rev) 859, 861.

[30] F Schulz, *Classical Roman Law* (Oxford, Oxford University Press, 1954) 4.

[31] Savigny, (n 18) §113; the translation appears in Patterson, (n 29) 861.

[32] Savigny (n 18) §114.

[33] ibid, §115.

[34] ibid, §112.

[35] ibid, §115.

[36] Patterson (n 29) 862.

determining force. The freedom of his choice between competing decisions was unrestricted; whatever advantage the error might (apparently) present to him, he could reject it, and hence the existence of a free declaration of the will is by no means destroyed by the influence of the erroneous impression.'[37] While an error in motive was insufficient to determine the will of the party, an error in expression was. An error in expression was legally consequential: it rendered the contract void. Where, therefore, there was an essential variance between the will and expression, no contract arose. The consequences of such a mistake was to render the contract void; in such circumstances, there could be no claim for damages even where the party in error was at fault. '[E]very transaction affected by an operative error must be regarded as null and void, irrespective of whether the party who had been labouring under the mistake wished this to be the case or not'.[38] In his treatment of mistake Savigny 'took a stand against prevailing practice';[39] many of his ideas as to the consequences of mistake were not accepted by the later pandectists.[40] A contract was formed only when the outward expression of the parties' will corresponded with their inner will: the essence of a contractual relation consisted in mutually conforming declarations of will as to the contents of the obligation. The difficulty with the division between motive and declaration, however, was that it was often impossible to separate the two.[41]

Sir Frederick Pollock

The principal protagonist in the introduction of Savigny's contract theories into English law was Sir Frederick Pollock. Although Pollock is now largely overlooked in legal circles, he was one of the pre-eminent jurists of the late nineteenth century.[42] He began the English tradition of treatise writing undertaken by men with academic, rather than practical, legal careers. Born into a family steeped in the law,[43]

[37] Savigny (n 18) §115; the translation appears in Patterson, (n 29) 862.

[38] R Zimmermann, *The Law of Obligations, Roman Foundations of the Civilian Tradition* (Cape Town, Wetton & Johannesburg, Juta & Co Ltd; 1990) 614–15. Zimmermann relies upon Savigny (n 18) §138.

[39] Zimmermann (n 38).

[40] A majority of the pandectists would have allowed only the party in error to invoke the invalidity of the transaction; towards the end of the nineteenth century, the term '*Anfechtbarkeit*' (rescindability) came into use, and one started to require a declaration of rescission. See Zimmermann (n 38) 615.

[41] ibid; translation in Patterson (n 29) 863. Patterson's criticisms extend to the entire will theory: he describes it as 'hopelessly vague'. He also directs criticism to the fact that Savigny's conceptions rested upon a now outdated psychology: 864.

[42] Something of Pollock's life, and a great deal of his contributions to the common law, can be seen in N Duxbury, *Frederick Pollock and the English Juristic Tradition* (Oxford, Oxford University Press, 2004); and RA Cosgrove, *Our Lady the Common Law: An Anglo-American Legal Community, 1870–1930* (New York and London, New York University Press, 1987) ch 5.

[43] The beginnings of the Pollock legal dynasty lay with Pollock's grandfather, Sir Jonathan Frederick Pollock (Chief Baron of the Exchequer 1844–66), and his brother Sir David Pollock (Chief Justice of Supreme Court of Bombay). While Pollock's father, Sir William Frederick Pollock, was the Queen's

Pollock had studied classics and mathematics at Trinity College, Cambridge and was elected a fellow at Trinity in 1868. It seems to have been assumed that his career would lie in law and he was called to the Bar by Lincoln's Inn in 1871. Lincoln's Inn was chosen by Pollock's father (and possibly his grandfather) as an appropriate Inn because it was thought that the Chancery branch of the profession would more suit Pollock's 'scholarly tastes' rather than the less academic common law side of the practice.[44] Pollock, 'shy, terse, taciturn, stolid, inclined not to speak when speech was expected',[45] almost never appeared in court. He described later that it became apparent that his bent did not lie in practice[46] and he concentrated his career as a jurist upon legal writing and lecturing.

His early legal experiences determined much of his later approach to the law. While his first pupillage at Lincoln's Inn was to a conveyancer, during which Pollock despaired of understanding the law, his next pupillage was to Nathaniel Lindley, who was noted for his skills as a pupil master. Under Lindley, Pollock flourished. Lindley was a meticulous barrister with an academic bent. He had studied in Bonn briefly and published a translation of the general part of Thibaut's *System des Pandekten Rechts*.[47] He published the translation to allow students and practitioners not only to acquaint themselves with the general principles of Roman law but also to facilitate the acquisition of a habit of classification and the ability to move from the general to the particular and so to bring together the great principles of English jurisprudence. Lindley thought English textbooks were poorly organised and 'a student is only too likely to be bewildered by the acquisition of particular facts which he is wholly unable to systematise'.[48] While his first pupillage left Pollock with a distaste for equity, his pupillage under Lindley inspired him to take up the study of Roman law and to employ Roman methods to develop law as a science. As he later explained to Lindley, it was 'in your chambers, and from your example, I learnt that the root of the matter which too many things in common practice conspire to obscure, that the law is neither a trade nor a solemn jugglery, but a science'.[49] While Pollock was persuaded of the value of

Remembrancer, because of the size of his grandfather's family (he had 21 children survive infancy), he also had a number of uncles in the legal profession. One of these was Charles Edward Pollock, an Exchequer Baron, and the other two were uncles by marriage, the judges Sir Samuel Martin and Sir Joseph William Chitty. In addition, Pollock's first cousin was Viscount Hanworth, MR. In short, the Pollocks were a byword for legal respectability. The general interest the legal profession took in Frederick Pollock can be seen by the interest expressed in the publication of his standing in the Cambridge Classical Tripos for 1867, which compared him favourably to his grandfather: *The Law Times*, 6 April 1867, 437.

[44] Sir Frederick Pollock, *For My Grandson, Remembrances of an Ancient Victorian* (London, John Murray, 1933) 160.

[45] Duxbury (n 42) 31.

[46] Pollock (n 44) 168.

[47] N Lindley, *An Introduction to the Study of Jurisrpudence; being a translation of the General Part of Thibaut's System des Pandekten Rechts* (London, William Maxwell, 1855).

[48] ibid, iv. The weak state of the common law as regards its jurisprudence and the value that Savigny might bring to this was noted by an American author as early as 1834: Anon, 'Life and Writing of Pothier' (1834) 12 *American Jurist & Law Magazine* 341, 374.

[49] F Pollock, *Principles of Contract: Being a Treatise on the General Principles Concerning the Validity of Agreements in the Law of England*, 4th edn (London, Stevens and Sons, 1885) iii.

Roman law to the study of the common law, he found a paucity of texts on the subject. England awaited Buckland, and Pollock found outdated the German texts employed by Lindley. James Bryce, then the Regius Professor of Roman Law at Oxford, recommended Savigny.[50] The effect of the German upon Pollock was profound: it was nothing short of an enlightenment. Even at the end of his long life, Pollock described Savigny as 'the greatest expounder of legal principles in modern Europe'.[51] After having read Savigny's *System of Modern Roman Law*, Pollock found that he had 'passed out of a cave of shadows into clear daylight. The vast mass of detail was dominated by ordered ideas and luminous exposition . . . the master proved, not by verbal definition, but by achievements in act, that the science of law is a true and living one'.[52]

Pollock's *Principles of Contract*

Pollock's *Principles of Contract at Law and in Equity* was an attempt to place law on a scientific basis. Pollock's conception of law as a science had a number of different aspects. The major aspect was to analyse the case law and in this fashion to seek out and ascertain the underlying normative principles upon which the law was founded. The process of analysis dedicated to formulating a rational result from the authorities could be difficult because the authorities were often ambiguous and sometimes conflicting on a first view.[53] These underlying principles, once identified, needed to be classified and placed within a system. In this process, one moved from the general to the particular. Pollock approved of the method of exposition employed by the German jurists of dealing with the principles and rules found in all or most of the subject under consideration so that they could be disposed of before the several branches of the particular subject were considered.[54] The actual divisions of the subject were formal rather than material, and many different possibilities presented themselves.[55] Another aspect of this science was to provide a terminology for these concepts within law in order to facilitate this process of classification. A third aspect to the science of law was prediction: 'the ultimate object of natural science is to predict events, to say with ultimate accuracy what will happen under given conditions'.[56] The object of a scientific law was thus to ensure that the same decision was given on the same facts. A fourth aspect of this scientific approach was that law should, as much as possible, be in plain English: it should be intelligible.[57]

[50] Pollock (n 44) 169. Bryce's relationship with Roman law is described by Cosgrove (n 42) ch 3.
[51] Pollock (n 44) 169.
[52] Pollock (n 49) iv.
[53] F Pollock, 'Has the Common Law received a Fiction Theory of Corporations?', reprinted in AL Goodhart (ed), *Jurisprudence and Legal Essays* (London, Macmillan & Co, 1961) 213.
[54] F Pollock, 'A First Book of Jurisprudence: Some General Legal Notions', reprinted in AL Goodhart (ed), *Jurisprudence and Legal Essays* (London, Macmillan & Co, 1961) 58.
[55] ibid, 46.
[56] F Pollock, 'The Science of Case Law', reprinted in AL Goodhart (ed), *Jurisprudence and Legal Essays* (London, Macmillan & Co, 1961) 169–70.
[57] ibid, 184. As to this scientific approach, see Pound (n 26).

Pollock, in his development of contract law as a science, sought to bring order to chaos. Savigny was his guide in this process. He admired Savigny's method of developing his subject, his lucid exposition, his classification and his ability to reconcile apparently dissimilar Roman cases. That Savigny achieved his system through a narrow focus upon an already ordered Roman legal system was not apparent to most nineteenth-century jurists.[58] A part of the personal appeal Savigny had for Pollock must have been his combination of two of Pollock's earlier studies: classics and mathematics. Savigny's reconciliation of historical truth with logical order struck a personal chord with Pollock. Savigny based his *System* on Roman law and he reduced it to a series of axioms which could be applied, like geometry, to resolve specific problems. At a more general level, there was an obvious attraction on the part of common law lawyers to a system which appeared to scientifically create a rational, relevant, internally consistent and functioning legal system out of a chaos of legal cases. The attraction is all the greater if the system can be created without time-consuming and difficult legislative processes.

It was not unusual at the time to turn to Germany for jurisprudential enlightenment: Germany was experiencing an intellectual and literary renaissance and its universities led the world.[59] German universities were at the height of their brilliance as English legal education was in the depth of darkness: Englishmen looked to Germans for assistance and for standards.[60] German scholars had made great advances in interpreting Roman law and were, generally, at the forefront of classical studies. Niebuhr's discovery of the Verona palimpsest of Gaius' Institutes had stimulated enormous advances in the subject in Germany. English lawyers were conscious of their deficiencies on this front: contemporaries wrote of 'the feebleness of our knowledge of the Roman law as a practical existing system, [which] has long been a subject for frequent comment with continental jurists'.[61] German universities had attracted English lawyers keen to learn more about German jurisprudence: Austin, Bryce and Lindley are amongst that small but influential group who spent a period of time studying in Germany. 'The German universities were viewed by both Germans and by foreigners, as international centers of legal scholarship and many made the pilgrimage there to study.'[62] While later writers have questioned how much these pilgrims understood of their German studies and the use to which they put this knowledge, there can be no doubt that the invocation of German legal science in whatever form was viewed by common law contempor-

[58] Reimann (n 9) 896. Few before Holmes and Pound recognised it as a grand illusion.

[59] These attractions are described in MH Hoeflich, 'Transatlantic Friendships & the German Influence on American Law in the First Half of the Nineteenth Century' (1987) 35 Am J Comp L 599.

[60] E Campbell, 'German Influences in English Legal Education, Jurisprudence in the 19th Century' (1959) IV *University of Western Australia Annual Law Review* 357, 357. When the 1846 Parliamentary Commission on Legal Education attempted to reform the Inns of Court they turned to German universities as inspiration for various models.

[61] FJ Tomkins and HD Jencken, *A Compendium of the Modern Roman Law founded upon the treatises of Puchta, Von Vangerow, Arndts, Franz Moehler, and the Corpus Juris Civilis* (London, Butterworths, 1870) xi.

[62] Hoeflich (n 59) 600.

aries as 'state of the art' learning. Pollock was presenting what appeared to be at the forefront of jurisprudence to most English lawyers. He was going farther than the earlier English contract writers who had relied upon Pothier's treatises for assistance. Pollock was ideally poised to present this learning; not only had he studied the classics at Cambridge but he also spoke German fluently at a time when most English lawyers would not have.[63] While English jurists distrusted Kantian legal theories, they were receptive to the synthesis of Roman law provided by German theorists, and Pollock was no exception to this trend.[64] There is an indication, however, that Pollock was somewhat more committed to Savigny's overall programme than has been suspected. It is possible to view as one of the ambitions of Pollock's writing on contract an attempt to clarify the law for later development: 'title by title, and chapter by chapter, the treasures of the Common Law must be consolidated into rational order before they can be newly grasped and recast as a whole' and in this recasting, the deficiencies of Pollock's own work might well be cast aside.[65] The outstanding oddity of his adoption of Savigny was that he did so 20 years after Savigny's original programme had begun to decline[66] and took a far less methodical interest in the analysis and ultimate abandonment of Savigny's work undertaken by later nineteenth-century German jurists.[67]

In *Principles of Contract at Law and in Equity* Pollock sought to present contract law in a scientific light. He regarded science as a system of divisions or classifications arranged according to underlying principles which could be used to predict the future application of the law to a given set of facts. This science of law was necessary to give coherence to a seemingly chaotic mass of common law cases which, if organised at all, were organised on crude arrangements. In this sense, Pollock's reliance upon Savigny's analysis was necessary for him to provide a synthesis of English law. Pollock's treatise was also attempting to grapple with two fundamental changes of the nineteenth century in contract law. One was the shift from a legal

[63] Pollock had learned his German on a summer vacation from Cambridge when he resided in Dresden in the summer of 1868; see Pollock (n 44) 116. Goodhart described him as having 'remarkable linguistic gifts' which aided his studies of foreign legal systems: 'Introduction', in AL Goodhart (ed), *Jurisprudence and Legal Essays* (London, Macmillan & Co, 1961) xvii. It is impossible to prove that nineteenth-century lawyers had an insufficient understanding of German to read Savigny in the original—but it is notable that references in English cases to Savigny's work were invariably to those of his works which had been translated into English. Additionally, writers on the subject felt compelled to translate the German works to make them accessible to English lawyers, and Pollock himself presupposed an understanding amongst his readers of Latin and French, but not of German, which he routinely translated into English. Hoeflich observes that while interest in German scholarship was high amongst English and American lawyers, few could read German fluently: 'Savigny and his Anglo-American Disciples' (1989) 37 Am J Comp L 17, 18. This topic is explored more broadly in MH Hoeflich, 'Translation and Reception of Foreign Law in the Antebellum United States' (2002) 50 Am J Comp L 753.

[64] See, eg, Duxbury (n 42) 190 and Campbell (n 60) 385. Pollock's disdain for German jurisprudence can be seen in his Oxford Lectures: *Oxford Lectures and Other Discourses* (London and New York, Macmillan and Co, 1890) 15, 16.

[65] Pollock (n 49) iv.

[66] Reimann (n 9) 864.

[67] Pollock was not alone in disregarding these later developments. EC McKeag, *Mistake in Contract: A Study in Comparative Jurisprudence* (New York, Columbia University Press, 1905) was an exception.

system based upon procedure to one based upon substance. Pollock sought to organise contract law around underlying substantive principles rather than the procedural forms of action or kinds of contracts. The second fundamental change, which Pollock anticipated, was the fusion of law and equity brought about by the Judicatures Acts 1873–75. The prior division of law and equity had also meant that treatises on contract law were, generally, similarly divided.[68] Common law writers wrote of contract at law and largely ignored the operation of equity; equity writers wrote of the operation of equity and largely ignored the law. In the future, the same courts would consider both law and equity; Pollock sought to ascertain the underlying principles of both bodies of law and present them as underlying normative principles of contract at law and in equity. While Pollock stated this purpose in academic terms,[69] the production of such a treatise would undoubtedly be a competitive advantage in the sales of such a work. As we shall see, Pollock's treatment of mistake in equity was less than satisfactory. Pollock also sought, in dealing with both law and equity, to consider matters of doubt and difficulty in contract law. Mistake was singled out as an area in which such consideration would be made.[70]

Pollock as Will Theorist

An intellectual influence is a difficult matter to ascertain with certainty. It can take many forms and it does not necessarily dictate a complimentary development within the system influenced. Savigny's influence upon Pollock's *Principles of Contract Law* is both apparent and elusive.[71] It is apparent in Pollock's statement that 'on points of Roman law (and to a considerable extent, indeed, on the principles it has in common with our own), I have consulted and generally followed Savigny's great work',[72] and it is also apparent throughout the first edition of his treatise in both text and footnotes. It is elusive in that it is an influence of uncertain extent: Pollock did not adopt Savigny's theories in their entirety, sometimes because they conflicted with the common law, other times through simple neglect. Because Pollock 'borrowed' from other sources and authors in addition to Savigny it is often hard to attribute a particular idea distinctly to Savigny as opposed to other German or even French jurists. Pollock was also influenced by Pothier; both directly through his treatises and indirectly through Pothier's reception into

[68] Leake's treatise on contract formed a partial exception: SM Leake, *The Elements of the Law of Contracts* (London, Stevens and Sons, 1867).

[69] F Pollock, *Principles of Contract At Law and in Equity: Being a Treatise on the General Principles Concerning the Validity of Agreements* (London, Stevens and Sons, 1876) v.

[70] ibid.

[71] This is not a subject which has been analysed in detail in English legal history nor have German scholars analysed the impact that Savigny exerted upon the development of English law. Reimann has considered the influence of Savigny in America and characterised it as both 'obvious and obscure at the same time': M Reimann, 'The Historical School Against Codification: Savigny, Carter, and the Defeat of the New York Civil Code' (1989) 37 Am J Comp L 95, 95.

[72] Pollock (n 69) viii.

English cases and through the Indian Contract Act 1872. The influence of Savigny was also one which diminished in subsequent editions of Pollock's *Principles*.

One of the greatest influences Savigny had upon Pollock was will theory and its conception of mistake. That there was nothing new about the will theory probably assisted Pollock in his adoption of portions of Savigny. When he sought to illustrate Savigny's theory, he was able to isolate within English cases instances in which the will theory was applied, particularly as Pollock sought to confine himself wherever possible to 'citing the latest and best authorities',[73] authorities which would have been decided after the writings of Pothier had become available to English judges and jurists at the beginning of the nineteenth century.

Pollock began his treatise in chapter one by considering the nature of contract, to define what a contract was. He stated the opinion that previous definitions of contract in English law books were unsatisfactory because no one definition was enough. A series of definitions was required and Pollock referred his readers to the definition supplied by the Indian Contract Act 1872, an Act greatly influenced by the work of Pothier. Pollock then plunged almost immediately into Savigny's consideration of *Vertrag*, agreement in its broadest sense. As we have seen, Savigny conceived of a contract as the union of several people who concurrently declare their will, which determines their legal relations. Without agreement, there was no contract. In addition, each had to be aware of the agreement; their wills had to be mutually declared and the will to form legal relations was the purpose of the people coming together.[74] Pollock accepted that an agreement was more than contract and that an agreement existed where two or more persons concur in expressing a common intention so that the rights and duties of those persons are thereby determined.[75] Pollock, following Savigny's lead, analysed contract on the basis of the contract of sale. Five elements were required: first, two or more parties; second, a distinct and shared intention; third, that each party was aware of the intention to agree; fourth, that the intentions must be directed towards legal consequences; and fifth, those consequences must be such as to confer rights or impose duties on the parties themselves. Having considered Savigny's *Vertrag*, Pollock returned without comment to the Indian Contract Act's definitions of contract. In addition to this somewhat odd mélange of theories, Pollock was not faithful in his reproduction of Savigny's theory. Savigny had concluded with a definition of contract after having considered the constituent components of will and the declaration of the will and the effect of mistake or duress upon these.[76] Pollock, however, followed the more traditional English approach, derived from Pothier, of considering the nature of an agreement as consensus and then examining the factors which disrupted consent.

[73] ibid, v.
[74] Savigny (n 18) §140, §308.
[75] Pollock (n 69) 2.
[76] Savigny (n 18) §114, §115, §137.

Pollock and Mistake

Having accepted Savigny's will theory, Pollock was bound to also accept that certain factors operating upon the declaration of the will could disrupt an apparent agreement. He agreed with Savigny that mistake did not itself affect the validity of the contracts but that it may be such as to prevent any real agreement from being formed. Pollock also followed Savigny's lead in finding that where the mistake prevented any real agreement from being formed, the contract was void, and in English law this was both at law and in equity.[77] Pollock, unfortunately, created something of a Frankenstein's monster, however, by introducing Pothieresque concepts of mistake preventing consent. Pollock considered mistake several chapters after he had considered the nature of contract, but he expressly linked his mistake chapter to the earlier chapter.[78] He had previously dealt with how the consent of the parties was ascertained and how this consent had been expressed. He turned now to those conditions which could remove consent and the first to be dealt with was mistake. He expressed difficulty in dealing with mistake 'the whole topic is surrounded with a great deal of confusion in our books',[79] although he could account for some of the difficulties in English law.[80] Given that there was an imperfect acceptance, if any, of mistake in the common law and that the dealings with mistake in equity were largely directed around particular remedies, it is no surprise that he found the subject confusing. It was also difficult to ascertain the effect of a misapprehension in equity.

Pollock acknowledged that some of the difficulties had been imported from the Roman law[81] and possibly for this reason felt himself justified in resort to Savigny, whom he believed had cleared the confusion in a 'masterly' manner.[82] Pollock was too meticulous a thinker and too deferential to the common law to completely adopt Savigny and recognised that not all of Savigny's solutions would be applicable to English law, which had already adopted a contrary position. It is wrong to think that Pollock was unaware of the differences between the civil law and the common law; he was aware of at least some of these differences[83] and consciously

[77] ibid.

[78] Pollock (n 69) 355.

[79] ibid, 357.

[80] Pollock was of the view that many of the difficulties in English law could be accounted for under one of three grounds: (1) the confusion of proximate with remote causes of legal consequences, because there had been a confusion of cases where the mistake had consequences of its own with those in which the mistake determined the presence of some other condition; (2) the assertion of propositions as general rules which ought to be taken with reference only to the particular effects of mistakes in particular classes of cases; and (3) the omission to assign an exact meaning to 'ignorance of law' in cases where the distinction between ignorance of fact and of law is material: Pollock (n 69) 358.

[81] ibid.

[82] ibid.

[83] See, eg, Pollock's admonition not to overlook the fundamental differences between the common law and the civil law in the passing of property in the sale of goods: Pollock (n 69) 394, fn (b). He referred his readers to C Blackburn, *A Treatise on the Effect of the Contract of Sale* (London, William Benning and Co., 1845) pt 2, ch 3. In this work the author (later to become Lord Blackburn) devoted this chapter to careful explanation on how the civil law differed in principle from the common law and

attempted to deal with these differences in his text. Pollock, however, also recognised that it was convenient to follow the 'arrangement and detail' of the subject according to the English practice. Pollock, as we shall see, also felt himself constrained by what he regarded as the already established English law regarding mistake. He was to find, and find himself bound, more by constraints imposed by law than by equity. In short, while there was a Savignian influence in the adoption of a mistake theory and in the conception of this theory, and to some extent in the development of it, this influence was tempered with a countervailing influence found within the English case law. While the resulting product created substantial and enduring difficulties in English law, it must not be forgotten that it did encourage English lawyers to look at law as a rational and coherent whole.

Orderly classification was critical to Pollock's legal science and he divided his chapter on mistake into three parts: first, mistake in general; second, mistake as excluding true consent; and third, mistake in expressing true consent. While the division of his chapter hints at Savigny's distinction between the will and declarations of the will, the actual treatment of the English law was not faithful to this distinction. It probably could not be. Pollock agreed with Savigny that consent formed under a vitiating factor was still consent; one had to look carefully to determine whether or not a contract arose despite this factor. While Savigny was far more precise in his treatment of mistake than Pothier had been, it really was not possible to entirely structure English contract law around his theories. The common law had already provided means for dealing with elements Savigny recognised as vitiating, such as fraud and duress. The result was that when Pollock considered those instances in which vitiating factors were present, he considered that the effect of each of these factors was dependent upon whether the state of mind created in one of the contracting parties by this vitiating factor was induced by the other party. Thus misrepresentation, fraud, coercion and undue influence were vitiating factors, but they were factors induced by the other contracting party, and the effect was thus to create a contract voidable at the option of the innocent party. Pollock distinguished between the mistake of one party caused by the fraud of another party and a mistake in which fraud was absent. Where there was the latter situation of mistake without fraud or misrepresentation, in other words, without the inducement of the other, then the contract was void. There was no question of the innocent party electing to affirm it; although Pollock was of the view that the innocent party could, upon discovery of the mistake, enter into a binding contract by continuing with his performance.[84] While Pollock followed Savigny's lead in finding that where mistake prevented a real agreement from being formed, the contract was void both at law and in equity, the invidious results which could occur in commercial practice do not seem to have occurred to him. Less problematic was where the mistake occurred in the expression of the

the enormous practical consequences that arose from these differences; the author was of the opinion that the differences have 'not been always kept in sight by the English judges': ibid, 171.

[84] Pollock (n 69) 404.

agreement, for here the common law, primarily through equity, provided a recognised form of relief in either rectification or interpretation.

After a lengthy outline of his topic, Pollock moved on to an examination of when relief would be given for a mistake in the common law. From this, he derived the general proposition that mistake on its own was of little consequence and not every mistake did vitiate a transaction (a conclusion Savigny himself had reached). Mistake was only of consequence in four classes of cases: (1) 'where mistake is such as to exclude real consent, and so—not avoid the contract but-prevent the formation of a contract, there the seeming agreement is void';[85] (2) where mistake occurred in the expression of a real consent, courts of equity would remedy the defect; (3) a renunciation of rights in general terms was not understood to include those rights of which the party was unaware (although this was really an instance of the second class); and (4) money paid under a mistake of fact could be recovered back. Of these four classes of cases, only the fourth class provided a real exception to the basic rule that mistake, in and of itself, had no consequence. Pollock confined his examination of mistake to mistakes of fact rather than of law for the general rule in English law was that relief was not given for a mistake of law.[86] While he thought that Savigny was right to state that legal consequences could attach to a mistake of law, the English position was too settled to change.[87] Two principal weaknesses present in Pollock's conception of mistake are that he not only failed to satisfactorily distinguish between fraud and mistake, but he also never managed to define with precision when a mistake was operative.

Where Mistake was Effective

Pollock conceived of two instances in which mistake had an effect in contract: first, mistake which prevented true consent (and in which no contract could be formed); and second, mistake in the expression of a true consent (and in which circumstances equity, and sometimes law, would operate to facilitate the expression of this true consent). Pollock was, throughout the remainder of his chapter, to deal with law and equity together. In his concern to unite the two bodies of jurisprudence into one on the basis of fundamental normative principles, Pollock did not engage with the question of the state of English law. He was not concerned to establish the role that mistake had played in courts of equity nor its tenuous existence in law. There was no attempt to examine either the equitable treatment of mistake, or the interface between courts of law and equity in instances where there had been a

[85] ibid, 367.

[86] ibid, 368.

[87] Pollock considered that while there was much to be said, in resolving the issue of whether or not to bar a mistake of law on the basis that citizens must be presumed to know the law to facilitate the administration of justice, hardship and injustice followed such a rule. He opined that there was much to be said for Savigny's treatment of the matter, which was to exclude relief for mistakes brought about by the negligence of a party, and ignorance of the law was presumed to be a form of negligence: ibid, 367.

factual misapprehension. The result was that the equitable treatment of mistake was sometimes overlooked, sometimes misunderstood and sometimes marginalised in Pollock's treatment of it. Pollock was never very keen on equity. In his view, the technical language of the equity jurists left much to be desired; in particular, there were too many words and phrases imbued with a mysterious value which did not correspond to any definite ideas.[88] The result was that Pollock's treatment of equitable cases concerned with mistake was far from accurate.

Mistake which Excluded True Consent

A court could only ascertain a common intention of the parties from an adequate expression of it. Where the parties each communicated different intentions there was no such expression. Pollock provided two circumstances where this occurred, and where it did the result was that 'we may say that the agreement is nullified by fundamental error'.[89] The first circumstance was where there was a variance between the offer of one party and the acceptance of another. One party meant one thing, the other party another thing. When this occurred there was no adequate expression of common intention and thus no contract.[90] In short, 'their minds never met . . . and the forms they have gone through are inoperative'.[91] In the second circumstance the apparent expression of common intention did not really exist because it was founded upon a common error which prevented, in substance, the common intention. Here, the common intention stood or fell upon the assumption upon which it was founded: 'an assumption made by both parties as to some matter of fact essential to the agreement'.[92] Where the assumption was wrong, the intention of the parties was from the outset incapable of taking effect. Pollock's quandary lay in adequately defining when a fact was sufficiently essential to realise a common intention.

Surprisingly, given his admiration for Savigny, Pollock did not adopt Savigny's treatment of an *error in substantia* to clarify this point. Savigny had taken particular care in his treatment of *error in substantia*, for such an error was an anomaly in his doctrinal edifice; he retained it out of respect for the Roman sources.[93] The passage in the Digest[94] had caused considerable consternation to earlier commentators. The passage seemed to be concerned with situations where a thing is thought to be one thing but is actually, in the sense of its essential physical properties, something else. Savigny approached the matter from a pragmatic perspective and did

[88] Pollock, 'The Science of Case Law', reprinted in AL Goodhart (ed), *Jurisprudence and Legal Essays* (London, Macmillan & Co, 1961) 184.

[89] ibid, 374. Pollock was keen to distinguish these instances where the result of the mistake was a nullity from those cases where the mistake was a ground for relief.

[90] ibid, 372.

[91] ibid, 373. Pollock found support for this position in s 13 of the Indian Contract Act 1872 and the decision of Hannen J in *Smith v Hughes* (1871) LR 6 QB 597.

[92] Pollock (n 88) 373.

[93] Zimmermann (n 37) 617.

[94] D.18.1.1.

not concern himself with the physical material of the subject matter. Savigny recognised that a contract may be void if the mistake relates to a substantial quality of the object in question. Where the substantial quality is such that it removes an object from one class of things and places it in the class of another object characterised by the utility of the object; the mistake as to this quality was an *error in substantia.*[95] Savigny reached this position by comparing four different instances considered by the Roman jurists in which the consent of the buyer could not be assumed.[96] By so strictly limiting when an *error in substantia* arose, Savigny devised a doctrine in which the demands of business were protected.[97]

Having ignored Savigny and having declined a precise definition of an essential fact, Pollock sought first to curtail the ambit of such a mistake in two ways. The first was that the 'error must be common to both parties'.[98] It is unclear from where Pollock derived this requirement that the error be common to the parties. It did not appear to come directly from either Savigny or Pothier. It may be that Pollock derived it from the Pothier-based Indian Contract Act 1872, which set out the requirement of a 'meeting of the minds'. Unusually, he did not provide a reference to English case law to support this requirement in any of the following nine editions of his treatise. The second requirement was that the misapprehension had to be one of great significance, a fundamental error. In an attempt to define when an error was fundamental, Pollock reverted to the common law treatment of a bargain. He considered that a mistake would be sufficiently important where it was 'as if the parties had made an agreement expressly conditional on the existence at the time of the supposed state of facts: which state of facts not existing, the agreement destroys itself'.[99]

If a fundamental error resulted in a void contract, the nature of a fundamental error and the means by which it is established are critical. Pollock made no attempt to establish an overarching set of criteria which defined such a fundamental error and, instead, explored fundamental error by examining different factual instances of fundamental error. In the construction of his analysis, Pollock borrowed from Savigny these instances of fundamental error. Pollock then proceeded to provide his readers with English cases which illustrated these kinds of fundamental error and the principles underlying each kind of error. That many of these cases had

[95] R Zimmermann, *The Law of Obligations, Roman Foundations of the Civilian Tradition* (Cape Town, Wetton and Johannesburg, Juta & Co Ltd, 1990) 617. Zimmermann relies upon Savigny (n 18) §137.

[96] The example of vinegar sold as wine was explicable not on the ground of value, but a difference in kind which determined the material mistake (*wesentlicher Irrthum*). Where the buyer thinks a female slave is a male slave, the sale will be void. The reason the sale is void has nothing to do with an abstract idea of substance or of comparative value but because a male slave undertakes different work than a female slave. Male slaves and female slaves are distinct lines in the slave trade: male slaves are in a different commercial category from female slaves. In contrast, a mistake as to the gender of a horse would be irrelevant because the use of a horse is not dependent upon its gender and thus a mistake as to gender would be irrelevant.

[97] Zimmermann (n 38) 617.

[98] Pollock (n 69) 373.

[99] Zimmerman (n 38) 617.

been decided in situations where there was no factual misapprehension or, in other instances where there was a factual misapprehension, they had nevertheless been decided on completely different legal grounds than mistake did not seem to bother Pollock. He may have felt justified in the former circumstances by drawing upon the cases since they were based on an underlying normative principle running throughout contract law, and such use might not have appeared bizarre or irrational. In the latter circumstances, Pollock may well have regarded these decisions as manifestations of a theory rather than the basis of them. By reconsidering these cases of factual misapprehension as instances of the doctrine of mistake in law, Pollock worked to disguise the substantive nature of the legal problem that had faced the earlier courts.

Categories of Fundamental Er ror

Error as to the Nature of the Transaction

Pollock divided the different instances of fundamental error into three categories: error as to the nature of the transaction; error as to the person of the other party to the contract; and error as to the subject-matter of the agreement. In the first of these categories, Pollock relied upon a series of cases starting with *Thoroughgood*'s case,[100] which had established that where a deed was not read to an illiterate or a blind man, or the effect of the deed was misrepresented, he was not bound by the deed. Pollock acknowledged that when these cases arose in equity, it was often difficult to separate them from fraud to determine 'was there any consenting mind at all?'.[101] While Pollock offered his readers no guidance as to how to separate mistake from fraud in these cases he had no doubt as to the similarity of principles applied by courts of law and equity to this question. Where there was a fundamental error as to the nature and the substance of the transaction, or where there was an error as to the legal character of the transaction, there was no agreement and thus no transaction.

Error as to the Person

Pollock referred to both Savigny[102] and Pothier[103] when he stated that where there was an error as to the person of the other party to the contract, such an error prevented any real agreement where the identity was important to the other contractor.[104] In most cases, knowledge of the identity of the other party was irrelevant and the contractor was indifferent as to the identity of the other party. Where, however, a party intended to deal with a definite person, this intention

[100] (1584) 2 Co Rep 9, 76 ER 408.

[101] Pollock (n 69) 376.

[102] Savigny (n 18) vol 3, p 269, in which Savigny dealt with the loan of money in which the borrower was mistaken as to the identity of the lender.

[103] RJ Pothier, *A Treatise on the Law of Obligations or Contracts*, trs WD Evans (London, A Strahan, 1806; reprinted Clark, NJ, The Law Book Exchange Ltd, 2003) §19.

[104] Pollock's views on mistake as to identity are examined more thoroughly in ch 8.

could not take effect unless that person was the party. The intention could not take effect where another was substituted. Pollock found common law support for this principle in *Boulton v Jones*[105] and *Mitchell v Lapage.*[106] While both cases involved a factual misapprehension of identity, neither established that a contract was void for such a mistake. The later case of *Boulton v Jones* had been decided, in part, with an eye to Pothier,[107] but the immediate concerns of the judges had been with agency and set-offs. Pollock concluded his discussion with an examination of various instances in the common law and equity in which identity was of relevance (satisfaction of the debt by a stranger, assignment of contracts, rights founded on personal confidence and agency) although none of these instances was concerned with the effect of a mistake as to identity on the formation of a contract.

Error as to the Subject Matter

Pollock divided his third fundamental error, as to the subject matter of the contract, into two sub-categories: first, an error as to the specific thing supposed to be the subject matter of the contract; and second, an error as to some aspect of the subject matter. The essential question in both sub-categories was: 'it is admitted that the party intended to contract in this way for something; but is this thing that for which he intended to contract?'[108] This rule was, for Pollock, fully explained in *Kennedy v Panama etc Mail Company.*[109] In his consideration of the meaning of these forms of error, he was keen to note the recognition of these instances in both law and equity, but without considering the differences between these two bodies of law. Where there was an error as to the specific thing (*error in corpore*) there was no contract, as could be seen from both the cases at law[110] and the cases in equity.[111] The difficulty that Pollock did not address is that there is little indication in the cases themselves that they had been decided on the grounds he advanced. What they do show is a different set of rules dealing with factual misapprehensions and a different system of dealing with the inter-relationship between law and equity. Once again, Pollock employed legal cases which involved factual misapprehensions but did not decide a doctrine of mistake.[112] The equitable cases relied upon by Pollock were decided on the basis of a mistake, but not a doctrine of mistake which prevented consent. Mistake in equity, in certain circumstances,

105 (1857) 2 H & N 564, 27 LJ Ex 117, 21 Jur 1156.

106 (1816) Holt 253, 171 ER 233. Pollock's grandfather had been counsel for the defence in the action.

107 See C MacMillan, 'Rogues, Swindlers and Cheats—the development of mistake of identity in English contract law' (2004) 64 *Cambridge Law Journal* 711, 716.

108 Pollock (n 69) 386.

109 (1867) LR 2 QB 580.

110 *Raffles v Wichelhaus* (1864) 2 H & C 906; 159 ER 375; *Phillips v Bistolli* (1824) 2 B & C 511; 107 ER 474.

111 *Malins v Freeman,* (1837) 2 Keen 25, 48 ER 537; *Calverly v Williams* (1790) 1 Ves Jun 210; 30 ER 306.

112 *Raffles v Wichelhaus* (n 110) was one that met the needs of the treatise writers regarding mistake, but a case in which there were no reasons for judgment given. *Phillips v Bistolli* (n 110) was a case in which the determination of whether or not a mistake had occurred was left to the jury.

were grounds upon which the court would not order a specific performance of the contract but would leave the other party to his remedy at law, namely damages.[113] These cases did not state that the apparent contract was void. Unsurprisingly, some of the equitable cases did not appear to support Pollock at all: those cases were rationalised on other grounds[114] or simply stated without any attempt to explain their relationship to the general principle.[115]

Pollock then turned to examine instances of fundamental error as to the kind, quantity or quality of the thing contracted for. 'A material error as to the kind, quantity, quality of a subject-matter which is contracted for by a generic description . . . may make the agreement void, either because there was never any real consent of the parties to the same thing, or because the thing or state of things to which they consented does not exist or cannot be realized.'[116] Pollock then followed his usual practice in isolating these instances within English cases; it was difficult, however, to find English cases that stated these principles as he would have liked. Pollock settled, instead, for finding a case which factually demonstrated the sort of error he was concerned with and either ignored the fact that it had been decided on a different basis or pointed out that although the point of principle he wished to assert had not come up, if it had, the case would have been decided in accordance with it.[117] At times, Pollock found a case which illustrated his point on the facts, but was decided on a different basis, a matter which he then acknowledged. An example can be seen in his treatment of a mistake as to kind which rendered the apparent contract void. He chose *Thornton v Kempster*,[118] a case in which the parties had not agreed as to the kind of hemp to be sold under the contract, but the case itself was decided on the basis that the parties had never agreed 'that the one should buy and the other accept the same thing' rather than the more general principle Pollock asserted. Pollock was forced to comment that it was 'perhaps rather the case of a variance in terms between the proposal and the acceptance'[119] It is odd that he resisted the opportunity to position the case, in Savignian terms, as one where the inner will of the parties had not matched the exterior manifestation of that will. Pollock sought here, as elsewhere, to unify the effect of mistake upon a contract at law and in equity. Thus he ignored the procedural context in which courts of equity operated: namely that their relief was granted or denied in the knowledge that there might still be a claim at law. Instead, he took the finding of a court of equity that mistake operated to provide relief and then stated that the agreement would have been void at law.[120]

[113] *Malins v Freeman* (n 111) [35] per Lord Langdale.

[114] See, eg, the treatment given to *Bloomer v Spittle* (1872) LR 13 Eq 427, *Harris v Pepperell* (1867) LR 5 Eq 1, *Garrard v Frankel* (1862) 30 Beav 961, 54 ER 961, discussed in Pollock (n 69) 388–89.

[115] See, eg, the treatment of *Dacre v Gorges* (1825) 2 S & S 454, 57 ER 420, discussed in Pollock (n 69) 389.

[116] Pollock (n 69) 391.

[117] See, eg, his treatment of *Henkel v Pape* (1870) LR 6 Ex 7 in Pollock (n 69) 391–92.

[118] (1814) 5 Taunt 786, 128 ER 901.

[119] Pollock (n 69) 391.

[120] *Webster v Cecil* (1861) 30 Beav 62, 54 ER 512, discussed in Pollock (n 69) 392–93. The defendant had mistakenly set the wrong sum for property he offered to sell and the plaintiff accepted this

In his dealing with mistakes as to a quality of the subject matter of the contract, Pollock sought to incorporate both Savigny and the authority of the English cases. The result was not a happy one. Although he did not apparently intend such a result, Pollock created an extremely restrictive ambit for such a mistake. A mistake as to quality raises particular problems because it is clear that the party has, in one sense, obtained what they bargained for. There is a very real risk of upsetting transactions and the contractual allocation of risks by avoiding a contract for a mistake as to quality. Savigny, as we have seen, sought to limit this in his consideration of an *error in substantia* by limiting it to attributes that placed the thing in one commercial category, whereas, absent that attribute, the thing would be in another category. The common law, to the extent it had considered this at all under the heading of mistake, insisted that the mistake be a bilateral one shared by both the parties.[121] Pollock postulated this fundamental error as to quality as follows:

> sometimes, even when the thing which is the subject-matter of an agreement is specifically ascertained, the agreement may be avoided by material error as to some attribute of the thing. For some attribute which the thing in truth has not may be a material part of the description by which the thing was contracted for. If this is so, the thing as it really is, namely without that quality, is not that to which the common intention of the parties was directed, and the agreement is void. An error of this kind will not suffice to make the transaction void unless—
>
> (1) It is such that according to the ordinary course of dealing and use of language the difference made by the absence of the quality wrongly supposed to exist amounts to a difference in kind;
> (2) and the error is also common to both parties.[122]

Strangely, Pollock was cognisant of the different treatment given to an error as to quality between the common law and the civil law, but thought that 'the whole of Savigny's admirable exposition of so-called error in *substantia* deserves careful study',[123] and that the primary differences between the legal systems lay in the conclusions in detail. Such differences ought not to 'affect the usefulness and importance of the general analogies'.[124] It does not seem to have occurred to him that different conclusions were reached because different principles and considerations were applied in reaching those conclusions. The common law was concerned that an objective standard prevail and that the reasonable expectations of the non-mistaken party be protected. As we shall see, this formed an underlying

mistaken offer. As soon as the defendant realised his mistake, he informed the plaintiff of it. In the circumstances, Romilly MR refused to order a specific performance of the agreement and compel performance of the agreement where the mistake was clearly proved and the land was undervalued in the mistaken offer. Instead, the plaintiff could bring such action at law as he was advised. For Pollock, however, 'it is submitted . . . that the agreement was void at law'. He does not reveal the basis upon which such a submission could be made.

121 *Smith v Hughes* (n 91).

122 Pollock (n 69) 393.

123 ibid, 394 fn (b).

124 ibid.

basis to the decision in *Smith v Hughes*[125] (1871). In addition, the common law had largely dealt with questions of quality on the basis of the terms of the contract: if the seller warranted a non-existent quality, damages lay for breach; absent a warranty, *caveat emptor* applied and the buyer bore the risk. Such an approach was completely opposite to the civilian. Different considerations applied in the common law where fraud was present and the law intervened because of the wrongdoing. The common law was less concerned with the preoccupation of the civilians as to the formation of the agreement and more concerned with interpreting the terms of the agreement. Equity, where it intervened in cases of mistake, was largely concerned with the conduct of the parties rather than the metaphysics of formation. In particular, Pollock seems not to have been aware of the problems in placing two checks upon the form of error into his postulation of an error as to quality. The first was the Savigny-inspired consideration that the quality define the subject matter, in itself a high threshold. The second was that the parties shared this mistake. This double limitation effectively prevented a case in which a mistake as to quality could succeed.

In dealing with a mistake as to quality, Pollock also sought to distinguish such a mistake from two other legal categories in the common law. The first was a warranty as to an attribute or a quality. Where the vendor had warranted that the good had such a quality, then the misapprehension as to the quality was not a fundamental error but a breach of contract on the part of the vendor which sounded in damages.[126] The contract stood. The second legal category was fraud. If the misapprehension was caused by the misdescription of one of the parties, the contract was voidable for fraud or misrepresentation.[127] Pollock was correct in the division of these two legal categories. What was awkward about his theory was the extent to which the two of them had previously dealt with most cases of factual misapprehension. Equally awkward was that in superimposing his newer theory of mistake over them, Pollock offered his readers scant guidance on how to distinguish a mistake from a material attribute (rendering the contract void) from a warranty or from fraud.[128]

Error as to the Existence of the Subject Matter

Finally, Pollock added another form of fundamental error which he had not outlined to his readers: an error as to the existence of the subject matter.[129] A contract was void if it related to a subject matter thought to exist which did not, but only in circumstances where the existence of the thing was presupposed as essential to the

[125] (n 91).
[126] ibid.
[127] ibid, 403–404.
[128] Readers were told that where there was a separate warranty as to a quality, the existence of such a warranty established that the warranty was not a condition or an essential part of the contract; ibid, 394. Less 'guidance' was offered as to how to distinguish mistake from misrepresentation or fraud although Pollock clearly recognised the similarities: ibid, 396–97.
[129] ibid, 397.

agreement. While 'no precise rule can be laid down . . . typical cases may be stated by way of illustration'.[130] No better form of illustrations could be found than those set out in the Indian Contract Act 1872[131] and Pollock then set these out, accompanied as always by a collection of case authorities which 'supported' the proposition.

Knowledge

A mistake, to be effective, needed to be a bilateral mistake. When there was ignorance on the part of one party and knowledge on the part of the other, different considerations applied. Here, Pollock followed *Smith v Hughes* in creating a narrow exception to his rule that mistake, to be effective, had to be bilateral. A unilateral mistake would avoid the contract where the party with knowledge knew that the second party without this knowledge lacked the knowledge and that the second party only intended to contract on the basis that the thing had the quality he ignorantly believed it to have.

Like Savigny, Pollock attempted to begin with general principles and move on to the particular applications of these principles. He dealt, at the outset, with the problem presented to all common law lawyers: how to square the essentially subjective nature of the will theory with the objective nature of English law. In Pollock's case, he ignored this in his treatise, but in a series of Indian lectures observed that it was not the inner thoughts of a party which were concerned with consent, but the outward acts of the party:

> As between man and man, the question is not, under normal conditions, what my inward thought or belief may have been. Rather it is what I have given another man just cause to expect of me. The law regards as my intention that intention which a reasonable man, in the given circumstances, would infer from my words or acts.[132]

Relief

Pollock concluded his discussion on mistake as affecting consent with an examination of the 'rights and remedies of [a] party to a void agreement'.[133] The remedy[134] was that the party could assert that the transaction was a nullity from the beginning and this right arose in various ways, depending upon the procedural position of the party. If the case was at law, a defendant pleaded that there was no agreement. A plaintiff who had paid money in performance of an apparent contract could recover his money in an action for money received; if he had not paid,

[130] ibid.

[131] s 20.

[132] Sir F Pollock, *The Law of Fraud, Misrepresentation and Mistake in British India* (Calcutta, Thacker, Spink & Co., 1894) 109.

[133] Pollock (n 69) 404.

[134] 'Remedy' was an odd choice for an author who was so scathingly critical as to what he saw as the unscientific remedial relief granted by courts of equity in cases of mistake.

he could resist paying by asserting that there was an absence of consideration. In equity, a defendant could resist the enforcement of any equitable right claimed under the transaction and as a plaintiff he could seek to have the transaction declared void. The thorny question of how, procedurally, to deal with mistake in law and in equity once the two bodies of law were administered by a single court after the Judicature Acts was not a question grasped by Pollock.

Mistake in Expressing Consent

Pollock's bifurcation of mistakes affecting consent and mistakes in expressing consent may have been inspired by Savigny's distinction between mistakes in the formation of the will and mistakes in the expression of the will. As we have seen, Savigny distinguished between the formation of the will and the declaration of the will. A contract was void only where the will and declaration of one party did not match that of another or where the will of one party did not match his declaration. Whether or not Pollock was so inspired, mistakes in expressing consent were seemingly similar to the equitable remedy of rectification. To a great extent, the last part of Pollock's chapter on mistake dealt with the traditional equitable relief for mistake, which Pollock almost invariably referred to as 'peculiar'. Pollock concerned himself with the case of parties who had formed a true consent unimpeded by mistake, but had mistakenly expressed this consent in terms which did not accurately represent their real intentions. In these instances, the law dealt with the situation in one of three ways: first, in those rules which were common to law and equity; second, in those 'peculiar' rules of construction in equity; and third, in a hodge-podge of 'peculiar' defences and remedies in equity.

In the first of these instances, courts of both equity and law would, without any special remedy, cure simple and obvious forms of mistaken expression by ordinary rules of construction. Where such construction did not apply, the rule was that 'greater regard is to be had to the clear intent of the parties than to any particular words which they may have used in the expression of their intent'.[135] Pollock's second instance of 'peculiar' rules of construction in equity involved general words, stipulations as to time and relief against penalties in which courts of equity could intervene to uphold the true intention of the parties, regardless of the manner in which they had expressed this intention. In his final instance of 'peculiar' defences and remedies in equity, Pollock considered the traditional equitable relief of refusing specific performance in instances where the written instrument did not accord with the intention of the parties, and the ability of a court of equity to rectify a mistaken expression of an agreement properly formed. Pollock at this point discussed briefly, in a paragraph, 'some cases of a rather peculiar kind'[136] which appeared to conflict with the rule already stated that the mistake had to be of both parties in

[135] Pollock (n 69) 407.

[136] ibid, 427. The cases were *Harris v Pepperell* (n 114), *Garrard v Frankel* (n 114) and *Bloomer v Spittle* (n 114).

order to rectify the instrument. These were those cases in which Romilly MR had allowed a party to reform an instrument on the ground that it did not conform with his intention and in which the court had granted the parties the option of either rescinding the agreement entirely or reforming it to express the agreement mistakenly thought to have been entered into. It will be observed by contemporary readers that these 'peculiar' cases were much the same as the approach of Lord Denning in his decision in *Solle v Butcher*.[137] Pollock appeared to have viewed the equitable cases as simply wrong. In 1894, Pollock, lecturing in India, gave a clearer insight into his views. He began his lecture on mistake by pointing out that historical causes had caused the word 'mistake' to be surrounded in English law 'with a kind of mysterious halo. Nay, more, it is possible to find in utterances of highly respected writers, and in judicial deliverances of English Vice-Chancellors, expressions which seem to ascribe to Mistake a kind of magical power enabling the Court to upset any transaction whatever.'[138] Pollock stated that it was best to forbear from any further reference to 'these loose and misleading phrases' and that the less 'an Indian student can hear about them the better'.[139]

The Changes in Pollock's *Principles*

Like Pollock himself, his treatise was enormously long-lived; he himself wrote a further nine editions and, following his death, Winfield produced three more editions. An essential question is the extent to which Pollock's theory, with the weaknesses discussed above, changed over this period from 1876 to 1950. The answer is astounding: it did not change.

That it did not change is all the more astounding when one considers the changes that Pollock made to his will theory of contract. It has been recognised that from the third edition of *Principles* the influence of Savigny began to wane.[140] The critical change came about in the first chapter, in which Pollock introduced his subject. In his third edition, Pollock almost entirely rewrote his first chapter dealing with definitions and the first conditions of contract. He explained that he had done so partly because of recent decisions and 'partly because the treatment of first principles appeared on revision to be in sundry respects inadequate'.[141] He had employed Savigny's concept of agreement (*Vertrag*), a concept which extended beyond contracts to all transactions based upon will, in his first two editions, and supplemented this with the definitions of contract found in the Indian

[137] [1950] 1 KB 671, [1949] 2 All ER 1107, 66 TLR (Pt 1) 448, [1949] EGD 346.

[138] Pollock (n 132) 108. Pollock delivered the Tagore Law Lectures of 1894.

[139] Pollock (n 132) 108.

[140] Kessler (n 17) 1070, and Duxbury (n 42) 194. Michele Graziadei in 'Changing Images of the Law in XIX Century English Legal Thought (The Continental Impulse)' in M Reimann (ed), *The Reception of Continental Ideas in the Common Law World 1820–1920* (Berlin, Duncker & Humblot, 1993) explores a general move of late nineteenth-century English and American jurists away from the influence of Roman law.

[141] F Pollock, *Principles of Contract Law: Being a Treatise on the General Principles Concerning the Validity of Agreements in the Law of England*,3rd edn (London, Stevens and Sons, 1881) vi.

Contract Act 1872. In his third edition, this disappeared. Pollock, his enthusiasm for Savigny only slightly dimmed, explained in an appendix that while Savigny's definition of agreement, and from this contract, was an admirable one, it should be confined to its own purposes and its own context. It had also occurred to Pollock that it might be inadvisable to apply Roman terminology to the common law. For the same reason, he was no longer content to adopt the Indian Contract Act 1872 to the same extent that he previously had.[142]

The result was that the focus in his first chapter moved away from contract as consensus, defined in relation to the will of the parties. For two editions, he was concerned to 'separate and analyse' the elements which must occur in the formation a contract. This was a somewhat circular exercise, beginning as it did with the statement that 'every agreement and promise enforceable by law is a contract'.[143] By the fifth edition, Pollock placed in his first chapter that which he had first considered in the introduction to his third edition:

> The law of contract may be described as the endeavour of the State, a more or less imperfect one by the nature of the case, to establish a positive sanction for the expectation of good faith which has grown up in the mutual dealings of men of average right-mindedness.[144]

Contract had transformed itself from the will of the parties to the protection of reasonable expectations.

What had happened to diminish the attraction of Savigny's light? A part of the answer lies in Pollock's realisation that contract law was a complex matter, not easily explained by use of the will theory alone.[145] Another part of the answer appears to lie in Holland's criticism of Savigny. Holland, a Professor at All Souls College, Oxford, considered Savigny's analysis of a contract. While Holland agreed with Savigny that the constituent elements of a contract were several parties, a mutual communication of agreement, and an intention to create legal relations, he was critical of Savigny's requirement that there be an agreement of the wills of the parties.

> Is it the case that a contract is not entered into unless the wills of the parties are really one? Must there be, as Savigny puts it, 'a union of several wills to a single, whole and undivided will?' Or should we not rather say that here, as elsewhere, the law looks, not at the will itself, but at the will as voluntarily manifested? When the law enforces contracts, it does so to prevent disappointment of well-founded expectations, which, though they usually arise from expressions truly representing intention, yet may occasionally arise otherwise.[146]

Holland stated that he put his view forward 'with some diffidence' because he expressed it against the current authority of, inter alia, Pollock and Anson, but

[142] ibid, App A.

[143] Pollock, *Principles of Contract Law: Being a Treatise on the General Principles Concerning the Validity of Agreements in the Law of England*, 4th edn (London, Stevens and Sons, 1885) 1.

[144] Pollock, *Principles of Contract Law: Being a Treatise on the General Principles Concerning the Validity of Agreements in the Law of England*, 5th edn (London, Stevens and Sons, 1889) 1, and 3rd edn (n 142) xx.

[145] Duxbury (n 42) 196.

[146] TE Holland, *The Elements of Jurisprudence*, 2nd edn (Oxford, Clarendon Press, 1882) 194.

noted that 'it is hard to see how it can be supposed that the true consensus of the parties is within the province of the law'.[147]

Yet another part of the answer lies in the fact that Pollock had discovered another bright light to whom he was attracted: Oliver Wendell Holmes. In 1881, Holmes published *The Common Law*.[148] Holmes recognised that the common law lacked an analytical foundation and was best explained as a historical and sociological phenomenon rather than a logical one. As he famously stated, 'the distinctions of the law are founded on experience, not logic'.[149] A particular focus for Holmes' criticism was the German theorists, notably Savigny. Holmes was among the first cognisant of the dangers of confusion that could arise from an indeliberate transfer of ideas from one legal system to another and was deeply sceptical of the task of imitating the German model within the common law.[150] Particularly in his dealing with contract law, Holmes attacked German legal formalism. Reimann has convincingly argued that such an attack was likely an oblique attack on Christopher Columbus Langdell, then the young scholar's Dean at Harvard Law School.[151] Langdell was a leading proponent of logic in the common law, and one who accepted the will theory into common law contract law. Holmes confided to Pollock that he thought Langdell's book on contract law 'a more misspent piece of marvellous ingenuity I never read, yet it is most suggestive and instructive'.[152] Holmes' polemic undoubtedly affected Pollock's perception of the common law generally, and contract law in particular.[153] While it cannot be established with certainty,[154] it seems likely that Holmes' attack upon the will theory had a particular resonance with Pollock. Early in 1881, Holmes forwarded a copy of his book to Pollock in the hope that it would receive attention in England.[155] Pollock had a deep respect for Holmes' work;[156] decades later he stated that 'Holmes has done for the Common Law [what] . . . Savigny did for modern Roman Law',[157] and it

[147] ibid, 195.

[148] OW Holmes, *The Common Law* (Boston, Little, Brown and Co., 1881).

[149] ibid, 312.

[150] MW Reimann, 'Holmes's *Common Law* and German Legal Science' in RW Gordon (ed), *The Legacy of Oliver Wendell Holmes, Jr* (Edinburgh, Edinburgh University Press, 1992) 90.

[151] ibid, 92–95.

[152] Holmes' reference to the work was in a letter to Pollock dated 10 April 1881: M DeW Howe (ed), *The Pollock–Holmes Letters* (London, Cambridge University Press, 1942) vol I, 17.

[153] He spent some considerable part of his introduction to the third edition of *Principles* discussing the work: Pollock (n 142) xi–xx.

[154] Pollock does not seem to have directly stated that he modified his opening chapter in *Principles* in relation to Holmes' work. Indeed, he states that he received a copy of *The Common Law* too late to make substantive amendments to his own third edition: ibid, xi. He had, however, received a copy of the book from Holmes early in 1881: Howe (n 152) 16. Pollock's letter, sent in response to Holmes' gift of the book, is missing: ibid.

[155] Howe (n 152) 16. Holmes' hopes were realised in Pollock's review in 51 *Saturday Review* 758 (11 June 1881). Pollock concentrated primarily upon Holmes' handling of tort, concluding that while he did not have space to consider his other subjects, that his research on contract dispelled many of the earlier obscurities: ibid, 759. There is no indication, however, that Holmes read Pollock's treatise: PJ Kelley, 'A Critical Analysis of Holmes's Theory of Contract' (1999–2000) 75 *Notre Dame Law Review* 1681, 1713.

[156] Cosgrove (n 42) 143.

[157] Sir F Pollock, '*Ad Multos Annos*' (1931) 31 Colum LR 349, 349.

influenced his own later work in both contract and tort.[158] Pollock himself observed in the introduction to his third edition that his views had changed once he had read Holmes' 'most acute and ingenious volume'.[159]

While it cannot be established with certainty, Holmes' work seems to have caused Pollock to back away from his will-based Savignian theory of contract as consent and to move towards Holmes' positivist view of contract. While Holmes recognised that the development of the law was logical, with each decision derived from prior precedents, it was in substance legislative rather than logical. Each judge faced with old precedents found new rules to justify those precedents.[160] Holmes examined contract through its antecedents and its consequences: contracts arose where there was a promise, followed by consideration: 'the root of the whole matter is the relation between reciprocal conventional inducement, each for the other, between consideration and promise'.[161] When the promised event failed to occur, the consequence was a court order to pay damages. Holmes rejected the entire concept of contract based upon will theory, 'the superfluous theory that contract is the qualified subjection of one will to another, a kind of limited slavery'.[162] Holmes regarded the adoption of a will theory in the common law of contract as a disastrous mistake, from which he must save his contemporaries.[163] Holmes' lectures on contract have been interpreted as a direct attack on that which Pollock speculated, namely Maine's evolutionary theory.[164] Pollock, who was at the beginning of a lifelong friendship with Holmes, seems to have accepted his influence here, as he had earlier with Savigny. It is curious that he did not mention it, either to Holmes or to the wider world. An explanation for this is that while Holmes' work changed Pollock's own perceptions of contract, this change did not result in an acceptance of Holmes' view. Pollock believed that he could not accept all of Holmes' theories and he could not reject those he did not accept on the ground that they were alien to the common law, a device he had employed in failing to accept some of Savigny's theories. Another explanation may lie in the fact that to change course in such an abrupt fashion would be to undermine his overall acceptance of Savigny, and this Pollock was not prepared to do. Instead, Pollock incorporated elements of Holmes' positivist, objective theory of contract into his

158 It has been observed that Pollock borrowed Holmes' categorisation of torts: Duxbury (n 42) 270.

159 Pollock, (n142) xi.

160 PJ Kelley, 'Oliver Wendell Holmes, Utilitarian Jurisprudence, and the Positivism of John Stuart Mill' (1985) 30 *American Journal of Jurisprudence* 189, 205. See, also, M DeW Howe, 'The Positivism of Mr Justice Holmes' (1951) 64 *Harvard Law Review* (Harv L Rev) 529, and the reply of HM Hart Jr, 'Holmes's Positivism—An Addendum' (1951) 64 Harv L Rev 929, with accompanying rejoinder by Howe.

161 Holmes (n 148) 293–94.

162 ibid, 300. He also rejected the definition in the Indian Contract Act 1872, s 2, a definition that Pollock was taken with.

163 See, eg, Reimann (n 9) 85. Reimann refers to the refutation of German legal science as a whole rather than simply will theory.

164 Kelley (n 155) 1716. Henry Maine had sought to explain the nature of legal development in Indo-European societies as one in which legal systems evolved from primitive to more sophisticated systems.

own[165] will-based theories. That the overall result was a disjointed affair did not seem to bother Pollock.[166]

Nowhere was this disjointed result more apparent than in relation to mistake. Holmes had dealt with mistake in *The Common Law*, finding that the apparent mistake cases were ones of 'dramatic circumstances' where the real problem was not the mistake but instances where the primary elements of the contract were not made out.[167] Thus, the case of *Raffles v Wichelhaus*[168] was one where each party had said a different thing;[169] *Smith v Hughes*[170] was really concerned with a situation in which, where one party knows that the other party assumes he uses a word in one sense rather than another, he will be bound to employ the first sense.[171] In other instances, the promise given would be meaningless where the terms of the supposed contract were contradictory in matters that went to the root of the contract.[172] In all of these cases, Holmes thought a subjectivist will theory to be irrelevant:

> there is no new principle which comes in to set aside an otherwise perfect obligation, but that in every such case there is wanting one or more of the first elements . . . either there is no second party, or the two parties say different things, or essential terms seemingly consistent are really inconsistent as used.[173]

While Pollock found attractions in Holmes' view and admired it as a 'thorough-going and concise' enunciation of the principles of contract law on a par with the enunciation that Pollock, guided by Savigny, had given to the principles of English law, he was unable to follow it. The sticking point, for Pollock, was that he could not agree with Holmes that fraud and misrepresentation ever rendered a contract void.[174] He also could not abandon his original consideration that the consequences that flowed from the misapprehension were dependent upon the knowledge of the person who had induced the misapprehension.[175] Pollock modified his view of contract in light of Holmes, but he could not modify his view of mistake.

In his original conception of contract, mistake, as dissensus, followed upon a state of contract, as consensus. When Pollock modified his conception of contract, and moved away from consensus, he not only left in his chapter on mistake but he left it virtually unchanged in every one of his subsequent editions of *Principles of*

[165] Pollock never was able to entirely reject the role of consent in contract, he merely subjugated it to a utilitarian view of the necessity of contract and the protection of reasonable expectations.
[166] While no one was to influence him as profoundly in his later editions, he was prone to reading new things and then simply inserting them into his treatise. This is particularly true of his later editions.
[167] Holmes (n 148) 308.
[168] (1864) 2 H & C 906; 159 ER 375.
[169] Holmes (n 148) 309.
[170] (n 91).
[171] Holmes (n 148) 310.
[172] ibid.
[173] ibid, 315.
[174] Pollock (n 142) xviii.
[175] ibid.

Contract. Nowhere in his first edition had he relied more upon Savigny than in regard to mistake, and, while he did prune many of his references to the master in his later editions, Savigny remained a dominant force in the mistake chapter. The chapter became a sort of intellectual orphan. As Pollock's interest in overseas legal development now looked across the Atlantic rather than to Germany, he did not keep himself abreast of German legal developments. He did not notice the irony when he commented favourably in a later edition that the German Basic Law had adopted a 'new and much simplified course on the whole matter. Any kind of "declaration of intention" is voidable on the grounds of fundamental error, even if the mistake is unilateral; but voidable only, and subject to the duty of compensating any party for damages incurred by relying on the validity of the act'.[176] Pollock had gone some way to placing part of the earlier German view of mistake into English law; once there, it proved impossible to remove. Future editions of *Principles* contained few substantive changes to the text; what additions were made were largely confined to footnotes. In his second edition, Pollock, post-Judicature Acts, necessarily removed the remaining divisions he had outlined between law and equity and varied accordingly his discussion of rights and remedies for mistake. Pollock's subsequent handling of mistake as to the person was odd in the extreme. He never did amend his chapter to base it upon the House of Lords' decision in *Cundy v Lindsay*[177] or even to discuss the case in the body of the text. He chose instead to confine such an eminent authority to a footnote. The footnote itself became increasingly crowded as Pollock spent several decades collecting subsequent decisions involving mistake of identity and re-examining them. Gradually he seemed to realise that the later cases were frauds,[178] although he resisted any revision of the topic for this would upset his original classification and this he was not prepared to do. The result was that the cases did not accord to the 'principles' upon which they were supposedly based.

One small set of changes Pollock did make in his subsequent editions was to obscure the remaining vestiges of the different treatment given to mistake at law and in equity. In his second edition, Pollock, post-Judicature Acts, necessarily removed the remaining divisions and altered his discussion of relief. He also reduced his consideration of equitable cases that had the effect of rendering a contract voidable upon terms. Following his fifth edition, these cases, of an 'anomalous character', largely disappeared from his treatise. By ignoring these cases, Pollock began the process of their disappearance.

Pollock was still writing treatises when the House of Lords decided *Bell v Lever Brothers.*[179] Privately, he wrote to Holmes that the decision was 'wrong in law . . . and I am sure is mischievous in fact as encouraging shifty people to say they

[176] *Principles of Contract: A Treatise on the General Principles Concerning the Validity of Agreements in the Law of England*, 8th edn (London, Stevens and Sons, 1911) 488.

[177] (1877–78) LR 3 App Cas 459; [1874–80] All ER Rep 1149; 26 WR 406; 47 LJ QB 481; (1878) 38 LT 573.

[178] Pollock (n 176), 474, in reference to *Gordon v Street* (1899) 2 KB 641.

[179] [1932] AC 161.

forgot the things it was their business to remember'.[180] Pollock discussed *Bell v Lever Brothers* within his category of a fundamental error concerned with a non-existent subject matter and expressed displeasure with the decision for several reasons. The first was the use of the term 'mutual mistake'. In a rather irritable aside he observed that 'the term "mutual mistake" has long been in common use to signify the fact of both parties holding and acting on the same erroneous belief. It is more correct to say "common".'[181] Second, the decision 'cannot be regarded as a satisfactory case; and I will even venture to hope that in the next generation our successors will put it on the shelf as one of those decisions on peculiar facts in which it is unsafe to put one's trust as settling any general principles'.[182] Third, Pollock vehemently disagreed with the finding that the mistake of Bell and Lever Brothers would not have mattered, for in this case 'the plaintiff company surely did not get anything like what it bargained for'.[183] Fourth, Lord Atkin's criterion could not be consistently applied 'without the aid of fine-drawn distinctions of a kind not desirable in matters of business'.[184] A final irony is Pollock's inability to discern the extent to which his own work had influenced Lord Atkin's decision.

Frederick Pollock died, aged 91, in 1937. He never did amend or revise his chapter on mistake. There are indications that while he had hoped to reconsider *Principles of Contract* as a whole, he became very busy writing other treatises, lecturing, and editing both the *Law Reports* and *The Law Quarterly Review*. A second reason for the lack of reconsideration is that most contract theorists of his era clung to a version of the will theory which necessitated a doctrine of mistake which vitiated this will. There was no countervailing ideological challenge to stimulate Pollock to develop another theory. A further reason is that the courts did not produce a decision greatly at odds with Pollock's theory of mistake until *Phillips v Brooks*[185] in 1919. By the time *Bell v Lever Brothers* was decided Pollock's age prevented him from reconsidering the matter as a whole. His *Principles of Contract* continued after his death, at the publisher's request, with his friend PH Winfield producing three further editions, the last in 1950. The importance of the treatise can be seen in the fact the publishers thought it desirable to produce an updated version. While Winfield introduced certain structural changes to the treatise, mistake remained largely unchanged. It thus ended where it began; replete with theoretical contradictions and largely 'supported' by cases decided on other grounds.

The internal inconsistencies, conceptual vagaries and the distortions worked upon the existing legal and equitable treatment of mistake would not have mattered

[180] Howe (n 152) 306. Holmes himself did not seem overly concerned about the case; aged 91, his reply was that 'I only desire repose'.

[181] *Principles of Contract: A Treatise on the General Principles Concerning the Validity of Agreements in the Law of England*, 10th edn (London, Stevens and Sons, 1936) 443.

[182] ibid, 498.

[183] ibid. It is interesting to speculate as to whether the mistake would have qualified under Savigny's formulation for an *error in substantia*; reasoning by analogy, it can be said that the release of a supposed claim to compensation is of a different commercial category altogether than the release of an actual claim to compensation.

[184] ibid.

[185] [1919] 2 KB 243.

if Pollock had not been viewed as the pre-eminent contract lawyer of his day. As Duxbury has pointed out, Pollock's unique position as editor of the *Law Reports*, also editor of *The Law Quarterly Review*, and the writer of a proliferation of treatises, gave Pollock an inordinate influence over the shape of English law. Something of the regard in which he was held by lawyers can be seen in Lord Wright's statement that 'the writings of a lawyer like Pollock, constantly cited in the Courts and quoted by the judges, are entitled to claim a place under his category of unwritten law, even in a system like ours which does not normally seek its law from institutional writers'.[186] For Lord Wright, Pollock's *Principles of Contract* was 'a legal classic and heralds a new period of English study . . . Pollock's book was for students of principles and legal thinkers'.[187] An author held in such light had the ability to disseminate a theory which was alien to the law he wrote about.

The theory that Pollock provided to the common law was a difficult one. He had blended the subjective approaches of Pothier with the objective approaches of Savigny, apparently without realising differences in the theories. Various common law concerns, such as objectivity and the protection of reasonable expectations, were built into Pollock's theory. The theory was difficult, if not impossible, to apply satisfactorily to problems. Worse, by his third edition, Pollock had abandoned his overall theory that contract was based upon consensus. Mistake remained, while the reason for it had disappeared. The irony was that Pollock had sought, in part, to explain contract law on a coherent basis: the task proved elusive. Apart from these larger theoretical difficulties, a further problem was that Pollock supported his conception of mistake with cases decided on different bases. The unique basis of the equitable cases was ignored, as were those cases that did not fit within Pollock's theory. In deciding that the effect of a mistake was to render the contract void, Pollock created a powerful disincentive for courts to find an operative mistake.

Sir William Anson and the Principles of the English Law of Contract

The other influential English treatise writer of the nineteenth century was Sir William Anson. Anson, like Pollock, was of a generation who found their initial introduction to the learning of law difficult. Anson matriculated from Balliol College, Oxford, and having read classics was elected to a fellowship at All Souls College. He then went into the chambers of the great special pleader, Thomas Chitty. He described his experiences thus: 'I learned nothing, and as I knew nothing to begin with, and was never taught anything, the result is not surprising'.[188]

[186] Lord Wright, 'In Memoriam' (1937) 53 LQR 12, 13.

[187] ibid, 15.

[188] HH Henson (ed), *A Memoir of the Right Honourable Sir William Anson* (Oxford, Clarendon Press, 1920) 18.

From Chitty's chambers, Anson went to become a pupil of Alfred Thesiger, whom he revered and under whom he flourished. Anson practised at the Bar for a brief period before his father died suddenly in a railway accident. Anson, the eldest of ten children, succeeded to the baronetcy and was suddenly placed at the head of his family and was 'compelled to shoulder the burden of large responsibilities'.[189] Anson managed these responsibilities by becoming an Oxford academic; he was elected to the Vinerian Readership in English Law in 1874. He took an active part in the revival of the study of law at Oxford.

He published the first edition of his *Principles of the English Law of Contract* in 1879;[190] the work is one of the most successful common law books ever written. Dicey wrote that no writer 'ever published a work more useful for the man just beginning his legal studies than Anson's *Principles of the English Law of Contract*'.[191] The book was written because the School of Jurisprudence in Oxford had introduced the subject of contract law in 1877 and the teachers felt a need for a book to which they could direct their students. Anson, considered by Dicey to be 'the best teacher of English Law to be found in Oxford from 1874 to 1898',[192] wrote his treatise as a guide to students in an age in which they had few guides. His intended readership was students and their teachers. His work was thus concise, clearly written, thorough in its coverage and with a minimum of cases: 'the special virtue of the book lies in its precisely meeting the wants of a student who begins reading the law of contract'.[193] Anson took great care in the arrangement and proportion of his subject; his care was rewarded by frequent and continuous later editions. Anson explained that 'neither Sir Frederick Pollock nor Mr Leake wrote for beginners, and I feared lest the mass of statement and illustration which their books contain, ordered and luminous though it be, might tend to oppress and dishearten the student entering upon a course of reading for the School of Law'.[194] Anson's early career at the Bar seems also to have given his treatise a practical bent rather than a theoretical one.

In one sense, Anson's ambition was more modest than Pollock's: Anson sought to provide an outline of the principles of English contract law rather than an exhaustive study. Possibly because his ambition was more modest, Anson was more successful in realising it. Anson was not concerned about grandiose expositions of theory nor about relating vast numbers of English cases to this theory. As he explained, he was indebted to both Mr Leake and Sir Frederick Pollock; he described the former as approaching the subject as a practitioner would in advancing his case, while the latter inquired into the nature of contract and how it was brought about. In a remarkably insightful comment, Anson explained that he gained the most information from Leake, but that Pollock started him on his way.

189 ibid, 42.
190 Sir WR Anson, *Principles of the English Law of Contract* (Oxford, Clarendon Press, 1879).
191 Henson (n 188) 93.
192 AV Dicey in Henson (n 188) 86.
193 ibid, 93.
194 Sir WR Anson, *Principles of the English Law of Contract*, 6th edn (Oxford, Clarendon Press, 1891) v.

Anson's ambition was, in another sense, greater than Pollock's, for Anson strove to set out the subject in simple propositions. Anson wrote to Thesiger that he had settled 'on a definiteness of statement as to the results of the cases which would have been presumptuous in a book of practice'.[195] While Anson, too, was influenced by Savigny's *System of Modern Roman Law* and by *Obligationrecht*, the influence was not nearly as pervasive as it was upon Pollock, and it was one which Anson came to circumscribe in its effect. It is possible that the brunt of the Savignian influence was filtered through Pollock and into Anson's work. One suspects that Anson's German was not as fluent as Pollock's. Shortly after he was elected to his fellowship at All Souls, Anson was offered a post in Berlin tutoring the boy who would later become Kaiser Wilhelm. The principal attraction of the post was the opportunity to learn German and to 'get the best possible German lectures on Law, &c at the University there'.[196] Anson declined the post upon the objections of his mother and resolved to improve his French.[197] Interestingly, his use of Pothier was far more oblique and Anson was not reliant upon the Indian Contract Act 1872, which he referred to as 'that unhappy experiment in codification' with 'pseudo-scientific' views,[198] for definitions and expositions.[199] As we shall see, Anson was forced to confront the Savignian will theories as they applied to English contract law. Unlike Pollock, Anson attained some success in doing this. Anson's success lay in the fact that he was concerned to discover what the structure of English law was in itself. He had an eye to the theorists, but he was not constrained by them. He was able to acknowledge that 'the law is still unsettled even on rudimentary points, and thus in such matters one feels the excitement of an explorer'.[200]

Anson and Mistake

Anson began by setting out a system of contract law; he took pains to deal with his topic logically. His system possessed a conciseness lacking in Pollock's. Anson began by relating the nature of contract to other obligations and then proceeded to consider the elements necessary to form a valid contract. At the heart of Anson's analysis of contract is a will theory. A contract was an obligation formed by agreement,

[195] Private letter, Anson to Alfred Thesiger, 20 March 1879. Anson enclosed a copy of his *Principles*, which he had dedicated to Thesiger. The letter is bound within the Institute for Advanced Legal Studies' copy of the work.

[196] Anson in a letter to his father, Sir John Anson: see Henson (n 188) 63. Anson had previously, however, spent time in Germany and seems to have had some understanding of the language: ibid, 36.

[197] Anson was to tutor another of Victoria's descendants; the young man who was to become Edward VIII learned his constitutional law from him.

[198] Sir WR Anson, *Principles of the English Law of Contract*, 9th edn (Oxford, Clarendon Press, 1899) 30.

[199] Anson listed the sources he principally relied upon as: Savigny's *System* and *Obligationrecht*; Pollock's *Principles*; Benjamin's *Sale of Goods*; SM Leake, *The Elements of the Law of Contracts* (London, Stevens and Sons, 1867); and Christopher Columbus Langdell's *Selection of Cases on the Law of Contracts*: Anson (n 198) xxxi.

[200] Anson to Thesiger (n 195).

'and Savigny's analysis of these two legal conceptions may with advantage be considered here with reference to the rules of English law'.[201] In both his definition of agreement, as the outcome of two or more consenting minds, and his definition of obligation, as a power of control exercisable by one party over another with reference to future and specified acts or forbearances, Anson was expressly indebted to Savigny.[202] If contract thus required the consent of the parties, then it was necessary to consider those circumstances in which consent was not present. This Anson did in a chapter entitled 'Reality of Consent'. In this chapter, he dealt with those elements which removed any real expression of intention: mistake, misrepresentation, fraud, duress and undue influence. Mistake took two forms for Anson: a mistake of intention, which went to the reality of the consent; and a mistake of expression, which could be a ground for rectifying the contract. Anson dealt with them in separate chapters of his treatise. A mistake of intention arose where the parties did not mean the same thing or where the parties meant the same thing but one or both formed this meaning under untrue conclusions as to the subject matter of the agreement. Where mistake had any operation at all, its effect was to render the contract void.[203] Anson was not as keen as Pollock to amalgamate legal and equitable doctrines in this area of law, probably because he was far more cognisant of the fact that law and equity seem to provide different consequences where a mistake has occurred. Anson shied away from stating that a court of equity avoided a contract entirely for a mistake. Anson did not state, as Pollock had, that contracts were void in equity as well as at law. In fact, Anson noted that in cases of mistake, courts of equity would refuse to order the performance of an obligation exacted through 'manifest inadvertence' and would, instead, leave the party to his claim for damages at common law.[204] The remedies available in law and equity were expressed differently; at common law, a person who had entered into an agreement which was void for mistake could repudiate an executory agreement and defend an action brought upon it; in equity, a party could resist specific performance of a contract and might, as plaintiff, be able to apply to the Chancery Division to have the contract declared void and to be freed of his liabilities.

Anson observed that there were two forms of confusion with regard to mistake. The first 'comes from a practice adopted even by the most learned and acute writers of blending the subjects of Mistake and Failure of Consideration'.[205] His observation demonstrates that Anson was aware that a larger role for mistake was being developed in treatises than the common law probably admitted at the time. He has a gentle chiding of Pollock for this. He noted that Pollock introduced into his text cases which dealt only with the performance of the terms agreed. These cases were concerned with the problem of whether or not the terms of the contract reflected

[201] Anson, *Principles* (n 190).
[202] ibid, 2 and 4, respectively.
[203] ibid, 127.
[204] ibid, 123.
[205] Sir WR Anson, *Principles of the English Law of Contract*, 2nd edn (Oxford, Clarendon Press, 1882) 123.

what one of the parties sought and whether those terms had been performed; these were not questions of mistake. As Anson observed later, if a man contracted and failed to keep his contract due to circumstances of which he was not aware, or upon which he did not calculate at the time, the rights of the promise were not determined by a mutual error of the parties, 'but on the somewhat elementary truth that a contract expressed in unequivocal terms gives a right of action to the party injured by its breach'.[206] The second form of confusion was the attempt to ascertain the state of mind of the parties and to distinguish a bilateral error from a unilateral error. If the mind of one party did not meet that of the other, it was immaterial as to what the state of the other's mind was.

Anson's treatment of mistake was largely similar to, albeit briefer than, Pollock's. Mistake removed consent, and thus there was no contract. Anson was at pains to establish that where mistake had this effect it was exceptional: as a general rule, a man was bound by his agreement where he had expressed his assent in unequivocal terms not induced by fraud or duress. It may be that because Anson paid greater attention to the decided cases than to the work of European theorists he envisioned a much narrower ambit for an operative mistake than Pollock had: 'it is perhaps safe to say that unless Mistake goes to the root of the contract, and is such as to negative the idea that the parties were ever *ad idem*, it will be inoperative'.[207] Anson did not supply a definition of mistake beyond this rudimentary one. Instead, he fell back on the traditional technique of considering factual instances in which a mistake would invalidate a contract. Here he seems to have been guided by Pollock both as to the instances and the order in which they should be presented: mistake as to the nature of the transaction; mistake as to the person; and mistake as to the subject matter. His treatment of mistake was not identical to Pollock's; in relation to a mistake as to identity, Anson formulated his proposition that where a party has in contemplation a definite person with whom he desires to contract and the definite person is not who he was thought to be, the result is a void contract, on the basis of the recent decision in *Cundy v Lindsay*.[208] His treatment of mistake as to the subject matter of the contract was not as confused as Pollock's. For Anson, where there was a mistake as to the existence of the subject matter (*Couturier v Hastie*[209]) or a mistake as to the identity of the subject matter (*Raffles v Wichelhaus*[210]) or where there was a mistake as to the quality of the thing promised, known to the other party (*Smith v Hughes*[211]) then there was no contract. Anson's text was more comprehensible than Pollock's because Anson did not admit as many sub-categories under this head as Pollock had.

[206] Sir WR Anson, *Principles of the English Law of Contract*, 5th edn (Oxford, Clarendon Press, 1888) 308. Lord Atkin, in *Bell v Lever Brothers Ltd* [1932] AC 161 was to adopt this approach.

[207] ibid, 116.

[208] (n 177).

[209] (1852) 8 Ex 40, 155 ER 1250 (Court of Exchequer); (1853) 9 Ex 102, 156 ER 43 (Exchequer Chamber); (1856) 5 HLC 673; 10 ER 1065 (House of Lords).

[210] (n 168).

[211] (n 91).

Anson did not attempt to place both mistake in forming the consent necessary to contract and mistake in expression in the same chapter. He dealt separately with the cases where an agreement had been formed, but the consent was mistakenly expressed in a later written document. Anson dealt with the topic of rectification for mistake in a chapter dealing with rules relating to evidence, in which he concerned himself with those instances where the parties disputed the meaning of the words of the contract. In these circumstances, equity would not only admit extrinsic evidence to ascertain the real agreement between the parties (in both oral and written agreements) but would also rectify a written agreement where it did not accurately record the agreement of the parties. Where, by a mutual mistake, the parties failed to express their true consent, equity would rectify the written instrument so that it would accord with their true intent. This would be the case even where the parties could no longer be restored to the same position.[212] Anson dealt with the *Garrard v Frankel*[213] line of authorities both as a part of the reality of consent and as a part of the rectification of mistaken instruments. For Anson, this line of authorities was not the anomaly it was for Pollock. Anson regarded them as the equitable equivalent of *Smith v Hughes*.[214] Where one party erred and the other was aware of this error, the result was that where there was a mistake, not as to subject matter of a contract, but as to the terms of the contract, then the party who is cognisant of the fact of the error will not be allowed to rely upon the agreement when he seeks to take advantage of the error. Anson thought that this was an instance where the contract was void at both law and equity.[215] This was not quite what the equitable courts had decided, and Anson is aware of this when he considers these authorities in relation to rectification. He points out that in these cases, where there is a unilateral mistake, a court of equity will allow the non-mistaken party the option to either be freed from the agreement altogether or abide by the agreement on the terms intended by the other party. He noted that these were cases which appeared to be ones in the nature of fraud. The mistake had to be caused by the party who sought to rely upon the mistake caused and it had to be known to him before his position was affected by the contract. Equity, however, would not use these powers unless the parties could be placed in the same position as they had been before the contract was formed.[216]

Anson Modifies his Treatment of Mistake

In the second edition of his work,[217] published in 1882, Anson considered two sets of objections which worked against his Savigny-inspired theory of obligations: the first was Holmes' and the second was Holland's. Anson set out the theory Holmes

212 Anson (n 206), 239.
213 (1862) 30 Beav 445; 54 ER 961; 31 Law Jo Eq 604; 8 Juris ns 985.
214 (n 91).
215 Anson (n 206), 127.
216 ibid, 240. Anson maintained this basic proposition in subsequent editions of his treatise.
217 Anson (n 205).

had advanced in *The Common Law*: there were no obligations arising from promises, simply a liability to pay if the thing promised did not occur: 'Thus every contract is the taking of a risk'.[218] While Anson found Holmes' work 'powerful and ingenious',[219] he disagreed with the theory advanced because it did 'not seem to represent either the attitude of the law towards the parties, or the attitude of their minds to one another'.[220] For Anson, English law recognised contractual obligation as something distinct from a liability to pay damages in the event of non-performance; the parties to a contract themselves did not contemplate liability to pay damages in the event of breach as anything other than a remote possibility.

While the objection raised by Holmes went to the nature of the contractual obligation when created, the objection of Holland went to the mode of creation. The objection went as follows.[221] Agreement was not necessarily the basis of contract because the consensus ad idem of two or more minds at the same moment was incapable of proof. Therefore, courts were forced to fall back upon a man's overt acts and ask whether, to a reasonable man, these acts were capable of any construction but that of an expression of intention as was necessary to form a contract: 'Thus if a man contract under a mistake, and then ask to be relieved of his bargain on the ground that he did not know the facts, or misinterpreted them, or was ignorant of the legal significance of his words, he will not, save in rare cases, be assisted by the courts'.[222] The suggestion drawn from this analysis was that 'the obligation created by contract does not spring from the agreement of both parties, but from the conduct of one'.[223] While Anson acknowledged that he feared that his 'attempted defence of Savigny's analysis has not convinced'[224] Holland, he refuted the proposition that the law enforced contracts on the basis of the conduct of one party by pointing out that such a view of agreement only reappeared in a different form. It might be that in some circumstances there was no real agreement between the parties but that in those circumstances 'their conduct must have been indistinguishable from Agreement'.[225] Anson opined that 'there is no doubt that in the history of legal ideas the conscious adoption of Agreement as the basis of Contract comes late'.[226] Consensus, he explained, was not the basis of the action; 'solemnity of form' was, whether it be the words of the *stipulatio* or the seal in covenant. Consensus, however, was always the essence of the transaction, 'though undetected by legal analysis'.[227] Anson concluded his discussion of Holland's analysis that while agreement was necessary to contract, it was clear that a court could not ascertain the state of the parties' minds and that, consequently, where

218 ibid, 9.
219 ibid, 8.
220 ibid, 9.
221 ibid, 10–11.
222 ibid, 11. A portion of Blackburn J's judgment in *Smith v Hughes* (n 91) was cited as support for this proposition.
223 ibid.
224 ibid, 10, fn 1.
225 ibid, 12.
226 ibid.
227 ibid.

parties exhibited all the phenomena of an agreement, the existence of the agreement was to be taken for granted. Having thus examined and refuted the counter-arguments, Anson was able to agree with the basic proposition he had set out in his first edition: 'Contract is an Agreement enforceable at law, made between two or more persons, by which rights are acquired by one or both to acts or forbearances on the part of the other'.[228]

In the third edition of his work, Anson removed the long discussion of the criticisms of his Savignian analysis. He observed, tersely, that 'these topics are better suited to a treatise on Jurisprudence than to an elementary book on the law of contract'[229] and simply confined himself to disagreeing with them. On the important question of formation, Anson stated that the law did require the wills of the parties to be at one, but where they presented all the phenomena of a single will, the same consequences followed, because 'they are not allowed to say that they were not agreed'.[230] He exhibited a certain crankiness in later editions regretting that Professor Holland was unable to alter his own view.[231]

Unlike Pollock, Anson introduced subtle changes and refinements to his conception of agreement and mistake in the later editions of his treatise. I have examined his criticisms of Holmes and Holland as to a will theory of contract. By the sixth edition of 1891, Anson changed his chapter on mistake by introducing subtle restatements 'for the sake of greater clearness and better arrangement'.[232] The effect of these restatements was to limit the ambit of mistake in contract law. These limitations came about in three ways. The first way was to clearly demarcate mistake from other areas of contractual doctrine. These were: instances in which the offer and the acceptance did not correspond, such that there was never any outward appearance of agreement; situations 'in which the assent of one party has been influenced by a false statement made by the other, innocent or fraudulent, by violence, or oppression on the part of the other'[233]; and situations in which there was a failure of consideration, those instances 'in which a man is disappointed as to his power to perform his contract, or in the performance of it'.[234] Even the most learned authors, Anson wrote, were apt to confuse mistake with a failure of consideration. Pollock, he noted, was one such author. Finally, it had to be assumed that the terms of the contract corresponded to the intentions of the parties. If performance did not accord with the terms of the contract, this was a question of breach, and not of mistake. The second way Anson limited the ambit of mistake was a narrower restatement of the doctrine:

228 ibid, 13.

229 Sir WR Anson, *Principles of the English Law of Contract*, 3rd edn (Oxford, Clarendon Press, 1884) 8.

230 ibid, 9.

231 Anson (n 180) 9: 'I fail to understand why Dr. Holland (ed 5. pp 222–226) continues to regard this view as of any real importance. A contract, as a legal transaction, can exist only in such a form as may be perceptible to a Court of Law.'

232 ibid, vii.

233 ibid, 125.

234 ibid.

> The cases in which Mistake affects Contract are exceptions to an almost universal rule that a man is bound by an agreement to which he has expressed a clear assent, uninfluenced by falsehood, violence or oppression. If he exhibits all the outward signs of agreement the law will hold that he has agreed.
>
> . . . Thus it will appear that operative mistake is very rare, and that the cases of genuine mutual mistake are rarer still.[235]

Anson clarified his restatement by declaring that mistake invalidated a contract in only three circumstances. These were: first, where the parties contracted through the fraud or negligence of another person and one of the parties entered a transaction he would not have otherwise entered; second, where one of the parties was dishonest in knowing the other party believed him to be someone else or attached a different meaning to the terms; and cases of 'genuine mutual mistake'.

The third way Anson limited mistake was to narrow his instances of mutual mistake. He did this through a series of observations. A mutual mistake as to the nature or existence of the transaction had to arise from deceit and be such that ordinary diligence would not discern. The mistake had to be caused by a third party because if it arose through an act of a party to the contract, the contract would be voidable for misrepresentation or fraud.[236] While this can be seen as a crude attempt to separate fraud from mistake, it was an imperfect attempt because he was then unable to reject the fraudulent identity cases as fraud rather than mistake. Anson also now (correctly) observed that cases concerned with a non-existent subject matter were really cases of antecedent impossibility. Nevertheless, he carried on to outline *Couturier v Hastie*[237] and *Cooper v Phibbs.*[238]

A similarly unacknowledged weakness of his doctrinal structure can be seen in Anson's later treatment of the equitable cases. Anson altered his concluding section on mistake. Previously he had contrasted the legal position with the equitable, pointing out that *Garrard v Frankel*[239] was the equitable response to the similar common law situation which arose in *Smith v Hughes.*[240] This he now changed and introduced a certain obliqueness to his analysis. While Anson appears to state that an operative mistake, whether in law or equity, rendered a contract void, he introduced without explanation two bodies of equitable cases in which this did not occur. The first was *Webster v Cecil,*[241] in which the court of equity refused specific performance of a contract on the grounds of mistake, but allowed the injured party to recover damages at common law. The second was a line of cases embodied in *Garrard v Frankel,*[242] *Harris v Pepperell*[243] and *Paget v Marshall.*[244] In these cases,

[235] ibid, 126.
[236] ibid, 129.
[237] (n 205).
[238] (1867) [LR] 2 HL 149.
[239] (n 208).
[240] (n 91).
[241] (1861) 30 Beav 62; 54 ER 812.
[242] (n 208).
[243] (1867) LR 5 Eq 1; 17 TLR 191; 16 WR 68.
[244] (1885) LR 28 Ch D 255.

admittedly 'not numerous', mistake was effective, although not a mutual mistake. Where one party knew of the other's error as to the nature or extent of his promise and sought to take advantage of this error, the court told the non-mistaken party that in substance 'his agreement must be either rectified, or cancelled, and that he may take his choice'.[245] Anson went further than Pollock in recognising these cases as good law, but he was unable to fit them within his wider theory as to the effect of mistake, for they amounted to creating contracts voidable for mistake. And, as Anson went on to conclude, 'the effect of Mistake, where it has any effect at all, is to avoid the contract'.[246] Maurice Gwyer, who prepared the twelfth edition under Anson's supervision, boldly set out that where mistake affected the formation of a contract, it meant that 'no true contract comes into existence; it is void *ab initio*'.[247] Equity, however, 'takes cognizance of Mistake in a wider sense than that given to it at common law'.[248] The effect was to highlight a contradiction Anson had elegantly glided over: mistake rendered a contract void, although equity did something else.

Anson was to write five more editions of his treatise and supervised the preparation of two more editions before his death in 1914. His views on agreement and mistake, as established in the sixth edition, remained unchanged. One reason for this lack of revision were the demands of his other endeavours;[249] another was that he did not regard the later cases as fundamentally changing the law nor, because he endeavoured to write a brief treatise, did he wish to include later cases he viewed as merely illustrative of the principle already enunciated. There are hints in the later editions that he was sceptical of the doctrine of mistake.[250] In short, Anson, by his sixth edition, came close to eliminating mistake. Conceptually he did by so limiting its application. Practically he did not, for he left it in place as a factor which could affect 'the reality of consent'. It is no wonder that many of the surviving texts bear the pencilled question marks of students.

Conclusions

Pollock and Anson held positions of prominence in late nineteenth-century contract law. As we have seen, they began by defining a contract as a form of agree-

[245] Anson (n 180), 138.

[246] ibid.

[247] Sir WR Anson, *Principles of the English Law of Contract*, 12th edn, ed M Gwyer (Oxford, Clarendon Press, 1910), 161.

[248] ibid, 162.

[249] In his tenth edition, he wrote that the pressures of work had left him little time to arrange the materials he had prepared: Sir W Anson, *Principles of the English Law of Contract*, 10th edn (Oxford, Clarendon Press, 1903) v. In addition to his other academic writings, Anson was elected the warden of All Souls College in 1881 (and took a prominent role in managing the College's finances during a time during which agrarian incomes fell), and he was elected Vice-Chancellor of Oxford in 1898, holding the position for a year until he resigned to become one of the two MPs for the university.

[250] He regarded *May v Platt* (1900) 1 Ch 616 as a failure of performance which demonstrated how easily a simple matter may be confused with an allegation of mistake: Anson (n 249) 155.

ment which existed because the will of the parties came together—two or more consenting minds met and a power of control was exercisable by one or more parties, or another. Both were attracted to aspects of Savigny's will theory in formulating this conception of contract. Once the will theory was adopted, mistake followed as a matter which could vitiate consent. It was clear by the time that Pollock wrote in 1876 that the simple statements in Pothier concerned with mistake were not sufficient to deal with the practical problems that arose. Pollock, partly because of this and partly for reasons of his own, turned to Savigny to help him construct a doctrine of mistake. Oddly, his adoption of Savigny was not complete nor did it operate to the exclusion of Pothier: Pollock, in particular, built a sort of Frankenstein's monster. Anson avoided this fate, but did so by quickly glossing over many of the joins in the body he constructed.

While both men moved away from a conception of contract dependent upon the will of the parties, their treatment of mistake remained largely the same. Anson seems to have realised the trouble that this caused and sought to limit the application of mistake drastically, to the point of non-existence. Four fundamental problems arose from their writings on mistake. The first was that the 'adoption' of a will theory necessitated an acceptance of mistake. While Savigny's conception of mistake was attractive because of the apparent resolution of the difficulties posed in Roman law, neither English author felt able to adopt it in its entirety. What they did adopt was the firm principle that the effect of mistake was to render a contract void. This put mistake at odds with other legal and equitable vitiating elements (misrepresentation, fraud, duress and undue influence) the effect of which was to render a contract voidable. The second problem was that their overlay of civilian theory obscured the workings of the common law and how courts had previously dealt with cases of factual misapprehension. This was particularly true of the equitable cases which had been decided because of the mistake but on a different basis. The equitable cases were particularly important as they pointed towards the result of a voidable contract rather than a void contract: a result which would address the disjunction of result between mistake and the other vitiating element. The methods employed by Pollock and Anson not only obscured the workings of the common law, but they impeded the development of the theory they advanced, for any scrutiny of the cases they cited revealed that they had been decided on other grounds. The third problem was that it appears that the course of development in equitable mistake was disrupted and ultimately altered by the treatises, particularly Pollock's. His dismissal of the more recent equitable cases as 'peculiar', and his characterisation of mistake as concerned with dissensus, worked to create twentieth-century confusion. The fourth problem was that the doctrine of mistake that was created was confusing and unworkable. It was not true to Savigny, and uncertainties arose when the theory was related to cases decided on other grounds. There was little guidance as to when an error was sufficiently fundamental to be 'operative'. The linking of different 'instances' was incoherent and self-contradictory, particularly with regard to mistake of identity. The distinction between fraud and misrepresentation, on the one hand, and mistake, on the other, was very poorly drawn. The result was an extremely restrictive ambit in which a doctrine of mistake would ever operate. An oddity of this process is that Pollock and Anson, having selected an already outdated German theorist around which to structure their doctrine, really took no interest in the ongoing debate in Germany. Had they followed this debate, many of the elements of their own scheme might have been workable.

Pollock and Anson sought to bring a system of organisation to English contract law. This they achieved, but at a cost of substance. Savigny's work, however, would tell us that such a step was only a necessary beginning until the principles were perfected.

7

The Creation of Contractual Mistake in Nineteenth-century Common Law

ENGLISH CONTRACT LAW recognises a small number of significant cases as the foundation of the doctrine of mistake: *Couturier v Hastie* (1856), *Raffles v Wichelhaus* (1864), *Kennedy v The Panama, New Zealand, and Australian Royal Mail Co* (1867), *Smith v Hughes* (1871) and *Cundy v Lindsay* (1878). These are the principal nineteenth-century common law cases upon which the later doctrine was built, albeit with judicial and academic questioning of the solidity of these foundations. The previous two chapters have scrutinised the theories of Pothier and von Savigny and how they were adopted by the principal treatise writers. This chapter returns to the cases of the common law and examines the first four[1] of these cases chronologically and in relation to the aspect of mistake they are said to have decided. An examination of the historical context in which they were decided reveals several factors. First, although all involved a situation of factual misapprehension, none was decided according to a doctrine of mistake. Second, the cases demonstrate how factual misapprehensions could be dealt with at common law before mistake. Third, none possessed any real innovation except *Smith v Hughes.* Given these factors, the chapter explores the process of common law reasoning and law making which came to make these cases the foundation of a new doctrine. An understanding of this process informs an understanding of why the resulting doctrine is problematic.

An Absence of Subject Matter: *Couturier v Hastie* (1856)

Couturier v Hastie[2] is said to stand for the proposition that a contract is void when the parties, mistakenly believing that a certain thing exists, make the thing the subject of their contract. Other interpretations exist[3]: that the contract was void for impossibility; or that there was an implied condition precedent that the goods

[1] *Cundy v Lindsay* is examined in ch 8.

[2] (1852) 8 Ex 40, 155 ER 1250 (Court of Exchequer); (1853) 9 Ex 102, 156 ER 43 (Exchequer Chamber); (1856) 5 HLC 673; 10 ER 1065 (House of Lords).

[3] All but the last were considered in PS Atiyah, '*Couturier v Hastie* and the Sale of Non-Existent Goods' (1957) 73 *Law Quarterly Review* (LQR) 340. Atiyah concluded that the case was not one of mistake.

existed; or that where one party is unable to perform he cannot insist upon the performance of another; or that the case was one where the consideration failed. The codified interpretation was that 'where there is a contract for the sale of specific goods, and the goods without the knowledge of the seller have perished at the time when the contract is made, the contract is void'.[4]

The case was not entirely decided on any of these grounds. The plaintiffs, Couturier and the Salzanis, were merchants in Smyrna who chartered a vessel, the *Keziah Page*, commanded by Captain Page, to carry 'fair average corn' from Salonica to an English port. Couturiers's English agents were Messrs Bernoulli, and it was they who hired the defendant cornfactors, Hastie and Hutchinson, to sell the cargo. Hastie advanced Bernoulli £600 in exchange for the bill of lading, the charter party, and the insurance policy. A fortnight later, Hastie sold the cargo to Callender. This sale, as was the cornfactors' custom, was on a *del credere* commission whereby the agent guaranteed the performance of the purchaser and was liable to the principal in the event of the purchaser's default. Messrs Bernoulli were notified of this sale, but not of the purchaser or the form of commission. Unbeknownst to these parties, the *Keziah Page* had encountered a tempest on her voyage which had slowed her passage, and the cargo became badly overheated and damaged. When she put in at Tunis, surveyors determined that three quarters of the cargo was damaged and that the remainder should be sold at auction.[5] The proceeds of £370 were given to Captain Page.[6] When Callender discovered this he repudiated the sale on the basis that the cargo did not exist. Callender became bankrupt, and Couturier brought an action against Hastie for the cargo price on the *del credere* guarantee; Hastie, in turn, brought an action against Bernoulli seeking the return of the £600 advance.[7]

The determination of the case followed the existing practice of pleadings; the Hilary Term Rules 1834. The action was brought in *assumpsit.* The plaintiffs declared that before the sale to Callender the corn had been shipped, deliverable to the plaintiffs or their nominees to an English port. They further declared that: (1) the cargo was insured; (2) the plaintiffs retained the defendants to sell the cargo on the terms that it was shipped free on board and at the purchaser's risk from loading. The agreement had been breached as neither the defendants nor Callender would pay. While it was clear to onlookers that the problem arose through a misapprehension, this misapprehension did not generate a legal response. Hastie pleaded *non assumpsit* but the Hilary Term Rules required Hastie to plead specifically each defence rather than rely upon the general issue.[8] Hastie was also unable to plead

[4] Sale of Goods Act 1893, 56 & 57 Vict, c 71, s 6.

[5] The day before the sale to Callender, the matter had been noted on the Lloyd's books, but none of the parties involved in the sale was aware of this entry: *Daily News*, Thursday, 18 December 1851, 5.

[6] Parliamentary Archives, Joint Appendix to the Two Several Cases of the Plaintiffs and Defendants, 24.

[7] ibid.

[8] 1851 [1389] Royal Com to enquire into Process, Practice and System of Pleading in Superior Courts, First Report, 15. Prior to the Hilary Term Rules, Hastie would have been able to plead the general issue, and the ability of defendants to do this in actions of *assumpsit* prevented the law from becoming mired in technical objections: ibid, 20.

alternative defences because this offended the rule against duplicity.[9] With his plea of *non assumpsit*, Hastie made a traverse which denied the promise and questioned the manner and form of the terms alleged.[10] Hastie made further pleas that went to the misapprehension: that Couturier had no property in the corn at the time of the agreement with Callender; and that Hastie and Callender were both ignorant of the sale which Bernoulli had withheld and concealed from them.[11] Hastie's pleas compelled Couturier to prove that the terms of the agreement were in substance accurate. If he could not, a variance arose, and Couturier's action would fail, for the jury would find against him on the particular issue.[12] The variance would arise not only where the proof at trial wholly failed to support the issue but also where it failed only on a particular point between the allegation and the evidence.[13] The dangers posed by a variance between the allegations and the evidence provided placed upon the special pleader the duty of ensuring 'great accuracy and precision in adapting the allegation to the true state of the fact'.[14]

The matter was heard before Baron Martin, sitting with a special jury at *nisi prius* in Guildhall.[15] Couturier appeared to have been unable to prove his pleas, and a variance appeared. Baron Martin stated that 'the question was entirely one of law, arising upon the traverse of whether the defendants did sell and dispose of the corn according to the terms of the declaration'.[16] He rejected Couturier's argument that the mercantile usage provided that a cargo sold 'free on board' meant that the purchaser bore the risk of loss from the vessel's loading. In his direction to the jury, Baron Martin ruled 'that the contract imported that, at the time of the sale, the corn was in existence as such, and capable of delivery'.[17] A verdict was entered for the defendants, who then succeeded in their action against Bernoulli to recover the amount paid in advance. This result was reversed by the Court of Exchequer, who found in Couturier's favour on the legal construction of the agreement between Hastie and Callender.[18] Mistake played no role in the determination of the construction to be placed upon the contract between Hastie and Callender. Baron

[9] ibid, 18–19. See also HJ Stephen, *A Treatise on the Principles of Pleading in Civil Actions; Comprising a Summary View of the Whole Proceedings in a Suit at Law*, 4th edn (London, Saunders and Benning, 1838) 415. The Commissioners identified this as one of the reasons that made the Hilary Term Rules impracticable.

[10] He also denied that he had sold the corn on the terms alleged and that the plaintiffs had notice of the *del credere* commission, for this was the effect of the form employed by Hastie's pleader when he set out the alleged agreements followed by *modo et formâ*. See Stephen (n 9) 215.

[11] Couturier joined issue on the first four pleas and, in turn, traversed the three further pleas of Hastie *de injuriâ*.

[12] Stephen (n 9) 215.

[13] Stephen (n 9) 94. Stephen gave as an example an instance where it had been pleaded that the covenant in a lease was to 'repair when and as need should require', and at trial the covenant in the deed appeared as 'when and as need should require, *and at the farthest after notice*': *Horsefall v Testar* (1817) 7 Taunt 385; 129 ER 154.

[14] Stephen (n 9) 216.

[15] A report of the proceedings appears in the *Daily News*, Thursday, 18 December 1851, 5.

[16] ibid.

[17] 8 Exch.40, 47; 155 ER 1250, 1254.

[18] Because Pollock CB dissented, a rule absolute for a new trial was made but with liberty for the defendants to bring the case before a court of error by a bill of exceptions.

Parke found that risk passed to the purchaser at shipping. Normally when there was a sale of a specific chattel, as distinct from a contract to sell and deliver a chattel in the future, there was an implied undertaking that the chattel existed. This situation was different because there were undertakings as to the quality of the corn at shipment and as to when shipment began. The sale was also accompanied by insurance to protect the purchaser from losses. The correct interpretation of the contract was that Callender purchased the cargo if it existed, but if it had been damaged or lost, he bought the benefit of the insurance. Hastie was liable for Callender's payment by reason of their *del credere* commission. The decision attracted no contemporary comment, and treatise writers were more impressed with a Statute of Frauds point[19] than the construction point; no account saw the case as a part of the doctrine of mistake. *The Times* declined to report the case and observed that 'the points involved were not of any public interest'.[20]

The Exchequer Chamber unanimously reversed the Exchequer Court. Coleridge J stated that the Exchequer's judgment rested upon the construction of the contract and that there was no evidence to explain the contract. The sale was of a cargo supposed to exist and thus capable of transfer. There was no insurable interest at the time of sale since the cargo no longer existed. In short, 'the basis of the contract in this case was the sale and purchase of goods, and that all the other terms in the bought note were dependent upon that'.[21] Contemporaries viewed the judgment as insignificant; *The Times* observed that it was 'too technical for notice'.[22]

Couturier went to the House of Lords. There are hints in his counsel's argument that mistake as a legal matter was mentioned. Couturier's counsel again argued that the sale to Callender was the sale of an expectation and not the sale of specific goods.[23] Counsel appears to have quoted Pothier's *Contrat de Vente*[24] to the effect that the contract of sale required a thing to be sold, and if the thing had been wholly destroyed prior to sale, there was no contract. Possibly this was to forestall an argument he expected from the defendant. Couturier's counsel then stated the position in English law that if a man bought a chance, he must abide by the consequences: he derived this proposition from an equitable mistake case.[25] Whether

[19] See, eg, WW Story, *A Treatise on the Law of Contracts Not Under Seal* (Boston, CC Little & J Brown, 1847) §351, and CG Addison, *A Treatise on the Law of Contracts and Rights and Liabilities Ex Contractu*, 4th edn ((London, V and R Stevens and GS Norton, 1856) 38. This was also the only contemporary judicial use of the case: *Wickham v Wickham* (1855) 2 Kay & J. 478; 69 ER 870.

[20] *The Times*, 27 June 1852, 7.

[21] 9 Ex 102, 110; 156 ER 43, 46–47.

[22] *The Times*, 27 June 1853, 7.

[23] Couturier's counsel, Frederick Thesiger and J Cowling, set out as their reason for allowing the appeal and affirming the direction of the Lord Chief Baron that the true meaning of the parties was the legal interpretation of the contract, which was based upon the circumstances of its creation and the information the mercantile world would employ in reading the contract: Parliamentary Archives, Case for the Plaintiffs in Error, 5.

[24] RJ Pothier, *Traité du Contrat de Vente*, in *Oeuvres de R-JPothier, contenant les traités du droit francais* (Brussels, AMJJ Dupin, 1829) 286, part I, s 2, art 1. He also appears to have cited L 57, ff *de Contrahenda Emptione* [D.18.1.57].

[25] *Hitchcock v Giddings* (1817) 4 Price 135; 146 ER 418.

this was coincidence or a deliberate attempt to foreclose an argument based upon mistake we do not know because Hastie was not called upon.[26] The Lord Chancellor rejected entirely Couturier's argument. This was not a case about consensus but about contractual construction: 'the whole question turns upon the construction of the contract which was entered into between the parties'.[27] Absent evidence that established mercantile usage as to the interpretation of such contracts, the court would construe the contract itself. This contract indicated that each party had contemplated that there was an existing thing to be sold. Absent such a thing, the Exchequer Chamber had come to the reasonable conclusion. The House of Lords, as with the lower courts, was concerned with the construction of the contract between Callender and Hastie because this was the issue the pleadings established for determination. The misapprehension was irrelevant to this determination and there was no need to create a doctrine of mistake to resolve the matter. Pothier was ignored. The matter was resolved on the variance between what Couturier had alleged in his pleadings, that the agreement was to take an expectation, and what was proved at trial. Contemporary reaction to the decision was muted and the case received little attention.[28]

This obscure case came to be viewed as an important mistake case by the treatise writers. Leake employed it first. Leake wrote that contracts founded upon agreement could be vitiated by certain circumstances which left the contract void of legal effect. Mistake was one of these factors. A form of mistake that Leake recognised was a mistake of both parties which induced the contract; a situation where, without the mistake, there would not have been a contract. The English authorities he provided for this proposition began with *Couturier v Hastie*.[29] He explained it as a situation in which the parties had contracted upon the mistaken supposition that the cargo existed and the question for the court was whether the contract was absolute or whether it was entered into upon the condition that the cargo existed. Once the court determined that the agreement was conditional upon the existence of the cargo, the contract was void. While this is one way of explaining the result in *Couturier v Hastie*, it is not the basis upon which the court

[26] Counsel stated, inter alia, that the 'contract in question was for the sale and purchase of an actual cargo, and at the time of the contract the cargo had ceased to exist, and the Plaintiffs had not any cargo to sell': Parliamentary Archives, Case of the Defendants in Error, 9. They also stated that the insurance would only cover part of the risks and would have ceased to have any effect before the contract of sale was made: ibid.

[27] (1856) 5 HLC 673, 681; 10 ER 1065, 1068. The other reports of the decision are consistent with this: 25 LJ Exch 253; 2 Jurist ns 1241.

[28] *The Times* outlined the procedural history of the case and noted, briefly, that the judges had seen no reason to disturb the judgment of the Exchequer Chamber: 28 June 1856, 11. *The Jurist* published the case in two sections of its Common Law Digest for 1857: the first under the heading 'Principal and Agent' to the effect that the defendant was not liable for the amount because it was the sale of a cargo which did not exist (2 Jurist ns 196); the second under Sale, 'Construction of Contract—Existence of Subject-matter of Sale', and there it was stated that the contract contemplated an existing thing to be sold and bought: because there was not, the factor was not liable (ibid, 221).

[29] SM Leake, *The Elements of the Law of Contracts* (London, Stevens and Sons, 1867) 176. He also cited a case which had been cited before the courts in *Couturier v Hastie*: *Strickland v Turner* (1852) 7 Ex 208; 155 ER 919.

decided the case. Leake's explanation was picked up by Benjamin. Benjamin, following Pothier,[30] wrote that a contract of sale required certain elements of which an object of the sale was one.[31] Without something to be transferred, there could be no sale, and Benjamin supported this proposition with *Couturier v Hastie.*[32] Pollock, two years later, wrote that *Couturier v Hastie* established that an agreement is void where the parties mistakenly believe that a non-existent subject matter is in existence.[33] Anson then described *Couturier v Hastie* as 'one of the leading cases' on the subject of a mistake as to the existence of the subject matter of the contract.[34] These were intelligent authors: why did they use the case in such a fashion? They did so because they needed support for the will theory they advanced. If consensus is a requisite for contract, dissensus must also be a requisite for no contract. *Couturier v Hastie* involved a factual misapprehension, and the court held that there was not an enforceable contract. It is clear that the effect of the case is the same as the authors stated. The problem is that the case was not decided upon these grounds. While the treatise writers no doubt felt justified in so using the case—to support the common law on principled and rational grounds—their use was to muddy the common law because the case clearly had not been decided upon these grounds.[35]

Mistake which Prevents Agreement—*Raffles v Wichelhaus* (1864)

Raffles v Wichelhaus[36] stands for the proposition that where the parties are at cross-purposes, in that one party meant one thing and the other party meant another such that no true agreement arose, there is no contract. What is remarkable about this is that *Raffles v Wichelhaus*, like *Couturier v Hastie*, was insignificant when decided; the Court of Exchequer did not even give reasons for its

[30] Couturier's counsel had relied on the same passage.

[31] JP Benjamin, *A Treatise on the Sale of Personal Property*, 2nd edn (London, Henry Sweet, 1873) 62.

[32] ibid.

[33] F Pollock, *Principles of Contract at Law and in Equity* (London, Stevens and Sons, 1876) 397–98.

[34] Sir WR Anson, *Principles of the English Law of Contract* (Oxford, Clarendon Press, 1879) 121. Sir Howard Elphinstone explained that the decision was made on the basis that the different ships meant that the parties were not *ad idem* and that there was thus no binding contract: (1886) 2 LQR 110, 111.

[35] A point noted by the High Court of Australia in *McRae v Commonwealth Disposals Commission* (1951) 84 CLR 377.

[36] (1864) 2 H & C 906; 159 ER 375; 160 LJ Exch 160. The case has been the subject of twentieth-century analysis: AWB Simpson, 'The Beauty of Obscurity *Raffles v Wichelhaus and Busch* (1864)', in AWB Simpson, *Leading Cases in the Common Law* (Oxford, Oxford University Press, 1995), and a fuller account of the same case appeared as 'Contracts for Cotton to Arrive: The Case of the Two Ships *Peerless*', (1989) 11 *Cardozo Law Review* 287; see also, RL Birmingham, 'Holmes on *Peerless*: *Raffles v Wichelhaus* and the Objective Theory of Contract', (1985) 47 *University of Pittsburgh Law Review* 183.

judgment.[37] Raffles sold cotton to Wichelhaus and Busch 'ex *Peerless* Bombay'. Unfortunately there were two ships *Peerless*, each sailing from Bombay, but one in October and the other in December. The sale was a substantial one[38] in a market of great volatility brought about by the American Civil War. English dependency upon high-grade American cotton had been disrupted by a Union blockade of shipping, and cotton prices were volatile as rumours of cotton running the blockade upset price stability.[39] Wichelhaus had contracted to take the cotton at 17¼d per pound after the arrival of the cotton. When the October *Peerless* arrived in Liverpool the market price for cotton was well below this agreed price; it is no wonder that Wichelhaus was unconcerned when he was not offered cotton in October. Raffles, however, probably had no cotton on the October *Peerless.*[40] When the December *Peerless* arrived, the market price was still below the contract price, but not by as much. Wichelhaus and Busch refused to take the cotton, and Raffles sued them for damages.[41]

Wichelhaus and Busch were foreign speculators and not regular cotton dealers. They sought to avoid any adjudication by members of the Liverpool community. They thus avoided the usual resolution of such dispute, arbitration,[42] and they framed their case in such a way as to avoid a trial by jury. The procedure of pleading had changed since *Couturier v Hastie*, and the Common Law Procedure Act 1852 allowed a party to take issue on either a point of law or fact.[43] Wichelhaus did not put in issue the facts alleged by Raffles and thereby avoided a jury trial. He

[37] There are two brief reports of the case and no contemporary discussion in the legal journals. *The Jurist* set down the case for hearing as '*Ruffles v Wichelhans*' (1864–65 10 Jurist n.s 11) and provided two brief entries in its Digest for that year (ibid, 84, 209). See Simpson, 'The Beauty of Obscurity' (n 36) 162.

[38] The total price was in the order of £3,593: Simpson, 'The Beauty of Obscurity' (n 36) 136.

[39] The volatility of the cotton market is described by Simpson in 'Contracts for Cotton to Arrive' (n 36) 310–11.

[40] As Simpson has observed, it seems unlikely that Raffles would not have tried to tender the cotton to Wichelhaus at the well-above-market price: Simpson, 'The Beauty of Obscurity' (n 36) 152. The *Law Journal*'s note observed that 'the plaintiff was not ready to deliver any goods which arrived by that [October] ship', presumably based upon the suggestion of Raffles' counsel: (n 37). The two reports in the Digest to *The Jurist* both repeat this: (n 37).

[41] Simpson has speculated that Raffles was quarrelsome; Wichelhaus and Busch were not cotton brokers (and thus outside the tight-knit trading community inhabited by Raffles) and were foreigners.

[42] Most cotton disputes were resolved through arbitration organised by the Liverpool Cotton Brokers Association and conducted by cotton brokers: AWB Simpson, 'The Origins of Futures Trading in the Liverpool Cotton Market', in P Cane and J Stapleton (eds) *Essays for Patrick Atiyah*, (Oxford, Clarendon Press, 1991) 182–84. The arbitration was voluntary at this time, and it appears that Wichelhaus and Busch refused arbitration. Simpson has concluded that if the matter had gone to arbitration, it seems likely that the defendants would have been compelled either to accept the later cotton or to have split the loss with the plaintiff, but that, in any event, it would have been unlikely that they would have escaped liability altogether: 'The Beauty of Obscurity' (n 36) 154.

[43] Common Law Procedure Act 1852, s 80. The process is discussed in E Bullen and SM Leake, *Precedents of Pleadings in Personal Actions in The Superior Courts of Common Law*, 2nd edn (London, V and R Stevens, Sons and Haynes, 1863) 692. In the older work of *Stephen on Pleading*, the author maintained that this process did not completely abrogate the common law rules because it required the leave of the court: J Stephen and F Pinder, *A Treatise on the Principles of Pleading in Civil Actions*, 6th edn (London, V and R Stevens and Sons, 1860) 307.

chose to proceed by demurrer, a recommended course of action[44] because the judgment upon the demurrer would be final and determine the matter 'in the simplest and cheapest manner'.[45] A demurrer, of course, meant that the court assumed the facts to be true for the purpose of the demurrer, and the question was whether or not they sustained the case in law. Wichelhaus followed another recommended action and did not raise the demurrer himself but pleaded the additional fact that there were the two ships '*Peerless*' and that he intended a different *Peerless* than Raffles. The effect of this was that Raffles had to bring the demurrer and had to admit the new facts.[46] In the words of Bullen and Leake, 'the party pleading [Wichelhaus] will thus gain the advantage of objecting upon the argument to the original defective pleading with the benefit of the added facts'.[47] To Wichelhaus's plea, Raffles thus demurred and the legal issue proceeded to the Court of Exchequer, sitting *en banc* without a jury. There the matter was determined quickly[48] and without a trial of the facts, as had been necessary in *Couturier v Hastie*, where Hastie was forced to choose to defend the case on either the law or the facts.[49] This stratagem achieved two objectives: lower costs and the avoidance of jurors who might have been less sympathetic to the foreign speculators who had quietly allowed the earlier cargo to be offloaded without query. Raffles' counsel argued that there was a contract for the sale of cotton of a particular description and that it was immaterial which ship the cotton was to arrive on as long as it was named '*Peerless*'. He seems also to have argued that if there had been a misapprehension, this had not harmed the defendants' speculation.[50] The defendants' counsel argued that once parol evidence was admitted to establish that there were two ships '*Peerless*', 'there was no consensus ad idem, and therefore no binding contract'.[51] At that point he was stopped by the Court, who stated that 'there must be judgment for the defendants'.[52] From the comments of Martin B and Pollock CB made in the course of the plaintiff's argument, it seems likely that they accepted that there was no agreement.[53] The court neither gave judgment on the basis of mistake nor did it hear argument on the point.

[44] Bullen and Leake (n 43) 691.

[45] ibid.

[46] ibid.

[47] ibid.

[48] *The Times* reported that all of the cases the Court heard that day were 'on paper', without a trial, and that the entire day was finished shortly after noon: *The Times*, 21 January 1864, 11.

[49] With the possibility that if he lost on the facts he could seek judgment *non obstante veredicto*. There was a disadvantage for Wichelhaus to do this once the Common Law Procedure Act 1852 existed because s 144 provided that a pleading defect could be later cured by the court and costs awarded to the successful party by s 145.

[50] The *Law Journal* (n 36) reported: 'if the defendants had said their speculation had fallen through in consequence, it might have been different'. See, also, Simpson, 'The Beauty of Obscurity' (n 36) 154.

[51] (n 36) 908; 376.

[52] ibid.

[53] 'It is imposing on the defendant a contract different from that which he entered into', per Martin B, (n 36) 907; 375, and 'it is like a contract for the purchase of wine coming from a particular estate in France or Spain, where there are two estates of that name', per Pollock CB, ibid. Pollock's statement has faint, but only faint, reminders of Ulpian's discussion of an *error in substantia*.

Once again, it was treatise writers who transformed the case from its inauspicious start to prominence as a leading mistake case. The case could be used to advantage in supporting the will theory of contract. If contracts were enforced because they represented the agreement of the parties, it was necessary to demonstrate that where there was no consent there was no contract. Mistake was accepted as an element which could vitiate consent, and *Raffles v Wichelhaus* supported this proposition. The case had the added advantage that the Exchequer gave no reasons to counter the theory advanced. Leake employed the case in his contract treatise and placed it in his chapter on mistake.[54] He used *Raffles v Wichelhaus* to support his proposition that a mistake of both parties as to the application of the agreement, where each intended different things, meant that there was 'no real agreement between them and consequently no contract'.[55] This saved the case from obscurity. Benjamin, undoubtedly working from Leake's treatise, included the case in his treatise on sale. Benjamin began from the proposition that contracts could only be formed by mutual consent. The corollary which followed was that a mistake of fact meant that each party assented to a different contract, and 'there is no real valid agreement, notwithstanding the apparent mutual assent'.[56] He cited *Raffles v Wichelhaus* as an instance of this corollary. Benjamin went further and devised 'reasons' for the judgment and stated that it had been held that 'on this state of facts there was no *consensus ad idem*, no contract at all'.[57] It is an astounding coincidence that Benjamin, who so greatly assisted in the rescue of *Raffles v Wichelhaus* from obscurity was, as the Confederate Secretary of State, greatly involved in the conflict which had created the market volatility in the case. Pollock followed Benjamin and employed the case as an example of one of his instances of mistake, namely an *error in corpore*. He described it as 'the most striking recent case of this kind'[58] and went even further than Benjamin in creating 'reasons' for judgment.[59] Accordingly, the defendant's plea succeeded because he had only bought cotton to arrive from a particular ship and to have held that he bought cotton from any ship bearing that name would to have imposed upon him a different contract. Three years later, Anson employed the case for exactly the same proposition and stated it in its now familiar form. In his usual concise fashion, he stated that a contract was void for mistake where two things have the same name and the parties enter into a contract in which each means a different thing. 'Under such circumstances there is a mistake in the identity of the thing contracted for, the

[54] SM Leake, *The Elements of the Law of Contracts* (London, Stevens and Sons, 1867). The case may originally have come to either his, or Edward Bullen's, attention on the pleadings points rather than the contract points.

[55] ibid, 178. Leake noted that the significance of mistake was that the Common Law Procedure Act 1854, ss 83–86 now allowed a party to plead the equitable defence of mistake in an action at law.

[56] JP Benjamin, *A Treatise on the Law of Sale of Personal Property; with References to the American Decisions and to the French Code and Civil Law* (London, Henry Sweet, 1868) 36.

[57] ibid, 37. He placed the case between two others: *Thornton v Kempster* (1814) 5 Taunt 786; 128 ER 901, and *Phillips v Bistolli* (1824) 2 B & C; 107 ER 474.

[58] Pollock (n 33) 387

[59] Pollock's grandfather was Chief Baron Pollock who sat in judgment in *Raffles v Wichelhaus.* It is possible, albeit improbable, that Pollock received an extrajudicial explanation from his forebear.

minds of the parties never really meet, and there is no true consent.'[60] Whatever the actual basis for the decision, assuming that the Exchequer judges even had a principled basis, the case had come to stand for the proposition that where mistake puts the parties at cross-purposes there is no contract.

Mistake as to a Quality of the Subject Matter—*Kennedy v The Panama, New Zealand, and Australian Royal Mail Company (Limited)* (1867)

Error in substantia had proven a tricky matter to define and to apply within Roman law. The passages from which Justinian's codifiers created the concept were disjointed and the principal passages the subject of interpolations so extensive as to render a coherent meaning almost impossible. Nevertheless, it says something about the state of nineteenth-century English contract law that the Roman law was seen as a useful elucidation of principle. The case which introduced *error in substantia*, or a mistake as to a quality of the subject matter, into English law was *Kennedy v The Panama, New Zealand, and Australian Royal Mail Company*.[61] When Blackburn J quoted Ulpian, later lawyers and jurists were able to make a direct connection to the Roman law of mistake.[62] The irony of this later connection is that Blackburn J was attempting to establish why English law had no such concept as a mistake as to a quality of the subject matter.

Blackburn J employed Ulpian to solve a practical problem rooted in the economic collapse of the 1860s. To understand what Blackburn J was attempting to do, it is necessary to examine inter-related legal developments in company law and misrepresentation and how legal changes were played out against the backdrop of a catastrophic banking collapse. English company law underwent a total reform between 1855 and 1862, it marked a 'sudden and sharp break' from the past.[63] The important reforms for this narrative are the recognition of the company as an entity separate from its shareholders and directors and, correspondingly, the rights of creditors to recover debts. The effect of the new nineteenth-century

[60] Anson (n 34) 123. Sir Edward Fry also added *Raffles v Wichelhaus* as a case in which the contract was avoided for a want of consent or failure of consideration: Sir E Fry and WD Rawlins, *The Specific Performance of Contracts*, 2nd edn (London, Stevens and Sons, 1881) 325, §722.

[61] (1867) LR 2 QB 580.

[62] See, eg, the comment of Lord Phillips in *Great Peace Shipping Ltd v Tsavliris (International) Limited* [2002] EWCA Civ 1407 at para 59.

[63] PL Cottrell, *Industrial Finance 1830–1914* (London and New York, Methuen, 1980) 54. On this development generally, see Cottrell, ibid, ch 3; BC Hunt, *The Development of the Business Corporation in England 1800–1867* (New York, Russell & Russell, 1936); M Lobban, 'Corporate Identity and Limited Liability in France and England 1825–67' (1996) 25 *Anglo-American Law Review* 397; and G Todd, 'Some Aspects of Joint Stock Companies, 1844–1900' (1932) 4 *The Economic History Review* 46. On the corporate legislation and speculation in the railways, see RW Kostal, *Law and English Railway Capitalism 1825–1875* (Oxford, Clarendon Press, 1994), pt I.

company legislation[64] was to move the concept of a company away from that of a partnership. It was recognised in 1856 that the company was a different entity from its members and it provided a form of limited liability which protected individual shareholders from the suits of creditors. Creditors could look only to the company for the satisfaction of their debts.[65] Prior to 1856, creditors had been able to single out a particular shareholder and sue him upon a *scirae facias* for the debts unpaid by the company.[66] Two modes of limiting liability were provided[67]: limitation by shares, whereby each shareholder was liable for an amount not exceeding the unpaid amount on their shares, and limitation by guarantee.[68] Courts were initially reluctant to allow a system which effectively permitted shareholders to 'avoid' a creditor's debts. The initial limitation of liability led to large increases in the registration of companies,[69] and the 1862 Companies Act led to a boom in company formations.[70] There was a particular increase in the number of joint stock bank companies, which created a stimulus to promoters generally.[71] Partly as a result of changes to company legislation, the 1860s were a turbulent decade of initial growth followed by later collapse. Life for many of these companies was 'nasty, brutish and short': of the companies formed between 1856 and 1868, only 41% were in existence at the end of the period,[72] and many of the new companies had a lifespan of less than 18 months.[73] By the end of the 1860s, courts were awash with the legal results of these companies' failures.

During the boom of the 1860s the well-respected banking firm of Overend, Gurney and Company was incorporated. Demand for shares was greater than the issue. The brief prospectus of 1865 failed to mention, however, that despite its excellent reputation the firm had sustained considerable losses since 1860. The directors' hope that an infusion of capital would shore up the concern proved misplaced.[74] The bank failed on 10 May 1866, causing a financial panic: 'the shock

[64] The Joint Stock Companies Act 1856, 19 & 20 Vict, c 47, and the Companies Act 1862, 25 & 26 Vict, c 89.

[65] Under the 1856 Act a creditor could seek a winding-up order for the company (s 82), which allowed a liquidator to be appointed (s 92).

[66] This change in the mechanism by which creditors could obtain satisfaction of their debts formed the backdrop to the litigation following the panic of 1866: Anon, 'Limited Liability', 11 *Solicitors' Journal*, 20 July 1867, 875, and 'The Decision on the Overend & Gurney Appeal', 11 *Solicitors' Journal*, 17 August 1867, 969.

[67] In s 7 and s 24.

[68] s 38.

[69] Todd (n 63) 62.

[70] Levi estimated that an average of 543 companies per year were registered in the years 1856 to 1868 in comparison with an average of 337 per year from 1844 to 1855: L Levi, 'On Joint Stock Companies', (1870) 33 *Journal of the Statistical Society of London* 1, 6. See also Hunt (n 63) 145, who observed that 3,500 companies had been formed in the four years between 1863 and 1866. Some of these were conversions of existing private firms.

[71] Hunt (n 63) 149.

[72] Levi (n 63) 22.

[73] ibid, 17. The short life-cycle is also discussed by Todd (n 63) 60.

[74] Malins V-C was later to find that the directors had not acted fraudulently in the incorporation of the company: *Re Overend, Gurney, and Company (Limited), Oakes' and Peek's Cases* (1867) 15 TLR 652, 654–55

which agitated the city of London yesterday afternoon will, before this evening closes, be felt in the remotest corners of the kingdom'.[75] The boom was brought to an abrupt end as other firms failed. Demand for shares fell away and many became unsaleable. Particular problems were caused by the way share capital had been raised. Shareholders generally paid up only ten per cent of the capital.[76] The shares were subject to the liability to pay the remainder upon further calls. Following the crash, few desired to purchase shares because they feared the unknown liability that might follow.[77] As companies failed, shareholders sought to remove themselves from the membership of the company and thus gain the return of their money and avoid further calls. It was drily observed that that 'difficulties occur but seldom in the dealings of a prosperous company with its shareholders'.[78] Shareholders brought applications under the 1862 Act to remove themselves from membership and rectify the company register on the basis that either there had never been a contract to take shares[79] or that the contract was voidable. Two arguments prevailed in the voidable cases. In the first, the shareholder argued that he was entitled to avoid the contract because he had purchased his shares on a misrepresentation in the prospectus. In the second, the shareholder argued that the misrepresentation arose from a variation between the prospectus and the later memorandum and articles of association, and that the shareholder had contracted to purchase shares in one sort of entity and another sort altogether had been formed.

The new company legislation and the economic conditions stimulated development in the law of misrepresentation, and the attitude of Chancery to claims that the share purchase was vitiated by fraud underwent substantial change.[80] Courts of law and courts of equity did not substantially differ in their treatment of misrepresentation cases.[81] Courts faced two problems in fraud claims. The first was whether the fraud of the promoters (or directors) bound the company such as to allow a shareholder to rescind his contract or whether the shareholder was restricted to an action in deceit against the promoter or director. In the mid-1850s, courts began to accept that a fraudulent misrepresentation made by an agent of the company could bind the company where this act was adopted by the company,

[75] *The Times*, 11 May 1866, 11.

[76] Levi (n 63) 22.

[77] Cottrell (n 63) 58. The problem was exacerbated since the Companies Act 1862 provided no mechanism by which companies could reduce nominal capital or subdivide shares; they could only wind themselves up and start again: Cottrell, ibid, 58.

[78] H Thring, *The Law and Practice of Joint-Stock and other Public Companies*, 2nd edn (London, Stevens and Sons, H Sweet, and W Maxwell, 1868) 49.

[79] A contemporary view of these cases can be seen in a series of articles in the *Solicitors' Journal*: 'Agreements To Take Shares in Joint-Stock Companies—No I', 15 September 1866, 10 *Solicitors' Journal* 1081; 'Agreements To Take Shares in Joint-Stock Companies—No II', 29 September 1866, 10 *Solicitors' Journal* 1112; 'Agreements To Take Shares in Joint-Stock Companies—No III', 6 October 1866, 10 *Solicitors' Journal* 1133.

[80] See M Lobban, 'Nineteenth Century Frauds in Company Formation: *Derry v Peek* in Context' (1996) 112 LQR 287, and 'Contractual Fraud in Law and Equity, c 1750–c 1850', 17 OJLS 441.

[81] Lobban, 'Nineteenth Century Frauds' (n 80).

although the problem was not entirely resolved.[82] In the early 1860s the company's liability was extended to include misrepresentations made in directors' reports when the reports were later adopted by shareholders and circulated.[83] These misrepresentations bound the company,[84] regardless of whether or not the body of the shareholders were aware of the fraud,[85] because where the representations were the proximate cause of the share purchase, it was inequitable to allow the company to retain the benefit for these shares.[86] The second problem was whether the actions of the company's agents had to have an element of positive fraud rather than mere negligence to succeed. At law, the plaintiff needed to establish both the falsity of the statement and an intention to deceive, a 'fraudulent mind and motive'.[87] Courts of equity were concerned to establish that fraud had to be shown,[88] although equity appeared willing to accept a less strict standard of proof than the common law where the representations were made in a company's prospectus. False statements (either negligent or fraudulent)[89] there which induced a person to take shares would be grounds for rescission. This opened a window in the 1860s for shareholders who sought to rescind their contracts. It could thus be asserted by 1866 that 'it is now well settled that, *prima facie*, a company cannot be allowed to profit by holding to his contract a person who has been induced, by the fraudulent misrepresentations of their agents, to become a purchaser of shares direct from the company',[90] although problems remained.[91] A

[82] ibid, 306–307. In *re North of England Joint Stock Banking Company, Dodgson's case* (1849) 3 De Gex and Sm 85, 64 ER 391, Knight-Bruce LJ observed that whatever fraud there was, it was attributable to the directors who could not be the agent of the shareholders to perpetrate a fraud: 90, 394; the decision was followed as late as 1852 in *In re North of England Joint Stock Banking Company, Bernard's case* (1852) 5 De Gex and Sm 283; 64 ER 1118.

[83] *New Brunswick and Canada Railway and Land Company v Conybeare* (1862) 9 HLC 711; 11 ER 907.

[84] ibid, 725; 913.

[85] ibid, 726; 913. Lord Westbury observed that the situation was different in common law, where proof was required that the maker of the representation was aware of, or should have been aware of, the representation's falsehood. Equity found it inconsistent with natural justice to allow the retention of property obtained by false representations even where the company was not party to the representations.

[86] ibid.

[87] Note (a) to *Bale v Cleland* (1864) 4 F & F 117; 176 ER 494 at 135; 502. Lobban, 'Nineteenth Century Frauds' (n 80) draws attention to those cases which indicated a relaxation from this strictness.

[88] *Burnes v Pennell* (1849) 2 HLC 497; 9 ER 1181. In this case Lord Brougham observed that a somewhat lower standard of fraud was needed in the case of an executory contract for which specific performance was sought than in those where rescission of an executed contract was sought: 529; 1194.

[89] Lobban, 'Nineteenth Century Frauds' (n 80) 309, citing *Jennings v Broughton* (1853) 17 Beavan 234, 51 ER 1023.

[90] Anon, 'Corporate Misrepresentation—No I', 10 *Solicitors' Journal*, 26 May 1866, 702.

[91] In addition to the problems already listed, a further problem was the nature of the document in which the misrepresentation appeared. Misrepresentations in prospectuses were actionable (*Smith v The Reese Silver Mining Company* (1866) 14 WR 606, and *Ship's case* (1865) 13 WR 450) because prospectuses were addressed to the purchaser 'in such a manner as to entitle him to act upon it': Anon, 'Corporate Misrepresentation—V' 10 *Solicitors' Journal*, 14 July 1866. However, where the shares were purchased from a third party, the shareholder could not seek the assistance of equity since it was not the company's misrepresentation which induced his purchase (*In re Liverpool Borough Bank Duranty's case* (1858) 26 Beavan 268; 53 ER 901). Where the misrepresentation was in a report, the question was whether or not the document had been made within the scope of the directors' duty, and whether the report had been directed at the purchaser to induce the purchase (*New Brunswick and Canada Railway Company v Conybeare* (n 82)).

significant limitation upon the shareholder's right to rescind his purchase of shares was that it required only a 'very slight degree of subsequent acquiescence on the part of the purchaser . . . [to] estop him from avoiding his contract'.[92]

The collapse of Overend, Gurney released a tumultuous torrent of actions as shareholders questioned the validity of their contract to take the shares. The law under the new Companies Act 1862 was still largely undefined and courts were forced to make difficult decisions in new areas. There were no obviously right answers to the questions facing the courts. The essence of the problem was that while courts of both law and equity sought to treat the contracts for the purchase of shares as a part of the general law of contract and determine the issues on broad principles of contract law rather than as a special, distinct form of contract,[93] these contracts had different consequences than a contract for the purchase of goods or land would have had. The purchase created ongoing relationships; shareholder qua company and shareholder qua shareholder. Possibly of even greater significance was the relationship with the firm's creditors, who could no longer look to shareholders to satisfy debts, but, it was said, had advanced credit on the strength of the shareholders and their liability to pay further calls upon shares. Courts had to consider these interlocking relationships in a context in which the relationships had changed because of the Companies Act 1862. Courts were also to become concerned about the financial and economic consequences of their decisions as the severity of the economic collapse became apparent. There were no easy or obvious answers available to the courts in resolving these problems, a point apparent when one considers the near irreconcilability of many of the cases. Over all of these various actions hung the litigation concerned with Overend, Gurney itself. So great were the potential liabilities[94] that the shareholders formed a Defence Association to resist the liquidator's calls by establishing that shareholders had purchased shares under fraudulent prospectus statements. While *The Law Times* greeted the defence with great scepticism,[95] the *Solicitors' Journal* took a more cautious approach and noted that because many legal issues had to be determined it could not be said that the shareholders' position was a hopeless one.[96]

[92] Anon, 'Corporate Misrepresentation—No II' 10 *Solicitors' Journal*, 2 June 1866, 722.

[93] *Re The Life Association of England (Limited)* (1865) 12 *Law Times Reports* 434; *The Directors &c of The Central Railway Company of Venezuela v Kisch* (1867) LR 2 HL 99; 36 LJ Ch 849, 858, per Lord Romilly.

[94] The prospectus had stated that the shares were of £50 each but that it was not intended to call up more than £15 per share: ibid. Levi later estimated that the liabilities of the firm were nearly £19 million: Levi (n 63) 17.

[95] '[W]e cannot anticipate for the shareholders any other result from an attempt to avoid payment of calls than a great increase of their loss by the addition of the costs of a useless litigation': *The Law Times*, 15 September 1866, 783. The anonymous writer acknowledged that while a fraudulent misrepresentation in a prospectus could avoid a contract, the difficulty facing the shareholders was that they had more than acquiesced to this in accepting dividends. Having taken the profits, they could not now seek to avoid the losses. The observation was prescient. *The Law Times*, however, was concerned with the rights of creditors, later observing that 'we considered the rights of creditors against the company subordinate to the equity of persons who had been unduly constituted members of it to be relieved from that position': Anon, 'Principle and Machinery in the Companies Act' 43 *The Law Times*, 6 July 1867, 137.

[96] *Solicitors' Journal*, 29 September 1866, 1109.

What was the state of the law in 1866 that two leading journals could be in such disagreement? The legal uncertainty was caused because courts had not yet established the complex relationships between a company (including its directors), shareholders and creditors under the new Companies Act. The disjointed manner in which these cases appeared before courts did not assist judges in establishing these relationships. The most significant case arose shortly before the collapse: *Ship's case*.[97] Ship bought shares in a bank on the strength of its prospectus. After Ship's application the company was incorporated and the memorandum and articles of association exceeded the objects in the prospectus. When the company failed, Ship discovered this variation and applied, before the winding-up order, to have his name removed from the register. Wood V-C in February 1865, directed that Ship's name be removed because 'as regards the company a gross fraud has been perpetrated, indeed, one of the grossest frauds conceivable',[98] since the prospectus invited Ship to apply for shares in a company of one particular description and then 'registered him as a member of a company of a totally different description'.[99] The decision was upheld on appeal, on the basis that Ship had never agreed to become a member of the company actually formed. While the company's creditors received some attention, this was outweighed by judicial concern for a shareholder who had been induced to purchase shares by a prospectus promising a limited endeavour only to become a member of a larger endeavour.[100] Ship's success encouraged shareholders in other companies to challenge their contracts on similar grounds.[101] Most applications were brought in equity, and the initial reaction was favourable to shareholders. Overend, Gurney's collapse generated an interest in the press about the 'release' of these shareholders on the basis of a misrepresentation. As the number of applications by shareholders increased, concerns were raised about the acceptability of allowing other 'innocent' parties to bear the risk of a company's failure: namely, the remaining shareholders and the creditors. Courts, having recognised that a misrepresentation in a prospectus was actionable even where the company's officers were not aware of its falsity,[102] began

[97] *Re The Scottish Universal Finance Bank (Limited), Ship's case* (1865) 12 TLR 256; 2 De Gex, J and S 544; 46 ER 486.

[98] 12 TLR 256, 256.

[99] ibid, 257.

[100] Before Wood V-C the creditors argued that in advancing credit they had regard to the names of the shareholders and that there must have been an authority to include the particular shareholder in this list. Wood V-.C replied that it must have been obvious to the creditors that since the authority to purchase the shares predated the articles of association, the authority was made with reference to the prospectus. On appeal, Turner LJ stated: 'the creditors of the company trust the company, and those who are or may be members of company. They do not trust individual members of the company otherwise than as being members of the company': 12 TLR 256, 259.

[101] *Re Scottish Universal Finance Bank, Breckenridge's case* (1865) 2 H & M 642; 71 ER 613; *Re The English, &c Rolling Stock Company, Lyon's case* (1866) 35 Beav 646; 55 ER 1048; *Ross v The Estates Investment Company (Limited)* (1866) 36 LJ Eq 54; 15 TLR 272; *Re The Russian (Vyksoundsky) Ironworks Company (Limited), Stewart's case* (1866) 14 LTR 659, aff'd (1866) 14 LTR 817; *Re Madrid Bank, Wilkinson's case* (1867) 15 WR 331; *Hallows v Fernie* (1867) 36 LJ Eq 267; 15 TLR 602; and *Re The Reese River Silver Mining Company (Limited), Smith's case* (1867) 16 TLR 549.

[102] In *Re The Reese River Silver Mining Company (Limited), Smith's case* (n 101) the promoters were defrauded by an American, and the promoters reproduced these representations without being aware

to restrict their initial generosity.[103] While some restrictions went to the misrepresentation,[104] most went to subsequent acts of the shareholder, interpreted as acquiescence which estopped him from rescinding the contract.[105] Ultimately, the House of Lords resolved the Overend, Gurney litigation by finding that the prospectus's statements were actionable but that, by their delay, the shareholders lost their rights of rescission.[106] The concern to protect the public from the speculative and fraudulent activities of company promoters gave way to a concern to protect other shareholders and creditors from shareholders who sought reasons to avoid their contracts as the value of shares dropped and further calls were made.

It is against this legal and economic background that Lord Gilbert Kennedy's case was played out. Ironically, Kennedy's dispute began long before the panic of 1866. His dispute concerned a respectable company. The Intercolonial Royal Mail Steam Packet Company (Limited) had been formed in 1858 'to provide steam communication between Australia and New Zealand, and to promote emigration to those colonies'.[107] New Zealanders desired a regular steam postal service from

of their falsity. Turner LJ observed that this did not excuse them because when they took it upon themselves to 'declare the authenticity' of the reports, they, took upon themselves the consequences of the reports being false. If they wished to be excused of the falsity of the reports, 'they should have framed their prospectus in a perfectly different mode': 551.

[103] Different judges also viewed the actions of shareholders subsequent to the purchase in different lights. The *Solicitors' Journal* observed that had *Re The Reese River Silver Mining Company* been heard by the Master of the Rolls, Smith's attempt to sell his shares would likely have prevented his release: Anon, 'Corporate Misrepresentation—V', *Solicitors' Journal*, 14 July 1866, 879.

[104] Eg, where the articles of association were not wholly incompatible with the prospectus the contract could not be rescinded for misrepresentation (*Re The Hop and Malt Exchange and Warehouse Company (Limited), ex parte Briggs* (1866) 14 LTR 39) and where the articles of association existed at the time the prospectus was distributed the person applying for shares had constructive notice of the articles and could not be relieved of liability on the basis of a variation (*Re Madrid Bank, Wilkinson's case* (n 101), aff'd (1867) 15 WR 499). It was the case that where a fraudulent misrepresentation lay, an action in deceit could be brought against its maker, and there were many who advocated this as the principal remedy of deceived shareholders: Thring (n 78) 53. The difficulty was that many of these makers had either disappeared or were without assets.

[105] A lapse of a reasonable time, in circumstances where there were questions raised about a company, barred a shareholder where the misrepresentations were 'the most wanton I ever saw', per Lord Romilly MR. in *Re The Breech-Loading Armoury Company (Limited), ex parte Blackstone* (1867) 16 TLR 273; or where a shareholder attempted to sell his shares once he was aware of the misrepresentation (*Re The Hop and Malt Exchange and Warehouse Company (Limited), ex parte Briggs* (n 104). Shareholders also lost their right to repudiate by delay (*Re The Cachar Company, Lawrence's case* and *Re The Russian Vyksounsky Iron Works Company (Limited), Kincaid's case* (1867) 16 TLR 223); or where a shareholder waited to see if the company would prosper (*Re Russian (Vyksounsky) Iron Works Company, Taite's case and Clavering's case* (1867) 16 TLR 343). That the decisions in *Ship's case* and *Stewart's case* were later limited was observed by contemporaries: 11 *Solicitors' Journal*, 9 March 1867, 425.

[106] *Oakes v Turquand and Harding* and *Peek v The Same* (1867) 36 LJ Ch 949. Their Lordships were particularly concerned in reaching this decision with the plight of the creditors. In doing so, they affirmed the judgment of Malins V-C (1867) 15 WR 397, which had distinguished *Ship's case* as a case in which the contract was void. His decision was not without contemporary critics, the *Solicitors' Journal* noting that 'the distinction thus drawn between *Ship's case* and a case of misrepresentation is insubstantial and illusory': 11 *Solicitors' Journal*, 16 February 1867, 355.

[107] 1864 (452) *Return of Names, Places of Business, Date of Registration, Nominal Capital and Number of Shares of Joint Stock Companies; Number of Shareholders and Number of Companies registered in City of London, to May 1864*, 46. The same source states that the company had been incorporated under the

Britain across Panama and sent their Postmaster General, Crosbie Ward, to Britain in 1863 to negotiate with the British government or a private company to carry out the project. Ward had received the agreement of the New Zealand government and a ministerial minute authorising Ward to negotiate on behalf of New Zealand for an extension of the postal service.[108] In November 1863, Ward accepted, on behalf of the New Zealand government, the tender of the Intercolonial, who then held the contract to deliver mail between Britain and New Zealand.[109] While questions were raised about Ward's authority to contract on behalf of the New Zealand government thes')e were decided in the affirmative. In December 1863, Ward entered into articles of agreement with the Intercolonial. The Intercolonial directors resolved to raise the necessary capital to perform the contract. The name of the company was changed to the Panama, New Zealand, Australian Royal Mail company (Limited) ('The Panama Mail Company') and a prospectus issued in March 1864 stated that new shares were to be issued to facilitate the contract entered into with the New Zealand government for a monthly mail service between Sydney, New Zealand and Panama.[110] Lord Gilbert Kennedy, having seen the prospectus and discussed the matter with his broker, applied for 1,600 shares. These were allotted to him and he paid £2 per share. In June 1864, the Panama Mail Company heard that the New Zealand government had declined to recognise the contract. The Panama Mail Company promptly informed its shareholders of this fact.[111] Kennedy, having received the circular, immediately wrote to the Panama Mail Company demanding the return of his money. Kennedy was not the only shareholder dismayed over the possible loss of the contract.[112] While Ward maintained that he had the requisite authority,[113] the New Zealand government set about ratifying the contract. The Panama Mail Company continued to proceed with the construction of the

Joint Stock Companies Acts of 1856 and 1857 with 183 shareholders at the date of the last return; the total amount of calls received was approximately £123,296 and with a nominal capital of £187,500.

108 The detailed facts of the matter are set out in the accounts in *The Times* on 3 June 1867, 10, and 5 June 1867, 10.

109 1863 [3155] *Postmaster General: Ninth Report*, 22. The Postmaster General's powers under the contract had been delegated to the New Zealand Governor. An annual payment of £24,000 was made to the company.

110 *The Times*, 26 February 1864, 10. It was recommended that 67,500 new shares of £10 each were created to provide the capital to carry out the project. New directors, including men from the two companies that the Panama Mail Company needed to work with to carry out the project, were appointed. The public announcement can be seen in *John Bull*, 12 March 1864; 171.

111 The circular began: 'the directors feel it their duty to inform the shareholders that, by the Australian mail just arrived, intelligence has been received that the present Government of New Zealand has declined to recognise in its present shape the contract': reproduced in *Daily Southern Cross*, 22 August 1864, 6. This reference, and all further references to New Zealand papers, has been drawn from the National Library of New Zealand (http://paperspast.natlib.govt.nz).

112 At an extraordinary meeting of shareholders in October 1864, a Mr Hudson moved to appoint a committee of inquiry to look into the Panama Mail Company's affairs. The motion was defeated, following allegations as to Hudson's motives: *Daily Southern Cross*, 23 December 1864, 5.

113 He explained this in a letter to the secretary of the Panama Mail Company reproduced in *The Times*, 3 June 1867, 10.

steamers they had ordered.[114] The Panama Mail Company refused to return Kennedy's money to him on the grounds that Ward assured them that the contract was binding and that, in any event, the New Zealand government would ratify the contract. Kennedy brought an action in October 1864 demanding the return of his money. In December 1864, the Panama Mail Company demanded the overdue instalments on his shares with interest (£4,917). In February 1865, the New Zealand government ratified substantially the same contract. The Panama Mail Company then brought an action against Kennedy to recover the overdue instalments in March 1865.

The Panama Mail Company delayed trial of the case. In February 1865, after the issue had been joined and the case set down for trial, the Panama Mail Company obtained an order for a commission to examine Ward and other witnesses in New Zealand as to Ward's authority. At the end of Trinity Term 1865, Kennedy's counsel received an order rescinding the commission, having argued that the documents were all in Britain and that the real object was to delay the trial until after the long vacation.[115] The case came up before Crompton J and a special jury in Croydon during the summer assizes in August 1865. There was an enormous amount of litigation before the court, mainly from London,[116] and two extra courts were established to get through the cases in a fortnight. Kennedy's case passed the reporters unnoticed. At the assizes a nominal verdict was taken in Kennedy's action for money had and received, and in the Panama Mail Company's action for the outstanding sums, subject to a special case. It may be that Crompton J suggested this course of action on the basis that the matter involved predominantly issues of law,[117] or it may be that the parties themselves were agreed that this was the best way of dealing with the matter, given that the volume of litigation soon meant that trying all the cases would be hopeless.[118] A verdict subject to a special case meant that the matter proceeded to the court for its opinion on the law.[119] A long delay then ensued before, two years later, the matter came before the Queen's Bench Division in June 1867. The delay likely ensured the Panama Mail Company's

[114] The Panama Mail Company apparently made clear that in so proceeding they did not relinquish the right to sue New Zealand for damages in the event of a breach of contract: *Nelson Examiner and New Zealand Chronicle*, 4 October 1864, 3.

[115] *The Times*, 16 June 1865, 11.

[116] '[T]he jurors of Surrey have good cause for complaint, that upon them is cast the burden of the civil business of the metropolis': 40 *The Law Times*, 12 August 1865, 494.

[117] He had suggested this as a means of dealing with a similar case in the same assizes: *The Consolidated Bank (Limited) v Smith* (1865) 9 *Solicitors' Journal*, 12 August 1865, 909. Kennedy had the same counsel as the defendant.

[118] *The Law Times*, 12 August 1865, 498. The matters raised were in documents: *The Times*, 3 June 1867, 10.

[119] *Chitty's Archbold's Practice of the Court of Queen's Bench*, 12th edn, S Prentice (ed) (London, H Sweet and Stevens & Sons, 1866) 452–55. Generally the case in such instances was that evidence was given at trial by each party to prove the facts upon which he relied and any disputed facts would be determined by the jury. The practice was not unusual where the case presented difficult issues of law: *Lush's Practice of the Superior Courts of Law*, 3rd edn, J Dixon (ed) (London, Butterworths, 1865) 957, and the court could give judgment without making inferences of fact: ibid, 959. The determination of Ward's authority was a legal one. Section 32 of the Common Law Procedure Act 1854 provided that error could be brought upon a judgment on a special case.

success, because the economy had changed entirely. Where, during the summer assizes of 1865, the market was buoyant and the papers carried accounts of persons disappointed not to have received Overend, Gurney shares,[120] by 1867 the courts were full of shareholders attempting to have themselves removed from the register. As the economy had changed, so, too, had the reaction of the courts to the shareholders' actions.

Kennedy was represented by Mellish QC, a prominent barrister in the shareholders' cases of the 1860s.[121] Mellish observed at the outset that the central question in both actions was whether or not Kennedy was a shareholder: if he was not, then he could recover the money he had paid and the Panama Mail Company's action for the outstanding calls would fail. The question involved three issues: first, whether Ward had authority to contract; second, if he did not, whether it was a condition of the contract to take shares that the mail contract existed; and third, whether there was a fraudulent representation by the Panama Mail Company that vitiated the shares contract. Common mistake was not raised, although clearly both parties laboured under a misapprehension. Mellish's arguments did not seek to transform the common law but to work within it. Mellish disposed of the first issue quickly: the legislation clearly indicated that any authority to contract for mail delivery was limited to an amount below the contract price and the Panama Mail Company could have entertained no doubt about this upon their counsel's opinion. The second issue was more difficult: whether the prospectus statement that a mail contract existed was a condition to the shares contract such that if the condition did not exist, there was no shares contract. Mellish argued that because Kennedy had been invited to take shares to fulfil the mail contract the mail contract was a condition of the shares contract: without the mail contract there was no means of providing profits to him. *Ship's* case supported this argument because it was based on the rule that a shares application must have reference to the prospectus. The situation here was the same; the purpose of the new shares was to meet a contract which did not exist, and thus the undertaking was entirely different from the one Kennedy had been invited to join. The mail contract was of the essence of the shares contract; the lack of the former gave Kennedy the right to repudiate the latter. 'He was not bound to wait for or accept a substituted contract.'[122] The argument 'was founded on a failure of the essential condition or consideration of the contract. It was not enough to say that the company had acted bona fide. The condition had failed, and Kennedy had a right to insist upon it.'[123] Mellish made clear that this ground arose independently of fraud. Mellish largely based his case on the failure of a condition and did not strenuously argue that the fraudulent representation of the company vitiated the contract:

[120] *Daily News*, 1 August 1865, 6.
[121] He also represented the liquidators in the Overend, Gurney litigation of *Oakes v Turquand*; *Peek v Turquand* (1867) LR 2 HL 325.
[122] *The Times*, 5 June 1867, 10.
[123] ibid.

> it was rather mentioned than strongly insisted on, and he [Mellish] appeared not strenuously to dissent from an observation made by one of the learned Judges, that the worst that could be said of the directors was that they had been in error, and had rashly, if erroneously, believed that the contract to be valid and binding when in strict law, perhaps, it was not.[124]

Manisty QC, for the Panama Mail Company, observed that the company's articles of association existed when Kennedy contracted to take shares, and these articles provided that the company's business was conducted under the Board's management. When Kennedy took shares he was in the same position as if he had signed these articles and thus agreed with the directors' powers to vary and alter contracts. Ward, Manisty argued, had authority to enter into the mail contract although 'the Court seemed very much against him'.[125] There was no absolute warranty that Ward had authority, only a representation which was only actionable if fraudulent. Alternatively, even if there had been a condition or warranty, there was no breach of it because there was a valid contract for the mail, and the only difficulty was created by a difference of opinion following the change of administration in New Zealand. In addition, even if there was a failure of the condition, this was not a total failure of consideration because it went only to part of the consideration: Kennedy had shares in a valid and subsisting company which was doing business and paying dividends. While Manisty submitted that there was no fraud, the Court declined to hear argument on the point.

At the conclusion of the arguments, *The Times*' reporter was of the opinion that the judges viewed the case as turning upon a condition or warranty and 'rather in the direction of judgment for Lord G Kennedy on the ground of a failure of condition or consideration'.[126] Cockburn CJ noted that it appeared that Kennedy had subscribed 'upon the faith of a certain state of facts which did not exist'[127]: the directors sought capital to apply it to a particular contract which would yield a profit when in fact they had no such contract. He implied that the mail contract was a condition of the shares contract. It did not matter if the directors believed the mail contract existed because they should have known whether it existed. 'Their business was to know a fact, if they stated it as a fact; and if they had only believed it they should have stated it as a belief.'[128] Had this been the decision in *Kennedy's case*, it would have had the effect of adopting into the common law the equitable decision in *Re The Reese River Silver Mining Company (Limited), Smith's case*. Blackburn J observed that this was not a case of fraud, for the worst that could be said was that the directors acted rashly, even erroneously, in believing the contract to be valid but this was not enough to sustain even a case of constructive fraud. Blackburn J appeared to be of the view that there was an implied condition

[124] ibid.
[125] ibid.
[126] ibid.
[127] ibid.
[128] ibid.

that the contract for mail existed. Had this been the decision in the case, it would have effectively implemented Blackburn J's decision in *Taylor v Caldwell* in relation to the formation of contracts. Mellor J stated that *Kennedy*'s case was different from the other cases before the courts because Kennedy had shares of some value, 'there was an existing company doing business under existing contracts, earning profits and declaring dividends'.[129] Kennedy, however, had undertaken to purchase shares issued for the express purpose of carrying out a particular contract which did not exist. Shee J noted that the position of the company was wholly different without the contract. Despite these statements which indicated support for Kennedy's argument, and to the surprise of *The Times*' reporter, the Court reserved their judgment.

Three weeks later the case was decided against Kennedy. What can explain the apparent change of opinion by the judges? The most likely explanation is that Kennedy's action was refused on policy grounds. By the time *Kennedy*'s case came before the Queen's Bench, the tide had shifted against the shareholders in Chancery. Where once courts had viewed with sympathy the claims of shareholders that they had taken out their subscriptions on the faith of false representations in the prospectus, this sympathy waned as increasing numbers of shareholders sought to set aside their subscriptions following the panic of 1866. Correspondingly, concern increased about creditors who faced unsatisfied claims for goods and services honestly advanced in the course of their own businesses. Creditors, unlike shareholders, were not speculators. Sympathy was also extended to those shareholders who stayed by their shares and honoured the later calls. Chancery did not shift in favour of these creditors and remaining shareholders by altering the criteria for an actionable misrepresentation but by two, interconnected, devices. The first was to categorise the contract in *Ship*'s case as entirely void because the purposes were completely different.[130] The second was to hold that a representation created a voidable contract which could no longer be rescinded because of the shareholder's acquiescence. Acquiescence was generally made out by the shareholder's delay, his attempts to sell the shares or his receipt of dividends. In *Kennedy*'s case, none of these bars existed: he had acted immediately to repudiate the contract, had not attempted to sell the shares nor had he accepted dividends. It seems likely that the Queen's Bench Division was unwilling to receive into the common law the overspill that might occur from Chancery if *Kennedy*'s case was admitted. In many instances, prospectuses had provided for things which turned out not to be the case: the floodgates would open if these were all seen as conditions of the contract. The practicalities of the situation forced the Court to deny *Kennedy*'s case by employing a variant of the first means used to limit *Ship*'s case. Kennedy's contract was not void, because what he had bought was not substantially different from what he had proposed to buy. And the fact of it was that by the time the matter appeared before the court, the

[129] *The Times*, 5 June 1867, 10.
[130] *Oakes v Turquand*; *Peek v Turquand* (1867) LR 2 HL 325 upheld this view.

company had a similar form of contract with New Zealand and it was delivering the mail.[131]

Blackburn J gave the decision.[132] Ward did not have authority to enter the mail contract and it did not bind the New Zealand government. The question of whether there was fraud or deceit on the part of the directors was one of fact. While the prospectus statement was intended to induce share purchases and Kennedy was so induced to purchase the shares, it could not be shown that there was any mala fides in the representation. The directors mistakenly, but honestly, believed, on the basis of counsel's opinion, that Ward had authority to contract on behalf of the New Zealand government. This was an honest mistake and not a fraudulent misrepresentation. In reaching this conclusion, the case turns away from considering whether there was a negligent misrepresentation; this likely occurred because the company had taken the advice of counsel. It was too much to find, in such circumstances, that the company ought to have known the representation was false or that they had been reckless in making it.

Having disposed of these issues, Blackburn J turned to an issue 'of much greater difficulty'.[133] He did not consider Mellish's condition precedent argument in the way in which it had been argued. Instead, Blackburn J considered that the issue was whether there was such a difference in substance between the shares of a company with a mail contract and shares in a company without such a contract as to allow the shareholder to return the shares, independently of any fraud. *Ship*'s case[134] meant that Kennedy could repudiate the shares contract if the invalidity of the mail contract meant that the shares received were different in substance. Blackburn J regarded the prospectus statement as an innocent misrepresentation made without fraud rather than a warranty, and thus there could not be a rescission 'unless it is such as to shew that there is a complete difference in substance between what it was supposed to be and what was taken, so as to constitute a failure of consideration'.[135] Blackburn J thus refused to extend the common law to provide relief to a person who contracted as a result of an innocent misrepresentation. While a contract could be rescinded for fraud, rescission would only occur for an innocent misrepresentation where there was a complete difference in

131 The Panama Mail Co had taken the money raised by its share issue and purchased vessels to enable it to carry out the contract. The matter was touched upon now and again in contemporary newspapers. The trial trip of the *Mataura*, a screw steamer built expressly for the purpose of the monthly mail service to New Zealand, was reported to have had 'very favourable results' in its trials in July 1866: *The Times*, 10 July 1866, 12. The *Ruahhino* was reported to have made a 'splendid trip' out to New Zealand, and the *Kaikoura* was reported to have left New Zealand with passengers, parcels and mail: *The Times*, 13 August 1866, 5. At the half-yearly general meeting of the company in December 1 866, the chairman 'congratulated the shareholders on the successful commencement of the Panama service' and stated that 'it certainly promised to be very prosperous': *Daily Southern Cross*, 23 February 1867, 5.

132 It seems likely that this decision was read from a written one. The wording of the surviving reports of the case are virtually identical.

133 LR 2 QB 580, 586.

134 According to Blackburn J. it was also the basis of *Gompertz v Bartlett* (1853) 2 El & Bl 849; 118 ER 985; and *Gurney v Wormersley* (1854) 4 El & Bl 133; 119 ER 51.

135 LR 2 QB 580, 587.

substance such that there was a complete failure of consideration. In doing this, Blackburn J had expressly declined to recognise that a mistake as to quality could vitiate a contract in English law.[136] Ironically, his next statement was to eventually have the effect of supporting the jurists' views that English contract law recognised mistake as to a quality. Blackburn J compared the English law to the position in Roman law concerned first with an *error in corpore*[137] and then with an *error in substantia.* He gave Ulpian's example concerned with the sale of slaves. There was no *error in substantia* where a female slave was sold under the mistaken belief that she was a virgin but there was when she was sold under the mistaken belief that she was male. In the latter case the contract was a nullity.[138] Blackburn J undoubtedly intended only to support the common law approach to a failure of consideration with an analogy to the elegance of Roman jurisprudence, for he then set out what he saw as the applicable underlying principle of English law:

> as we apprehend, the principle of our law is the same as that of the civil law; and the difficulty in every case is to determine whether the mistake or misapprehension is as to the substance of the whole consideration, going, as it were, to the root of the matter, or only to some point, even though a material point, an error as to which does not affect the substance of the whole consideration.[139]

Blackburn J, one of the 'creative minds in a creative age',[140] was aware of the differences between English and civil law.[141] He had taken the same approach in *Taylor v Caldwell,*[142] in which he compared English law to Roman law.[143] Blackburn J did not decide *Kennedy's case* on the basis of *error in substantia*; he employed the Roman law to illustrate an analogous principle which supported the common law position that there was not a failure of consideration. While Mellish had argued this on the basis that the stipulation in the prospectus was a condition precedent to the contract, Blackburn J rejected this argument as only 'remotely analogous' to the real question of whether or not consideration had failed. The effect of Blackburn J's innovative use of the Roman *error in substantia* was to prevent the rescission of a contract to take shares where the representation was innocent or negligent but not fraudulent. It neatly solved the court's dilemma. It was true that while Kennedy (through no fraud of the directors) had not got exactly the shares he bargained for, he had got shares in a functioning company paying

[136] He expressly cited *Street v Blay* (1831) 2 B & A 456; 109 ER 1212, and observed that in the absence of an express warranty or fraud, there could be no rescission where the parties were mistaken as to a quality of the horse.

[137] D.18.1.9–11 ('De Contrahenda Emptione') discussed earlier, in ch 2.

[138] Savigny explained this on the ground that there was an *error in substantia* because there was a complete difference in the work undertaken by slaves of different sexes: ch 6.

[139] LR 2 QB 580, 588.

[140] CHS Fifoot, *Judge and Jurist in the Reign of Victoria* (London, Stevens and Sons, 1959) 135.

[141] He was at pains to point out in his *Treatise on the Effect of The Contract of Sale* (London, William Benning & Co, 1845) the differences between Pothier's *Du Contrat de Vente* and English law: 172.

[142] (1863) 3 B & S 826; 122 ER 309.

[143] *Digest,* 45.I. 23, 33. His use of the Roman law was inapposite. See C MacMillan, '*Taylor v Caldwell* (1863)' in C Mitchell and P Mitchell (eds) *Landmark Cases in the Law of Contract,* (Oxford and Portland, OR, Hart Publishing, 2008).

dividends. By the time the judges considered his case, the company had a contract to deliver mail to New Zealand which was very similar to the first contract attempted.[144] Kennedy, unlike many other shareholders following the 1866 collapse, had shares of some value. If Kennedy had been able to rescind his contract, it is likely that large numbers of other shareholders in the Panama Mail Company, and other companies, would have been able to rescind their contracts, leaving their fellow shareholders and company creditors to hold an even greater loss. Blackburn J's use of the Roman *error in substantia* provided a useful tool to distinguish cases in which the contract to take shares was not good (and *Ship*'s case was applicable) and where it was good. The analogy of the Roman *error in substantia* also acted to severely curtail the actionability of innocent misrepresentations in the common law. It was this aspect which contemporary observers noted. *The Law Times*, ever eager to reduce the number of circumstances in which shareholders could repudiate their contracts, seized upon the case as a further limitation to their ability to do so.[145] The utility of the case, for *The Law Times*, lay in Blackburn J's elucidation of the circumstances in which an apparent shareholder could relieve himself of his shares because this acted to limit ambit of *Ship*'s case.

[144] In an obscure twist to this case, the first indications of financial difficulties with the Panama Mail Co occurred a fortnight after the court's decision. It was reported that the company would be unable to declare a dividend due to a shortfall in its receipts: *The Times*, 9 July 1867, 10. An outbreak of yellow fever in the West Indies greatly disrupted traffic through Panama and created further problems: *The Times*, 16 June 1868, 10; *The North Otago Times*, 14 February 1868, 2. Fear of sickness greatly diminished passenger numbers, and the line became far less profitable: *Nelson Examiner and New Zealand Chronicle*, 10 December 1868, 4. By October 1868, there was an extraordinary meeting of the company in which the chairman, Lord Claud Hamilton, proposed to wind up the affairs of the company. This was rejected: *Otago Witness*, 12 December 1868, 2. The value of shares had slumped considerably, and shares were then trading at 15s for £5 fully paid up and 30s for £10 paid up: *North Otago Times*, 8 December 1868, 2. A later problem that the company faced was a rival steam service via Suez, a service generally favoured by the Australian colonies. In 1866 and 1867, three to four times the amount of mail was delivered via Suez than via Panama: (1868–69) (227) Correspondence with Australian Governments on Postal Communications since Establishment of New Postal Service with India and China, App A. The inability of the colonists in New Zealand (who generally favoured the Panama route) and the Australian colonies, notably Queensland and Victoria (who generally favoured the Suez route), to co-operate in the deliveries by the company was a continuing problem and contributed to the company's demise. The end appears to have come about in early 1869 when creditors (a rival, the Royal Mail Steam Packet Company) seized and sold some of the steam vessels, an action which prevented the company from functioning effectively: *Daily Southern Cross*, 18 January 1869, 4; *Daily News*, 13 February 1869, 6; *Daily News*, 29 April 1869, 7. The Panama Royal Mail Co sent its last vessel from Sydney on 2 December 1868. In February 1869, the post office announced a discontinuance of mail service via Panama and that, henceforth, mail would be delivered via Suez: *The Pall Mall Gazette*, 16 February 1869. At the request of the Panama Mail Company, Malins V-C made a winding-up order on 18 February 1869. The company was reported to have substantial assets: *The Times*, 19 February 1869, 10. The company appears to have been honestly run until the end, with reports that the contributions of shareholders given with the intention of improving the company's position would be returned: *Liverpool Mercury*, 1 February 1869. Lord Gilbert Kennedy's demise was somewhat later; he died in Chelsea in November 1901, at the age of 79: *The Times*, 26 November 1901, 1.

[145] Anon, 'Relief from Shares', *The Law Times*, 16 November 1867, 40. The digest of the case in the *Weekly Reporter* was that the difference in the shares subscribed for and the shares allotted on the supposed existence of the mail contract was not so different as to justify repudiation in the absence of fraud: (1866–67) 15 *Weekly Reporter* col 59.

In particular, *Kennedy's* case provided a clear distinction between innocent and fraudulent misrepresentation. Where the misrepresentation was fraudulent, any material difference rescinded the contract but where it was innocent, only a substantial difference entitled a shareholder to rescind the contract, because he received 'in substance, though not in degree or particulars, what he bargained for'.[146] Although *The Law Times* made no mention of a doctrine of mistake (or even the reference to Roman law), the *Solicitors' Journal* made more of the use of Roman law and wrote about 'mistake', but by this the author appeared to have meant a mistake in fact rather than a doctrine of mistake in law.[147] Again, for this author, the significance of the case lay in the distinction of when a contract to take shares could be rescinded for an honest misrepresentation. The case also illustrated that it was open to the parties 'to make it a part of the bargain that if there is any mistake as to quality, or any mistake of any kind, the contract shall be at an end, but in the absence of such a stipulation a mistake as to the quality of goods, not caused by fraud, is not a sufficient ground for rescinding a contract'.[148] Because Kennedy's mistake was as to quality, the author explained, he was denied relief. In short, 'no new point of law is decided by this case'.[149] In later nineteenth-century litigation, *Kennedy v Panama Royal Mail Co* was cited by counsel and utilised by judges as support for the proposition that an innocent misrepresentation did not entitle a party to rescission unless the misrepresentation was as to something which fundamentally changed the nature of the contract.[150] Blackburn J, as Lord Blackburn, returned to the case in the Scottish case of *Mackay v Dick*[151] and explained that it had been decided in *Kennedy v The Panama Royal Mail Co* that a party could return a thing which had been delivered to him in fulfilment of a contract if it substantially differed from that which was contracted for. It is significant that over a decade later, Lord Blackburn did not explain the case as one in which the basis of the decision was a doctrine of mistake.

The treatise characterisation of *Kennedy's* case as one based on mistake occurred a decade later, although Anson refused such a characterisation.[152] Leake,

[146] ibid.

[147] 12 *Solicitors' Journal*, 9 November 1867, 28.

[148] ibid.

[149] ibid.

[150] As to reliance by counsel in argument, see *Oakes v Turquand*; *Peek v Turquand* (1867) LR 2 HL 325, 338; *Ross v Estates Investment Company* (1867–68) LR 3 Ch App 682, 684; *New Sombrero Phosphate Company v Erlanger* (1877) LR 5 ChD 73, 87; *Sharpley v Louth and East Coast Railway Company* (1875–76) LR 2 ChD 663, 672; *Edgington v Fitzmaurice* (1885) LR 29 ChD 459, 464; and *Arnison v Smith* [1889] LR 41 ChD 348, 353. The case was so employed by the judiciary in *Newbigging v Adam* [1887] LR 34 ChD 582, 592 per Bowen LJ, and *In Re Addlestone Linoleum Company* (1888) LR 37 ChD 191, 196 per Kay J. It was even so used by Bucknill J as late as 1910 in *Angel v Jay* [1911] 1 KB 666, 673.

[151] (1880–81) LR 6 App Cas 251, 265. Lord Blackburn said that other judges had accepted his view and he had no reason to change it.

[152] Anson and the authors of subsequent editions of his treatise firmly held the view that the case was not about mistake but about the performance of the terms agreed upon: he made no mention of the case in his first and second editions, and in his third edition he warned that Pollock's treatment of the case was 'misleading': Sir WR Anson, *Principles of the English Law of Contract*, 3rd edn (Oxford, Clarendon Press, 1884) 122.

writing the same year, made no mention of the case.[153] Possibly because of this omission Benjamin ignored the case in his first edition. In his second edition he included *Kennedy's* case but the treatment was a confused one. He appeared to view it as a case of both mistake and an innocent misrepresentation, although the point was never clear. The case was placed in the mistake chapter with the marginal note that it was an 'innocent misrepresentation causing mistake'. Benjamin urged the use of Roman law to explain the common law, underlining that where there was a mistake as to the substance of the whole consideration going to the root of the matter, error affected the contract.[154] The implication was that an innocent misrepresentation could create a mistake which was actionable. The writers of later editions of his treatise were to explicitly employ *Kennedy's* case as support for a number of propositions about mistake.[155] Pollock was the first to strongly advocate that the case was one of mistake and he made much of it because it appeared to support his proposition that a fundamental error as to some quality of the subject matter avoided the contract. As he noted, the difficult question in this case was whether the thing the party intended to contract for was, in absence of the quality, the thing he received. And for Pollock, 'the rule governing this whole class of cases is fully explained' in *Kennedy v Panama Mail Company*.[156] It is perplexing that Pollock did not incorporate Savigny's much-admired[157] analysis of *error in substantia*. Two decades after it had been decided, *Kennedy v Panama Mail Company* was so firmly established as a case of a mistake as to a quality that it crossed the Atlantic and was relied upon by the Supreme Court of Michigan in *Sherwood v Walker*.[158] The result was that while *Kennedy's* case prevented the development of liability at common law for innocent misrepresentations it was used to develop a principle that a mistake as to a quality could render

[153] Leake added the case to his mistake chapter in the second edition of his treatise, noting that the decision was authority for the proposition that Kennedy's contract was absolute and that the mistake did not affect the substance or validity of the shares contracted for, nor was there a failure of consideration: SM Leake, *An Elementary Digest of the Law of Contracts*, 2nd edn (London, Stevens and Sons, 1878) 345. Sir Edward Fry, writing of equitable mistake, accepted that the case was one where the common law avoided the contract on the ground of want of consent or a total failure of consideration: Fry (n 60) 324, §722.

[154] JP Benjamin, *A Treatise on the Law of Sale of Personal Property*, 2nd edn (London, Henry Sweet, 1873) 328–29.Benjamin also considered the case in relation to warranties.

[155] WAC Ker wrote that the case stood for the proposition that only a mistake as to an essential matter, such that 'there must be a difference in substance between the thing contracted for and that actually existing, so as to constitute a failure of consideration': JP Benjamin, *A Treatise on the Law of Sale of Personal Property*, 6th edn, WAC Ker (ed) (London, Sweet and Maxwell, 1920) 113. The point was also explicitly made that an innocent misrepresentation could create a mistake: 491–92. The proper conception of the case, however, was one falling 'under the head of mistake': 495.

[156] Pollock (n 33) 336. In fairness to Pollock, he did recognise (at 394) that the case was concerned with an innocent misrepresentation, although in so doing he seemed to suggest that the case was voidable whereas his earlier implication was that such a contract was void. No attempt was made to reconcile this difference.

[157] J Mackintosh, *The Roman Law of Sale* (Edinburgh, T & T Clark, 1892) 31.

[158] (1887) 66 Mich 568, 33 NW 919, 11 AmStRep 531. Morse J, for the majority, accepted this (at 576–77), and the dissenting judge, Sherwood J, accepted this proposition but disagreed as to its application to the facts before him: 582. It seems likely that the case was drawn from either Benjamin's or Leake's treatises, both of which were cited in the judgments.

a contract void. That the case denied liability for an innocent misrepresentation at common law made a doctrine of mistake (which carried no fault) all the more desirable.

Unilateral Mistake rarely renders a Contract Void—*Smith v Hughes* (1871)

The mistake of one party alone presented particular challenges. On the one hand, theoretical consistency seemed to require that such a mistake can operate to prevent the consensus of the parties; Pothier likely accepted that a unilateral error was sufficient to avoid a contract.[159] On the other hand, practical considerations work against the acceptability of most unilateral mistakes. These considerations include the need for commercial certainty and the protection of the non-mistaken party's reasonable reliance. English contract law had largely developed around caveat emptor. At common law, absent a warranty or fraud, the buyer assumed the risk of a unilateral mistake. Equity might provide relief for unilateral mistakes which affected conscience. English common law had long taken an objective approach to contractual formation; the subjective intentions of the parties were rejected in favour of the objective appearance of an agreement. The development of this objective approach existed in a system in which facts were decided by jurors. *Smith v Hughes*[160] is the case in which these two positions are, somewhat uneasily, reconciled. The case was to be an important building-block in the doctrine of mistake for treatises and was frequently relied upon in later cases.

Smith v Hughes concerned circumstances so routine as to escape most commentators. The case concerned a sale of oats by sample. The plaintiff, Smith, was a local farmer, and the defendant, Daniel Hughes, was a gentleman 'and the owner of a large stud of race horses'.[161] In July 1869, oats were in short supply in England and price was correspondingly high. Smith took a sample of oats to the defendant's manager, David Hughes, and offered oats for sale at 35s a quarter. Smith left the sample with Hughes, who wrote shortly thereafter that he would take the oats. After Smith sent the first 16 quarters, the defendant complained that the oats were new oats and not old oats. New oats, the defendant explained, were useless to him.[162] He sent back the oats and refused to take any more; Smith sued him for the price of the oats sent, the storage cost of the oats and the loss on resale of the

[159] See ch 5.

[160] (1871) LR 6 QB 597; 40 LJQB 221; 19 WR 1059. The case has received recent consideration by John Phillips in '*Smith v Hughes* (1871)', in *Landmark Cases in the Law of Contract* (n 43).

[161] *Bell's Life in London and Sporting Chronicle*, Wednesday, 20 October 1869, 2.

[162] New oats could not be fed to horses and were considered a health threat to them: see Phillips (n 160) 207. Phillips relies upon contemporary manuals of horse husbandry: JH Walsh, *The Horse; in the Stable and the Field*, 4th edn (London, 1862), and G Armatage, *The Horse; its Varieties and Management in Health and Disease* (London, 1893).

remaining oats. It appears that the plaintiff had committed sharp practice, although the defendant was unable to establish this. It seems unlikely that Smith was unaware that horse trainers wanted old oats and not new oats; in addition, he had carried sample in his pocket, a notorious means of 'ageing' oats.[163] The evidence established that the plaintiff had also sought a price well above the then market price for new oats[164] and at the going price for old oats.[165] David Hughes, on the other hand, contradicted himself in evidence as to whether or not he had sought only old oats. The defendant was unable to establish that a deception had been practised or that the plaintiff was aware of his misapprehension.

The case came before the Surrey County Court in October 1869. The judge put two questions to the jury: first, whether the term 'old' had been used in connection with the sale of the evidence (a matter upon which the judge had his doubts); and, second, whether they were of the opinion that the plaintiff believed the defendant to believe, or to be under the impression, that he was purchasing old oats. If the answer to either question was in the affirmative, verdict was to be for the defendant. The jury gave a general verdict for the defendant. The matter proceeded as a special case on appeal to the Queen's Bench sitting *en banc*: the question was whether or not the ruling and direction of the judge to the jury was correct. The court thought the point raised by the case sufficiently important to take time to consider their judgment.[166] The importance of the case lay in the relationship between caveat emptor and deceit. If the seller had not warranted the oats to be old, was his behaviour such as would amount to deceit or was his knowledge of the situation such that the contract should be set aside? Pollock QC, for Smith, argued that the judge's second direction was wrong, for this was a sale by sample and caveat emptor applied. If the defendant was under any doubt as to the subject matter of the contract, he could have sought a warranty. In absence of such a warranty or representation by the plaintiff, the plaintiff was under no duty to 'undeceive'[167] the defendant as to his mistaken belief. A promise, as Paley had observed, was to be interpreted 'in the sense in which the promiser apprehended at the time that the promise received it'.[168] Pollock argued that only where a special obligation or trust existed between the parties was mere silence an act of deception. He relied upon the recent work of his former pupil, Judah Benjamin, and also *Story on Contracts*,

[163] Phillips (n 160) 208–209.

[164] (1871) 40 LJQB 221, 222.

[165] *Bell's Life in London and Sporting Chronicle*, Wednesday, 20 October 1869, 2.

[166] *The Times*, 3 May 1871, 11.

[167] LR 6 QB 597, 599.

[168] W Paley, *The Principles of Moral and Political Philosophy*, Boston school edn (Boston, Benjamin B Mussey & Co, 1852) Book III, ch 5. Pollock borrowed the use of Paley from *Chitty on Contract*: Chitty had employed the same passage from Paley to support a theory of objective agreement: J Chitty, *A Practical Treatise of Contracts not under Seal*, 2nd edn (London, S Sweet, 1834) 62. Paley settled upon this proposition on the basis that it was justifiable because the promisor was to be bound to the expectations which he voluntarily and knowingly created: Paley (above) 92. It seems a strange omission on Pollock's part, had he worked from the entirety of Paley's work, that he did not cite the proposition set out in Book III, ch 6: 'whatever is expected by one side, and known to be so expected by the other, is deemed to a part or condition of the contract': ibid, 101.

for this proposition. *Story on Contracts* went further, and indicated that where the silence pertained to a defect in relation to the intrinsic circumstances of the subject matter of the contract (such as its nature, character or condition), mere silence was not fraudulent where proper diligence by the buyer would have revealed the defect. Finally, Pollock referred to Cicero's distinction between concealment and mere silence and concluded that there was no dishonesty where the seller knew of something the buyer did not.[169]

Counsel for Hughes, Arthur Wilson, argued that the parties were not *ad idem*: the plaintiff contracted to sell new oats, and the defendant contracted to purchase old oats. This was the substance of the judge's direction. That there was a sale by sample was immaterial because this went only to the quality, provided that the subject matter of the contract was the same. There was here a tacit representation, an inference of a warranty, that the oats were old oats.[170] The real question was whether the plaintiff led the defendant to believe that the oats were old oats. Wilson then relied upon the proposition set out in *Chitty on Contracts* that where one party to a contract stood by and knowingly allowed the other to contract under a delusion which he might have corrected, the contract was void.[171] Chitty's proposition was based upon *Hill v Gray*,[172] and Blackburn J questioned whether or not the case had been followed.[173] Pollock, in reply, addressed this concern and argued that later authority[174] established that *Hill v Gray* was no authority for Chitty's proposition since the case dealt with a positive deceit. Based on the questions of the Lord Justices it appeared that they were divided as to whether the plaintiff was aware of the defendant's misapprehension.[175]

Written decisions were given a month later.[176] Contemporaries were attracted to Cockburn CJ's judgment[177] because he viewed the central question as whether the passive acquiescence of the seller in the self-deception of the buyer entitled the latter to avoid the contract. He answered this in the negative on the basis that at common law the rule of caveat emptor applied. Where a specific article was sold without an express warranty and in circumstances in which the law did not imply a warranty and where the buyer examined the article to form his own opinion, the buyer's self-created misapprehension did not allow him to avoid the contract for 'he has himself to blame'.[178] Here oats were offered for sale by a sample that

[169] *Cicero de Officiis*, Lib III. Cap XII, xiii.

[170] 19 WR 1059, 1060.

[171] J Chitty, *A Practical Treatise of Contracts Not Under Seal*, 5th edn, JA Russell (ed) (London, S Sweet, 1853) 593.

[172] (1816) 1 Stark 434; 171 ER 521.

[173] 40 LJQB 221, 224.

[174] *Keates v Cadogan* (1851) 10 CB 591; 138 ER 234; 20 LJ CP 76, per Jervis CJ.

[175] Blackburn J stated that the jury 'must have been of the opinion that the defendant was contracting for old oats, and that the plaintiff knew it': 40 LJQB 221, 223, while Cockburn CJ stated that he saw no evidence that a term of the contract was that the oats used were old and that the plaintiff appeared not to know that trainers used only old oats: ibid.

[176] *The Times*, 7 June 1871, 11.

[177] ibid.

[178] LR 6 QB 597, 603.

Hughes had the 'fullest opportunity' of inspecting. The plaintiff said nothing about the age of the oats. There was nothing to create 'any trust or confidence' between the parties such that the plaintiff was obliged to communicate that these were new oats. There was also nothing to indicate that the defendant was acting on anything other than his own judgement; if there was, it might be that the plaintiff's silence amounted to a fraudulent concealment. The argument that the parties were not *ad idem* was rejected because it proceeded on the fallacy of confusing the buyer's motive for purchasing with one of the essential conditions of the contract. The essential condition was the sale of a particular parcel of oats; the motive of the buyer was that these were old oats. For a contract to be valid, the minds had only to be *ad idem* as to the essential condition.

Smith v Hughes marks the point at which the mistake doctrines of the will theorists entered common law cases. It occurred in the decisions of Blackburn J and Hannen J, both of whom on their own initiative had clearly referred to Benjamin's treatment of mistake. Blackburn J agreed with Cockburn CJ that caveat emptor applied; however, he was also of the view that where the parties were not *ad idem* as to the terms of the contract there was no contract 'unless the circumstances are such as to preclude one of the parties from denying that he has agreed to the terms of the other'.[179] In reaching this conclusion, Blackburn J was influenced by Benjamin's view that for a mistake to be operative, it had to be a bilateral mistake because the unilateral mistake of one party would not avoid the contract where the mistaken acceptance had been communicated on unconditional and unequivocal terms.[180] The words of Blackburn J's decision echo Benjamin's:

> if, whatever a man's real intention may be, he so conducts himself that a reasonable man would believe that he was assenting to the terms proposed by the other party, and that other party upon that belief enters into the contract with him, the man thus conducting himself would be equally bound as if he had intended to agree to the other party's terms.[181]

Blackburn J supported this proposition with the same case; oddly, for the development of a doctrine of mistake, it was a case dealing with estoppel.[182] While Blackburn J did not decide the case on the basis of mistake, he had clearly referred to Benjamin's doctrine, and this aspect of the case was re-incorporated and built upon by later writers.

Hannen J began with the proposition that a contract required that both parties 'should agree to the same thing in the same sense',[183] echoing Benjamin's requirement of mutual assent.[184] Benjamin had concluded that a unilateral mistake,

[179] ibid, 607.

[180] Benjamin (n 56) 306: 'For the rule of law is general, that whatever a man's *real* intention may be, if he *manifests* an intention to another party, so as to induce that other party to act upon it, he will be estopped from denying that the intention as *manifested* was his *real* intention.'

[181] LR 6 QB 597, 607.

[182] *Freeman v Cooke* (1848) 2 Ex 654; 154 ER 652.

[183] LR 6 QB 597, 609.

[184] Benjamin (n 56), 36, 302.

unknown to the other party, did not avoid the contract for mistake. He observed that in *Raffles v Wichelhaus* there was no contract because there were two ships 'Peerless'. Had there been only one ship 'Peerless', and a mistake was made by B who, when offered goods by A from this ship ('Peerless'), intended the goods to come from the ship 'Peeress', the contract would be good if A's proposal was unmistakeable and B's acceptance unequivocal and unconditional. In such an instance B was bound regardless of what he really thought. The reason for this was stated in the passage paraphrased by Blackburn J, that when one manifested an intention to another, one was estopped from denying that the intention manifested was the real intention. Hannen J did not carry the analysis this far, but relied upon *Raffles v Wichelhaus* to establish that where there was not an agreement to the same thing, then there was no contract. Hannen J then cited a case used by Benjamin in a corollary passage concerned with mutual assent, *Scott v Littledale.*[185] Benjamin advanced the case as an instance in which the vendor's unilateral mistake was as to the warranty of quality, a collateral matter which could not prevent a contract from coming into existence.[186] Hannen J used the case to illustrate the proposition that Benjamin had discussed immediately prior to this, that where one party had manifested one intention to the other party, he could not then deny that intention. The fault of the vendor precluded him from avoiding the contract. Neither explanation of the case was the actual decision of Campbell CJ, who had held that the contract was not avoided by the mistake and that a court of law could not give effect to an equitable defence because equitable relief in these circumstances would be partial or conditional.[187] Hannen J stated that the rule of law was that an intention manifested by one party to another could not avoid a contract, although the intention might be mistaken. Paley's statement showed that this legal rule had a moral corollary: a promise is to be performed in the sense in which the promiser apprehended at the time the promisee received it. Here, if Smith knew that Hughes dealt with him for oats on the assumption that these were old oats and he was thus aware that Hughes apprehended the contract in a different sense to that which he offered it, then Smith could not insist that Hughes was bound by the apparent bargain. In short:

> in order to relieve the defendant it was necessary that the jury should find not merely that the plaintiff believed the defendant to believe that he was buying old oats, but that he believed the defendant to believe that he, the plaintiff, was contracting to sell old oats.[188]

This passage came to define the conditions of an operative unilateral mistake. The basis and effect of *Smith v Hughes* in allowing relief for a unilateral mistake was very similar to the grounds upon which equity would allow relief for a unilateral mistake. This underlying similarity was to prove important after the fusion of law and equity.

[185] (1858) 8 E & B 815; 120 ER 304; 27 LJQB 201.

[186] Benjamin (n 56) 40. Benjamin's discussion of the case seems to contemplate a contract which would be voidable in equity rather than void at law.

[187] See ch. 4 above.

[188] LR 6 QB 597, 611.

Contemporary commentators concentrated upon Cockburn CJ's decision and viewed the case as an application of caveat emptor.[189] It was not seen as introducing a new doctrine, and the *Solicitor's Journal* commented that 'this case establishes no new principle'.[190] The anonymous author also observed that the decisions of Blackburn and Hannen JJ dealt with 'a proposition, probably of more curiosity than practical importance, but which possesses a certain scientific interest'[191] and examined how these judges dealt with the question of the seller's knowledge of the buyer's mistake as to the nature of the seller's promise. Recognising that there were subtle differences between the two decisions, the author impliedly favoured Blackburn J's approach: if the parties meant different things they were not *ad idem* and there was no contract. If, however, circumstances precluded one party from saying that he did not agree with the terms of the other, a contract would be formed by an estoppel. Scepticism was expressed about Hannen J's use of Paley because it gave no basis upon which one could distinguish between the moral rule and the legal rule. The author was of the view that the importance of the case lay in the fact that where one party allowed the other to contract under a misapprehension as to the meaning of the contract, the first party could only assert the contract on the basis that the other party understood it. The acquiescence of the one party in the misapprehension of the other amounted to an active deception. No doctrine of mistake was recognised by the author, who concluded that the case would be of limited future utility because of the difficulty of proving the knowledge of the other party.

Benjamin retained his treatment of unilateral mistake in his second edition and added *Smith v Hughes* as support for it.[192] Other treatise writers adopted a similar interpretation of the case. Leake employed Hannen J's decision to allow a contract to be avoided for mistake where one party allowed another to agree to a contract under a mistake.[193] Pollock used the case to formulate a series of questions to be answered in order to establish that a contract was binding in instances where one party was ignorant of some material fact of which the other party was not.[194] Anson also included the case in his chapter on mistake, and his statement of the principle upon which the case was decided is what has become the modern treatment of the case: that where one party misapprehends the nature of the promise made by the other party in circumstances where the other party is aware of the first party's misapprehension, the contract is void.[195] The decision in *Smith v Hughes* was attributable to the influence of Benjamin's treatise upon the court of Queen's Bench. The decision, in turn, was used by later treatise writers as an important support for the doctrine they devised, ignoring that the actual basis of the case was

[189] (1871) 4 Alb LJ 285; (1872) 8 Can LJ ns 98; and (1872) 2 *US Jurist* 59. *The Glasgow Daily Herald* used the case to illustrate that law and justice were mere 'matters of opinion': 12 June 1871, 4.

[190] 15 *The Solicitors' Journal and Reporter*, 21 October 1871, 899.

[191] ibid.

[192] Benjamin (n 154) 388–89.

[193] SM Leake, *An Elementary Digest of the Law of Contracts* (London, Stevens and Sons, 1878) 317–18.

[194] Pollock (n 33) 402.

[195] Anson (n 34) 125.

the application of caveat emptor. *Smith v Hughes* was important to these writers for two reasons: the first was that it re-affirmed the objective nature of contract and allowed the doctrine of mistake received into the common law to follow, more or less, the existing objective nature of contract law as a whole; the second reason was that it resolved the thorny question of when a unilateral mistake would avoid the contract. The treatise writers appeared oblivious to the reality that few cases would fit within the decision because of the difficulty of proving two mental states. The underlying oddity of the case is that the common law used the case to receive a civilian-inspired doctrine of mistake based upon a traditional common law concept of estoppel. The case worked on the premise that the promiser was estopped from denying a contract where he knew the promisee intended something else. The common law, in short, received a doctrine on a basis it already understood.

Conclusions

The most significant conclusion to be drawn from the examination of these four cases is that none was decided on the basis of a doctrine of mistake. All presented factual misapprehensions but in none of these cases were courts concerned to either apply or devise a doctrine of mistake as a matter of law by which the problem could be resolved. In *Couturier v Hastie* the focus was upon the terms of the agreement, because this was what the pleadings, framed under the Hilary Term Rules, set for determination. While there is a hint in counsel's argument that civilian theory was possibly applicable to this case, it is no more than a hint. In *Raffles v Wichelhaus*, the court decided only that there was no real agreement between the parties. *Kennedy v The Panama Mail Co* decided that a contract for shares could not be rescinded for an innocent misrepresentation where the representation did not change the essential nature of the subject matter but pertained only to a quality of the subject matter. Blackburn J sought to limit the shareholders' actions in the aftermath of the 1866 panic by refusing relief for a negligent misrepresentation. Roman *error in substantia* was a useful analogy to the English law employed to refuse the relief. The court was actually concerned with the application of common law warranties to a new 'thing'—company stocks. *Smith v Hughes* is best seen as a failed deception case. The question to be determined in the case was whether, if deception could not be made out by words, could it be made out by conduct in the face of silence? The court sought to determine what constituted a deception. A related question for determination was as to the nature and extent of a seller's warranty and how a contract could be formed—the very reverse of the question of how a contract could be vitiated. In each of these cases the 'doctrine' of mistake was established by the explanations of the treatise writers.

A second conclusion is that the later decisions, in *Kennedy v The Panama Mail Co* and in *Smith v Hughes*, occurred at a point when judges began to consider cases for determination on substantive principles rather than procedural points.

Interestingly, they neither devised a doctrine of mistake nor relied entirely upon civilian ones. Read carefully and in context, *Kennedy*'s case actually refuted the existence of an operable mistake as to quality. The quotation from Roman law, however, ensured that the future of the case lay in support for mistake. Contemporaries thought the case established the proposition that a mere mistake as to qualities did not avoid a contract. In *Smith v Hughes*, Blackburn J and Hannen J clearly had recourse to the treatment of mistake in Benjamin's treatise (and possibly Leake's) in reaching their decisions. Benjamin dealt with the subject they were concerned with as part of a doctrine of mistake. In this context, it is significant that the judges resisted decisions based on a doctrine of mistake.

A third conclusion is in the nature of an observation. These four cases, decided in the quarter-century between 1856 and 1871, demonstrate the concerns of common law courts when faced with contract cases. The pattern that emerges is as follows. Contract is based upon agreement and an initial question is whether or not there is an agreement. Are the parties '*ad idem*'? The question is whether, as a matter of observable fact, agreement has occurred and not whether a mistake has prevented it. If agreement can be said to have occurred, focus shifts to determine the terms of the contract. This is the concern of the court in *Couturier v Hastie.* According to the terms of the contract, was a definite cargo sold or was an adventure sold? Once it is decided that it is the former and not the latter, the plaintiff's case fails on a procedural ground—a variance has emerged between what has been found and what he pled. It is clear that lawyers and judges are aware that a factual misapprehension may occur and this is seen most clearly in the cases of sale. The resolution of such a problem is simple. Do the terms of the contract provide a warranty by the seller that purports to warrant the misapprehension exists as fact? If they do, then the seller is liable, regardless of his own lack of knowledge. If there is no warranty by the seller, caveat emptor applies and the buyer bears the risk occasioned by the misapprehension. The statements made by one party to another in this process are important because where there is a deception, such deception allows the other party to rescind the contract. Both *Kennedy v The Panama Mail Co* and *Smith v Hughes* can be seen as failed misrepresentation cases; a fact which is more than coincidence. Courts came to fashion a doctrine of mistake which avoided contracts where misrepresentation could not be made out. While courts of equity had long done this, it was a new development in the common law. Ultimately, in the twentieth century, misrepresentation came to be so broadly applied[196] that it effectively absorbed those cases where this doctrine of mistake would have operated.

A fourth conclusion is that these cases all illustrate the concern that nineteenth-century common law judges had as to the essential conditions of a contract. Where a party failed to perform these conditions, the contract was at an end. Factual misapprehensions complicated this operation but did not prevent it. As new theories

[196] Following the decision in *Hedley, Byrne v Heller* [1964] AC 465 and the passing of the Misrepresentation Act 1967.

of a mistake as to quality entered the common law these were closely allied to the pre-existing questions about conditions. The treatise writers explained these cases as being decided on a doctrine of mistake when their actual basis lay in the terms, the conditions, of the contract. Interpretation was transformed into the process of agreement. The readers of the cases looked in vain for a doctrine of mistake. The process by which the common law received new concepts was interesting. New concepts were considered in relation to the underlying substance of the common law. New ideas were understood by their relationship with, and in comparison to, existing common law concepts.

A fifth conclusion is that these cases illustrate the emergence of the influence of the treatises, with concepts of will and the effect of mistake upon the will. It is no coincidence that the three cases decided before the treatises show no concern with the process by which agreement is formed. *Couturier v Hastie*, and to some extent, *Raffles v Wichelhaus*, are decided by technical rules of procedure. Traces of Pothier are present in the former case, but the House of Lords thought this so insignificant as to decline to hear all of the argument. In *Kennedy*'s case, Roman law is referred to but not determinative. Once the treatises begin to be published, their influence becomes discernible. The influence of the treatise writers can be seen in *Smith v Hughes* and this began a cycle by which treatise writers had an influence upon the cases and then employed these cases in later editions of their treatises to buttress and support the (purported) doctrine. In short, a doctrine of mistake began in the treatises, influenced the cases, and was then reinforced in the treatises. The process was strengthened by the fact that the treatise writers tended to borrow from each other and thus reinforce the doctrine. As can be seen in Anson's objection to the characterisation of *Kennedy*'s case, the majority view generally prevailed.

Confusion arose at the doctrinal level, where absence of consensus prevented a contract from arising but the law required both parties to produce this absence of consensus. At a practical level, problems arose because the cases were not decided on the basis of mistake and it was difficult for treatise readers to square the reasons for judgment with the doctrine enunciated by the treatise writers. The final conclusion to an examination of these nineteenth-century cases supports the argument put forward earlier in this work: mistake as a legal doctrine was created by English theorists and not English judges. That its creation was imperfect and its judicial acceptance less than complete only served to confuse rather than clarify English contract law.

8

Mistake of Identity

WHILE COURTS OF common law in the nineteenth century moved slowly towards the development of a general doctrine of mistake, they were reasonably quick in developing a doctrine of mistake in relation to a specific form of mistake—a mistake as to identity.[1] When the doctrine did enter the common law in the 1870s, it did so through the works of the treatise writers, commencing with Judah Benjamin.

An Absence of Mistake of Identity in English Law

Before the mid-nineteenth century, treatise writers, both of equity[2] and of common law,[3] had ignored mistake of identity. This was not unusual, given that English courts had not considered misapprehensions regarding identity in this way. Cases had arisen, both in equity and at common law, where there were such misapprehensions, but the cases were not resolved on the basis of a mistake as to identity. In Chancery, little attention was paid to a mistake of identity. Instances exist where one party assumed the identity of another person for the purposes of engaging another in contract, but relief was infrequent[4] in absence of fraud.[5] Such

[1] I have considered this topic in an earlier article: C MacMillan, 'Rogues, Swindlers and Cheats: The Development of Mistake of Identity in English Contract Law' (2005) 64 *Cambridge Law Journal* 71. This chapter draws upon this earlier work. I have had the advantage of reading Michael Lobban's draft chapter on mistake, to be published in vol 12 of *The Oxford History of the Laws of England 1820–1914* (Oxford, Oxford University Press, forthcoming). I am indebted to him for explaining the changing approaches of judges to the effect of a fraudulent representation upon contracts during the nineteenth century.

[2] See, eg, *A Treatise of Equity* (sometimes attributed to Henry Ballow) (London, Nutt and Gosling, 1737), and J Fonblanque, *A Treatise of Equity. With the addition of marginal references and notes*, 2nd edn (London, W Clarke and Son, 1799).

[3] See, eg, J Chitty, *A Practical Treatise on the Law of Contracts not Under Seal*, 5th edn, JA Russell (ed), (London, S Sweet, 1853); CG Addison, *A Treatise on the Law of Contracts and Rights and Liabilities Ex Contractu*, 4th edn (London, Stevens & Norton, 1856), and SM Leake *The Elements of the Law of Contracts* (London, Stevens and Sons, 1867).

[4] In *Phillips v Duke of Bucks* (1683) 1 Vern CC 227; 23 ER 432 the court refused to execute an agreement to purchase land where one party assumed the identity of another person and thereby obtained a lower price in the purchase of land.

[5] *Lord Irnham v Child* (1781) 1 Bro CC 92, 95; 28 ER 1006, 1008; *Nelthorpe v Holgate* (1844) 1 Coll 203; 63 ER 384.

little concern as existed about identity in these cases went to the question of whether or not the party who had assumed the identity had obtained a lower price for the purchase rather than whether or not the mistaken party would have been concerned about the personality of the real purchaser.[6] At common law there were few instances in which a mistake of identity would arise as a question deserving legal consideration. Commercial sales were generally effected through brokers using bought and sold notes, a practice which provided little opportunity to dispute the identity of the parties.[7] In instances where a seller delivered goods to the wrong buyer, who kept them, the seller could recover the value with an *indebitatus assumpsit* count.[8] In those instances where a mistake of identity did arise, courts of common law were, like courts of equity, concerned to work out whether the mistaken party had suffered a prejudice related to price.[9] At times, the question arose as to whether or not evidence of agency was admissible to contradict the terms of the written agreement.[10]

In contrast to this lack of interest, civilian jurists were concerned about mistakes of identity. While Roman jurists gave little consideration to a mistake as to identity, and the topic was poorly developed within Roman law,[11] later theorists such as Pothier and Savigny were at pains to develop the subject. For Pothier, an error as to the person with whom one contracted, where identity was a material consideration of the contract, destroyed consent and consequently annulled the agreement.[12] Savigny had also considered a mistake as to identity of the other party significant. Where the identity of the person was essential, it could operate to produce a variation between the will and its declaration in such a way that consent was excluded, with the result that there was an invalid juristic act. In these circumstances a contractual obligation was void where one party thought he was dealing with someone else.[13] The entry of these ideas into English law was only partial and occurred over two decades. It appears to have begun in *Boulton v Jones*.[14] The case arose from poor business practices: the purchaser, Jones, bought goods thinking that he was dealing with Brocklehurst when, due to an earlier sale of the business on the same day, he dealt with Boulton. Jones had a set-off against Brocklehurst but not Boulton, and refused to pay Boulton. Jones defended the action brought by Boulton on the grounds that he had intended to contract with Brocklehurst and should not be compelled to submit to contract with Boulton, for

6 *Harding v Cox*, referred to in *Phillips v Duke of Bucks* (n 4) and *Fellowes v Lord Gwydyr* (1826) 1 Sim 63, 66; 57 ER 502, 503.

7 M Lobban (n 1).

8 ibid.

9 *Mitchell v Lapage* (1816) Holt 253; 171 ER 233.

10 *Humble v Hunter* (1848) 12 QB 310; 116 ER 885.

11 See ch 2 above.

12 RJ Pothier, *A Treatise on the Law of Obligations or Contracts*, WD Evans (trs) (London, A Strahan, 1806; repr Clark, NJ, The Law Book Exchange Ltd, 2003) pt I, ch I, s I, Art III §1, p 13. The matter is discussed in ch 5 above.

13 FC von Savigny, *System des heutigen römischen Rechts* (Berlin, Veit und Comp, 1840–49) vol 3, §136. The matter is discussed in ch 6 above.

14 (1857) 2 H & N 564; 27 LJ Ex 117; 21 Jur 1156; 6 WR 107.

Boulton knew of the advantages which attended the contract with Brocklehurst.[15] If Boulton suffered loss as a result of the sale of goods, he had only himself to blame.[16] Jones succeeded for 'if a person intends to contract with A, B cannot give himself any right under it'.[17] B could only sue upon the contract where there was no disadvantage to the other person,[18] and here there was disadvantage to A. The case was decided more upon procedure[19] and pragmatism than principle, yet it is possible to discern Pothier's mistake of identity. Bramwell B declined to find that only the person with whom the contract was made, although performed by another, could sue. Such a rule would only apply where the personality of the individual who performed the contract was of 'the essence of the contract',[20] an example of which would be where there was a contract to have a portrait painted. Bramwell B's proposition and illustration echo Pothier's and it is likely that it was an unattributed, possibly even unconscious, borrowing. While the case was not immediately regarded as having been decided on the basis of a mistake of identity[21] it was similar enough to the civilians' concern to be employed later as support for such a principle.

Identity Frauds: Criminal Law and the Law of Obligations

While *Boulton v Jones* did not involve fraud, the other cases which came to support a mistake of identity did. In these cases the rogue assumed the identity of another person in an attempt to contract with a merchant or supplier of goods to obtain goods on credit. Once the goods were obtained, the rogue sold them on to a third party without paying the owner. The problem was not new and it had consequences in both the civil law of obligations and in the criminal law of theft. An explanation of both bodies of law is necessary to understand the changes that came about in the law in the nineteenth century. Nineteenth-century English criminal law distinguished between larceny and obtaining goods by false pretences. Larceny, a felony, required the wrongful taking of goods without consent from the possession of another. However, the courts had managed to extend larceny to cover a consensual handing over of possession of goods where that consent was

[15] 6 WR 107, 108. Boulton had been Brocklehurst's foreman prior to the sale of the business.

[16] *The Times*, 26 November 1857, 8.

[17] Per Pollock CB, 2 H & N 564, 565.

[18] 21 Jur 1156; 6 WR 107, 119.

[19] Sir Frederick Pollock (Pollock CB's grandson) explained that what was really wanted was the power to add Brocklehurst as a party. This, however, was not possible at common law: Sir F Pollock, *Principles of Contract At Law and in Equity* (London, Stevens and Sons, 1876) 429.

[20] 6 WR 107, 108.

[21] See, eg, Leake's treatment of the case in 1867: Leake (n 3) 14–16, 306. William Macpherson in *Outlines of the Law of Contracts as Administered in the Courts of British India* (London and Calcutta, RC Lepage and Co, 1860) omitted to utilise the case as support for a mistake of identity.

induced by fraud. Their reasoning was that the victim was consenting to pass possession only, whereas the rogue's intention from the outset was to take ownership, to which the victim was not consenting. This form of larceny became known as larceny by a trick. But it could not further extend to the situation where the victim was duped into consenting to pass full ownership; that is to say, both property and possession of the goods. This had necessitated the creation by statute in 1757 of the crime of obtaining by false pretences.[22] The fine distinction between these two was difficult to maintain, and it became increasingly illogical in eighteenth-century Britain as the opportunities for deception increased in a nation with burgeoning mercantile trade. As Stephen explained, 'the distinction between the fraudulent conversion of property the possession of which was obtained by fraud, and the fraudulent acquisition of property as distinguished from possession, is hard both to understand and to apply to particular states of fact'.[23] The difficulties of conceptual distinction were compounded by procedural difficulties: a person indicted for obtaining goods by false pretences could not be acquitted if it turned out that his actions were theft, but a person indicted for theft could be acquitted if his actions amounted to obtaining goods by false pretences.[24]

Criminal prosecutions were brought by private individuals. To encourage such initiatives, it had long been provided since the reign of Henry VIII that the victim of a theft could recover his property if he prosecuted the felon to conviction.[25] By Henry's statute, the owner was given a writ of restitution and could recover the property from whoever was then in possession of the property.[26] Such a right occurred even where the sale had been made to an innocent third party in a market overt. Restitution, however, could only be made from the party in possession of the goods 'at the time of or after the felon's attainder'.[27] If a party had purchased stolen goods in a market overt and sold them on again before conviction, trover would not lie against him even where the owner had given him notice of the theft whilst the goods were in his possession.[28] In short, an intermediary could not be sued in trover. Five years later, a case arose before Lord Kenyon, *Parker v Patrick*,[29] in which the goods had been obtained fraudulently by false pretences, and a different result followed. The right to recover goods did not extend to goods

[22] By 30 Geo 2, c 24, s 1. In 1827 the Act was repealed by 7 & 8 Geo 4, c 27, and re-enacted by 7 & 8 Geo 4., c 29, s 53. See Sir JF Stephen, *A History of the Criminal Law of England, vol III* (London, Macmillan and Co, 1883) 161.

[23] ibid, 161.

[24] ibid, 162.

[25] 21 Hen 8, c 11.

[26] See Stephen (n 22) 132–34 for a description of the development of this process. Edward Hyde East, in his *A Treatise of the Pleas of the Crown* (London, A Strahan, 1803), stated that the writ of restitution had fallen into disuse, but that upon production of the goods at trial, the court ordered them to be restored to the owner, and if they were not restored, the owner could maintain trover; ibid, vol II, 788. Trover was an action for damages based upon a fictitious loss of the goods and a subsequent conversion of them by the defendant.

[27] ibid.

[28] *Horwood v Smith* (1788) 2 TR 750; 100 ER 404.

[29] (1793) 5 TR 175; 101 ER 99.

obtained by false pretences because this was not an offence in Henry VIII's reign. Accordingly, Lord Kenyon distinguished the case from that of the felony on the basis of the statute and found that where the goods were obtained by a fraud an action of trover would not lie against the third party purchaser. By the early nineteenth century, the similarity between larceny and obtaining goods by false pretences was apparent; and the lack of restitution for goods obtained by false pretences was well recognised.[30]

In addition to such restitution the owner of goods could pursue civil remedies to recover his property. As regards the civil law, the eighteenth-century cases concerned with instances in which a rogue fraudulently obtained goods by assuming the identity of another were divided upon the question of whether the owner of the goods intended to pass property in them or not. If the owner did, then property passed.[31] If the owner intended to part with possession only, a larceny by a trick, then property did not pass.[32] It was during the early nineteenth century that the attitudes of judges shifted in favour of owners as they came to see the effect of fraud as rendering the contract void.[33] The shift may have been more apparent than real, because the determination of this issue was often obscured by the procedures by which it was considered or the nature of the action in which it arose. A further complication was that in all of these cases courts were asked to decide as between two innocent parties which one should bear the risk of the loss occasioned by the fraud of another. The answer to this had a tendency to differ depending upon the relationship of the innocent parties to the rogue. Another factor which influenced courts was a consideration of which of the innocent parties bore greater responsibility for the problem. One means by which victims of swindles attempted to recoup their losses was to sue the carrier of the goods for negligence, breach of duty and trover in delivering the goods to the swindler.[34] In one such case, the judges looked at the intentions of the customer: where the customer did not intend to pay for the goods but went with the intention to commit a crime, the property in the goods did not leave the owner.[35] In a number of cases, courts in the 1820s stated that fraud had the effect of vitiating the sale if the purchaser obtained goods with the preconceived notion of not paying for them.[36] This change was not long-lived. Courts clearly had reservations about declaring that the

[30] East (n 26) 789, 816, 839.

[31] Lobban (n 1), relying upon East (n 26) vol II, 668, and *R v Parks* in Old Bailey Sessions Papers (online), ref: tl17940115-17, *R v Catherine Coleman*, in East (n 26) vol II, 672. See 30 Geo 2 c 24, 7 & 8 Geo 2 c 29, s 53.

[32] ibid, relying upon *Pear's Case* (1779), in East (n 26) vol II, 685; Old Bailey Sessions papers (online), ref: tl17790915-22.

[33] Lobban (n 1).

[34] ibid.

[35] *Stephenson v Hart* (1828) 4 Bing 476; 130 ER 851 per Park J at 483; 854.

[36] *Earl of Bristol v Wilsmore* (1823) 1 B & C 514; 107 ER 190; *Abbotts v Barry* (1820) 2 Brod & B 369; 129 ER 1009; *Ferguson v Carrington* (1829) 9 B & C 59; 109 ER 22 per Lord Tenterden at 60; 23, although the case demonstrates the extent to which these issues could be overlaid by procedural matters. See also *Hawse v Crowe* (1826) R & M 414; 171 ER 1068 (no property passed where the 'purchaser' had no reasonable expectation at the time he gave the cheque that it would be honoured).

contract was void in circumstances where the goods would be sold on by the swindlers to innocent third parties. Although he decided that the contract passed no property in the case before him, Tindal CJ expressed concern in establishing a general proposition that where a person purchased commodities which he was conscious that he could not pay for these commodities could be traced into the hands of subsequent purchasers,[37] a concern shared by Park J that an absolute rule should not be laid down.[38]

While part of the reason for such reservations was the realisation of the harsh results which could follow such a general rule, Parliament had also acted to ameliorate the great differences in criminal law between larceny and obtaining goods by false pretences. In 1826, Sir Robert Peel had introduced major reforms to the criminal law. Peel regarded the law as it pertained to false pretences as ineffectual and stated that it was hopeless to try to obtain a conviction for obtaining property under false pretences.[39] Peel observed that 'the object of the man [the rogue] in either case [larceny or false pretences] is the same—namely to cheat'.[40] Peel's Larceny Act 1827 extended the right of restitution beyond the felony of larceny to include the misdemeanour of obtaining goods by false pretences. It was thus enacted that where the owner of property indicted an offender for either the felony or the misdemeanour, the property of the owner was restored to him upon the conviction of the offender.[41] The result was the same even where the offender had sold the property on to an innocent third party for value. The desire to remove the prosecutorial and restitutionary anomalies between larceny and false pretences, and to encourage prosecutions, overshadowed the effect upon possible third parties who bought goods in good faith from a rogue. It also obscured, to some extent, the difference between the two offences. When the felony of larceny had been committed, there was no intention to part with the property in the goods, and thus the owner could follow his property into the hands of other purchasers unless the goods had been sold in a market overt. In that event, the owner relied upon the statute of Henry VIII to recover the property. The misdemeanour of false pretences, however, involved an intent to part with property in the goods. The restitution granted in 1827 therefore created theoretical problems involving the ownership of the goods: had property actually passed upon the false pretences or not?

The courts began to answer that question in the negative in the 1840s as it was asserted that the effect of the fraud was to render the contract voidable rather than

[37] *Irving v Motly* (1831) 7 Bing 543; 131 ER 210 at 551; 214.

[38] ibid, 553; 214.

[39] HC Deb, Vol XV, cols 1157–58 (13 March 1827). The reason that it was difficult to obtain a conviction was because an offender who was charged with obtaining goods by false pretences (a misdemeanour) would plead to the felony of larceny, and 'your aim is defeated': Peel, ibid, col 1158. The resulting Larceny Act 1827, 7 & 8 Geo IV, c 29, attempted in s 53 to overcome these difficulties by providing that while there was a subtle distinction between larceny and fraud, the offender would not be acquitted of the misdemeanor in situations where his actions amounted to the felony of larceny.

[40] ibid, col 1158.

[41] Larceny Act 1827, 7 & 8 Geo IV, c 29, s 57.

void. In a series of cases which (unlike most of the cases in the 1820s) involved an innocent third party purchaser, courts found that the fraud of the swindler rendered the contract voidable. In a significant decision in 1841, Lord Abinger found that an action for trover by a vendor would lie against a fraudulent purchaser but not necessarily against all those who acquired the goods from him. Whether or not the action lay against third parties who subsequently acquired the goods depended upon whether or not they took with notice of the fraud.[42] In *Load v Green*, Parke B defended the 'doubted' decision in *Parker v Patrick* on the grounds that the seller could elect to treat the transaction not as a contract and act to set it aside.[43] This view prevailed in *White v Garden*,[44] where the third party purchaser who bought goods obtained by fraud retained them, and also in *Stevenson v Newnham*.[45]

The importance of these decisions to the certainty of commercial transactions emerged in 1856 from the mercantile reaction to *Kingsford v Merry*.[46] The case concerned a fraudulent purchase. The plaintiffs sold goods through a broker, Leask, to a rogue trader, Anderson, who falsely told the broker that he was acting in the purchase as a factor to J & C Van Notten & Co, a firm for which he had acted as an agent. He obtained delivery orders, dock warrants, for the goods from the plaintiffs, telling them that he had really bought the goods for himself, despite the purchase being in Van Notten's name. Anderson then pledged the goods with the defendants Merry as security for a loan. Anderson's business had been maintained on forged bills of exchange. After he had been convicted of these forgeries the plaintiffs sued in trover. Initially, it was held that the third party purchaser without notice, Merry, had acquired title from Anderson. While the Exchequer Chamber accepted this view of the effect of fraud upon the contract, it also found that in the circumstances, the relationship of vendor and purchaser did not exist between the plaintiffs and Anderson, with the result that property did not pass to Anderson and that he could not, therefore, pass title to the defendants. While the effect of the decision was to protect the original owners, the mercantile community expressed indignation at the effect of the decision. The consequences of the decision were disseminated by Merry himself in an attempt 'to expose the insecurity in which all transactions are involved by the judgment'.[47] Merry's concern, picked up by the mercantile community, was that the dock warrants upon which he had bona fide advanced the sums to Anderson were regarded by the mercantile community as a valid form of security 'hitherto looked upon only as second to bank-notes in point of security'.[48] The effect of the judgment was that the warrants were liable to be impugned and thus efforts would have to be made to establish through the course of trading in such warrants that they were good at all stages to

42 *Sheppard v Schoolbred* (1841) C & M 61.
43 *Load v Green* (1845) 15 M & W 216; 153 ER 828 at 219; 829.
44 (1851) 10 CB 919; 138 ER 364.
45 (1853) 13 CB 285; 138 ER 1208.
46 11 Exch 577; 156 ER 960.
47 *The Times*, 24 December 1856, 5.
48 ibid.

verify the title by which each document was held. The judgment established the law as at odds with what the mercantile community had understood it to be.[49] Great concern was expressed over the ability to transact business without impeachment: 'the city is in a ferment . . . a panic has been raging'.[50] While the decision resulted in a meeting of merchants, bankers, brokers and traders, chaired by Baron Lionel Rothschild MP, which called for legislative changes to the law, nothing came of these proposals.[51] Lawyers and judges were of the view that the case did not effect a change in the law and that the case had been 'greatly misunderstood and misapprehended'.[52] What the reaction did clearly show was that the mercantile community, in deciding which of two innocent parties should bear the loss occasioned by a rogue, were of the view that it should be the original owner who had made possible the series of transactions carried out by the rogue. Third party purchasers who contracted bona fide should be protected from such possible loss. While courts initially moved in the opposite direction, this view was ultimately to prevail in law as well.

Kingsford v Merry established the possibility that the effect of the fraud was that no contract came into being, and this was to form the basis of the cases which came to be associated with a mistake of identity.[53] Within months of the decision in *Kingsford v Merry*, the Exchequer gave judgment in *Higgons v Burton*.[54] The case was concerned with a fraud upon the plaintiff silk merchants. The plaintiffs had been accustomed to dealing with a merchant in Cork and knew Dix as the merchant's agent. After Dix was discharged by the Cork merchant, Dix proposed to purchase silks from the plaintiffs in the merchant's name. The silks were sent; Dix forwarded them to the defendant for sale and received an advance. After the advance, but before the sale, the plaintiffs notified the defendant that the silks had been fraudulently obtained and demanded their return. The defendant refused to return them, sold them, and claimed a right to retain most of the proceeds to cover his advance to Dix. The defendant argued that the goods could not be recovered from a bona fide transferee at common law; on the basis of *Horwood v Smith*[55]

[49] A steady stream of letters reached *The Times* on this topic in the weeks following the decision. See, eg, *The Times*, 27 December 1856, 5.

[50] *The Daily News*, 19 January 1857.

[51] *The Times*, 20 January 1857, 6. *The Times*, 11 February 1857, 6 reported the calls of Robert Lowe in Parliament for legislation to satisfy the mercantile community that a fair trader pledging and selling goods in the course of business would have more protection than was enjoyed since the decision in *Kingsford v Merry*. See, also, (1857) 3 Jur (ns) 17.

[52] Per Cresswell J in *Mariot v The London and South-Western Railway*, *The Times*, 15 January 1857, 11. *The Jurist* opined that the law was 'left only as it was before, and commercial men need not feel alarmed by reason of the decision in the Exchequer Chamber': (1857) 2 Jur (ns) 557, 558. A second conversation on the case appeared the following week: 2 Jur (ns) 565.

[53] Lobban (n 1) has pointed out that the Exchequer Chamber's decision in *Collen v Wright* (1857) 8 E & B; 120 ER 241, which had the effect of providing that an agent who acted without authority did not personally enter into a contract such that property could pass, would have been present in the minds of the Exchequer judges who heard these mid-century cases which led to the development of mistake of identity.

[54] (1857) 26 LJ Exch 342.

[55] (1788) 2 TR 750, 755; 100 ER 404.

such a recovery could only be upon the statute of Henry VIII after the conviction of the offender. The Court of Exchequer refused this argument and distinguished between instances in which the rogue had defrauded an owner out of his goods and where the owner had no intent to contract with the rogue or to give him possession of the goods, and those instances in which there was a sale, albeit one affected by fraud. This case was within the former category because the plaintiffs never intended to either give Dix possession of the goods or to enter into a contract with him. They had intended to contract with the Cork merchant. In the circumstances, no property passed: 'there was no sale at all, but a mere obtaining of goods by false pretences; the property, therefore, did not pass out of the plaintiffs'.[56] Bramwell B was at pains to explain the importance of the decision in *Kingsford v Merry*; had the case been decided otherwise it would have established a proposition that would have been dangerous to trade—namely, that whenever a person was entrusted with possession of goods he could dispose of them.

Hardman v Booth: A Turning Point

Kingsford v Merry and *Higgons v Burton* were cases where the fraud had been perpetrated by a person known to the vendor of the goods, who was someone that the vendor had done legitimate business with, as an agent, in the past. The situation was otherwise with the cases that came to establish a mistake of identity, for these were cases in which the vendor was swindled out of his goods by someone he did not know. The 1860s saw the growth of what became known as 'long firm frauds'.[57] Orders were placed, generally from London, for goods to be delivered by rail from the provinces. The orders were either fraudulently given in the name of a well-known firm or under the name of a fictitious firm. Once delivered the goods were sold on or pawned immediately without payment to the supplier. The supplier was then left in the difficult position of trying to locate the swindler and, possibly, his goods. *Hardman v Booth*,[58] a case which came to be identified with mistake of identity, arose from the fraudulent operations of two men, Edward Gandell and his partner Henry John Todd. Their fraud upon the Hardman brothers bears many of the hallmarks of a long firm fraud, although the beginnings of it lay in a 'short con' in which the rogue met personally with his victim.[59]

[56] (1857) 26 LJ Exch 342, 344, per Pollock CB.

[57] Michael Levi provides an informative summary of these swindles in ch 2 of M Levi, *The phantom capitalists: The organization and control of long-firm fraud*, 2nd edn (Aldershot, Ashgate, 2008). Levi observes a comparative rarity of prosecutions for long firm frauds before 1850: 16.

[58] (1863) 1 H & C 803, SC 32 LJ Ex 105; 9 Jur (ns) 81; 11 WR 239; 7 LT 638.

[59] The frauds attracted interest in the Bankruptcy Court and were well publicised in the newspapers of the day: *The Times*, 22 September 1860, 11; 9 November 1860, 9; 8 January 1861, 9; 16 January 1861, 11. See, also, *The Morning Chronicle*, 16 January 1861, 3; 6 February 1861, 8. The trials were covered in *The Times*: 26 February 1861, 11; 28 February 1861, 11; and 1 March 1861, 11.

The Hardman brothers were woollen manufacturers from Rawtenstall. One brother travelled south to London, seeking business, and there he sought out a long-established firm known to him by reputation, Gandell & Co. The family firm was run by its elderly proprietor, Thomas Gandell, who, being in poor health, had entrusted the management of the firm to his son, Edward. It is not clear from the surviving reports why the failing Thomas had not given over the business to his son, then aged 58: it may have been that he was able to foresee his son's lack of business acumen or it may have been because Edward had previously been bankrupted. Hardman met Edward, whom he mistakenly, but reasonably, decided was capable of contracting on behalf of the firm. Edward did all he could to further this erroneous belief and purchased Hardman's serge in July 1860. Within days Gandall sent two further orders for packing linings. The goods were collected by Gandell & Co's porter, but diverted to the premises used by Edward and his partner, Todd. The pair pledged the goods to an auctioneer, Booth, who provided them with £300 and took a power of sale. Edward Gandell and Todd, almost immediately afterwards, filed a petition for bankruptcy and were found to be in a hopeless state of insolvency with debts estimated at around £20,000. The auctioneer, Booth, sold the goods at auction, and Hardman purchased the goods back. It subsequently emerged that Edward had been in partnership with Todd since 1857 for the purpose of obtaining goods and sending them abroad, although without his father's knowledge.[60] A range of criminal charges were brought against Gandell and Todd upon the committal of the Bankruptcy Commissioner. The Hardmans were active in these prosecutions. The more serious charges were levied against Gandell, who was accused of forging bills of exchange with intent to defraud. Both men were charged with a lesser offence, a misdemeanour, under the Bankruptcy Law Consolidation Act 1849,[61] of obtaining goods on credit within three months of bankruptcy under the pretence of carrying on business and with intent to defraud. Finally, Edward Gandell was indicted on two separate counts of obtaining goods by false pretences. The prosecution did not go well. Gandell was acquitted of forging a bill of exchange.[62] Three days later, he was back in the Central Criminal Court with Todd. At this point, something in the nature of a plea bargain was struck with the prosecution.[63] Gandell and Todd pleaded guilty to the charges under the Bankruptcy Consolidation Act 1849—Todd in relation to Hardman, Gandell in relation to another merchant, Galbrath.[64] In exchange, the prosecution offered no evidence in relation to various forgery charges, and Gandell was found not guilty.[65] Gandell also pleaded guilty to two charges of unlawfully obtaining goods by false

[60] The reason for the partnership was that Todd had thrice been adjudicated bankrupt and found it impossible to obtain any credit, and Todd exploited the relationship in such a way as to allay any suspicions of his involvement.

[61] s 253.

[62] Old Bailey Sessions Papers (online) (www.oldbaileyonline.org), ref: t18610225-245.

[63] *The Times*, 1 March 1861, 11; *The Era*, 3 March 1861.

[64] Old Bailey Sessions Papers (on line), ref: t18610225-257.

[65] ibid, t18610225-260.

pretences, for which he was sentenced to two years without hard labour.[66] It seems likely that the Hardmans were amongst the victims contained in these convictions.

The problem for the Hardmans at this point was how to recover the money they had spent in purchasing back their goods from the auctioneer, Booth. The purchase must have been out of necessity, for the Hardmans would have justifiably feared the disappearance of the goods. The sale was made months before Gandell was convicted and *Horwood v Smith* meant that the Hardmans could not recover their goods from Booth until a conviction was made nor could they prevent him from selling. Booth, of course, had every incentive to sell. *Scattergood v Sylvester*[67] provided that the property automatically revested upon conviction, but the Hardmans must have realised that by the time that occurred, their goods, packing linings, were likely to have disappeared. The lot of an original owner who knew where his goods were but was unable to take any effective action before the rogue's conviction was a precarious one.[68] The surviving record does not disclose why the Hardmans brought their action in trover 14 months after the conviction because, on the basis of the existing law, they ought not to have recovered. The restitution under the Larceny Act 1827 would not have been of use to them because they were in possession of the goods at the time of Gandell's conviction. When they brought their civil action, however, the Larceny Act 1861 had been enacted and it may be that this change affected the perception of these cases. The Act was a consolidating statute, and it largely re-enacted this restoration provision.[69] The effect of the 1861 Act was that while the rogue could pass title to a third party purchaser without notice, this purchaser 'lost' title when the rogue was convicted because property revested in the owner.[70] The 1861 Act also included an interpretation section which defined 'property' to include not only the original property but also any property or thing which the original property might have been converted into or exchanged for.[71] The interpretation section raised the possibility that where the property had been sold the proceeds of the sale might be recovered by an original owner. Before the 1861 Act it was clear that where the third party purchaser sold goods on to another before the conviction of the rogue, no liability attached to the third party. This placed the original owner in a difficult position, because prior to the conviction he could neither recover his goods from a third party nor prevent the third party from disposing of them (and the third party had every incentive to sell the goods).

This was to form the backdrop for the Hardmans' action in trover against the auctioneer. The action in trover was, of course, 'an action for damages based upon a fictitious loss and finding and a subsequent conversion to the use of the

[66] ibid, tl18610225-258; tl18610225-259.
[67] (1850) 15 QB 506.
[68] See, eg, the actions of the owner in *Nickling v Heaps* (1870) 21 LT 754.
[69] 24 & 25 Vict, c 96, s 100.
[70] *Scattergood* v *Sylvester* (1850) 15 QB 506, 117 ER 551, SC 19 LJQB 447; 14 Jur 977. The matter is discussed by JWC Turner in *Russell on Crime*, 12th edn (London, Stevens, 1964) 1032.
[71] s 1.

defendant'.[72] The court confined Hardman to seeking only the proceeds of the sale.[73] To maintain his action, Hardman had to establish that he had never parted with the property in his goods. Two issues were presented: first, was there a valid contract by which title to the goods passed to Edward Gandell; and, secondly, was there a subsequent conversion of the goods by Booth? The resolution of these civil issues was influenced by the completed criminal proceedings. At a procedural level, the judges were aware that if the goods had still been possessed by Booth, then title to the goods would have been restored to the Hardmans at the time of Gandell's conviction. It would be known that in the future an owner might be able to claim the proceeds of the sale under the Larceny Act 1861. In the determination of whether or not property had passed to Gandell, the judges were concerned that the effect of the law in the civil proceedings accorded with the law in the criminal proceedings. There could not be a revesting of title under the Larceny Act 1861 and a loss of title at common law. A related concern was the effect of the conviction upon the status of the 'contract'. Since Gandell had been convicted of obtaining goods by false pretences, was it open to the court in the civil suit of trover to find that there had been a contract with him? The defendant argued that although there had been a criminal fraud on the part of Gandell, this did not preclude the creation of a contract, albeit one which was voidable at the option of the plaintiff.[74] Wilde B. interrupted counsel to ask: 'can a man effect a real sale, and be at the same time liable for obtaining money by false pretences?'[75] Counsel replied in the affirmative and, it is suggested, correctly. The offence of obtaining goods by false pretences necessitated that the rogue obtained not just the possession of the property but a transfer of the property itself.[76] The problem was that, even at criminal law, the distinction between theft and false pretences as it applied to different states was difficult to maintain. In this civil case, a difficulty the defendant faced was the view that Gandell's actions amounted to theft, which necessarily meant that no property in the goods would pass. Ballantine Serjt for Hardman argued that no property passed to Gandell and Todd because 'it was no more than if the plaintiff's pocket had been picked'.[77] Once it was viewed that Gandell's actions were akin to theft, then the civil consequence was that no property had passed.

The plaintiffs had argued that there was no contract at all, because there was no assent: 'it was a mere obtaining of the goods by false pretences. No property ever passed out of the plts. When was there ever a contract; or two consenting minds to

[72] FW Maitland, *The Forms of Action at Common Law* (Cambridge, Cambridge University Press, 1948) 71. Following the reforms of the Common Law Procedure Act 1854, the court could order the restitution of the chattel and the option of paying the value or restoring the chattel was no longer left to the defendant.

[73] Hardman first sought first £459 18s, the amount invoiced to Gandell and, when this was non-suited, he then sought the return of the £344 he had paid at the sale to the auctioneer: 7 LT Rep NS Ex 638, 639.

[74] The point is clearly made in the report published in *The Law Times*: ibid, 638: 'For, although Gandell and Todd may be liable criminally for the fraud, yet still there was a contract, and a contract upon which the plts may have sued.'

[75] 9 Jur (ns) 81. The reasoning was based upon *Higgons v Burton* (n 54).

[76] Stephen (n 22) 160–62.

[77] *The Law Times*, 15 November 1862, 40.

the same terms of the agreement?'[78] The plaintiffs relied on the recent decisions in *Kingsford v Merry* and *Higgons v Burton*, which established that where a person obtained goods by false pretences by pretending to deal for another, no property passed as no contract arose. The concern in these cases was that if a rogue could pass a title that he did not himself have, this would be a principle 'very dangerous to trade'[79] in that anyone entrusted with the possession of goods could convey title to the goods. The defendant replied that a contract had arisen between Hardman and Edward Gandell, albeit one which was voidable for fraud. Once an innocent party, such as the defendant, acquired rights, the contract could no longer be avoided. Many of the authorities seemed to support this position.[80] While the defendant raised an argument akin to raising the presumption of *inter praesentes* or face-to-face dealings, that Hardman intended to contract with the party physically before him,[81] Pollock CB rejected this argument.[82] Hardman succeeded. In the determination of the first issue, the non-existence of a contract, the judges did not mention mistake as to identity which prevented contractual formation. Pollock CB based his opinion on a lack of consensus:

> There never was that contracting mind, which is formed by the convergence of two intentions to a common object, and which is required by law to constitute an agreement. The plaintiffs thought they were dealing with Gandell & Co, the packers, and to them they sent the goods. That was the form of the contract. It had no substance.[83]

In the words of another report, 'at no period of time were there two consenting minds to the same agreement'.[84] Martin B. and Wilde B. were of the same opinion. Martin B. seemed to be of the opinion that the contract would have been voidable for fraud if the fraud had been perpetrated by Gandell & Co; but as it was not, none of the fraud cases cited by the defendant were relevant.[85]

[78] 7 LT Rep NS Ex 638, 639.

[79] *Higgons v Burton* (n 54) 344, per Bramwell, B. The basis of the decision in *Hardman v Booth* seems to have been *Higgons v Burton*, which had been argued by Hardman's counsel. The most popular report of the case in *Hurlstone and Coltman* does not record this, and it then appears to be separate authority for the same proposition. When *Cundy v Lindsay* (1877–78) LR 3 App Cas 459 reached the House of Lords, Lord Hatherley, at 468–69 pointed out that *Hardman v Booth* must have been correctly decided because *Higgons v Burton* reached the same conclusion. The comments are made without apparent recognition that the former case was based upon the latter.

[80] *Stevenson v Newnham* (n 45); *White v Garden* (n 44); *Sheppard v Schoolbred* (n 42); and *Milne and Seville v Leister* (1862) 1 H & N 786.

[81] This appears in the report of the judgment of Pollock CB in 9 Jur (ns) 81: 'Mr Hawkins says it was a contract personally between the individuals who constituted the parties to the conversation of the subject of the goods.' See also 7 L Rep NS Ex 638,, where it was reported that counsel argued that because the dealing was with Edward Gandell only, 'He was the individual person with whom the contract was for them made'.

[82] 9 Jur (ns) 81.

[83] ibid, 82.

[84] 1 H & N 803, 806. *The Weekly Reporter* recorded that 'there were, in fact, no two consenting parties. No minds drawn together so as to amount to an agreement. There was the form, it is true, but there was no contract': (n 58).

[85] 1 H & N 803, 807. It is difficult to understand his judgment on this point since the facts of *White v Garden* (n 44) are particularly close to *Hardman v Booth*. It is possible that the rogue in *White v Garden* was not attempting to impersonate anyone else and thus the fraud was operative to render the contract voidable.

The second issue remained: had there been a conversion of the goods by the auctioneer? The auctioneer here was more than a mere conduit pipe, since he had advanced money on the goods. He was, however, unaware of the criminal manner in which the goods had been obtained. The judges agreed unanimously that there had been a conversion. The auctioneer was responsible to the plaintiffs to the extent of the money realised.[86] *Hardman v Booth* received a significant amount of attention in the contemporary legal press because of the ability to recover the value of the goods in trover from a party who had advanced money in good faith. This was the distinct change made to the law. The importance of *Hardman v Booth* at the time was that it established that the innocent auctioneer, without any wrongful intention, had committed a conversion of the plaintiff's goods and was liable to pay the value of the goods to the plaintiff. That this was the case was later recognised by the House of Lords in *Hollins v Fowler*.[87] *Hardman v Booth* was affirmed in *Hollins v Fowler*, one of the cases whereby it 'came to be the law that a voluntary dealing in good faith with the goods of another could nevertheless constitute a conversion . . . and it could then be said that 'trover is merely a substitute of the old action of detinue . . . [it] is not now an action *ex maleficio*, though it is so in form, but is founded on property'.[88]

It was Judah Benjamin's pen that transformed the case into one of a mistake of identity. As we have seen,[89] Benjamin was guided in writing his *Treatise on the Law of Sale* by Pothier. Adopting Pothier's error as to the person, which could prevent the parties from assenting, Benjamin employed *Hardman v Booth* and *Higgons v Burton* to support this position in English law:

> A mistake as to the *person* with whom the contract is made, may or may not avoid the sale, according to circumstances . . . where the identity of the person is an important element in the sale . . . a mistake as to the person dealt with, prevents the contract from coming into existence for want of assent.
>
> Where a person passes himself off for another [*Hardman v Booth*], or falsely represents himself as agent for another, for whom he professes to buy, [*Higgons v Burton*] and thus obtains the vendor's assent to a sale, and even a delivery of goods, the whole contract is void; it has never come into existence, for the vendor never assented to sell to the persons thus deceiving him. The contracts in the cases cited below were held void, on the ground of fraud, but they were equally void for mistake, or the absence of the assent necessary to bring them into existence.[90]

This brief passage marks the entry of mistake of identity into English contract law.

86 1 H & C 803, 806; 9 Jur (ns) 81, 82; 11 WR 239.
87 (1874–75) LR 7 HL 757. Blackburn J was particularly clear on this point, at 764.
88 JH Baker, *An Introduction to English Legal History*, 4th edn (London, Butterworths, 2002) 399.
89 In ch 5.
90 JP Benjamin, *A Treatise on the Law of Sale of Personal Property* (London, Henry Sweet, 1868) 36.

Cundy v Lindsay: The Beginning of Mistake of Identity

The case said to establish the doctrine, *Cundy v Lindsay*, was decided on the basis of Benjamin's explanation. The case, concerned with the civil consequences of a long firm fraud, was described in the newspapers as 'a curious case, of considerable interest to the commercial world'.[91] Alfred Blenkarn was a swindler who operated a classic long firm fraud operation over several decades. A bankrupt[92] described as 'a respectable-looking, middle aged man'[93] at the time his fraud was perpetrated, he had established himself in an office on Little Love Lane, Cheapside, London.[94] The office overlooked Wood Street, and Blenkarn had stationary printed up which described his address as '37, Wood Street' and styled himself 'Messrs Blenkiron & Co'. The purpose of these exercises was to make himself look like the long-established firm of W Blenkiron & Sons, manufacturers of collars, cravats and braces, located at 123 Wood Street. Blenkarn wrote to Robert Lindsay & Co, linen merchants, in Belfast and requested samples of handkerchiefs. These were duly sent out, although Lindsays had difficulty making out his name by his signature. A few days later, Blenkarn ordered 150 dozen handkerchiefs, received those, and then, ingeniously complaining about the packing of these goods, ordered a further 200 dozen. Lindsays, thinking they were sending these to the reputable firm at 123 Wood Street, filled these orders and invoiced Blenkiron & Co. Despite the lack of payment, a further 100 dozen handkerchiefs were sent out at Blenkarn's request. Blenkarn worked with his son, also named Alfred Blenkarn, and the younger Blenkarn sold the first and third lots of handkerchiefs when they arrived to his former employer, Cundy, who carried on a glovemaking business at 97 Wood Street.[95] After several months the swindle came to light. Lindsays had their lawyers, Ashurst, Morris and Co, attempt to attach any funds Blenkarn had with his bankers. When it was discovered that these amounted to 9s 5d, they prosecuted him for obtaining goods on false pretences. Blenkarn was convicted of obtaining goods by false pretences and sentenced to 18 months with hard

91 *The Times*, 4 December 1876, 10.

92 Evidence of Robinson at the trial of Blenkarn for false pretences: Old Bailey Sessions Papers (online), ref: tl18740407-305. Blenkarn had previously been bankrupted in 1863 (*The Law Times*, 21 February 1863, 231; *The Times*, 28 May 1863, 13); this appears to have arisen from another long firm fraud involving deliberate confusion over addresses: (1863) 11 WR 304. In 1865 Blenkarn had been imprisoned for debts which had arisen when he had ordered goods and had not paid for them: *The Times*, 3 August 1865, 9; 17 August 1865, 11. The Bankruptcy Commissioners expressed suspicions about the nature of his transactions on this latter occasion.

93 *The Illustrated Police News*, 11 May 1872. The description appears in an account of an appearance before the Central Criminal Court in which Blenkarn was discharged over allegations of embezzlement in connection with his employment as a purchasing agent.

94 Old Bailey Sessions Papers (online), ref: tl18740407; Parliamentary Archives, vole 316, Appeal Cases 1878.

95 The younger Blenkarn, who had already been acquitted on earlier charges of embezzlement (Old Bailey Sessions Papers (online), ref: t18720506-381), purported to sell the handkerchiefs on behalf of Moss, Ryland & Co—another fictitious firm created by his father to look like an existing, reputable firm. Cundy was a partner in the firm, which traded as Dent, Allcroft & Co.

labour.[96] An order for the restitution of the goods under the Larceny Act 1861 was made. Lindsay recovered 200 dozen handkerchiefs from a pawnbroker, but Cundy had already sold the handkerchiefs. Cundy no doubt felt justified in refusing to pay Lindsay for the handkerchiefs because by the time Blenkarn had been convicted they no longer possessed the goods.

The plaintiffs then sought a declaration that the defendants had converted their handkerchiefs. The jury found that the handkerchiefs were sold by the plaintiffs and that the defendants were bona fide purchasers. Two issues were presented to the Queen's Bench to determine if the action was maintainable.[97] First, had any property ever passed from Lindsay to Blenkarn? Second, if it had passed, was there a right to the handkerchiefs or the proceeds of their sale because it revested to the plaintiffs upon the conviction of Blenkarn? It was in relation to the first issue that Benjamin's theory of mistake was argued by the plaintiffs. Their counsel argued that there was no contract of sale because there had never been any intent to deal with the rogue. There was 'an entire mistake as to the person to whom they were selling'[98] and counsel supported this with Benjamin's comments[99] and his explanation of *Hardman v Booth* as a mistake of identity case. This was the first ground on which the plaintiffs claimed they had never lost property in their goods. The second ground was the Larceny Act 1861, section 100. The plaintiffs argued that because of the recent decision in *Nickling v Heaps*[100] their property was restored to them not upon the conviction of the rogue, but from the time the fraud was perpetrated. This was important because by the time Blenkarn was convicted, the handkerchiefs had already passed through the hands of Cundy and into the pockets of many different gentlemen. An argument was also made in the alternative that if the property had been resold, the proceeds of the sale revested by reason of the interpretation section's definition of 'property'. Blackburn J thought so little of the mistake point that he asked not to hear the defendant's argument on this issue. In relation to the Larceny Act 1861, the defendants argued that in the case of false pretences (as opposed to larceny) property passed under the contract until, and unless, the contract was avoided. Thus, any property restored was restored at the point of conviction and not at the time of the fraud. The property could only be recovered from those parties who held it at the conviction. And this was not the defendants.

Both bench and bar saw the civil law as interlinked with the criminal law. This is apparent in the characterisation of the issues. First, if there had been a conviction for false pretences, had property in the goods ever passed? Second, under the restitution provision of the Larceny Act 1861, who held the property in the goods,

[96] The punishment appears not to have deterred him from such activities for he was to carry on with long firm frauds following his release, this time as 'Bower and Co'. He was convicted of obtaining goods by false pretences and sentenced to five years in 1882: Old Bailey Sessions Papers (online), ref: t18820327-408.

[97] *The Times*, 16 February 1876, 11.

[98] *Cundy v Lindsay* (1875–1876) LR 1 QBD 348, 350.

[99] (n 88).

[100] (1870) 21 LT (NS) 754.

and at what point in time? The interaction of the conviction for false pretences and the effect that this had upon any transfer of property was significant. Blackburn J did not find that this conviction prevented the passing of title. The contract was voidable for fraud, but once a bona fide purchaser had acquired an interest, the original contract could not be avoided. The situation was otherwise where the felony of larceny had occurred, for there no title was conferred. Such an approach is consistent with the difference between larceny and false pretences. The decided authorities, however, went both ways on this point. In some cases courts had accepted that property could pass where there was a conviction for false pretences.[101] In other cases, courts had refused the possibility that title could be transferred where there had been a conviction for false pretences.[102] As any transfer of property occurred by contract, the conviction for false pretences was thus relevant to whether the contract was voidable or void.

With regard to the first issue, the plaintiffs faced the difficult precedent of *Horwood v Smith*[103]: that an action in trover did not lie against an innocent purchaser who acquired goods from a felon and sold the goods to another prior to the felon's conviction. The goods could only be recovered from the person in possession at the time of conviction, because the owner could not have his remedy against more than one person.[104] Lindsay employed two arguments to overcome this case. First, *Nickling v Heaps* held that upon the conviction of the perpetrator of fraud the restoration of property in the goods occurred at the time of the fraud. Cundy thus had no property since, upon the rogue's conviction, property was restored to Lindsay from the time of the fraud. Second, the new definition of property in the 1861 Act included anything that the goods had been converted into or exchanged for. Cundy no longer had the handkerchiefs; he did, however, have the proceeds from their sale, and Lindsay sought restitution of these proceeds. The Court of Queen's Bench refused both these attempts to circumvent *Horwood v Smith*. *Nickling v Heaps* was doubted as the Larceny Acts of 1827 and 1861 used the word 'restored' in relation to the time of conviction, not of the fraud. The authorities supported this position.[105] Property was restored at the time of the conviction: and this had occurred after Cundy had disposed of the goods. With regard to the argument that property restored included its proceeds, the judges found that the interpretation section could not possibly be intended to apply to the resti-

[101] *Parker v Patrick* (1793) 5 TR 175 (explained further in the related criminal proceedings of *Rex v De Veaux* (1793) 2 Leach 585); and *White v Garden* (n 44).

[102] *Noble v Adams* (1816) 7 Taunt 5; 129 ER 24; *Earl of Bristol v Wilsmore* (1823) 1 B & C 514; 107 ER 190; *Irving v Motley* (1836) 7 Bing 543, 5 M & P 380; 131 ER 210, *Kingsford v Merry* (n 46), *Higgons v Burton* (n 54); and, now, *Hardman v Booth* (1863) 1 H & C 803; 158 ER 1107, 32 LJ Ex 105; 9 Jur (ns) 81, 11 WR 239, 7 LT 638. The difficulties these divergent lines of authorities placed upon commercial law were considered by Benjamin in his second edition in 1873: JP Benjamin, *A Treatise on the Sale of Personal Property*, 2nd edn (London, Henry Sweet, 1873) 9–10, 342–43.

[103] (n 55).

[104] ibid, 755, per Lord Kenyon.

[105] *Scattergood v Sylvester* 15 QB 506; 19 LJ (QB) 447; and *Horwood v Smith* (n 55).

tution section.[106] In short, the case was not within the restorative provision of the Larceny Act 1861.

Blackburn J found that the conviction for false pretences meant that the contract was voidable. It is at this point that mistake of identity became relevant, and Blackburn J rejected the argument based on Benjamin's treatise and *Hardman v Booth*. While *Hardman v Booth* was good law, it was distinguishable: 'the facts of the present case . . . are not the same at all'.[107] In *Hardman v Booth* there was never any contract: Hardman sought out Gandell & Co, was given the card of this firm to send the goods to, and did send the goods to this address.[108] Lindsay, in contrast, had always intended to deal with the person at 37 Wood Street. The result was that Lindsay had a contract, albeit one he could avoid because of this person's fraud. Blackburn J attached significance to two points. First, the rogue's signature did not clearly read 'Blenkiron': Blackburn J opined that it read 'Blenkurn',[109] while Lindsay had originally sent samples to a 'Benkwood'.[110] The plaintiffs were aware of the reputable firm, but clearly had not even attempted to ascertain its address. Second, the plaintiffs had initially pursued the rogue before Cundy, because they had commenced proceedings in the Mayor's Court to attach Blenkarn's bank account.[111] The Court also sought to establish, as between two innocent parties, which of the two was more responsible for the loss which had arisen. This they found to be the plaintiffs: 'in this particular case the real original fault was in the plaintiffs' so readily taking up with the notion he [the rogue] was another person than he actually was'.[112]

The Court of Appeal allowed Lindsay's appeal. They disagreed with the lower court on the question of whether or not property had passed to Blenkarn. The jury's conviction for false pretences meant that Lindsay had only intended to deal with the reputable firm of Blenkiron & Co. The case was directly within *Hardman v Booth*. Blenkarn's fraud was not to induce Lindsay to deal with him but to induce Lindsay to deliver the goods to him in the belief that he was dealing with the legitimate firm. It would be a contradiction of the criminal conviction to find that

[106] Blackburn J went so far as to describe the interpretation clause as 'a modern innovation and [it] frequently does a great deal of harm, because it gives a non-natural sense to words which are afterwards used in a natural sense': (1875–76) LR 1 QBD 348, 358. It was not until the enactment of the Larceny Act 1916 that property came to include that which the original property had been converted into or exchanged for. See JWC Turner, *Russell on Crime, vol 2*, 12th edn (London, publisher?, 1964) 1035.

[107] (1875–76) LR 1 QBD 348, 354, per Blackburn J.

[108] The implication is that Hardman's beliefs were reasonable and that Lindsay's were not.

[109] Evidence given at Nisi Prius—First day, Parliamentary Archives (n 92) 33.

[110] ibid, evidence of Robert Thomson, 29–30. Thomson sought to reproach the author for his sloppy handwriting.

[111] ibid, Respondent's Case, 8. The jury found that there was no intention on the part of the plaintiffs in so doing to adopt the rogue as their debtor. This was merely something they had done on the advice of their solicitors, Ashurst, Morris & Co. It appears that they may have sworn the affidavit of debt for the proceedings against the rogue in the Mayor's Court before they had begun the criminal indictment. The jury found, however, that the plaintiffs did not intend to accept the rogue as their debtor when they swore the affidavit. This was a special jury and it is likely that the businessmen on the jury were acutely aware of the difficulties of a manufacturer in the plaintiffs' position.

[112] *Lindsay v Cundy* 24 WR 730, 732, per Mellor J.

property had passed to Blenkarn, even in a voidable contract: 'having regard to the nature of the false pretences, we think it necessarily follows that the property in the handkerchiefs never passed'.[113] Indeed, had Lindsay intended to deal with the person at 37 Wood Street, the criminal conviction was unsound. The Court of Appeal was concerned to ensure that the result in the criminal law was consonant with the result in civil law. Since the criminal conviction preceded the civil decision, it was thus the civil law that followed the criminal law. By finding that no property passed to Blenkarn, the Court of Appeal declined to decide the issue of restoration under the Larceny Act 1861 and did not hear counsel upon this issue.

When the case appeared before the House of Lords it was largely argued on the question of whether or not there had been a (voidable) contract between Lindsay and Blenkarn such that property passed to the latter. The determination of this question was resolved with reference to the offence of false pretences. Cundy was represented by a number of barristers, including Judah Benjamin. Benjamin was cast in the odd role of personally arguing against the position he had taken in his treatise. Cundy's argument was that *Hardman v Booth* was distinguishable because Hardman had intended to contract only with Thomas Gandell & Co whereas Lindsay intended to contract with the person at 37 Wood Street and did so. Credit was thus given to A Blenkarn & Co at 37 Wood Street. While the title might be impeached for the fraud, it could not be so impeached once the property had been purchased bona fide by a third party. Property had therefore passed to Cundy. In the event that it had not so passed and that it revested upon the conviction of Blenkarn, the appellants had already parted with the goods at that time (and at a point when they had good title). The respondents were not entitled to the proceeds of the sale.[114] Lindsay argued that there was no contract because there were never two minds consenting to the same thing. *Bolton v Jones* and *Hardman v Booth* established that in such circumstances there was no contract. Delivery under a mistake would not pass property to Blenkarn. In the event that property had passed to Blenkarn, however, the property revested in Lindsay upon Blenkarn's conviction. Counsel was interrupted by Lord Cairns at this point as he observed that it was probably unnecessary for their Lordships to consider the point.[115]

The judgment of the Court of Appeal was affirmed on the basis that there was never a contract between Lindsay and Blenkarn. In reaching this consideration, their Lordships were also concerned to ensure conformity between the criminal law and the civil law: namely, with the effect of the criminal conviction upon the existence of the contract. The Law Lords accepted the line of authority that a conviction for false pretences necessarily meant that there was no passing of property.[116] If

[113] (1876–77) LR 2 QBD 96, 101, per Mellish L.J.

[114] *Manchester Times*, 9 March 1878.

[115] *The Law Times*, 6 July 1878, 6. *The Weekly Reporter* was somewhat more forthcoming and reported that the defendants argued that the Larceny Act 1861 assumed that a person who sold goods which he was later convicted of obtaining by false pretences could pass property in such goods to a bona fide purchaser: 26 WR 406.

[116] (1877–78) LR 3 App Cas 459, 467–68, per Lord Hathersley, and his acceptance of *Higgons v Burton* (n 54); Lord Penzance at 471; and Lord Cairns at 465 (although he deals with this problem obliquely).

there was no passing of property, the contract was void because the proprietary consequences had, as a matter of civil law, to be determined by contract. The defendants' argument, that a voidable contract was created by the rogue's fraud, was rejected. The plaintiffs succeeded because there had never been a contract between them. As Lord Cairns LC stated: 'of him [Blenkarn] they [Lindsay] knew nothing, and of him they never thought. With him they never intended to deal. Their minds never, even for an instant of time rested upon him, and as between him and them there was no consensus of mind which could lead to any agreement or any contract whatever'.[117]

The absence of the Larceny Act 1861 in the Law Lords' decisions has obscured the essential background to the case and the understanding of why the Law Lords found that the contract was void because there was no intent to deal with the rogue and thus no contract was formed with him. Consensus, as understood by the civilian theorists, is the justification put forward to support a decision made on other grounds and to serve other ends. Because the Law Lords sought to ensure that the criminal law and the civil law were not in conflict, there is no erudite exposition of a doctrine of mistake. Indeed, their Lordships did not consider mistake as such. Contemporary accounts of the case are consistent with this view. The case did not attract as much attention as *Hardman v Booth* had done. The contemporary importance of the case lay in the interaction of fraud, a conviction for false pretences and the operation of the restitution provision under the Larceny Act 1861.[118] There is no apparent significance, for practitioners, of 'mistake' as an independent doctrine. In the only brief note of the case, *The Law Times* presented it as one where the major issue was which of two innocent parties should bear the cost of the fraud of another. They expressed concern, but not surprise because of *Hardman v Booth*, that Blenkarn's fraud meant that there was no sale and thus no property passed.[119] There was no mention of mistake.

That *Cundy v Lindsay* was primarily about the reconciliation of criminal and civil results can be seen in another decision given in the same year: *Moyce v Newington*.[120] This case also involved obtaining goods by false pretences and highlights the difference between the trial and appellate decisions in *Cundy v Lindsay*. The offender was convicted of obtaining goods by false pretences and the question then arose as to who, between the original owner and the innocent third party purchaser, had property in the goods. The Court opined that on 'abstract principles'

[117] (1877–78) LR 3 App Cas 459, 466.

[118] The *Weekly Reporter Digest* placed the case at trial and at the Court of Appeal under the general heading of 'FRAUD', with the sub-heading of 'Goods obtained by fraud—Bona fide purchaser of-Conviction of fraudulent seller—Restitution-24 & 25 Vict, c 96, ss 1, 100':, vol 24, p 109; and vol 25, p 115. The entry for the decision of the House of Lords was under 'TROVER', with a similar sub-heading, 'Goods obtained by false pretences—Passing of property—Larceny Act 1861 (24 & 25 Vict, c 96), s 100': *The Weekly Reporter Digest*, vol 26, p 246.

[119] *The Law Times*, 6 July 1878, 170. The article concluded: 'Perhaps it is a misfortune that our law does not recognise a middle course, such as would be attained by distributing the loss between the two innocent parties, rather than suffer one to bear the whole.'

[120] (1878) 4 QBD 32. An insight into the process of restitution can be seen in the decision of *The Queen v The Justices of the Central Criminal Court* (1886) 18 QBD 314.

it might be better to find that there was no contract between the original owner and the rogue, because the rogue buyer never intended to purchase the goods but only to defraud the original owner. The Court found, however, that the authorities were against such a position and that in the circumstances a voidable contract arose. If the contract was not avoided, a bona fide purchaser could acquire property in the goods.[121] The question then arose as to the effect of the restitution provisions of the Larceny Act 1861. Here, the Court made a bold decision. The restitution provision applied only where property had not passed to a third party purchaser. This, Cockburn J explained, was the construction of the statute accepted by the Queen's Bench in *Cundy v Lindsay*, and this construction remained unchanged by the House of Lords.[122] Consequently, the innocent third party purchaser succeeded. Although the House of Lords had avoided construing the Larceny Act's restitution provision in *Cundy v Lindsay*, within the decade they disagreed with the interpretation placed upon it in *Moyce v Newington*, and it was overruled in *Bentley v Vilmont.*[123]

The contract law created in *Cundy v Lindsay* was largely determined by the influence of the criminal law. The influence is twofold. First, the harsh result to the bona fide third purchaser would generally occur anyway because of the restitution provision of the Larceny Act 1861. Second, the majority of judges who heard the case were influenced by the criminal conviction of the rogue for obtaining the goods by false pretences. This, they believed, prevented the passing of property. Working backwards, this meant that there had never been a contract which could pass property. This could be explained as an absence of consensus (and by inference a mistake of identity) prevented any contract. In this process, the court was not concerned with mistake as such; while it is possible to find this in the decisions, and it is thus part of the case; mistake is arrived at as a result of, not as a reason for, the decisions made.

The Treatise Writers and the Development of Mistake of Identity

It did not, however, take long for *Cundy v Lindsay* to become a case which stood for the proposition that a mistake as to identity meant that no contract existed. The second edition of Pollock's treatise came out a year after the House of Lords' decision, and *Cundy v Lindsay* was added as further support for the proposition

[121] Cockburn J for the court found that the principles underpinning this were unsatisfactory but adopted the approach that preference would be given to the innocent purchaser because of the equitable principle that where one of two parties must suffer from the fraud of a third, the loss should fall upon he who allowed the third party to commit the fraud; ibid, 35.

[122] ibid, 36.

[123] (1887) 12 App Cas 471.

that a mistake as to identity prevented contractual formation.[124] Pollock's treatise was widely used by practitioners and judges, and citations to it were frequently made. A second influential treatise, written by Anson, appeared at much the same time, and he employed *Cundy v Lindsay* as his authority for the view that a mistake as to identity prevented contractual consensus.[125] Anson relied upon the passage of Lord Cairn's speech in which he explained that there was no meeting of the minds and thus no contract, as a basis for the existence of this principle of mistake as to identity. The apparent contract was thus void for mistake, not voidable for fraud. Indeed, Anson conceived of a fraud pertaining to the person as an exception to the general rule that a contract procured by fraud was voidable at the option of the defrauded party.[126] This early characterisation of *Cundy v Lindsay* as exceptional, without explaining that the exception resulted from the criminal conviction of Blenkarn for obtaining goods by false pretences, went some way towards explaining why a fraud perpetrated with regard to a mistake as to identity created a void contract, and not a voidable one which would have resulted from a fraud as to the subject matter of the contract. The majority of judges seemingly accepted the proposition that the criminal conviction for obtaining goods by false pretences necessarily meant that the contract was void. This fact was ignored by the treatise writers when they employed the case to support the writings of the civilian jurists. In turn, the treatise writers appeared to advance a principled reason why some of these contracts were held to be void and not voidable.

These two treatise writers, upon whom so many others relied for guidance, established mistake as to identity in English contract law. There was little explanation of the doctrine, and it did not match what the case law had decided. In particular, the underlying concerns about the effect of the criminal law and proceedings had been stripped away; necessarily so since these were treatises about contract, and not crime. The concerns about the operation of trover and its use as a proprietary remedy have also disappeared; again, necessarily so, as Pollock and Anson wrote about the substance of contract law, and not of the forms of action or restitution in the criminal law. The result, however, was the beginning of confusion in the construction of a doctrine that was difficult to apply and resistant to scrutiny.

Once mistake as to identity received an existence as a category within the principles of contract law, it was comparatively easy to find other cases which illustrated the principle and expounded upon it. There was nothing new in the facts of these cases; what was new was how the law explained the resolution of these problems. Mistake of identity was used to explain a legal problem which had been infrequently considered and in which the law had difficulty finding a clear exposition of the principles of mistake as to identity. It is possibly for this reason

[124] F Pollock, *Principles of Contract at Law and in Equity*, 2nd edn (London, Stevens and Sons, 1878) 409.

[125] Sir WR Anson, *Principles of the English Law of Contract* (Oxford, Clarendon Press, 1879) 118–19.

[126] ibid, 154–55.

that in the next prominent case of mistake of identity, *Smith v Wheatcroft*,[127] Fry J explicitly introduced and applied Pothier's considerations on identity. Fry J was familiar with Pothier's views on identity and had employed them in his own treatise.[128] While Fry J apparently employed Pothier to provide further support for his decision, he modified the application of Pothier's theory. Pothier had conceived of identity as significant in a positive sense: that one might contract with a particular party and that party alone. Fry J employed Pothier in a negative sense: that the defendant intended to contract with all the world except, possibly, the type of person to whom the plaintiff had assigned his contract. Once Pothier had been directly referred to, and quoted, a form of link with the civilian theories was made. Thereafter, in a series of cases, reference was made directly to Pothier. Unusually, these cases tended to involve negative personality considerations: *Gordon v Street*,[129] where Street was willing to borrow money from anyone bar the notorious Gordon; *Said v Butt*,[130] where the theatre owner would not sell a ticket to the plaintiff, a critic; and *Sowler v Potter*[131] where the lessor would not lease premises to the woman convicted of running a disorderly tea room. It was through these cases that Pothier's test began to bear direct judicial and academic scrutiny. The difficulty with this process was that it all appeared to be based upon the fragment of Pothier quoted by Fry J and without any further reference to Pothier's *Treatise on Obligations*.[132] This impeded an understanding of Pothier's considerations on identity. One result of this impediment was the long controversy over whether or not Pothier formed a part of English law: as has been seen from the arguments made above, his influence had actually entered English law unobtrusively some time earlier in *Boulton v Jones*.

New Legislation and a Changed Judicial Approach

While long firm frauds continued to operate after *Cundy v Lindsay* there were surprisingly few cases in which actions were brought to recover property or the proceeds of the property on the basis that, by mistake or otherwise, no property

127 (1878) 9 ChD 223.

128 He wrote that 'it is an obvious principle of Natural Law, that where the learning, skill, solvency, or any personal quality of one of the parties to the contract is a material ingredient in it, then the contract can be performed by him alone': E Fry, *The Specific Performance of Contracts* (London, Butterworths, 1858) 52.

129 [1899] 2 QB 641.

130 [1920] 3 KB 497.

131 (1939) All ER Ann 478.

132 That this occurred was first identified by JC Smith and JAC Thomas in 'Pothier and the Three Dots' (1957) 30 *Modern Law Review* 38. Fry J's translation accords with neither of the published translations of Pothier's work. Smith and Thomas speculated that Fry had translated the work himself. Later judges and academics simply referred to Fry's quote—leading to the inevitable conclusion that they had not read Pothier at all. The fact that Fry translated the work illustrates the process of borrowings made by lawyers and judges.

had passed to the rogue. It is hard to explain why something does not happen. It may be that the decision in *Moyce v Newington* inhibited further development of this area of law for a period of time. It may also be that the enactment of the Prosecution of Offences Act 1879[133] made it financially more attractive to owners to seek restoration of their property following a criminal conviction rather than bringing their own civil proceedings. The decision in *Bentley v Vilmont*, which allowed restoration under the Larceny Act 1861, would have encouraged owners to pursue criminal processes. Whatever the reason it was 20 years before another long firm fraud was characterised as a mistake. In *King's Norton Metal Company v Edridge, Merrett, and Company*,[134] the rogue, Wallis, adopted a fictitious persona when ordering the goods from the plaintiff. Once he had acquired possession of the goods, he sold them to the defendants. It appears that there was never an order under the Larceny Act 1861, which may be why the plaintiffs were forced to bring an action for the conversion of the goods. Two things had changed since *Cundy v Lindsay*. The first was the judicial attitude towards the effect of the fraud upon the initial contract. In *Bentley v Vilmont* Lord Watson had stated that where the goods were obtained by false pretences, the original owner had intentionally given his fraudulent purchaser a title which later bona fide purchasers without notice of the fraud were entitled to rely upon.[136] Fraud rendered the contract voidable, not void. It was only by operation of the Larceny Act 1861 that the original owner recovered his goods. The second thing that had changed was the restitution provision in Larceny Act 1861. The Sale of Goods Act 1893[137] had the effect of partially repealing the provision in the Larceny Act 1861. Section 24 of the Sale of Goods Act 1893 uncoupled the link Peel had first made in the Larceny Act 1827 in allowing an owner to recover property in goods where the offender was convicted of false pretences. Courts had proven unwilling or reluctant to apply the provision where to do so would force the bona fide purchaser without notice of the fraud to bear the cost of the fraud. This reluctance underscores the decisions in *Moyce v Newington* and *Bentley v Vilmont*. Sir Mackenzie Chalmers, draftsman of the Sale of Goods Act 1893, corrected this inequitable result.[138] Subsection 24(2) was introduced by amendment in committee 'to restore the old state of the law and to override sect 100 of the Larceny Act, 1861'.[139] While the Sale of Goods Act

[133] 42 & 43 Vict, c 22. Section 7 of the Act placed the financial burden upon the new Director of Public Prosecutions (DPP), but also provided that where the owner had given all reasonable information and assistance to the DPP in the prosecution, the owner could still obtain restitution of his property.

[134] (1897) 14 TLR 98. It is unfortunate that there is only one report and that it contains some obvious inaccuracies. The author is unable to locate references to the case in contemporary legal journals.

[135] Either Wallis was never convicted or, because of the changes made by the Sale of Goods Act 1893, detailed below, no order was made.

[136] *Bentley v Vilmont* (n 121) 477.

[137] 56 & 57 Vict, c 71.

[138] Chalmers described the result of the extended operation of s 100 of the Larceny Act 1861 as 'anomalous' and noted the regret of the Law Lords in *Bentley v Vilmont*: Sir M Chalmers, *The Sale of Goods Act, 1893 including the Factors Acts, 1889 & 1890*, 2nd edn (London, Clowes and Sons, 1894) 53.

[139] ibid, 54. This return was noted by other contemporary accounts: WCA Ker and AB Pearson-Gee, *A Commentary on the Sale of Goods Act, 1893, with Illustrative Cases and Frequent Citations from the Text of Mr Benjamin's Treatise* (London, Sweet & Maxwell, 1894) 158–59. See also the testimony of

preserved the power of the court to make an order for restitution if the restitution was just in the circumstances,[140] this no longer followed as a matter of right. The Court of Appeal in *King's Norton Metal v Edridge* was not, therefore, faced with the difficulty of reconciling the civil law result with the criminal law result of the restoration of the goods upon conviction. In light of the changed attitude towards the effect of a fraud involving false pretences on a contract and the new legislative framework, it is no surprise that the Court of Appeal dismissed the plaintiffs' argument that the contract was void on the basis of *Cundy v Lindsay* and *Hardman v Booth* because they had never intended to deal with the rogue. AL Smith LJ, who adopted Pothier's comments in *Gordon v Street* two years later, ridiculed the proposition that a long firm fraud was a case where there was a contract void for a mistake of identity.[141] He appeared not to appreciate that this had been exactly the situation in *Cundy v Lindsay*. But then, attitudes towards the effect of the fraud on the contract, in relation to the offence of false pretences, had changed: in *Cundy v Lindsay*, following *Hardman v Booth*, the House of Lords accepted that the false pretences were like theft and no property could pass. This was the wrong conclusion to make on the criminal law. AL Smith LJ's decision that 'the indictment against a long firm was always for obtaining the goods by false pretences, which presupposed the passing of the property' reflected the later view of the effect of the offence upon the contract. It had come to be accepted that false pretences rendered the contract voidable and not void.

King's Norton Metal v Edridge was ignored by contemporaries and had no immediate impact upon the consideration of a mistake as to identity. The same was not true of the next case of a mistaken identity based upon fraud. *Phillips v Brooks*[142] concerned a rogue who called upon a jeweller, selected certain items and introduced himself as someone else. The jeweller accepted a cheque in the name of this other person and allowed the rogue to take away a ring. The rogue sold the ring to the defendant, a pawnbroker. The rogue was convicted of obtaining goods by false pretences. In the jeweller's action against the pawnbroker for damages or the ring's return, Horridge J held that there was a contract between jeweller and rogue, although this was voidable at the jeweller's option. Upon the sale to a third party without notice, the jeweller lost the ability to avoid the contract and the third party acquired good title. The case is consistent with *King's Norton Metal v Edridge* because Horridge J heard argument on the interrelationship of the substance of the criminal conviction and the passing of property by a contract obtained by fraud, and also the previous possibility of property revesting upon a criminal conviction. Horridge J also heard argument, based upon Pothier and to a lesser extent

HD Roome before the Joint Select Committee which considered the Larceny Bill 1916: *Report from the Joint Select Committee of the House of Lords and the House of Commons on the Larceny Bill [H.L.] together with the proceedings of the committee and the minutes of evidence*, 17 July 1916, 45.

[140] Ker and Pearson-Gee (n 139), 159. By way of example, the authors provide situations where no third party has obtained title or where the third party has obtained a good but voidable title.

[141] (1897) 14 TLR 98, 99.

[142] [1919] 2 KB 243.

upon Pollock's treatise, that where identity was a material element to the contract, a mistake as to identity rendered the contract void. This position, it was argued, was the basis of the decisions in *Cundy v Lindsay*, *Hardman v Booth* and *Smith v Wheatcroft*. Horridge J refused to follow these authorities and, instead, applied a US case[143] to establish that where the rogue appeared in person before the owner, the contract was voidable. Pothier's principle did not apply where 'the seller intended to contract with the person present, and there was no error as to the person with whom he contracted, although the plaintiff would not have made the contract if there had not been a fraudulent misrepresentation'.[144] The argument which had been rejected in *Hardman v Booth* had now come to form a legal presumption.

The case was dismissed by contemporary accounts as incorrectly decided. Pollock, in particular, was of the definite view that the decision was wrong.[145] Subsequent writers were equally disparaging[146] and Viscount Haldane, in *Lake v Simmons*, explained the case on the basis that the contract was concluded before identity became an issue.[147] Why did Horridge J reach this conclusion, based upon a US trial decision?[148] The answer, once again, lies in the criminal law and the recent enactment of the Larceny Act 1916.[149] The 1916 Act clearly stated, following upon and further developing the position of the Sale of Goods Act 1893, that any goods obtained by fraud did not revest in the original owner by reason of the offender's conviction.[150] The law had, here, been specifically amended to cure these anomalies.[151] The law had largely[152] returned to its pre-1827 state; restitution was

[143] *Edmunds v Merchants' Despatch Transportation Co* 135 Mass 283.

[144] [1919] 2 KB 243, 248–49.

[145] Pollock in his last edition as editor of the *Law Quarterly Review* observed that the *inter praesentes* argument was 'a nice point, and, without denying the weight of the authority, we should like to see it dealt with in the Court of Appeal': (1919) 140 LQR 288. The same edition contained the observations of a 'learned correspondent' who concluded that it was 'difficult to believe' that a disguise as to an identity created 'the difference between a good title and no title': ibid. Pollock relegated the case to a footnote in the next edition of his treatise and observed that it was contrary to Pothier: Sir F Pollock, *Principles of Contract*, 9th edn (London, Stevens and Sons, 1921) 509. Pollock's views were shared by others: *The Law Times*, 17 May 1919, 51, in which the anonymous author was of the view that Pothier's observations were dismissed, although they seemed very much to the point.

[146] ECS Wade, 'Mistaken Identity in the Law of Contract' (1922) 38 LQR 201; CK Allen, 'Mistaken Identity' (1928) 44 LQR 72.

[147] [1927] AC 487, 501–502.

[148] *Edmunds v Merchants' Despatch Transportation Co* (1883) 135 Mass 283. An author no less eminent than Pollock had doubted the correctness of this decision and noted that it did not accord with Pothier's principles of mistake of identity: Sir F Pollock, *Principles of Contract: A Treatise on the General Principles concerning the Validity of Agreements*, 8th edn (London, Stevens and Sons, 1911) 497.

[149] 6 & 7 Geo 5, c 50.

[150] s 45(1).

[151] *Report from the Joint Select Committee of the House of Lords and the House of Commons on the Larceny Bill [HL] together with the proceedings of the committee and the minutes of evidence*, 17 July 1916, 7–8.

[152] Section 45 of the Larceny Act 1916 did reserve a power of restitution to the court where there was a conviction for obtaining goods by false pretences, but this seems to have been intended only for the exceptional circumstances considered in relation to the Sale of Goods Act 1893: see Ker and Pearson-Gee (n 139).

available for larceny, but not for false pretences. The ownership of goods acquired by false pretences was now determined by the general rules of contract law, and the conviction of the offender was irrelevant to this determination.[153] Horridge J had no need to reconcile two possibly different results between the civil and criminal outcomes. There was, however, nothing new about an *inter praesentes* transaction, for the same situation had arisen in *Hardman v Booth*. What was new was, first, the restitution provision of the criminal law and, second, the interaction of the civil law (now in the Sale of Goods Act 1893) with this criminal law. Again, this change is not apparent in a reading of the law reports or of descriptions of the case. This created a difference between *Cundy v Lindsay* and *Phillips v Brooks* which was difficult to explain solely on the basis of contract law. The placement of these cases within the category of mistake impeded contemporary understanding of the cases. The inconsistency between *Phillips v Brooks* and the earlier cases was noted at the time, and doubt was expressed that the decision was correct.[154] Shortly thereafter, in *Lake v Simmons*[155], this doubt continued and the case was distinguished from *Cundy v Lindsay* on grounds that Horridge J had not advanced. With the benefit of hindsight, it is now apparent that it would have been preferable for the Law Lords to have declared the case either right or wrong. The treatise writers who had done so much to develop a doctrine of mistake as to identity had ignored the criminal law aspects to these cases. The result was that, when the criminal law changed and removed the crucial underpinning of the early cases of *Hardman v Booth* and *Cundy v Lindsay*, there was no acknowledgement of why this had happened.

Conclusions

Mistake of identity was the one type of mistake which can accurately be said to have existed at the end of the nineteenth century in that the doctrine was accepted and considered by the judiciary in the determination of cases. It was recognised both at law, in *Cundy v Lindsay*, and in equity, in *Smith v Wheatcroft*. The theoretical origins and affinity of this new doctrine, such as they were, were based upon Pothier's theory that where the personality of the other party was a significant element in the formation of the contract and there was a mistake as to that personality, there was no contract.[156] All the major contract treatises after *Cundy v Lindsay* treated the subject in this fashion. And yet, a close reading of the House of Lords' judgments in *Cundy v Lindsay* does not reveal the acceptance of a doctrine of

[153] A point observed by Ker in the first edition of Benjamin's treatise to appear after the Larceny Act 1916: JP Benjamin, *A Treatise on the law of the Sale of Personal Property*, 6th edn (London, Sweet, 1920) 27.

[154] See n 145.

[155] [1927] AC 487.

[156] A close reading of *Smith v Wheatcroft* would indicate that Fry J probably thought that a mistake of identity rendered the contract voidable rather than void.

mistake of identity so much as an agreement between their Lordships that there was never such consensus as was required to contract. Equally, *Smith v Wheatcroft*, despite directly introducing Pothier's considerations into English law, was not decided on the basis of a mistake of identity. At the point at which courts did accept such a mistake, in *King's Norton Metal v Edridge* and *Phillips v Brooks*, they declined to apply the doctrine and found that the contracts before them were voidable for fraud rather than void for mistake. How could this be?

The answer lies in the way in which mistake of identity developed within the common law. In all of these cases, courts were faced with two innocent parties, one of whom would have to entirely bear the loss caused by the rogue's fraud. In determining this central issue, courts were faced with conceptual problems not only in contract law, but also in tort law and in the criminal law. The hazards of the litigation process meant that the way in which these problems were resolved was sometimes happenstance: which parties appeared before the court with which claims often influenced who succeeded. Turning to the criminal law first, throughout the nineteenth century the legislature and the courts struggled to provide an incentive to individuals to prosecute criminals by allowing the restitution of their property. At the beginning of the nineteenth century, while obtaining goods by false pretences was a crime, it was not one for which an order for the restitution of property could be made. It was, therefore, acceptable for courts in considering the nature of the agreement made under the rogue's false pretences, to find that the contract was voidable. The enactment of the Larceny Act 1827 created a change in the criminal law. To provide the victim with an incentive to prosecute, the 1827 Act provided that the goods could be restored upon conviction. It became more difficult for a civil court to maintain that the contract was voidable because it was clear that title could be recovered. There seems to have been doubt amongst judges as to where the title did reside between the offence and the conviction. Initially, the judicial attitude appeared to favour the owner. In conceiving of the effect of the false pretences, for which the rogue had been convicted, upon the contractual process, judges equated the offence with that of larceny by a trick. Looking at the matter from this perspective, the false pretences were seen as something in which the victim never intended to part with his property—it was a form of theft. This view prevailed in *Hardman v Booth* and in *Cundy v Lindsay* in the House of Lords. And yet, as Blackburn J had stated in *Cundy v Lindsay* in the Queen's Bench, the effect of the conviction for false pretences should have meant that a contract existed but that it was voidable for fraud. Gradually this view came to prevail.

As these changes in the substantive relationship between the offence and the putative contract occurred, there were also ongoing changes in the restitution provisions of the Larceny Act 1861. It had not been intended by the legislature that an innocent third party should bear the risk of the rogue's fraud. The injustice of this was apparent. In *Moyce v Newington*, the statute was misconstrued to protect the third party; in overturning this decision, the House of Lords in *Bentley v Vilmont* was at pains to point out the injustice of this provision. In *Bentley v Vilmont*, the House of Lords was willing to state that it was only by reason of the statute that the owner re-acquired the property. Simultaneously, there was a growing public responsibility for prosecutions after the 1879 Act, which established the Director of Public Prosecutions. The commercial uncertainty and the injustice which could arise from a third party bearing the cost of the crime were no longer outweighed by the need to encourage prosecutions. The Sale of Goods Act 1893 effected a partial repeal of the restitution provision of the Larceny Act 1861, and the section was completely repealed by the Larceny Act 1916. Thereafter, courts were not concerned with a problem that was present in the mid-nineteenth century—namely, that title could not be simultaneously held by one party as a result of the criminal law and by another as a result of the civil law.

Judges changed their own views as to the effect of a fraudulent misrepresentation as to identity throughout the nineteenth century. At the beginning of the century, the problems posed by these cases were often obscured by a system of justice which resolved many issues by procedure rather than substance. Other routes of recompense were available at the beginning of the century, such as a suit against the carrier. As these other routes decreased and, from the mid-century, procedural reforms meant that many of these cases had to be decided on a substantive basis, courts vacillated between finding that the contract was voidable or that there was no contract at all. It is clear that, to some extent, courts were concerned to establish as between the two innocent parties which one was most responsible for the loss occurring. The party most responsible generally bore the loss. The determination of whether the contract was void or voidable was also affected by whose intention the judges examined. When judges focused upon the owner, they generally found no intent to part with property in the goods and usually found that there was no contract. Interestingly, based upon the reaction to *Kingsford v Merry*, courts appeared relatively impervious to mercantile criticism. They seemed, instead, to be more concerned with internal consistency in the law—although there were struggles to balance the various factors of crime and contract. This was, to some extent, exacerbated by the fact that the actions brought by owners were in tort. Initially, these were in trover, and part of the process at play in these cases was the development of trover whereby it was extended to cover situations in which there was voluntary dealing in good faith with the goods of another.

The treatise writers wrote of a mistake of identity which prevented a contract from arising or rendered it void. They achieved a synthesis between the common law and the theory of Pothier and they placed this within the common law. Despite its weak foundations in the case law, later courts accepted this doctrine, although they resisted applying it by the beginning of the twentieth century. While it proved a convenient means of explaining why some contracts were void, its existence and seemingly arbitrary application created uncertainty in this area of the law.

9

Mistake after Fusion

THE FINAL, AND most significant, nineteenth-century procedural reform was the 'fusion' of law and equity brought about by the Supreme Court of Judicature Act 1873.[1] Before fusion, mistakes had received different treatment in courts of common law from that in courts of equity. Courts of common law largely failed to accord a legal response to mistakes, although some slight recognition can be discerned immediately before fusion; courts of equity could provide particular relief if they thought the circumstances, related to a broad conception of conscience, right to grant such relief. To a great extent there was no need for the common law to be concerned with mistake as a legal doctrine. The common law did not need to accord a legal response to mistake as such because the available procedures allowed the resolution of such cases for other reasons. These procedures were reinforced by the possibility of relief in equity for a mistake. Equity provided such relief in circumstances where the participants recognised that the contract was valid at law, which gave no legal recognition to the mistake. Indeed, it was this validity at law which brought the litigants to equity for assistance. Surprisingly little judicial consideration was given to the treatment of mistake following the amalgamation of courts of common law and equity. The ideas developed by the treatise writers from the 1860s entered the law slowly: it was only with the 1931 decision in *Bell v Lever Brothers* that mistake was authoritatively recognised as a part of English law. This chapter charts the post-fusion development of mistake until 1949.

The Judicature Act 1873

The Judicature Act 1873 was, of course, designed to 'make provision for the better administration of justice' rather than to create a new substantive body of law. Ashburner's awkward metaphor, that 'the two streams of jurisdiction, though they run in the same channel, run side by side and do not mingle their waters'[2] largely describes the new Supreme Court's treatment of contractual mistake until well into the twentieth century. To a great extent, this lack of co-mingling was brought

[1] 36 & 37 Vict, c 66.
[2] W Ashburner, *Principles of Equity* (London, Butterworth & Co, 1902) 23.

about by the provisions of the Judicature Act 1873, which operated to keep the common law and equitable treatments of mistake separate. While some sections of the 1873 Act could have formed the basis for a substantive fusion of mistake,[3] the allocation of specific business to particular divisions of the new Supreme Court worked against such a substantive fusion. The development of a legal concept of mistake in equity had arisen largely because of Chancery's unique remedial powers of rectification, specific performance and rescission. Specific performance and rectification were assigned exclusively to the Chancery Division of the new High Court.[4] This allocation acted to confine mistake cases largely to the Chancery Division, where a distinct equity bench and bar continued to resolve mistake cases in much the same way as before fusion. As Professor Polden has observed in a skilful analysis of the selection and deployment of judges after 1875, the full potential for fusion was not realised.[5] The new High Court saw a rapid and thorough recreation of the divide between equity judges and common law judges.[6] Writing a quarter of a century after fusion, Augustine Birrell observed that if Lord Eldon were suddenly to come back to life, having survived the shock of the Judicature Acts, he would find little difference in the rectification of an instrument for mistake or in orders of rescission or specific performance.[7] Before the common law divisions, the common law judges had been disinclined to consider mistake as a defence when given the power to do so by the Common Law Procedure Act 1854.[8] In these circumstances it is unsurprising that there was no substantive fusion of equitable mistake with the limited forms of mistake recognised at common law.

Equitable Mistake in the Chancery Division of the High Court

Cases in which contracts were formed under a mistake were, as before fusion, infrequently litigated before the new Chancery Division. Most mistake cases still arose out of the core jurisdiction of the old Court of Chancery: the sale of land, the

[3] The principal provisions were s 24 (which provided that the High Court or Court of Appeal could provide equitable relief against, inter alia, any contract or deed in the same way as Chancery could have done), and s 25(11), which provided that where there was any conflict between law and equity the latter would prevail.

[4] s 34(3).

[5] P Polden, 'Mingling the Waters: Personalities, Politics and the Making of the Supreme Court of Judicature' (2002) 61 *Cambridge Law Journal* (CLJ) 575. Underhill, in 1937, wrote that there still existed 'a strong feeling of distinction between the Common Law barrister and his Chancery brother': Sir A Underhill, *Change and Decay: The Recollections and Reflections of An Octogenarian Bencher* (London, Butterworth & Co, 1938) 87.

[6] Polden (n 5) 592.

[7] A Birrell, 'Changes in Equity, Procedure, and Principles', in *A Century of Law Reform* (London, Macmillan, 1901) 197.

[8] See ch 4.

arrangement of leases and family settlements. The existing equitable practice with regard to mistake underwent an evolution rather than a revolution. While the process by which this evolution occurred is by no means clear, a number of trends can be discerned. One was a procedural necessity: if the Chancery Division refused to grant specific performance it needed to consider awarding damages. A second trend was the eventual acceptance that a party could rectify, or in the contemporary term, 'reform', a contract and then seek specific performance of it. Linked to this was a third trend, an increasing insistence that equity would intervene only upon a bilateral mistake. A fourth trend was the slow erosion of Lord Romilly's rescission on terms cases.

The Impact of Procedural Unity upon Substantive Law

An early point for determination was what the Chancery Division should do if it refused an order for specific performance because of a mistake. *Tamplin v James*[9] concerned a vendors' action for the specific performance of a sale of land. The purchaser's defence was that he had signed the contract under a mistake as to the extent of the property offered and he refused to accept a smaller parcel. This was a unilateral mistake to which the vendors had not contributed, nor were they aware of it. Baggallay LJ stated that it was well established that a court of equity would refuse specific performance of an agreement entered into under a purchaser's mistake where it would cause injustice to enforce the agreement. In these instances the mistakes usually arose through a vendor's unintentional misrepresentation or where ambiguities in the agreement caused the parties to give different interpretations to it. At times, cases such as *Malins v Freeman*[10] went further. In the case before him, however, Baggallay LJ found that there was neither misrepresentation nor ambiguity. A defendant could not successfully deny his liability on the grounds that he had made a mistake for such a denial would mean that specific performance was rarely enforced upon a defendant who was unwilling and unscrupulous. The defendant brought an appeal from Baggallay LJ's order for specific performance. The appeal was heard by a combination of two Chancery judges, James and Cotton LJJ, and one common law judge, Brett LJ. It was the latter who observed that where specific performance was refused because of mistake the court then had to consider the question of damages,[11] a point with which his Chancery brethren agreed.[12] The case formed the basis of the practice that where specific performance was not refused for mistake, damages had to be considered,[13] and this practice was approved of by Pollock.[14] Significantly, their Lordships

[9] (1879, 1880) 15 Ch D 215.

[10] (1837) 2 Keen 25; 48 ER 537.

[11] (1879, 1880) 15 Ch D 215, 219.

[12] ibid, 222 per Cotton LJ, and 223 per James LJ.

[13] *Bell v Balls* (1897) 76 LT ns 254, 256.

[14] Sir F Pollock, *Principles of Contract*, 5th edn (London, Stevens and Sons, 1889) 599. Curiously, Pollock contrasted the effect of this decision with what he viewed as the unsuitable practices of the

treated the two bodies of law and equity as completely distinct as regards to mistake. Where a mistake had occurred, this could be a reason to refuse to compel the performance of a contract but their Lordships clearly did not view the contract as void at common law by reason of this mistake. Indeed, the contract was valid at law, but might, because of the mistake, be one which would prevent the specific enforcement of it in equity. The case indicated clearly that the fusion effected was a procedural one, rather than a substantive one.[15] Having refused specific performance, their Lordships made no attempt to consider the effect of the mistake at law for this was not a concern at law.

Tamplin v James was also the modern origin for two further developments in English law of mistake. The first was the refusal to grant relief where the defendant's mistake arose as a result of his failure to take reasonable care: 'if a man makes a mistake of this kind without any reasonable excuse he ought to be held to his bargain'.[16] To allow the defendant relief for his careless mistake would be to deprive the vendors of a sale they could have made to another. The second was that the court evinced an unwillingness to intervene in cases of unilateral mistake unless there was unconscientious behaviour by the non-mistaken party, such as occurred in *Webster v Cecil*,[17] 'where a person snapped at an offer which he must have known perfectly well to be made by mistake.'[18] This approach was not dissimilar to that of the Queen's Bench in *Smith v Hughes.*[19] *Tamplin v James* received the approval of both judges[20] and jurists[21] in these restrictions of unilateral mistake.

Reform and Perform

Prior to 1875, Chancery had always refused to order specific performance of a contract which had been rectified.[22] Story[23] and Fry were both critical of this refusal; the latter questioned whether the prohibition existed in English law.[24] The Judicature Act 1873 provided Fry with a convenient ground to deny the future

courts of equity which 'from . . . habit or etiquette . . . down to recent times, never decided a legal point when they could help it': ibid.

15 A point strongly made in the decision of Cotton LJ, who spoke of the situation not as a fusion of the doctrine of law and equity but as one where both equitable and legal remedies are dispensed within a single court: *Tamplin v James* (n 9) 222.

16 ibid, 221, per James LJ.

17 (1861) 30 Beav 62; 54 ER 812.

18 *Tamplin v James* (n 9) 221 per James LJ.

19 (1871) LR 6 QB 597; 40 LJQB 221; 19 WR 1059.

20 See, eg, the decision of Kay J the following year in *Goddard v Jeffreys* (1881) 45 LT ns 674, 675, and also *Aspinalls to Powell and Scholefield* (1889) 60 LT ns 595; *Ellis v Hills and the Bright and Preston ABC Permanent Benefit Building Society* (1892) 67 LT 287.

21 See, eg, Pollock (n 14) 464–65.

22 *Woollam v Hearn* (1802) 7 Ves Jun 211; 32 ER 86, discussed in ch 3.

23 J Story, *Commentaries on Equity Jurisprudence as Administered in England and America, vol I*, 2nd edn (London, A Maxwell, 1839) 141–43.

24 E Fry, *A Treatise on Specific Performance* (London, Butterworths, 1858) 229–34.

application of the prohibition. On the convenient basis that section 24(7) allowed the High Court to grant all such remedies whatsoever as the parties were entitled to, Fry asserted that 'the High Court could have no difficulty in entertaining an action for the reformation of a contract, and for the specific performance of such reformed contract, in every case in which the Statute of Frauds did not create a bar'.[25] After an initial acceptance of this assertion,[26] English courts reverted to the original prohibition.[27] The unease with which they applied this prohibition could not be contained, and in *Craddock Bros v Hunt*,[28] the majority reasoned that rectification only corrected the written document to accord with the earlier contract. The document so rectified should thus have the same force as if the mistake had not been made, and the Statute of Frauds would be no defence to such a rectification. The rectified instrument was one continuing contract, and specific performance could be ordered in such circumstances. In dissent, Younger LJ observed that this had not been the Chancery practice before fusion and that while the Judicature Act 1873 allowed parties to do in one action what had previously been done in two, it did not allow parties to do what could not have been done at all.[29] Younger LJ's conclusion that the Judicature Act 1873 was not intended to create new remedies[30] was correct, but so useful was the Act as a basis to effect this change that the Privy Council accepted the majority's decision the following year.[31] The proposition Fry had advanced in his treatise had become law.

Fry's proposition was adopted for three reasons. All are indicative of a greater concern by courts of equity with the reasons for intervention on the grounds of mistake. The first reason was that if the mistake was one of transcription rather than agreement it was illogical not to specifically perform this agreement. Earlier Chancery judges had not viewed the matter in this light, partly because they were less concerned with providing principled reasons for the intervention and partly because of two further changes that entered the equitable treatment of mistake in the late nineteenth and early twentieth centuries. These changes are the second and third reasons for the acceptance of Fry's proposition; their importance is such that they are also considered in detail below. The second was that by the 1920s courts insisted that only a common mistake shared by the parties would warrant rectification. The third was that the flexibility of the equitable relief for mistake in the twentieth century began to diminish as practices became rules.

[25] ibid, p 355, §799.

[26] In *Olley v Fisher* [1887] LR 34 Ch D 367, North J accepted Fry's assertion in obiter dicta.

[27] *May v Platt* [1900] 1 Ch 616. This decision was followed in *Thompson v Hickman* [1907] 1 Ch 550, although Neville J expressed considerable disquiet at 561–62. In *Forgione v Lewis* [1920] 2 Ch 326, Eve J expressed doubt about the rule and held that it did not apply to the facts before him: 329.

[28] [1923] 2 Ch 136.

[29] ibid, 167.

[30] A point made by Brett LJ in *Britain v Rossiter* (1879) (1882–83) LR 11 QBD 123, 129.

[31] *United States of America v Motor Trucks* [1924] AC 196.

The Growing Necessity for the Mistake to be Bilateral

While Chancery had found it easier to grant relief in circumstances where the mistake was bilateral, this was not an invariable requirement. In the area of marriage settlements, in particular, Chancery had rectified mistakes in situations where the mistake was either unilateral or where the evidence of a common mistake was exceptionally weak. In the second half of the nineteenth century it was increasingly accepted that the mistake should be a bilateral one. Romilly MR appeared to accept this as a requirement and after fusion this was increasingly accepted as correct.[32] The requirement was necessary in the case of rectification, for the court acted to reform the instrument to accord to the antecedent agreement of the parties: if only one party had been mistaken, there could not have been an antecedent agreement. In *Paget v Marshall*,[33] Bacon V-C was concerned with a claim to rescind a lease on the ground of mistake. The lessor was mistaken and the lessee probably was not. After stating that common mistake was a ground for rectification and that a unilateral mistake could be a reason to refuse specific performance, Bacon V-C refused to find that the lessee had sought to take advantage of the mistake and found that the mistake must have been common to both parties. This common mistake provided the basis upon which the lease could be rescinded. Bacon V-C offered the lessee the election of either rescission or acceptance of the contract on the terms as understood by the lessor. The lessee elected the former.

Later cases accepted that rectification could only occur where the mistake was bilateral. That this was a departure from the previous equitable practice can be seen in the marriage settlement cases in which a wife in a disadvantageous position was assisted through rectification although the mistake was unilateral. This could occur in circumstances where the behaviour of the husband was suspiciously close to fraud.[34] In some instances where the wife's interest was not preserved after the death of her husband, equity intervened to rectify the settlement on what seems to be the unilateral mistake of the wife and often in cases where her testimony was the only evidence of this mistake.[35] This intervention generally, although not invariably, occurred when the expectations of others were not impinged. Frequently, the wife testified that she did not understand the terms of the settlement,[36] a position accepted in marriage settlements where it was rejected in commercial arrange-

[32] *Earl of Bradford v Earl of Romney* (1862) 30 Beav 431; 54 ER 956, 439; 959.

[33] (1885) LR 28 Ch D 255, 262–63. Bacon V-C's statement was addressed to the argument of counsel, which had been based upon William Williamson Kerr's *A Treatise on the Law of Fraud and Mistake*, 2nd edn (London, W Maxwell & Son, 1883) 498. Although Bacon V-C praised Kerr's treatise, it provided a somewhat confused and unprincipled account of the mistake cases.

[34] *Clark v Girdwood* (1877) 25 WR 575.

[35] *Edwards v Bingham* (1879) 28 WR 89; *Hanley v Pearson* (1879) 41 LT 673; *Johnson v Bragge* (1900) 83 LT 621. Husbands appear to have had a more difficult course in receiving rectification of a settlement they did not understand: *Rake v Hooper* (1900) 17 TLR 118, in which Kekewich J asserted that the court would only rectify a settlement where both parties had been in error (at 119) and that to do otherwise would be 'mischievous' (at 120).

[36] See, eg, *Cordeaux v Fullerton* (1879) 41 LT 651.

ments. In *Coganv Duffield*,[37] Bacon V-C explicitly stated that his intervention was for the purpose of 'completing' a settlement entered into in such haste that the proper form of the settlement had not been created. The underlying reason for intervention in all such cases was the unconscionability of depriving a wife of her property, particularly in circumstances where the settlement had been brought about by the undue influence of others who breached their fiduciary duties to the wife.[38] These became, in the end, cases dealt with as undue influence, where the law examined the relationship between the parties and the behaviour of the stronger actor, rather than examining the misapprehension or misunderstanding of the weaker party.

In cases where rescission was sought, Lindley LJ stated that a common mistake was a basis for rescinding an agreement.[39] Gradually, in response to the arguments made asserting this, courts came to accept that rescission required a bilateral mistake, described variously as a mutual or common mistake.[40] Relief for a unilateral mistake, in the form of rescission or a refusal of specific performance, would only occur in circumstances where the mistake was induced by the other party[41] or where the non-mistaken party 'snapped' at a mistaken offer.[42] The role of treatises is not apparent in this judicial process and it may only be coincidental that throughout the nineteenth-century writers had written of the necessity of a bilateral mistake in cases of rectification or rescission.[43]

[37] (1875) LR 20 Eq 789, 803. Similarly, in *Clark v Girdwood* (n 33) Malins V-C stated that a 'proper' settlement would not have done what the one before him had.

[38] In *Lovesy v Smith* (1880) 43 LT ns 240, a widow married her solicitor. The solicitor prepared the marriage settlement the night before their wedding, presenting it to his bride at 5 o'clock on the morning of their wedding. She signed the settlement, having waited all night for his return, and only discovered after his death that a moiety had been settled upon him absolutely. Her testimony (which included the statement that she would never have married him had she been aware of this) was the only evidence of the error.

[39] *Huddersfield Banking Co. Ltd v Henry Lister and Son, Ltd* [1894] 2 Ch 273, 280–81.

[40] See, eg, *Debenham v Sawbridge* [1901] 2 Ch 98, 109–10, per Byrne J; *Scott v Coulson* [1903] 1 Ch 453, 455 per Kekewich J; and *Scott v Coulson* [1903] 2 Ch 249 (CA), 252 per Vaughan Williams LJ, and 253 per Romer LJ.

[41] *Wilding v Sanderson* [1897] 2 Ch 534.

[42] See, eg, *Aspinalls to Powell and Scholefield* (1889) 60 LT ns 595.

[43] Few authors concerned solely with equity asserted this unequivocally but they chose instead to consider it in relation to either types of mistake or forms of relief. Joseph Story (n 23) indicated that a unilateral mistake could be grounds for the refusal of specific performance but that for rescission or rectification the mistake had to be bilateral, and this was echoed by Grigsby in his later English edition of Story: *Commentaries on Equity Jurisprudence*, 2nd English edition, WE Grigsby (ed) (London, Stevens and Haynes, 1892) 70, 71, 86–87, 92. Fry (n 26) wrote that a unilateral mistake could be a ground for refusing specific performance but that rectification and rescission required a bilateral mistake (214, 216, 221); Leake followed this treatment (SM Leake, *The Elements of the Law of Contracts* (London, Stevens and Sons, 1867) 170) but Pollock and Anson emphasised the necessity for the mistake to be bilateral: Pollock (n 14) 434, 465, 498, and Sir WR Anson, *Principles of the English Law of Contract*, 7th edn (Oxford, Clarendon Press, 1894) 131.

The Increasing Rigidity of Equitable Relief

The flexibility of equitable relief had allowed Chancery to fashion a remedy to suit the circumstances. Some of these practices may well have been built around the procedures of the old Court of Chancery. Thus, while a mistaken party could not obtain specific performance of a contract with a variation, if he refused to perform the contract, the other party might bring a bill seeking specific performance. If the mistaken party asserted the mistake in his defence, the Court of Chancery could present the plaintiff with a choice. This choice was an election between either having his bill for specific performance dismissed or having specific performance of the contract on the terms understood by the (mistaken) defendant. Once the oddities of repeated appearances in different courts seeking justice were swept away by the Judicature Act 1873, the acceptability of such a convoluted practice would appear questionable. The flexibility of equity diminished as the Chancery Division was less willing than the old Court of Chancery to put parties to these elections. Chancery had sometimes an enforced an agreement formed at the court when one party was given an election between two courses of action. Romilly MR had extended this practice in *Garrard v Frankel*[44] by offering the lessee an election between having the lease rectified or giving up the lease and paying an occupation rent. He followed this in *Harris v Pepperell*;[45] the correctness of neither decision was questioned by contemporaries.[46] A decade after Romilly MR's death the actual basis of his decisions, and the correctness of them, was challenged in *Paget v Marshall*.[47] The plaintiff lessor sought the relief granted in *Harris v Pepperrell*. The defendant based his case partly on *Kerr on Fraud and Mistake*,[48] a curious treatise written largely without a unifying treatment of the subject, for the proposition that *Harris v Pepperell* was a rectification case and that rectification could be granted only for a common mistake, of which this was not. He also based his case on the argument that *Garrard v Frankel* and *Harris v Pepperell* were explained by Sir George Jessel as explicable only on the basis of frauds which Romilly MR had omitted to mention out of delicacy.[49] The lessor's counsel replied that these obser-

[44] (1862) 30 Beav 445; 54 ER 961; 31 Law Jo Eq 604; 8 Jur (ns) 985.

[45] (1867) LR 5 Eq 1; 17 TLR 191; 16 WR 68.

[46] See, eg, JH Dart and W Barber, *Dart on the Law of Vendors and Purchasers*, 5th edn (London, Stevens and Sons, 1876) 744, where the author observed the effect of the decisions in *Garrard v Frankel*, *Harris v Pepperell* and *Bloomer v Spittle* (1872) 13 Eq 427 without questioning them. Fry, in the second edition of his treatise, took a similar approach and commented in a footnote that Lord Romilly himself had pointed out the distinction between *Garrard v Frankel* and *Earl of Bradford v Earl of Romney* (n 31): Sir E Fry and WD Rawlins, *A Treatise on the Specific Performance of Contracts*, 2nd edn (London, Stevens and Sons, 1881) 340, §760, and Sir E Fry and EP Fry, *A Treatise on the Specific Performance of Contracts*, 3rd edn (London, Stevens and Sons, 1892). See, eg, *Burchell v Clark* (1875–76) LR 1 CPD 602, where neither opposing counsel nor the judges questioned the accuracy of the decisions when employed in argument; the same occurred in *M'Kenzie v Hesketh* (1877) 38 LT ns 171 and in *Bloomer v Spittle* (above).

[47] (1884) 28 Ch D 255.

[48] WW Kerr, *A Treatise on the Law of Fraud and Mistake*, 2nd edn (London, W Maxwell & Son, 1883). Counsel relied upon the passages set out at 499–500.

[49] (1884) 28 Ch D 255, 260.

vations of Romilly MR, if made, had not been reported. Although Bacon V-C applied the earlier cases and did not question the correctness of them, this was to be the last such application. The characterisation of fraud was seen in future to be their actual basis.

The reason for this lies in a parallel development in Scottish law, in *Brownlie v Campbell*.[50] The case concerned a contract for the conveyance of land in which the terms of the contract imposed upon the purchaser the risk of all errors in the particulars. The vendor's particulars erroneously described the property. The House of Lords refused to set aside the contract on the basis that this could only be done where the misrepresentation amounted to fraud. In reaching this decision, their Lordships approved of the statement in *Bell's Principles of Scottish Law* that, where there was doubt as to a conveyance, the purchaser should seek a warranty. Absent such a warranty, the conveyance could only be set aside where there was fraud on the part of the vendor or an *error in substantialibus* 'sufficient to annul the whole contract'.[51] While Lord Selborne LC stated that the law in England and Ireland was to the same effect, there was no consideration of the equity cases, such as *Cooper v Phibbs*,[52] in which a conveyance had been set aside for a mistake short of fraud. *Brownlie v Campbell* was accepted into English law apparently without the realisation that the decision was dependent upon the contractual allocation of a risk of error and that mistake had been expressly rejected.[53] The decision led English judges to the conclusion that an executed conveyance could only be set aside where fraud was established.

This unwitting acceptance was to cause problems in later English equity cases. In *May v Platt*,[54] Farwell J refused to admit evidence of the parties' mistake.[55] The evidence could only be admitted for one of two purposes. The first would be to rectify the contract, and what was actually sought was rectification followed by specific performance and this was prevented by *Woollam v Hearn*.[56] The second was to show that the parties were not *ad idem* and to put the purchaser to the election of either accepting rectification or rescinding the contract. Farwell J rejected this as well. Rectification required a bilateral mistake and was allowed for unilateral mistake only where there was fraud or misrepresentation. *Garrard v Frankel*,

[50] (1880) 5 App Cas 937.

[51] ibid, 937.

[52] (1867) [LR] 2 HL 149.

[53] *Soper v Arnold* (1888) LR 37 ChD 96, 102 per Cotton LJ (oddly, the appellant's argument based on *Cooper v Phibbs* was ignored, probably because of the peculiar facts of the case); *Re Tyrell; Tyrell v Woodhouse* (1900) 82 LT 675 per Cozens-Hardy J; *Debenham v Sawbridge* [1901] 2 Ch 98, 110 per Byrne J; and *Seddon v The North Eastern Salt Company* [1905] 1 Ch 326, 331 per Joyce J (who observed that the rule was the same in law as could be seen in the case of *Kennedy v Panama, New Zealand and Australian Royal Mail Co*). *Brownlie v Campbell* formed a part of Lord Herschell's reasons in *Derry v Peek* (1889) LR 14 App Cas 337, 374.

[54] [1900] 1 Ch 616.

[55] The parties to a conveyance were mistaken as to the exact extent of the estate; it was marginally smaller than the vendor had held it out to be. The real mistake, however, was likely that of the vendor's solicitor, who probably forgot to qualify the vendor's 'interest' in the particular land with the words 'if any'.

[56] 2 Ves Jun Supp 24; 34 ER 981.

Harris v Pepperell and perhaps *Paget v Marshall* were cases of fraud. In so characterising the cases, Farwell J echoed the criticism of the cases found in Dart's sixth edition on *Vendors and Purchasers*,[57] but in doing so he misconstrued the earlier mistake cases. Rescission of land, Farwell J stated, could only be granted where there was unfair dealing, following the decisions of *Brownlie v Campbell* and *Soper v Arnold* (in which the court had applied the former case). While the decision to reject the *Garrard v Frankel* line of cases was a departure that was not warranted by the case, there were other signs of judicial discontent with the cases.[58]

A second factor worked against the survival of the *Garrard v Frankel* line of authorities, and this was their treatment at the hands of treatise writers. Pollock, in particular, led the criticism of these cases because he viewed them as peculiar and anomalous.[59] For Pollock's Savigny-inspired theory, which dictated that the effect of mistake was to render a contract void *ab initio*, these cases were peculiar because it was impossible to deny that both law and equity regarded the contracts as valid despite the mistake but that equity might regard the contract as voidable. The presence of terms simply underscored the fact that the contract was voidable and not void. Pollock's criticisms were to gain hold in the case law[60] and also in the works of treatise writers[61] concerned with equitable doctrines and practices. It is unlikely that Pollock's criticisms were the sole reason for the decline of these cases but, coupled with a changed approach to mistake by equity judges, the result was that these cases became submerged without being overturned. It was in this manner that they became, as Pollock had described them, 'peculiar'.

Substantive Fusion of Mistake

Two factors explain the lack of an attempt to effect a substantive fusion of common law and equity to create a coherent doctrine of mistake in the half-century following fusion.[62] The first is that the allocation of jurisdiction under the

[57] *A Treatise on the Law and Practice Relating to Vendors and Purchasers of Real Estate* by the late J Henry Dart (6th edn, W Barber, RB Haldane and WR Sheldon (eds) (London, Stevens and Sons, 1888) vol II, 839: 'it is, however, difficult to understand the grounds of these decisions. Either there has originally been a contract, in which case the Court cannot make a new one, or there has been no contract, in which case neither at Law or in Equity is there anything to enforce').

[58] In *Beale v Kyte* (1907) 96 LT 390, Neville J opined that *Bloomer v Spittle*, another Romilly MR decision which applied *Garrard v Frankel*, was wholly unintelligible and wrongly reported: 391.

[59] See ch 6 above.

[60] In the nineteenth century, recourses to Pollock were generally made by counsel. See, eg, JM Riggs' adoption of Pollock's interpretation of *Cooper v Phibbs*: *Soper v Arnold* (n 49) 97. By the twentieth century judges also began to have recourse to Pollock, a point examined below.

[61] Even equitable treatise writers relied upon Pollock. See, eg, Grigsby (n 43) 70, and *Dart's Treatise on the Law and Practice of Vendors and Purchasers of Real Estate*, 8th edn, EP Hewitt and MRC Overton (eds) (London, Stevens and Sons, 1929) vol II, 618, fn (*t*), which referred readers to Pollock's comments on the 'anomalous character' of *Garrard v Frankel* and the cases decided upon it.

[62] The lack of such an attempt, and the adherence of Chancery lawyers to their own practices, can be seen in *Archer v Stone* (1898) 78 LT 34, in which a purchaser fraudulently deceived the seller of a lease as to the real identity of the purchaser. The case is not dissimilar from the sort of frauds perpetrated in cases such as *Cundy v Lindsay* (1877–78) LR 3 App Cas 459; [1974–80] All ER Rep 1149,

Judicature Act 1873 ensured that most equitable mistake cases were heard before the Chancery Division, which followed the pre-existing equitable precedents and developed its own doctrine largely without common law influences. The second factor is that the common law, apart from mistake of identity, had little in the way of a doctrine of mistake until well into the twentieth century.

At times judges[63] made comparisons between the different treatment a particular case would receive at law and in equity, although they made no attempt to harmonise these different treatments. An example is Lindley LJ's judgment in *Huddersfield Banking Company, Ltd v Henry Lister & Son, Limited*,[64] where he observed that while equity, in cases such as *Bingham v Bingham*,[65] set aside contracts for mistake and restored the money, the common law provided much the same result in cases such as *Strickland v Turner*,[66] in which an action for money had and received was allowed on the ground of a total failure of consideration.[67] That these comparisons were made indicates three points. First, judges were far more concerned that the results of the equitable and legal cases were the same than they were that the same principles were applied: fusion was procedural and not substantive. Second, the comparisons indicate the extent to which the legal and equitable treatment of mistake in the system before fusion was largely complementary rather than contradictory. Third, they indicate the extremely limited extent of equitable borrowing of common law cases immediately after fusion. *Smith v Hughes* was a notable exception. That it successfully 'crossed over' from law to equity is not surprising given that the case was concerned to prevent sharp practice, a concern that underscored the equitable jurisdiction for mistake. *Smithv Hughes* itself appears to have been introduced to the Chancery Division by the argument of counsel, who relied upon Pollock's treatment of the case.[68] The case was used in the Chancery Division both to limit the ambit of unilateral mistake and to attempt to prevent a non-mistaken party from taking an unconscionable advantage of the mistaken party.[69]

(1878) 42 JP 483; (1878) 14 Cox CC 93; (1878) 26 WR 406; (1878) 47 LJQB 481; (1878) 38 LT 573., but no reference is made to this case or the newly emergent English mistake of identity. The arguments of counsel and North J's decision addressed the earlier equitable cases, although these had a civilian influence in the form of Pothier due to Fry J's decision in *Smith v Wheatcroft* (1878) 9 Ch D. 223, 230.

63 See, eg, *Cochrane v Willis* (1865) 1 LR Eq 58, 63 per Knight Bruce LJ, and 64 per Turner LJ

64 [1895] 2 Ch 273, 280–81. Other instances can be found in *Clayson v Leech* (1889) 61 LT ns 69, 70 per Bowen LJ, and *Scott v Coulson* [1903] 2 Ch 249, 252 per Vaughan Williams LJ.

65 (1748), 1 Ves Sen 126; 27 ER 934, Ves Sen Sup 79; 28 ER 462.

66 (1852) 7 Exch 208, 155 ER 919.

67 It may be that Lindley LJ was influenced by Pollock's treatise (which was dedicated to Lindley LJ), because Pollock used the same cases to similar effect as illustrations of instances at law and in equity of a mistake as to the existence of the subject matter: Pollock (n 14) 469–73.

68 This process began early: *M'Kenzie v Hesketh* (1877–78) LR 7 Ch D 675, 679; 38 LT ns 171.

69 *London Holeproof Hosiery Company, Ltd v Padmore* (1928) 44 TLR 499, 501, and *Blay v Pollard* [1930] 1 KB 628, 636.

A Reduced Ambit for Mistake in Equity

It was earlier observed that Chancery's core jurisdiction was property management and that in the nineteenth century misapprehensions were bound to arise in a system dominated by settlements and operated in absence of any registered title. The late nineteenth century saw an increasing number of legislative changes, designed to effect substantive changes in land-owning, to increase the alienability of land and to maximise its economic utility. During the nineteenth century somewhere between a half and three quarters of English land had a strict settlement imposed upon it.[70] Strict settlements were complex matters in which the risk of an inadvertent error was ever present. The strict settlement was designed to ensure that land was held by a single male heir and maintained within a family for successive generations. To facilitate these ends, the heir was necessarily a life tenant and, as the century wore on, the demands of scientific agriculture, which required a level of expenditure not foreseen when many settlements had been devised, necessitated changes to the powers of this life tenant.[71] The result was legislative reform to the powers of the life tenant. The Settled Land Act 1882 gave the tenant for life a power of sale which had the effect of undermining the principal objective of the strict settlement: the retention of the estate.[72] The policy of the 1882 Act was ultimately adopted and somewhat extended by the Settled Land Act 1925.[73] The effect of these increased powers was ultimately to lead to the sale of large amounts of land; by 1921, over a quarter of English land had changed hands.[74] Changes in taxation which attracted revenue charges to settlements acted to further reduce the viability of strict settlements.[75] The untimely deaths of young men in the Great War acted to disrupt further the process of settling land, and by the 1920s, settlements of land were drafted to protect wealth rather than land.[76] It seems likely that as strict settlements became less viable, so, too, did marriage settlements become less attractive. The Married Women's Property Act 1870, followed by the more

[70] MR Chesterman, 'Family Settlements on Trust' in GR Rubin and D Sugarman (eds), *Law, Economy and Society, 1750–1914: Essays in the History of English Law* (Worcester, Professional Books Limited, 1984) 130; A Underhill, 'Changes in the Law of Real Property' in *A Century of Law Reform* (London, Macmillan, 1901) 282 wrote that it was not an exaggeration to state that nearly all the great estates of England held their land upon a strict settlement.

[71] E Spring, 'Landowners, Lawyers, and Land Law Reform in Nineteenth-Century England' (1977) 21 *American Journal of Legal History* 40, 44. Spring has also observed, however, that there appear to have been a wide variety of settlement structures employed by different families: E Spring, 'The Settlement of Land in Nineteenth-Century England' (1964) 8 *American Journal of Legal History* 209.

[72] The reasons for the 1882 Act and its application are described by one of the property lawyers who contributed to its enactment: Underhill (n 70).

[73] The changes to strict settlements and trusts for sale are outlined in RE Megarry and HWR Wade, *The Law of Real Property*, 3rd edn (London, Stevens and Sons, 1966) ch 6. The changes brought about by the 1925 legislation have been described as the final stage in the dismantling of the Victorian strict settlement: B English and J Saville, *Strict Settlement A Guide for Historians* (North Humberside, University of Hull Press, 1983) 112.

[74] Spring, 'Landowners' (n 71) 40.

[75] Chesterman (n 70) 166.

[76] BW Harvey, *Settlements of Land* (London, Sweet and Maxwell, 1973) 5.

wide ranging Married Women's Property Act 1882, effected 'a great and revolutionary change in the relations of husband and wife'[77] and allowed married women to control their own property. Marriage settlements had been designed to protect the wealth of a wife from a potentially rapacious or dissolute husband; once a wife could hold her own property, the reason for such a settlement diminished. It is known that the 1870 Act caused substantial changes in the nature of property owned by women[78]; it seems equally likely that the effect of the legislation was to contribute to the disappearance of the marriage settlement itself as its protective measures were no longer needed.

Ultimately the entire property regime was simplified with the major enactments of 1925 which were designed to simplify conveyancing. The principal objectives addressed in this simplification process were to allow the purchaser to satisfy himself that his vendor was capable of passing title and in ascertaining the legal and equitable interests charged against the property.[79] The means by which these objectives were achieved ultimately acted to reduce those circumstances in which a mistake would operate. As mistake was recognised in common law courts, the traditional jurisdictions in which it had appeared in equitable courts were diminished.

Common Law Mistake in the High Court

Mistake cases at common law, apart from those of mistake of identity, were a rare occurrence in the half-century following fusion. Argument about mistake was absent in cases where one would have expected it,[80] and most cases in which it was considered arose from bizarre circumstances and little judicial consideration was given to mistake.[81] In one such case where an argument was attempted that the parties were at cross purposes and no contract arose, the Privy Council abruptly dismissed the claim because 'an intelligent child would have understood

[77] Underhill, *Change and Decay* (n 5) 81.

[78] MB Combs, '"A Measure of Legal Independence": The 1870 Married Women's Property Act and the Portfolio Allocations of British Wives' (2005) 65 *The Journal of Economic History* 1028. Combs concludes that while the legislation did not allow women to increase their total wealth, it allowed them to shift their wealth-holding away from realty to personalty and that this shift was attributable to the legislation: ibid, 1053. The property regimes of marriage are discussed in S Cretney, *Family Law in the Twentieth Century* (Oxford, Oxford University Press, 2003) ch 3.

[79] A contemporary description of these changes is given in GC Cheshire, *The Modern Law of Real Property* (London Butterworth & Co, 1925) 65–83; the historical background is outlined in WR Cornish and G de N Clark, *Law and Society in England 1750–1950* (London, Sweet & Maxwell, 1989) 166–79. The opposition to such legislation by provincial solicitors, fearful that a simplified system would lead to a reduction in their business, is described by Avner Offer in 'The Origins of the Law of Property Acts 1910–1925' (1977) 40 *Modern Law Review* 505.

[80] See, eg, *Holmes v Payne* [1930] 2 KB 301.

[81] *Pope and Pearson v Buenos Ayres New Gas Company* (1892) 8 TLR 516; appeal dismissed (1892) 8 TLR 758; *Ewing and Lawson v Hanbury & Co* (1900) 16 TLR 140; *The Steam Herring Fleet (Limited) v Richards and Co (Limited)* (1901) 17 TLR 731.

it. Business cannot go on if men of business are allowed to shelter themselves under such a plea'.[82] The postponed coronation of Edward VII gave rise to comparatively few mistake cases. In a rare exception, *Clark v Lindsay*,[83] Scrutton K.C. raised an argument based on *Kennedy's* case, and Alverstone LCJ held, apparently on the basis of a mutual mistake of fact, that the procession was not merely the object and motive of the contract but went to the very substance of the contract, without which there was no contract. This implied acceptance of a doctrine of mistake, whatever it might be, was repeated on the eve of the First World War in the strange circumstances of *Galloway v Galloway*.[84] In a briefly reported decision, Ridley J held that the terms of the agreement were based on a mistaken assumption, and 'the law clearly was that if there was a mutual mistake of fact which was material to the existence of an agreement, the agreement was void'.[85] The rarity with which these cases arose indicates that mistake, if it existed as such, was largely peripheral to the operation of the common law of contract.

It was not until 1930 that a case arising in the King's Bench Division which directly raised an issue of mistake received any significant judicial consideration. Two parties had contracted to terminate an existing contract when, unbeknown to either party, the existing contract was terminable at the option of one of the parties. Coincidentally this case, *Munro v Meyer*,[86] not only raised the same issue as *Bell v Lever Brothers* but it was also heard by the same trial judge only days before the trial of the latter case. Munro contracted to sell cattle meal to Meyer, a Hamburg merchant. Difficult financial circumstances in Germany meant that Meyer lost the market for this meal, and the pair contracted to terminate the supply contract. After this termination contract was completed, Meyer discovered that adulteration of the meal meant that he would have been able to reject the shipment. He then refused to make further payments under the termination contract. His counsel argued that the termination contract was not enforceable because it had been entered into on the assumption that certain facts existed which did not. The argument was supported with *Bingham v Bingham*, *Cooper v Phibbs*, and *Kennedy*'s case. Wright J considered that mistake arose both at common law and in equity. At common law, in certain circumstances, a mistake could prevent a supposed contract 'from being any contract at all'; there was an appearance of a contract, but the contract was 'void'.[87] Wright J provided two such circumstances. The first was where the contract was for a subject matter which had perished at the time of the contract; there was no contract and any money paid was recoverable as money paid under a consideration which had failed. No rights could arise out of a

[82] *Falck v Williams* [1900] AC 176, 180 per Lord Macnaghten.

[83] (1903) 19 TLR 202.

[84] (1914) 30 TLR 531. A couple who believed themselves to be married, but were in fact not married due to an earlier marriage of the man, entered into a separation deed. The man later successfully argued that he was not bound under the deed because of a common mistake as to the assumed validity of the marriage.

[85] ibid, 532.

[86] [1930] 2 KB 312.

[87] ibid, 332.

contract which was a nullity. An illustration of this could be found in section 6 of the Sale of Goods Act 1893 and *Couturier v Hastie*.[88] The second was *Scott v Coulson*, in which the same result occurred in relation to a chose in action. Wright J did not appear to realise that this was an equitable case, for he then went on to contrast the 'clear' treatment of mistake to be found at common law with mistake in equity:

> certain other cases which are not so clear as those to which I have referred, in which a Court of equity has exercised jurisdiction to declare, on the ground of some material and vital mistake, that the contract is rescinded *ab initio*, but the Court has only exercised that equitable jurisdiction if satisfied not only that there was a mistake but also that the circumstances were such that the mistake could be undone, and ought to be undone, and that there might be a *restitutio in integrum*.[89]

Equity intervened to set aside a contract where there was, as in *Cooper v Phibbs*, a mistake as to the relative and respective rights of the parties. The contract before Wright J was not one which could be justifiably set aside, because of the complexities present in Meyer's claim that the supply contract was terminable. These complexities meant that it was far from certain that he would have succeeded in his claim for termination and, in these circumstances, it seemed likely that he would have settled the claim, possibly on the same terms as it had been mistakenly settled.

The significance of this obscure case is that it demonstrated Wright J's understanding that contractual mistake existed at both common law and in equity; and that equity did not declare the contract to be void, but might possibly rescind it for mistake. The case also demonstrated that a leading commercial judge of the day was unconcerned with the basis of the equitable relief for mistake and provided a weak description of instances of mistake at common law.

The Importance of *Bell v Lever Brothers*

This was the unresolved state of the English law of mistake when Lever Brothers sued Bell and Snelling. The resulting House of Lords' decision was to form the foundation for English contractual mistake; unfortunately, this foundation is dangerously unstable for a number of reasons. First, the case was not about mistake but about asserting an acceptable standard of behaviour for senior corporate managers at a time when companies came increasingly to rely on these managers.[90] Second, the decisions in the case were circumscribed by procedural rules which constrained the conduct of the case in such a way as to produce an artificial issue for resolution.[91] Third, a critical scrutiny of the decisions indicates that the largely

[88] (1856) 5 HLC 673, 10 ER 1065.

[89] [1930] 2 KB 312, 334.

[90] This aspect of the case is dealt with in detail in C MacMillan, 'How Temptation Led to Mistake: An Explanation of *Bell v Lever Bros Ltd*' (2003) 119 *Law Quarterly Review* (LQR) 625.

[91] The procedural aspects of this care are dealt with in detail in C MacMillan, 'The Trial: How Procedure Shapes Substance' (2008) 19 KLJ 465.

commercial judges who decided this case were guided in their decisions by the principal treatises of the day. In receiving this guidance, the judges unwittingly adopted a theory of mistake which, as we have seen, was both substantively flawed and grounded upon cases which were not support for this theory.

It was only by mistake that *Bell v Lever Brothers*[92] became the principal English case on mistake. The case received as much judicial attention as it did because of the plaintiff's determination to set corporate standards of behaviour and its ability to fund this litigation. Bell and Snelling had been hired by Viscount Leverhulme to run a West African commodities company, the Niger Company, a subsidiary of Lever Brothers. The pair achieved such success in this endeavour that Lever Brothers formed an amalgamation with a rival company. Lever Brothers entered into contracts with each man to terminate his employment in exchange for the payment of handsome amounts of compensation to each man. Within months of their departures, Lever Brothers discovered that the pair had been trading in cocoa on their own account, using the company's broker and in breach of the cartel agreement to which the Niger was a party. The effect of their actions had been to render their employment contracts terminable at Lever Brothers' option. Lever Brothers demanded the return of the termination payments; the refusal of this demand led Lever Brothers to issue a writ seeking the recovery of the payments. The action was brought as a matter of principle: Lever Brothers' head, Sir Francis D'Arcy Cooper, was of the firm view that such corrupt conduct, if left unchecked, would destroy a business.[93]

The action was framed on the principal bases of fraudulent misrepresentation or concealment, and breaches of duty and of the contracts of service.[94] A brief alternative claim of mistake was alleged but as monies paid under a (unilateral) mistake of fact by Lever Brothers rather than a mistake which affected the formation of the contract. The defendants' solicitor sought particulars of the nature of the mistake of fact alleged, notably 'who was under what mistake of what fact or facts'.[95] Lever Brothers' solicitor replied with a broader allegation, that the mistake was that the defendants 'had acted honestly in their conduct of the affairs of the Niger Company Limited and had not dealt in cocoa on their own account and/or in so dealing on their own account had not acted contrary to their duty and/or the terms of their respective contracts'.[96] Counsel who prepared the further particulars, Wilfrid Lewis, privately expressed to his client that, although these particulars 'should suffice', the essential difficulty they faced in this claim was that 'the plea in order to succeed must establish a mutual mistake of fact and I take it that the defendants will say that they were under no misapprehension at all as to what they

[92] [1932] AC 161.

[93] Testimony of Cooper, transcript p 20, to be found in the records kept by the Parliamentary Archives, [1931] AC *Bell v Lever Brothers* (vol 858).

[94] The writ can be found in the Parliamentary Archives (n 95). The writ is described in greater detail in MacMillan (n 91) 468.

[95] Parliamentary Archives (n 93), App 4.

[96] ibid, App 5.

had done or that their dealing in cocoa on their account was contrary to their duty'.[97] Lewis directed that no further particulars as to the mistake should be given.[98] It does not seem to have occurred to him that there was a body of equitable cases in which rescission would be allowed for a unilateral mistake where it would be unconscionable to allow one party to obtain an advantage from the mistake. Nor, apparently, was *Smith v Hughes* considered applicable to the case. Counsel's opinion was clear that only a bilateral mistake would allow a court to rescind a contract entered into under a mistake of fact. The rules of civil procedure effectively prevented Lever Brothers from establishing such a bilateral mistake before trial. While documentary discovery was available, Bell and Snelling had destroyed virtually all the documents which pertained to the trades, rendering the affidavit of documents largely useless. Only three people had knowledge of the alleged fraud: Bell, Snelling and Fontannaz, the broker. There was no procedure by which these people could be orally examined before trial, and Lever Brothers had trouble in establishing the nature of their case before the trial opened.

Lever Brothers had an uneasy relationship with Fontannaz, and each party was suspicious of the other. Lever Brothers recognised that Fontannaz was the only source from which they might obtain information about the trades,[99] and they served him with a *subpoena duces tecum* requiring him to attend at trial with a large number of documents pertaining to commodity trades.[100] Only at this late stage did Lever Brothers' accountants examine the documents. Following this examination, Lever Brothers' counsel sought to amend their pleadings to allege even further fraudulent activities on the part of the defendants: that they had appropriated the proceeds of profitable Niger trades and left the company with the unprofitable ones and that they had used Niger money to cover their trades. In view of the seriousness of these allegations,[101] Wright J decided to adjourn the trial. When the trial resumed in May 1930, Lever Brothers withdrew the allegations of appropriation, a matter which was to later work against them. Worse was to come for Lever Brothers because, as the trial wore on, it became increasingly apparent that the evidence did not support a finding of either fraudulent misrepresentation or concealment. The documentary evidence was sparse, Fontannaz's evidence proved to be of dubious value and the only means of proving these allegations was through the defendants' testimonies. The defendants, astoundingly, each testified that they had not realised that the trades breached the cartel agreement and that they had forgotten the trades when they entered the termination agreements.[102] The effect of these surprising testimonies was to force Lever Brothers to their alternative claim of mistake (a claim perceived to be so insignificant it had not been addressed

[97] Unilever Archives and Records Management (hereafter 'UARM'), Acc 1996/48, box 138, file 2063, Opinion of Wilfrid Lewis, 21 January 1930.

[98] ibid.

[99] MacMillan (n 90) 642.

[100] A description of these is in MacMillan (n 91) 474.

[101] The defendant's counsel, Sir Leslie Scott, described the allegations as 'criminal' in nature: *Financial Times*, 28 March 1930, 10.

[102] See MacMillan (n 91) 478, and MacMillan (n 90) 644–46.

in opening arguments). Over the vociferous objections of Pritt for the defendants, Wright J allowed questions pertaining to mistake to be put to the special jury. In his summing up to the jury, Wright J made clear that the central problem in the case was the acceptability of Bell and Snelling's conduct and that what the jury had to determine was whether or not the termination agreements should stand in light of this conduct. The action had been brought to seek a declaration that the termination agreements were no longer binding and return of the money. Wright J stated that there were two routes by which this end could be reached. The first was fraudulent misrepresentation or concealment; the second was mistake. With regard to the first route, Lever Brothers' case was a difficult one to establish in law and also on the facts, which required them to prove the defendants' mental states. Wright J expressed doubt that fraudulent concealment or misrepresentation had been made out and guided the jury towards mistake.[103] The jury found that the defendants had breached their contracts or duty in undertaking the secret trades, that Lever Brothers were entitled to terminate the contracts of employment and would have done so had they known; that Lever Brothers were unaware of the secret trades when they entered into the termination agreements; that if Lever Brothers had been so aware of the trades, they would not have entered into the termination agreements; and that at the date of their respective meetings before the termination agreements, neither Bell nor Snelling had in their mind the secret trades. The jury negatived any finding of fraudulent misrepresentation or concealment in relation to the termination agreements. The result was that Lever Brothers' claim to rescind the termination agreements now depended solely upon mistake.

Davies, for Lever Brothers, addressed the legal issue of when and how mistake affected a contract. Wright J's puzzlement as to the law in this area complicated Davies' meandering argument. Wright J had been a common law lawyer, noted for his commercial law expertise, and stated at the outset that mistake of fact was 'one of the most difficult questions in the law of Contract'.[104] He was greatly puzzled by two things. The first was the lack of authority. He was of the view that 'there must have been many cases in the past where an Agreement has held not to be binding on the ground of mistake, where the money has been paid, and the Court has said that there must be what they call *restitutio in integrum*'.[105] He called repeatedly on Davies to 'cite some cases . . . I have seen no case which throws any light on that question [of mistake in contractual formation]'.[106] The second was the difficulty he and Davies encountered in trying to extract underlying principles from the decided cases. As Wright J observed, there were many possible varieties of mistake and 'each variety carries a little different consequence'.[107] Wright J did

[103] MacMillan (n 91) 478–80.
[104] Parliamentary Archives (n 93), App 33, 1447.
[105] ibid, 1444.
[106] ibid, 1466.
[107] ibid, 1456.

not appear to realise that in deciding the case on the basis of a common mistake he was breaking new ground.

Wright J had forgotten what he had decided in *Munro v Meyer*; Pritt, for the defendants, had Munro's counsel attend as an *amicus curiae* to read out his notes of the decision.[108] Curiously, Wright J did not repeat his attempt to consider the effect of mistake at law and in equity. The observations he made in the course of Davies' argument indicated little knowledge of either the reasons underlying equitable intervention in cases of mistake nor the relief offered. Wright J was of the view that the difficulty before him was that the parties intended to contract but the mistake went to what he labelled the 'inducement' to contract.[109] Davies struggled to locate cases which dealt with this point. He used the categories listed in *Halsbury's Laws of England* under mistake and noted that where there was a mistake of a fundamental character, a unilateral mistake of fact would be grounds for rescission. The problem, as Wright J recognised, was that there was no indication of when a mistake was fundamental.[110] Davies cited *Paget v Marshall* as an authority for allowing rescission for a unilateral mistake. Davies omitted the equitable basis for the decision, and Wright J stated he 'should not feel very strongly disposed to follow, because I do not understand it'.[111] He struggled to accept the proposition that a contract could be rescinded where one party, through his own mistake, did not get what he had bargained for, because if this was allowed, 'no contract would ever stand'.[112] Inexplicably, Davies failed to explain that the basis of the decision was that the non-mistaken party sought to obtain an unconscionable advantage. Wright J found *Paget v Marshall* of little help.[113] Davies turned to *Gun v M'Carthy*,[114] which set out Lord Romilly's election in *Garrard v Frankel* and *Harris v Pepperell*, and on this basis argued that bilateral mistake might be a ground for rectification and unilateral mistake could be a ground for rescission. Davies also pointed out that in *Garrard v Frankel* and in *Harris v Pepperell* rectification had been allowed on a unilateral mistake, but only where the non-mistaken party was given the option of having the contract rescinded.[115] Pritt, for the defendants, accurately observed that the cases in which rescission had been granted on terms had all been subsequently said to have been supported only on the ground of fraud.[116] Davies stated that these cases could only be supported on the ground that the contract was reformed at the option of the party against whom the decision was taken, and that this was allowed because the other party had intended to do something else. This last suggestion disturbed Wright J because if this was correct and it were applied to commercial transactions then 'anybody

[108] ibid, 1499.
[109] ibid, 1454–55.
[110] ibid, 1455.
[111] ibid, App 23, 144.
[112] ibid, App 33, 1459.
[113] ibid, 1467.
[114] 13 Ir Ch D 304.
[115] Parliamentary Archives (n 93), App 33, 1468.
[116] ibid, 1469.

might come and say that he had made a mistake in his own mind and did not intend what the contract says'.[117] Wright J seemed to be of the view that the equitable jurisdiction for mistake extended as far as refusing specific performance in the conveyance of land but no further.[118] Davies, again without explanation of the equitable jurisdiction upon which the *Garrard v Frankel* cases were based, argued that they established that where the non-mistaken party sought to retain the contract it could be rescinded.[119] Davies summarised his argument that the mistake of Lever Brothers had begun as a unilateral one, as a mistake as to the subject matter of the contract, and this was a fundamental mistake. The findings of the jury indicated that the mistake was a mutual one and that therefore the termination agreements should be rescinded because they 'would never have been entered into had the true facts been known'.[120] It is difficult to gauge from the surviving record why Davies did not argue his case more strongly. What is clear from the surviving record is that the participants struggled at the trial to analyse mistake in English law.

When Wright J gave judgment in the case the following week some of these confusions had been clarified. It is possible that he had recourse to Anson's or Pollock's treatises: when the former had been briefly cited to him in argument, he found it helpful.[121] He held that the effect of mistake could be to remove the true consent of the parties. Where the written contract did not correctly express the actual contract, a court could rectify it. This mistake was in neither category but a mistake described:

> as being mistake of subject matter, or substance, or essence, or fundamental basis . . . what is meant is some mistake or misapprehension as to some facts (which . . . includes private rights, as held in *Cooper v Phibbs*) which, by the common intention of the parties, whether expressed or more generally implied, constitute the underlying assumption without which the parties would not have made the contract they did.[122]

While Wright J appeared to have been describing a mistake as to a quality of the subject matter, he then supported this with *res extincta* examples.[123] *Huddersfield Banking Co v Henry Lister & Son*[124] provided that in equity a common mistake would set aside a transaction. *Kennedy v Panama, New Zealand and Australian Royal Mail Co*[125] (*Kennedy*'s case) set out the applicable test: was the mistake as to

117 ibid, 1470.
118 ibid.
119 ibid.
120 ibid, 1503. Davies also advanced, briefly, the argument that there had been a complete failure of consideration since Lever Brothers were not bound to keep the pair in their employ.
121 ibid, 1461–62. It is curious that Davies did not attempt to build upon Anson, although it appears that he had not considered the work carefully and quoted from the seventh edition published in 1894. Wright J observed that he preferred a more up-to-date volume because he had been a freshman in 1894 and 'a lot has happened since then'.
122 [1931] 1 KB 557, 564.
123 Sale of Goods Act 1893, s 6, the principle of which, he asserted, had been applied in *Couturier v Hastie*, *Strickland v Turner* and *Scott v Coulson*.
124 [1895] 2 Ch. 273.
125 (1866–67) LR 2 QB 580.

the whole substance of the consideration, going to the root of the matter, or only to some point which did not affect the whole substance? While Wright J implied that the test was based upon the Roman distinction between an *error in corpore* and an *error in substantia*, he did not consider the Roman law. Following this somewhat confused discussion of mistake, Wright J purported to apply what he saw as the reasoning in *Kennedy's* case. The essence of the bargain between Lever Brothers and Bell was the existence of the service agreement as a binding obligation, and the bargain was intended to be a purchase by Lever Brothers for a consideration of the rights Bell was assumed to have against them, 'just like the purchase of a chattel or a chose in action'.[126] The complication in this case was that Lever Brothers had not terminated the service agreement but only had an election to terminate the agreement. Nevertheless, the jury had found that, had they been aware of the trades, they would have terminated the agreement. Thus, 'the mistake or misapprehension here is as to the substance of the whole consideration, and goes "to the root of the whole matter," in the words of . . . *Kennedy's* case'.[127] The same considerations applied to Bell's bargaining. While Bell's counsel raised *Smith v Hughes* as a barrier to relief, Wright J rejected this because the case 'seems to be a long way from the present case . . . [where] . . . there was a complete difference in substance in the nature of the actual thing or chose in action the subject of the service agreement, as compared with the common understanding of both parties as to what they were dealing about'.[128] Wright J's discussion indicates that he did not understand that neither case was decided on the basis of mistake. Indeed, he seems to have assumed that both were decided according to some doctrine of mistake at common law. While Wright J was of the view that the agreement was probably void for mistake, which would allow a common law claim for money had and received, a court of equity could do all that was required to constitute a *restitutio in integrum*. Wright J seems to have decided that the agreements must be rescinded in equity and that the court would do what was 'practically just'. The judgment left a great deal to be desired. Mistake was fashioned according to the theories of the treatise writers, supported by the same decisions but without a close examination of the bases of these cases. Little understanding of equitable mistake is provided, and while the basis of intervention was expressed as equitable, the reason given is a failure of consent. While Roman law considerations were borrowed, they were equated to a failure of consideration. The judgment was not only a departure from previous English law but one that did so in a questionable manner.

The Court of Appeal

Bell and Snelling brought an appeal from the decision. The panel which heard the appeal consisted of noted commercial judges more accustomed to the common

126 [1931] 1 KB 557, 567.
127 ibid, 568.
128 ibid, 570.

law than equity. The appellants now modelled their mistake argument on Anson's treatise.[129] The sixteenth edition stated that the law recognised mistake in three instances: mistake as to the subject matter's existence; an error as to the identity of the party; and error as to the identity of the subject matter. None of these applied here. While the service agreements were voidable they were not void, and it was not possible to determine that the respondents would have terminated them. The cases relied upon by Wright J were inapplicable as they dealt with instances where the subject matter had ceased to exist. *Kennedy*'s case supported the appellants not the respondents, because it was a case which dealt with an innocent misrepresentation. As long as the service agreements had not been terminated, any misapprehension as to their terminability did not go to the subject matter of the agreements but only some incidental matter.[130] From the authority cited, it may also have been argued that an executed contract could be set aside only where there was fraud.[131] Although not reported, the appellants appear to have argued that the respondents could not rely upon mutual mistake as it had not been pleaded.[132] Unilateral mistake could only vitiate a contact where there were elements such as fraud.[133] This, the appellants argued, was a completed contract and, in such circumstances, neither law nor equity would interfere to disturb a concluded bargain:

> If that type of error was enough to vitiate a contract, why were not the law books full of such cases; if the fact that people's minds, when making a perfectly specific agreement in clear terms, were in error was sufficient to upset the bargain, there must, day by day, be cases in which such contracts would be attacked.[134]

The appellants' argument skilfully avoided the equitable cases and the possibility that there was an *error in substantia.* It is no coincidence that Anson's treatise was cited, because it had restricted mistake to the point of non-existence. Curiously, the appellants relied upon a passage in the older sixteenth edition of 1923; the then current seventeenth edition,[135] under two new authors (Miles and Brierly), had changed the treatment of mistake. Gwyer had written of three limited forms of mutual mistake, none of which, as the appellants argued, affected the termination agreements. Miles and Brierly wrote broadly of two cases of operative mistake: those cases in which the parties contracted on the mistaken belief that some fact which lies at the root of the contract was true, and those cases where, although there was an outward appearance of agreement, the law treated the apparent

[129] Sir WR Anson, *Principles of the English Law of Contract*, 16th edn, ML Gwyer (ed) (Oxford, Clarendon Press, 1923) 163.

[130] The argument appears in the judgment of Lawrence J at 590.

[131] The authority was *Seddon v North Eastern Salt Co* [1905] 1 Ch 326, in which Joyce J had considered that *Brownlie v Campbell* and *Soper v Arnold* established that an executed contract could be set aside only where there was fraud, and that *Kennedy*'s case established that this was a rule of law as well as equity.

[132] This appears in the judgment of Scrutton LJ at 582.

[133] *The Times*, 22 October 1930, 5.

[134] ibid, reporting the argument of Miller for the appellants.

[135] Sir WR Anson, *Principles of the English Law of Contract*, 17th edn, JC Miles and JL Brierly (eds) (Oxford, Clarendon Press, 1929).

contract as void for a lack of consensus.[136] The respondents' case would have been stronger had the later edition of Anson's treatise been used. It is impossible to discern why it was not.

The respondents focused upon the appellants' wrongdoing and sought to establish that it was the duty of the appellants to abstain from personal cocoa speculation and that they owed a duty to disclose and account for any profit so obtained. Their failure to perform this duty was an important fact inducing the respondents to enter into the termination agreements. The difficulty as to whether this was a unilateral or a bilateral mistake returned to haunt the respondents here, and they made no clear decision as to which it was, arguing that whatever it was, the contract was void for mistake. If this was a case of a unilateral mistake, *Smith v Hughes* applied. If this was a mutual mistake, *Cooper v Phibbs* provided that where parties contracted under a mutual mistake as to their relative and respective rights, the result was that the contract was liable to be set aside as having proceeded upon a common mistake. This contract was not merely liable to be set aside, it was actually void.

This flimsy argument was enough to succeed, and the Court of Appeal unanimously dismissed the appeal. Scrutton LJ, the former pupil master of both Wright J and Lord Atkin, and a common law lawyer with a formidable commercial law expertise, analysed the problem in comparison to the newly emergent doctrine of frustration and provided a different explanation for the mistake cases. The law was that:

> where at the time of making the contract the circumstances are such that the continuance of a particular state of things is in the contemplation of both parties fundamental to the continued validity of the contract, and that state of things substantially ceases to exist without fault of either party, the contract becomes void from the time of such cessation, the loss falling where it lies.[137]

The contract was valid when made because the implied foundation existed; once this was destroyed, the contract was void. Where the implied foundation is assumed by both parties to exist when the contract is made, but does not exist, the result is that the contract is void because of an implied term that its validity shall depend upon the existence at the time of the contract and during its performance of a particular state of facts. This state of facts had to be essential to the existence of the contract, 'a fundamental reason for making it'.[138] Scrutton LJ viewed the basis of the decision in *Krell v Henry*[139] to be the same as *Cooper v Phibbs.* While Lord Westbury, in the latter case, had used language which indicated the contract was voidable, later authorities had shown that the contract was void. Scrutton LJ did not refer to what these later authorities were, probably because there were no such authorities, but contented himself with a reference to a case in which few

[136] ibid, 153.
[137] [1931] 1 KB 557, 584.
[138] ibid.
[139] [1903] 2 KB 740.

reasons for judgment had been given.[140] Scrutton LJ concluded by stating that he entirely agreed with the judgment of Wright J on this point and with the authorities he cited in support of it. He did, however, question whether or not *Kennedy*'s case, in so far as it decided that an innocent misrepresentation was not grounds for rescission, was still good law following the fusion of law and equity, and he expressed doubt as to whether an executed contract could not be rescinded for an innocent and material misrepresentation.[141] His analysis of an implied foundation to the contract, while appearing to solve the problem before him, avoided the essential problem of when something would form an implied foundation and when it would not.[142]

Lawrence LJ identified the issue as a non-existent subject matter. He agreed with Pollock's *Principles of Contract*[143] that in such cases the question was whether or not the existence of the thing contracted for or the state of things contemplated was or was not presupposed as essential to the agreement. He also agreed with the decision in *Cooper v Phibbs*, although he followed Pollock's view[144] that the lease was not voidable but void. *Cooper v Phibbs* applied here to render the termination agreements void for mistake. No other case was on all fours with the present one. Greer LJ observed that the real problem was a mutual mistake as to a quality of the subject matter. While this point had not previously been determined, he asserted that 'a mistake as to the fundamental character of the subject matter of the contract is one which, if mutual, the law will regard as rendering the contract void'.[145] He reached this conclusion by reference to Salmond and Winfield's *Principles of the Law of Contracts*,[146] which declared that the *res extincta* cases were illustrations of a general principle that where the parties to a contract had mistakenly assumed a certain fact as the basis of the contract, the law will read into the contract an implied condition that the fact exists. Greer LJ qualified this proposition with *Kennedy*'s case, which required that the mistake had to be such as to constitute a complete difference in substance between the thing as it was supposed to be and what it was such that there was a failure of consideration. Greer LJ agreed with Wright J that what Lever Brothers had paid for was the right to terminate the service agreements and this they could have done without compensation. The jury had found that they would have terminated the service agreements and, con-

[140] *Galloway v Galloway* (1914) 30 TLR 531.

[141] The point raised by *Seddon v North Eastern Salt Co* [1905] 1 Ch 326 and *Angel v Jay* [1911] 1 KB 666, the latter a case which arose again in *Solle v Butcher* [1950] 1 KB 671, [1949] 2 All ER 1107, 66 TLR (Pt 1) 448, [1949] EGD 346 (see text at n 204).

[142] Although the work does not appear to have been cited in the Court of Appeal, Scrutton LJ's reasoning as to an implied foundation is similar to the argument advanced by Salmond and Winfield that the general principle of essential error was 'that when the parties to a contract have assumed as its basis and presupposition the existence of a certain fact the law will in proper cases, by way of necessary implication, read into the contract an implied condition, imputed to the constructive intention of the parties, that such a fact exists': Sir J Salmond and PH Winfield, *Principles of the Law of Contracts* (London, Sweet & Maxwell, 1927) 195.

[143] Sir F Pollock, *Principles of Contract*, 9th edn (London, Stevens and Sons, 1931) 530.

[144] ibid, 532, 535.

[145] [1931] 1 KB 557, 595.

[146] Salmond and Winfield(n 142) 195.

sequently, there was such a difference in substance between what was supposed to be and what was as to constitute a failure of consideration. The termination agreements were void for mistake. Neither Lawrence LJ nor Greer LJ thought much of the pleadings point.

Three observations can be made about these judgments. The first is that while the judges accepted that a doctrine of mistake existed they differed as to the basis for this doctrine. Each judge was perplexed by the lack of authority on the particular issue presented. At common law the nearest equivalents were cases concerned with warranties and failure of consideration. Although they did not distinguish between legal and equitable treatments of mistake, equity presented few precedents for a mistake as to a quality.[147] A second observation is that each judge proceeded on the basis that the position at law was the same as it was in equity. This was a change from earlier post-fusion cases in which judges recognised that while law and equity might each find that a contract entered into under a misapprehension was not binding, they also recognised that different bases existed in each body of law to reach this result. In *Bell v Lever Brothers*, the Court of Appeal accepted that there was a doctrine of mistake in both law and equity and that the effect of an operative mistake was to render the contract void. The difficulties with the judgments are obvious. The judges are disagreed even as to how to characterise the mistake: is it a mistake as to the subject matter or merely a quality of the subject matter? The majority state it to be the former, and this characterisation may occur because the principal treatises, Anson and Pollock, did not consider a mistake as to a quality of the subject matter. Had Pollock's adoption of mistake included Savigny's theory of *error in substantia*, their Lordships might have found the decision easier to reach. While Salmond and Winfield had considered something they termed an *error in essentia*, something which related 'to some matter which is of the essence of a contract',[148] they provided little case law to support such a definition, and the cases they did provide were used by the other authors as instances where there was a failure as to the subject matter.[149] This points to the third observation. While the judges accepted that English law recognised a doctrine of mistake, they were concerned to establish this doctrine on the basis of precedents and not the theories advanced by jurists. It seems probable that each of the judges did utilise treatises in formulating his judgment,[150] and the fact that these treatises presented different approaches to the problem did not help to

[147] The issue arose infrequently in courts of equity because in the case of a sale of land, a mistake of quality was invariably compensated in damages. Courts were reluctant to intervene in settlements unless the mistake was fundamental.

[148] Salmond and Winfield (n 142) 192.

[149] *Strickland v Turner, Couturier v Hastie, Scott v Coulson* and *Galloway v Galloway* were used. Part of the reason for the sparseness of precedent was that there were few cases in English law that could support such a proposition; another part of the reason was that Salmond had died before the treatise was complete and had left few citations for his propositions: Salmond and Winfield (n 132) iv.

[150] Lawrence LJ and Greer LJ expressly referred to Pollock, and Salmond and Winfield respectively: [1931] 1 KB 557, 590, and ibid, 595. Scrutton LJ's judgment bears resemblance to Salmond and Winfield's discussion of an essential error amounting to a failure of condition: Salmond and Winfield (n 142) 192–95.

clarify what mistake was or why it vitiated a contract. The problem was compounded by the fact that any scrutiny of the cases indicated that they were not decided on grounds that supported the treatise writers' theories. It does not seem to have occurred to the judges that perhaps English law did not recognise the doctrine of mistake that the treatise writers asserted.

The House of Lords

The judicial confusion as to what effect mistake had upon contractual formation was shared by Lever Brothers' lawyers. Their solicitor, William Glasgow, had concerns as to the uncertainty around mistake. A week before the hearing in the House of Lords, he wrote to Lever Brothers' secretary, the barrister LV Fildes, and expressed concern about whether the mistake had to be bilateral or only unilateral.[151] He discussed two equitable cases, *Cooper v Phibbs* and *Cochrane v Willis*, without recognition that these *were* equitable cases. Glasgow observed that it was difficult to ascertain from these cases whether a common mistake or a unilateral mistake was sufficient to allow relief. He was sure that a distinction between the two forms of mistake existed and that it was to be found in *Cochrane v Willis*. He referred to the decisions of Knight Bruce LJ and Turner LJ in which they observed that the essence of the case was that where a party in ignorance of his rights gave up property for no consideration, the agreement was not effective at either common law or equity. Fildes replied that he had discussed the matter with Lever Brothers' counsel, Clement Davies, who found that 'the cases are by no means clear'.[152] Part of the lack of clarity arose from fact that the borderlines between mutual mistake, fraud and failure of consideration appeared unclear. Fildes was much impressed with Pollock's treatment of mistake (described as 'masterly') but did not seem to realise that Pollock was one of the figures who had employed cases concerned with matters such as fraud or a failure of consideration and used them to support his theory of mistake. Glasgow was less impressed with Pollock's efforts and was of the view that 'it does not seem possible to collect from the cases or any of them a clear principle to apply to our facts'.[153]

While it appeared from Glasgow's letter and the case for the respondents that Lever Brothers would argue that the termination agreements could be rescinded on the basis of *Cooper v Phibbs*, a different argument was advanced by Sir John Simon. It is not clear why this change occurred. The appellants raised substantially the same argument made before the Court of Appeal: first, there was no mutual mistake such as to avoid the termination agreements for there was no mutual mistake as to the existence or identity of the subject matter of these contracts; second, there was no duty to disclose the dealings; and third, mutual mistake had not been pleaded in a case fought upon fraud. While Simon's response still made no

[151] UARM, Acc 1996/48, box 35, file 2063B, letter from Glasgow to Fildes, 17 June 1931.
[152] ibid, letter from Fildes to Glasgow, 19 June 1931.
[153] ibid, letter from Glasgow to Fildes, 21 June 1931.

distinction between common law and equitable cases, he sought to reconcile the cases said to deal with mistake around a single principle which could be applied to the issue at hand. The difficulty, Simon argued, lay in distinguishing in a particular case between a mistake as to the subject matter and a mistake as to a quality of the subject matter. Simon's argument recognised that the cases said to be decided on mistake were at times resolved on other bases, and he attempted to classify these cases to ascertain from them the underlying principle upon which they had been resolved. He classified cases in which contracts had been avoided for mistake or 'analogous' grounds under four heads: mutual mistake; impossibility of performance; commercial frustration; and implied condition. The principle applicable to these cases was that the parties had contracted upon a 'contractual assumption' which was false and lay at the very root of the contract. If the assumption were not true, the contract was avoided. The contract was avoided *ab initio* if the assumption was of present fact, for this was a mistake not of quality but of essence. If the assumption were of a future fact then the contract ceased to bind when the assumption was shown to be untrue. A distinction was drawn between those cases in which the parties had reached a consensus and those in which they had not.[154] Simon's proposition applied only to cases where consensus had been reached. Lever Brothers had contracted to obtain the right to terminate the appellants' employment agreements. The erroneous assumption was that they did not have this right when they did. This mistake was essential to the contract, and the contract should thus be avoided. While Simon relied upon *Anson on Contracts* in his arguments, the origin of his argument likely lies in Salmond and Winfield. These authors wrote that an essential error, about either an express or an implied condition of the contract, was an operative mistake which invalidated the contract. An essential error was an error as to the essence of the contract—a matter which, if it were an obligation to be performed by one of the parties, would entitle the other party to rescind the contract should the obligation not be performed.[155]

Their Lordships considered these arguments for nearly six months before deciding, by a narrow majority, that the contracts were binding. The majority allowed the appeal for different reasons. Lord Blanesburgh decided that because Lever Brothers had not pleaded mutual mistake they could not rely upon this ground without an amendment to their pleadings, and this Lord Blanesburgh refused to allow.[156] He considered mistake only in so far as to state that he agreed with Lords Atkin and Thankerton on the point. Lord Thankerton held that for mistake to avoid a contract, it had to be a mutual one which went to the root of the contract because of *Kennedy*'s case. The mistake here was not sufficiently fundamental because the mistake went only to the possibility of terminating the agreements by other means. He found that there was no obligation upon the appellants

[154] Such as *Raffles v Wichelhaus* (1864) 2 H & C 906; 159 ER 375; 160 LJ Exch 160.

[155] Salmond and Winfield (n 142) 192–95.

[156] Lord Blanesburgh was indignant at Lever Brothers' behaviour in raising new allegations of fraud after having opened their case. He was deeply influenced by the Appellant's Case, a matter reflected in his judgment.

to disclose their breaches to the respondents. Accordingly, Lever Brothers were bound even though they would not have entered into the contracts had they known of the breaches of the employment agreements. In addition, for a mistake as to an 'underlying assumption' to avoid a contract it could 'only properly relate to something which both [parties] must necessarily have accepted in their minds as an essential and integral element of the subject-matter'.[157] While this was a probable assumption in the case before their Lordships, they were not necessarily forced to this assumption. On this basis, Lord Thankerton distinguished the decisions in *Cooper v Phibbs*, *Scott v Coulson*, *Couturier v Hastie* and *Strickland v Turner* because it was clear on the face of those contracts that 'the matter as to which the mistake existed was an essential and integral element of the subject-matter of the contract, or it was an inevitable inference from the nature of the contract that *all* the parties so regarded it' (emphasis added).[158] In a highly artificial manner, Lord Thankerton then held that nothing in the termination agreements or the circumstances attending them provided any indication that the appellants regarded the indefeasibility of the service agreements as an essential and integral element of the subject matter of the termination agreements.

The definitive judgment on mistake was given by Lord Atkin. This marks, in English law, the birth of a doctrine of contractual mistake based on a failure of consent. Lord Atkin made the theories of the treatise writers law, although not in a way which pleased the only living member of the original writers.[159] Lord Atkin sought to provide a coherent and unifying principle to the confused state of law in this area;[160] an effort similar to, although not nearly as successful as, the one he would undertake five months later in *Donoghue v Stevenson*.[161] For Lord Atkin the applicable rules of law appeared to be established with 'reasonable' clearness: 'if mistake operates at all it operates so as to negative or in some cases to nullify consent'.[162] English law recognised three classes of mistake: mistake as to the identity of the contracting parties; as to the existence of the subject matter of the contract; or as to a quality of the subject matter. Mistake could be of one party or of both, and the effect of the mistake depended upon the class of mistake. Where there was a mistake as to identity and A thought he was contracting with B (and would contract only with B) whereas he was in fact contracting with C, the mistaken belief of A negatived consent, and the contract was void. If the parties mistakenly contracted with regard to a subject matter which was, unbeknown to them, no longer in existence, consent was nullified and the contract was void.[163] In *Cooper*

[157] [1932] AC 161, 235.

[158] ibid, 236.

[159] Pollock thought little of the judgment, as discussed below.

[160] In doing this, he fulfilled the private sentiment of Lever Brothers' solicitor that 'the House of Lords now have the opportunity to make the law clear and this they presumably will do': letter from Glasgow to Fildes (n 153).

[161] [1932] AC 562.

[162] [1932] AC 161, 217.

[163] Lord Atkin was of the view that if the seller was aware that the subject matter had perished this would also prevent a contract arising.

v Phibbs the mistake as to title had the same effect as a mistake as to the existence of the subject matter. The parties intended to effect a transfer when this was impossible. Lord Atkin approved of the case with one criticism: that the lease must have been void rather than voidable. The most difficult problems, however, arose in relation to a mistake as to a quality of the subject matter. Two elements were necessary for such a mistake to be legally effective: first, the mistake had to be of both parties; and second, it had to be 'as to the existence of some quality which makes the thing without the quality essentially different from the thing as it was believed to be'.[164]

The applicable principles were found in two cases treated as authoritative expositions of the law, from which he quoted extensively: *Kennedy*'s case and *Smith v Hughes. Kennedy*'s case established that a mistake as to quality was of no effect unless there was a difference in subject matter such that there was a complete difference in substance between what it was supposed to be and what it was 'so as to constitute a failure of consideration'.[165] *Kennedy*'s case, according to Lord Atkin, was an instance where the misapprehension, although a material part of the motive inducing Kennedy to apply for shares, did not change the substance of the shares. *Smith v Hughes* was cited for the proposition that where a party contracted on the basis that the subject matter of the contract possessed a certain quality which it did not, the contract was good absent fraud or a warranty as to the quality. In addition, the non-mistaken party was under no legal obligation to inform the other of his mistake. Oddly, Lord Atkin did not offer many insights into either case.

Lord Atkin then proceeded to apply the principles. It would be wrong to decide that a contract to terminate a specified contract is void if it turns out that the specified contract has already been broken and could have been terminated otherwise:

> The contract released is the identical contract in both cases, and the party paying for release gets exactly what he bargains for. It seems immaterial that he could have got the same result in another way, or that if he had known the true facts he would not have entered into the bargain.[166]

Lord Atkin dismissed Simon's argument that there was no such thing as a mistake as to a quality of the subject matter, and his formulation that linked 'mistake' and 'frustration'. Lord Atkin rejected the formulation that whenever consensus was based on a contractual assumption which was not true the contract was avoided whether the assumption was as to a present or future fact. Such a formulation did little to assist the determination of what was a fundamental assumption. It is difficult to see, however, how Lord Atkin's own formulation of an operative mistake as to a quality of the subject matter assisted in the determination of when this

[164] [1932] AC 161, 218. Where the requirement of the particular quality formed a part of the contract, the inquiry was as to whether the quality was a condition or a warranty: this was a different branch of law altogether. Lord Atkin did not appear to realise that this, along with *caveat emptor*, had been the common law treatment of many earlier cases of factual misapprehensions.

[165] Per Blackburn J, reproduced at [1932] AC 161, 220.

[166] ibid, 223–24.

occurred, particularly after the denial that it existed in the case before him. It was possible, however, to link the 'mistake' and 'frustration' cases in those instances where an implication was necessary for giving business efficacy to the contract, and a condition could be implied where, both as to existing facts and future facts, a new state of facts 'makes the contract different in kind from the contract in the original state of facts'.[167] The critical question was: 'does the state of new facts destroy the identity of the subject-matter as it was in the original state of facts?'.[168] Here it did not.

Two factual points underlie Lord Atkin's decision. First, he did not view this case as one concerned with the appropriate standards of managerial conduct, and incorrectly viewed Lever Brothers' concern as financial.[169] Second, Lord Atkin was concerned with sanctity of contract: it was 'of paramount importance that contracts should be observed, and that if parties honestly comply with the essentials of the formation of contracts—ie, agree in the same terms on the same subject-matter—they are bound, and must rely on the stipulations of the contract for protection from the effect of facts unknown to them'.[170] Wright J, as Lord Wright, explained this in Lord Atkin's obituary as the reason for his decision.[171] When Lord Atkin gave his judgment the Great Depression had begun; many events had occurred which would have rendered many bargains undesirable.[172]

Lord Warrington, with whom Viscount Hailsham agreed, held that the agreements were liable to be set aside because of a mistake of fact common to both parties, which, by their common intention, constituted the underlying assumption without which the parties would not have made the contract. This principle existed both at common law (and was the basis of *Strickland v Turner*) and in equity (and was the basis of *Scott v Coulson*). *Kennedy*'s case limited this principle by confining it to circumstances where the mistake was as to the substance of the consideration, where it went to the root of the matter. A second limitation was that the mistake had to be mutual: *Smith v Hughes.* Lord Warrington concluded that the principle applied to the termination agreements. It was clear that each party believed that the service agreements were binding and could only be terminated upon compensation. The real question was whether or not this erroneous assumption was of such a fundamental character as to be an underlying assumption without which the parties would not have entered into their contract. Lord Warrington was of the view that it was; particularly because the jury had found that Lever Brothers would not have entered into the termination agreements had they been

[167] ibid, 227.

[168] ibid.

[169] MacMillan (n 91) 653–54.

[170] [1932] AC 161, 224.

[171] 'Lord Atkin of Aberdovey, 1867–1944', *Proceedings of the British Academy, vol 32* (1951) 322. Geoffrey Lewis, in his biography of Lord Atkin, used it to illustrate Lord Atkin's conviction that 'bargains made by traders must stand' and that it is not the job of judges to change these: G Lewis, *Lord Atkin* (London, Butterworths, 1983) 68.

[172] In September 1931 Britain left the gold standard, and sterling had depreciated by 30% by December: CP Kindleberger, *The World in Depression 1929–1932* (London, Penguin, 1987) 158–59.

aware of the conduct which had made the service agreements terminable. This was the root and basis of the termination agreements. A critical passage at the end of Lord Warrington's judgment indicates that their Lordships had not considered the position of mistake in equity:

> This case seems to me to raise a question as to the application of certain doctrines of common law, and I have therefore not thought it necessary to discuss or explain the special doctrines and practices of Courts of equity in reference to the rescission on the ground of mistake of contracts, conveyances and assignments of property and so forth, or to the refusal on the same ground to decree specific performance, though I think, in accordance with such doctrines and practice, the same result would follow.[173]

The statement is important, for Lord Warrington alone had come from the Chancery Bar and, indeed, had been counsel in *Scott v Coulson.* The House of Lords was attempting to create a doctrine at common law, and in this endeavour, the utility of the equitable cases was that these were the only cases which had been expressly decided on the basis of mistake. The reasons for these decisions was ignored by their Lordships.

It is difficult to establish what the House of Lords decided in *Bell v Lever Brothers.* While all the Law Lords recognised a doctrine of mistake at common law, it is equally clear that they effectively produced this doctrine for the first time. This was done with greater attention to the treatise writers than it was to earlier cases, which were largely misinterpreted. Curiously, their Lordships generally ignored direct reference to the treatises and attempted to construct their judgments from the cases. The result was the birth of a doctrine formed from cases which did not sustain it. Both Lord Thankerton and Lord Warrington were clearly influenced by the treatises and their differences were on the application of the propounded doctrine to the case before them.[174]

Lord Atkin's judgment created the modern doctrine of contractual mistake, a creation delivered from the treatises rather than the earlier cases. An analysis of the judgment reveals the pervasive influence of Pollock's and Anson's treatises[175] upon this new doctrine. The first influence is that, although Lord Atkin probably thought he was giving a judgment at common law, he clearly saw no distinction between the treatment of mistake at common law and in equity. While equity practitioners had realised in the past that a contract might be unenforceable for mistake both at common law and in equity, they also generally recognised until into the twentieth century that different bases created this result in each body of law. Lord Atkin, from his treatment of *Cooper v Phibbs*, clearly saw no difference between the operation of the two bodies of law. Pollock had begun his chapter on

173 [1932] AC 161, 210.

174 Lord Warrington held that the jury's findings that Lever Brothers would not have entered the termination agreements had they known of the trades meant that the mistake was sufficient to avoid the agreements; for Lord Thankerton it was not. While Lord Warrington thought the mistaken belief about terminability relevant to the appellants' decisions to enter the termination agreements, Lord Thankerton did not.

175 Lord Atkin's rejection of Sir John Simon's argument and the decision of Scrutton LJ in the Court of Appeal is also a rejection of the theory of mistake put forward by Salmond and Winfield.

mistake by stating that 'it is now seldom, if ever, necessary or useful to consider the former differences between the doctrines of the common law and those of equity'.[176] The second influence is that this doctrine is expressed in different terms than had been recognised by courts of equity. Legal consequences attach to mistake because mistake disrupts the consensus necessary to form a contract. In Lord Atkin's words, 'if mistake operates at all it operates so as to negative or in some cases to nullify consent'.[177] The dependence upon Pollock is particularly striking. Although Pollock had, by the time of the then contemporary edition of his work, abandoned an overall dependence upon consensus as the basis for contract, he still retained it in his mistake chapter.[178] Lord Atkin followed Pollock's lead that not every mistake would be effective[179] and adopted Pollock's term of 'nullity'.[180] Having established the legal basis as a failure of consent, Lord Atkin then proceeded to explain mistake as occurring within different classes. While this was a method common amongst civilian and Roman jurists, it was a late entrant to the common law. This is a further influence, for Lord Atkin borrowed his classes from Pollock. Pollock had written of three kinds of fundamental error which excluded true consent[181] and modified this somewhat by replacing one of these kinds with a mistake as to a quality of the subject matter, something Pollock had regarded as a sub-category of an error as to subject matter.[182] Lord Atkin agreed with both Pollock and Anson that for a mistake to affect consent, it had to be as to a fundamental assumption or a fact which went to the root of the contract.[183] Lord Atkin relied greatly upon two cases, *Kennedy*'s case and *Smith v Hughes*, in association with this concept. Again, these were cases used by Pollock to convey this requirement of a fundamental error.[184] That Lord Atkin relied upon Pollock's interpretation of these cases is apparent in his statement that these cases were really decided on bases other than mistake.[185] The final, and most significant of the influences Lord Atkin derived from the treatise writers was that where mistake was effective, it rendered the apparent contract void *ab initio*.[186] Because Lord Atkin had not distinguished between mistake at common law and mistake in equity, and the

[176] Pollock (n 143) 478.

[177] [1932] AC 161, 217.

[178] Pollock (n 143) 476. Anson's treatise also explained mistake as a failure of consensus: Anson (n 135) 169.

[179] Pollock (n 143) 478.

[180] ibid, 499. Lord Atkin apparently devised the concept of consent being 'negatived', although it is impossible to ascertain what, if any, difference arose between 'nullified' and 'negatived'.

[181] Pollock (n 143) 500. Pollock's kinds of fundamental errors were: (a) as to the nature of the transaction; (b) as to the person of the other party; and (c) as to the subject matter of the agreement.

[182] ibid, 515. Also, like Pollock, Lord Atkin observed the similarities between a mistake as to quality and that which would be a condition or a warranty within the contract: ibid, 516. The authors of Anson had also classified forms of 'operative mistake' which were most frequently encountered as: mistake as to identity of the person; mistake as to the identity of the subject matter; and a mistake by one party as to the intention of the other, known to that first party: Anson (n 135) 156.

[183] [1932] AC 161, 218. Anson (n 135) 153; and Pollock (n 143) 498–99.

[184] Pollock (n 143) 499, 515–17.

[185] [1932] AC 161, 222.

[186] ibid, 217–18.

different bases for these mistakes, both were considered void (not voidable). This was a radical, and apparently unseen, departure from the pre-existing equitable case law. It was to prove problematic.

While Lord Atkin served as midwife at the birth of this new doctrine of mistake, the doctrine was stillborn. The principles enunciated, and their particular application, were a matter of dissatisfaction to contemporary lawyers.[187] Lord Atkin's decision did not lessen 'the difficulty of drawing a distinct line between fundamental and non-fundamental mistake'.[188] Gutteridge observed that the case marked the apex of the development of the law of mistake upon contractual formation.[189] The case could not be regarded as satisfactory, because it was difficult to reconcile with the earlier cases and also because the authority of the case rested in large part upon the pleadings points.[190] It was also clear that the commercial world, as seen in the findings of a City of London jury, took a very different view of the conduct of Bell and Snelling.[191] Commentators expressed concern that the case had been brought upon the wrong grounds with the result that the statements of law with regard to contractual mistake were *obiter dictum.*[192] Other commentators agreed with the principles established but disagreed with their application to the particular facts.[193] Pollock, in his last edition, noted that Lever Brothers 'surely did not get anything like what it bargained for', and that the release of an imaginary claim for compensation was of no value in law.[194] He also stated that Lord Atkin's criterion could not be applied 'without the aid of fine-drawn distinctions of a kind not desirable in matters of business'.[195] Publicly, Pollock agreed with Lord Warrington and hoped that future lawyers would recognise that the case did not settle any general principle and would confine the case to its peculiar facts.[196] Privately, he observed to Oliver Wendell Holmes that the case was 'wrong in law' and 'mischievous in fact', as it encouraged 'shifty people' to forget things that it was their business to remember.[197] The next edition of *Chitty on Contracts* largely ignored the decision[198] but in subsequent editions *Chitty* included a chapter on

[187] R Champness, *Mistake in the Law of Contract* (London, Stevens and Sons Limited, 1933); Champness described the decision as 'not entirely satisfactory' and one which had 'given rise to considerable discussion' on reconsidering aspects of the law relating to mistake as a vitiating element upon contractual formation: vii. Champness wrote his book in an attempt to rectify this situation and, in particular, to arrive at some guiding principle consistent with the decided cases on the subject. Sadly, this object was not achieved.

[188] HAE, 'Contract—Mistake in Formation' (1932) 4 CLJ 370, 371.

[189] HCG, 'Notes *Bell* v *Lever Brothers, Ltd*' (1932) 48 LQR 148.

[190] ibid.

[191] ibid.

[192] PA Landon, '*Bell v Lever*' (1935) 51 LQR 650, 652.

[193] PH Winfield, 'Review of *Principles of Contract*' (1936) 52 LQR 429, 430. CJ Hamson, '*Bell v Lever Bros*' (1937) 53 LQR 118 described the case as 'disliked': 123.

[194] Sir F Pollock, *Principles of Contract*, 10th edn (London, Stevens and Sons, 1936) 498.

[195] ibid.

[196] ibid.

[197] Letter to Holmes, 23 March 1932, *The Pollock–Holmes Letters*, vol 2, Mark DeWolfe Howe (ed) (Cambridge, Cambridge University Press, 1942) 306.

[198] *Chitty's Treatise on the Law of Contracts*, 19th edn, H Potter (gen ed) (London, Sweet & Maxwell Limited, 1937).

mistake which stated that 'it is extremely doubtful whether the case decided any principle or indeed whether on its facts the decision can be regarded as in any sense satisfactory'.[199]

Wright J, elevated shortly after the decision to the House of Lords, regarded Lord Atkin's enunciation of principle as correct but the application of it to the particular facts as incorrect. In giving the Privy Council's opinion in *Norwich Union Fire Insurance Society v WH Price*[200] he was at pains to observe that the effect of the decision in *Cooper v Phibbs* that a contract entered into by parties under a mutual mistake as to their respective rights was liable to be set aside, had not been overruled or contradicted by their Lordships in *Bell v Lever Brothers.*[201] While it was essential that the mistake be an objective one which was fundamental to the transaction itself, whether or not a particular mistake could be so described was often 'a matter of great difficulty'.[202] Writing extrajudicially, he explained the difference in *Bell v Lever Brothers* between the lower courts' decisions and the majority decison of the House of Lords as attributable to the resolution of the 'real problem' of 'whether the mistake was sufficiently basic'.[203]

The Importance of *Solle v Butcher*

Given the difficulties which clearly attended mistake cases it is unsurprising that mistake did not arise in a major case until *Solle v Butcher*[204] in 1949. The case is a fragment from a larger history.[205] The problem was whether or not the Rent Restriction Acts applied to Flat 1, Maywood House. The effect of the Rent and Mortgage Interest Restrictions Act 1939 was to fix the annual rent chargeable to £140. Maywood House was badly damaged during the Blitz and rendered uninhabitable. After the war, Butcher, a builder, acquired a long lease of the property and repaired the flats to let. London had suffered an acute housing shortage due to the depredations caused by the Luftwaffe's aerial bombardments. Solle, Butcher's partner in an estate agency, assumed a managerial role in rebuilding Maywood House and was in charge of letting the flats. One of the partners' concerns was

[199] *Chitty's Treatise on the Law of Contracts*, 20th edn, H Potter (gen ed) (London, Sweet & Maxwell Limited, 1947) 242. The chapter author was Sir Charles Odgers. Scepticism was also presented by JC Miles and JC Brierly in Anson's *Principles of the English Law of Contract*, 18th edn (Oxford, Clarendon Press, 1937) 146–49, in which the decision was said to restrict English mistake only to cases involving a non-existent subject matter.

[200] [1934] AC 455.

[201] ibid, 463. The case itself was concerned with a mistaken payment.

[202] ibid.

[203] Lord Wright of Durley, 'Williston on Contracts' in *Legal Essays and Addresses* (Cambridge, Cambridge University Press, 1939) 214.

[204] [1950] 1 KB 671, [1949] 2 All ER 1107, 66 TLR (Pt 1) 448, [1949] EGD 346. All further references to the case are to [1950] 1 KB 671. Interesting comparisons to this case can be made to the decision in *Nicholson & Venn v Smith Marriott* (1947) 177 LT 189, in which Hallett J applied Lord Atkin's test yet seemed to have believed that the effect of mistake was to render the contract voidable.

[205] The larger historical picture is explained in C MacMillan, '*Solle v Butcher* (1949)' in C Mitchell and P Mitchell (eds), *Landmark Cases in the Law of Restitution* (Oxford, Hart Publishing, 2006).

whether or not the refurbished flats were so substantially altered as to be new entities and thus outside the Rent Acts. This, in 1947, was not an easy question to answer. Solle showed Butcher counsel's opinion that the flats were outside the Rent Acts because there had been a 'substantial structural alteration' to the flats such that they had become new dwelling-houses.[206] It was on this basis that the five flats were let. Solle rented Flat 1 at the market rate of £250 per annum. Butcher did not serve upon Solle a notice of increase of rent in the prescribed form[207] because both thought the flat was outside the Rent Acts. Had he done so he would have been able to recover almost all of the agreed £250. By entering into the lease without the prescribed notice, Butcher was barred from recovering any of the increases that would have been permitted for the entire currency of the lease. Butcher was also barred from evicting Solle from the flat for the seven years of the lease. A small procedural defect, based upon a shared mistake, had enormous consequences. A year later Solle and Butcher had a falling out and Solle, fortuitously, discovered a rent receipt which showed the previous tenant's rent to have been £140 per annum. Solle sued Butcher in the county court and alleged this to be the standard rent and sought to recover the overpaid rent. Butcher's defence was that he had rented the flat on Solle's assurance that it was outside the Rent Acts and not subject to rent restrictions. Alternatively, Solle was estopped by his conduct from asserting that the rent restrictions relieved him of his obligation to pay the agreed rent. Butcher also brought a counter-claim to rescind the lease on the ground that it had been entered into under a mutual mistake of fact. Sir Gerald Hurst, in the county court, was sympathetic to Butcher's situation but found that the flat had not undergone a change of identity and was thus subject to rent restrictions. Butcher brought an appeal from this decision.

The Court of Appeal had little sympathy for Solle, a surveyor and an estate agent; he caused the mistake which gave rise to the difficulties. Aware of the 1939 rent, he agreed to pay the higher market rent and did not then mind if this was the controlled rent or not, and he intended to pay it for seven years. It was only after his falling out with Butcher that he attempted to seek Rent Act protection. Jenkins LJ found for Solle but described his case as 'being as completely devoid of merit as any case could well be'.[208] Solle admitted that he was 'taking advantage of our mistake to get the flat at £140. for seven years'.[209] Such a situation was, it will be recalled, precisely the sort of situation in which courts of equity had intervened to prevent one party from obtaining an unconscionable advantage at the expense of the other party by reason of a mistake. This jurisdiction was, however, largely

[206] RE Megarry, *The Rent Acts*, 6th edn (London, Stevens and Sons, 1951) explains the judicial development of the doctrine of change of identity whereby a dwelling place subjected to substantial structural alterations could become a new dwelling-house in fact, such that the new premises shed all the attributes of the old. Such a change had to be of a radical nature and beyond 'mere improvements or structural alterations': 61–62. The determination of such a change of identity was one of fact, and one attended by uncertainty.

[207] Increase of Rent and Mortgage Interest (Restrictions) Act 1938 (1 & 2 Geo VI c 26), s 7(4).

[208] [1950] 1 KB 671, 699.

[209] ibid, 683 per Bucknill LJ. See also the comments of Denning LJ at 694.

forgotten and the case arose in the county court as a Rent Acts case, not as a case for equitable relief before the Chancery Division.

While the case was not framed on the basis of the older equitable jurisdiction,[210] it was clearly unfair in the circumstances that Solle should be able to benefit from the mistake.[211] To allow Solle to benefit from the mistake would not only allow him to unjustly enrich himself at Butcher's expense, but it would also mean that the other four tenants in Maywood House would also have grounds to lower their rents. Butcher, having expended considerable sums in the improvement of the property, and providing vital post-war housing, would now find himself considerably out of pocket. The difficulty facing the court was how to prevent this injustice. Butcher's counsel suggested four possible options: first, to find that the county court judge had erred in finding that the flat had not undergone a change of identity; second, that Solle was estopped from relying on his legal rights under the Rent Acts; third, that the contract should be rescinded since Butcher was induced to contract with Solle because of the latter's innocent misrepresentation; and fourth, that the contract should be rescinded because of a common mistake of the parties.

The court quickly dismissed the argument that the county court judge had erred in finding that the flat had not undergone a change of identity. This was a finding of fact and not of law. To find that these alterations created a change of identity would have been to set a precedent that, in post-war London, would have removed vast swathes of housing stock from the very protection Parliament intended to confer. Estoppel presented legal problems. To find that Solle was estopped from relying upon his legal rights would create a rule of general application to other cases and it would facilitate the removal of housing from the Rent Acts. The recent case of *Welch v Nagy*[212] had decided that the jurisdiction of the Rent Acts could not be ousted by an estoppel. The Lord Justices applied this case and the Rent Acts[213] to reject the estoppel argument. Rescission on the basis of misrepresentation presented challenges. Bucknill LJ rejected the claim on the basis that the county court judge had not found that there was such a misrepresentation as would allow rescission. His decision avoided a problem dealt with specifically by Jenkins LJ and Denning LJ as to whether or not, as a matter of law, an executed lease could be set aside for an innocent misrepresentation. The problem was the decision in *Angel v Jay*,[214] which held that an executed lease could not be rescinded for misrepresentation unless the misrepresentation was fraudulent. This decision was based upon Joyce J's decision in *Seddon v North Eastern Salt Co*,[215] although

[210] Although Butcher's counsel advanced, in the alternative, that the lease was voidable on the basis of Lord Westbury's decision in *Cooper v Phibbs*, it does not appear from the reports that the argument was any more developed than that.

[211] [1950] 1 KB 671, 690 per Denning LJ.

[212] [1950] 1 KB 455.

[213] Section 1 of the 1920 Act expressly provided that parties to a lease could not exclude the provisions of the Act by their own contractual terms: Increase of Rent and Mortgage Interest (Restrictions) Act 1920. If an express promise by a tenant to preclude the operation of the Acts was prohibited, then so, too, should be a promise made by the tenant's words or conduct.

[214] [1911] 1 KB 666.

[215] [1905] 1 Ch 326.

the case probably did not represent the law.[216] Joyce J had relied upon *Brownlie v Campbell* (which had also limited the authority of *Garrard v Frankel*), in which the House of Lords held that an executed contract for the conveyance of land would not be set aside unless there had been a fraudulent misrepresentation, and a similar statement in *Wilde v Gibson.*[217] Both cases concerned the sale of land and conveyancing practices, which meant that they were of dubious value outside this area of law. Conveyancing practice was that misrepresentations as to a quality of the land were dealt with by the terms of the conveyance. Where there were misrepresentations as to the title, other factors were significant. It was expected that the purchaser would investigate the title fully before purchase and, if he wished, might seek the additional security of a covenant from his vendor as to the nature of the title.[218] These practices occurred in a system of unregistered titles in which it was highly undesirable that a conveyance would be upset on anything other than fraud.[219] *Angel v Jay* had applied these cases beyond their original ambit. Jenkins LJ, although noting recent doubts about *Angel v Jay*, was not prepared to depart from it.[220] Denning LJ doubted the supposed rule that rescission was available for an executed agreement only where there had been fraud.[221]

The Lords Justice were divided on the issue of whether or not rescission could be granted for a common mistake. Jenkins LJ held that it could not because the trial judge had not found that there was a mistake of fact, although possibly one of law. It was impossible to find a mutual mistake of fact: Butcher intended to grant and Solle took a lease on the terms intended. They knew all the material facts; their misapprehension was the effect of the Act upon these facts. There was no question of a mistake as to a private right, as had arisen in *Cooper v Phibbs.* Furthermore, to allow rescission would be to frustrate the whole purpose of the Rent Acts. Parties were prohibited from contracting outside the Acts, and the Act operated irrespective of the intention of the parties. It was dangerous to allow a right of rescission in this case for it would mean that other tenants might be turned out if such a mistake were discovered. Jenkins LJ's judgment is curious on two fronts. The first is the relationship with the Rent Acts: early courts of equity had not debarred relief from mistake simply on the grounds that a statute was present. The second is Jenkins LJ's concern that a curious result would arise where a contract would be rescinded even if the tenant did not claim the benefit of the Rent Acts overlooks the discretionary nature of the equitable relief. What this indicates is how strange

216 HA Hammelmann, '*Seddon v North Eastern Salt Co*' (1939) 55 LQR 90, 100.

217 (1848) 1 HLC 605; 9 ER 897.

218 *Clare v Lamb* (1875) LR 10 CP 334, 339, per Grove J.

219 Hammelmann (n 216) 96–97. See, also, *Dart's Treatise on Vendors and Purchasers, vol II*, 8th edn, EP Hewitt and MRC Overton (eds) (London, Stevens and Sons, 1929) 600–01. *Dart's Treatise* stated that there could be a rescission of an executed contract where there was a mutual mistake: ibid.

220 [1950] 1 KB 671, 703.

221 He thought *Angel v Jay* wrongly decided, if it did hold that an executed lease could not be set aside except for fraud. *Seddon v North Eastern Salt Co* had lost all authority since Scrutton LJ threw doubt upon the decision in *Bell v Lever Brothers*, and *Wilde v Gibson* should be confined to conveyancing cases. The Privy Council had set aside an executed lease in *Mackenzie v Royal Bank of Canada* [1934] AC 468, 475, per Lord Atkin.

arguments sounded to judges who had become barristers half a century after the treatise writers had written of their version of mistake, even to a judge who had come from a Chancery practice.

Denning LJ and Bucknill LJ both held, although for different reasons, that the lease could be rescinded in equity for mistake. Denning LJ's decision went well beyond the authorities argued by Butcher's counsel and was premised upon statements of law that sounded strange to his contemporaries. For Denning LJ there were two kinds of mistake: first, mistake as dealt with by courts of common law, which rendered the contract void, a nullity from the very beginning; and second, the kind of mistake dealt with by courts of equity, where the effect of the mistake was to render to contract not void but voidable, liable to be set aside on such terms as the court thought just. Much of the difficulty surrounding mistake arose because before fusion courts of common law extended mistake beyond its proper limits to include circumstances where the contract was really voidable and not void. *Cundy v Lindsay* was such a case. Since the fusion of law and equity there was no need to continue this practice and it was now the case that a contract was void for mistake only where the mistake prevented the formation of the contract. This general statement of law is partly correct when viewed in light of the history of mistake. Denning LJ's statements about the practices of courts of common law in according legal effects to mistakes are not accurate. While courts of common law had found that there was no contract in cases involving misapprehensions, this had been done on grounds other than mistake before the treatise writers. While not relying upon the treatises himself nor explaining their limitations, Denning LJ adopted their rationalisations for these cases. His use of *Cundy v Lindsay* as a case where the mistake was extended to render the contract void rather than voidable was, again, partly correct, for Blackburn J had found at first instance that the contract was voidable—but for fraud.[222] His statement that *Cundy v Lindsay* was a dubious precedent after fusion because there was no reason to continue this process of extension indicates the underlying purpose of his judgment: it was an attempt to provide clarity to the law of mistake in way that both recognised the doctrine as an operative doctrine and simultaneously prevented injustice rather than creating it. Equitable relief, granted on a discretionary basis, was key to this approach. An underlying difficulty with Denning LJ's approach was that his explanation of mistake was not only partial but also only partly correct.

Denning LJ began by considering mistakes at common law which rendered the contract a nullity. He recognised that 'all previous decisions . . . must now be read in light of *Bell v Lever Bros Ltd*',[223] which stood for the principle that once an objective agreement had been reached with sufficient certainty of terms and on the same subject matter there was a contract. It was irrelevant if one party was under a mistake which 'was to his mind fundamental',[224] and that the other party knew

[222] *Lindsay v Cundy* (1875–76) LR 1 QBD 348, 357.
[223] [1950] 1 KB 671, 691.
[224] ibid.

of this mistake or even if this mistake was shared. This explanation was overly broad because it failed to consider the effect of *Smith v Hughes.* Denning LJ characterised cases in which goods have perished as cases of an implied condition precedent.[225] He denied Pothier's influence upon mistake in English law on the weak basis of *King's Norton Metal v Edridge.*[226] When he applied the restrictive criteria he had set out to the case before him he found that there was a contract: 'the parties agreed in the same terms on the same subject-matter'.[227] The mistake about the application of the Rent Acts was not a ground for declaring the lease void *ab initio.* To find that such a lease was a nullity from the outset would be to remove the incentive for tenants to seek a reduction in their rents.

Denning LJ then considered mistakes which rendered a contract voidable, 'liable to be set aside on some equitable ground'.[228] In these cases a court of equity proceeded on the basis that the contract was not void at law but that equity would relieve a party from the consequences of his own mistake provided that this could be done without injustice to third parties. Denning LJ, accurately, stated that this intervention occurred where it was unconscientious for a party to avail himself of the legal advantage obtained.[229] He gave three examples: where the mistake was induced by a material misrepresentation;[230] where one party allowed another party mistaken as to the terms of the contract or as to the first party's identity to contract with him and did not correct the mistake;[231] and where the parties contracted under a common misapprehension either as to facts or as to their relative and respective rights, provided that the misapprehension was fundamental and the party seeking to set it aside was not himself at fault. This third category was well established, beginning with *Lansdown v Lansdown,* extending through *Bingham v Bingham* to *Cooper v Phibbs.* The principle in *Cooper v Phibbs* had been 'repeatedly acted on'[232] and was in no way impaired by *Bell v Lever Brothers,* where the House of Lords had treated *Cooper v Phibbs* 'as a case at law'.[233] In any event, the principle had been fully restored by the Privy Council in *Norwich Union v Price.*[234] In the present case, Solle was a surveyor employed by Butcher to arrange finance, to negotiate with the rating authorities, and as a letting agent. Solle had formed the

225 This was a sustainable interpretation of *Couturier v Hastie*; however, the point disingenuously ignores Lord Atkin's rejection of such a principle in *Bell v Lever Brothers.* The approach of the common law to impossibility cases resolved on the basis of implied conditions in relation to subsequent impossibilities, begun in *Taylor v Caldwell* (1863) 3 B & S 826, 122 ER 309; SC 32 LJQB 164; 8 LT 356; 11 WR 726, was about to be rejected by Lord Radcliffe in *Davis v Fareham Urban DC* [1956] AC 696.

226 (1897) 14 TLR 98.

227 [1950] 1 KB 671, 692.

228 ibid.

229 ibid. Denning LJ based this on *Torrance v Bolton* (1872) LR 8 Ch 118.

230 Denning LJ opined that this would have been how *Smith v Hughes* would have been decided in the twentieth century: [1950] 1 KB 671, 693.

231 Denning LJ opined that this would have been how *Cundy v Lindsay* would have been decided in the twentieth century: ibid.

232 [1950] 1 KB 671, 694. Denning LJ referred to two nineteenth-century cases: *Earl Beauchamp v Winn* (1873) LR 6 HL 223, 234 and *Huddersfield Banking Co Ltd v Lister* [1895] 2 Ch 273.

233 ibid.

234 [1934] AC 455.

view that the building was not rent controlled, and he had told Butcher of his view. Butcher relied upon him and let the five flats on that basis on long leases. Solle now sought, by his own admission, to take advantage of the mistake. In this instance, the established rules would allow equity to intervene. That the lease had been executed was not a bar to rescission, as could be seen in *Cooper v Phibbs* itself. As observed above, Denning LJ doubted the authority of *Seddon v North Eastern Salt Co* and *Angel v Jay*. The real question was whether or not the parties could be restored to substantially the same position as the one they were in before the contract was made.[235] This was what had been done in *Cooper v Phibbs* by imposing terms 'so as to do what was practically just'.[236] This situation was similar to that faced by Romilly MR in *Garrard v Frankel*, a decision both followed and explained by Bacon V-C in *Paget v Marshall* as an instance where the court put the parties into the same position they would have been in if the mistake had not been made. Applying this to the case before him, Denning LJ thought that the court should rescind the lease on terms which enabled Solle to either stay at the agreed rent or to leave.[237] On this basis, Denning LJ allowed the appeal. Bucknill LJ agreed that the appeal should be allowed on the terms proposed by Denning LJ on the simple basis that the case was within Lord Westbury's principle in *Cooper v Phibbs*.

Solle v Butcher was to become a controversial decision. Lawson both recognised the equitable basis for Denning LJ's decision and approved the result.[238] Although Lawson recognised the unsatisfactory nature of the proposition asserted (because it did not receive the agreement of Jenkins and Bucknill LJJ) he welcomed it as the starting point in a new development which would reduce the severity of the common law finding that the contract was void.[239] Other contemporaries viewed the equitable bases of the case as being largely without precedent and, accordingly, a case in which law was extended or created rather than applied. Goodhart wrote of it that 'this extension of equitable powers is rather a startling one, for none of the books seems to have recognised it'.[240] The decision prompted Grunfeld to write a lengthy article in which he examined the case and considered the merits of applying a doctrine of mistake in equity.[241] While he favoured the substitution of mistake in equity for mistake at common law, he was critical of what he saw as the vague nature of Denning LJ's 'restatement' of the law of mistake and noted that

235 A proposition premised upon Lord Blackburn's statement in *Erlanger v New Sombrero Phosphate Co* (1878) 3 App Cas 1218, 1278–79.

236 [1950] 1 KB 671, 696.

237 The Rent Acts complicated the terms which could be imposed but Denning LJ suggested that the lease would be set aside if the defendant gave an undertaking that he would permit the plaintiff to remain as a licensee pending the grant of a new lease. During this licence period the appropriate notices could be served to allow a permitted increase in the rent to the originally agreed rent.

238 FH Lawson, *The Rational Strength of English Law* (London, Stevens & Sons, Limited, 1951) 65–67.

239 ibid.

240 ALG, 'Rescission of Lease on the Ground of Mistake' (1950) 66 CLJ 169, 171. He was similarly critical of the case as not having been subsequently applied in his review of Denning's *The Changing Law*: AL Goodhart, 'Review Alfred Denning *The Changing Law*' (1954) 17 MLR 86, 87.

241 C Grunfeld, 'A Study in the Relationship between Common Law and Equity in Contractual Mistake' (1952) 15 MLR 297, 304, fn 48.

there seemed to be little basis for equity's concern about conscientiousness. Both commentators faced the same shortcoming of, apparently, referring primarily to the contract treatises rather than the older treatises on equity and the cases themselves. The result was that Denning LJ was credited with rather more innovation than he had undertaken. Grunfeld was, however, correct in his characterisation that Denning LJ was attempting to set the law of contractual mistake on a clearer footing following the decision in *Bell v Lever Brothers.* Writing extrajudicially three years later, Denning LJ wrote that *Solle v Butcher* had caused 'the most remarkable change . . . in the doctrine of mistake'.[242] The change was that an 'infusion of equity' allowed courts to adopt a middle course between either declaring the contract formed under a mistake a nullity, void from the beginning, or allowing it to stand. The middle course was to set the contract aside on terms which 'were fair to both parties'[243] and which could also act to protect the rights of any innocent third parties.

It is clear that Denning LJ was attempting to restate the law of mistake which, following *Bell v Lever Brothers*, effectively precluded any recognition of a mistake as to quality. It is also clear that, unlike his immediate predecessors, he did so without recourse to a contract treatise. Why did he attempt this? At the time his decision was given the House of Lords could not overturn its own decisions.[244] It was equally clear that the area was a conceptual minefield and the cases were difficult to reconcile. The result of finding a case void was so harsh as to dissuade most courts from this action. Denning LJ's attempt to explain mistake suffers from a number of shortcomings; there is, for example, no reason given as to why mistake vitiates a contract. Nevertheless, he did outline a way around the difficulty posed by *Bell v Lever Brothers*, fixing a practical problem by invoking equity, a method he had successfully employed in *High Trees House*[245] and was to employ less successfully in *National Provincial Bank v Ainsworth.*[246] Denning LJ's judgments have to be approached critically because it is acknowledged that while he sought to do justice, this sometimes occurred at the expense of precedent.[247] In *Solle v Butcher*, this gives rise to two important questions: first, did the equitable jurisdiction that Denning LJ claimed to exist actually exist; and, second, if this jurisdiction did exist, had it been overruled by the decision in *Bell v Lever Brothers*? Although neither point was convincingly addressed by Denning LJ in his decision, good reasons exist to answer the first in the affirmative and the second in the negative.

The question of the effect of *Bell v Lever Brothers* upon *Cooper v Phibbs* has been discussed above. It was also the case that earlier courts of equity had intervened to

242 A Denning, *The Changing Law* (London, Stevens and Sons, 1953) 60.

243 ibid, 61.

244 *Practice Statement* [1966] 3 All ER 77.

245 *Central London Property Trust v High Trees House Ltd* [1947] KB 130.

246 *National Provincial Bank v Hastings Car Mart* [1964] Ch 665; reversed *National Provincial Bank Ltd v Ainsworth* [1965] AC 1175.

247 R Goff, 'Denning, Alfred Thompson [Tom]', in *Oxford Dictionary of National Biography* (Oxford, Oxford University Press 2004-).

set aside agreements which were unconscientious, were akin to fraud or failed to implement the intentions of the parties. The injustice of Solle's claim was recognised by all the judges who heard it, and it was the sort of case in which courts of equity had provided relief for mistake. Courts of equity had not allowed statutes to prevent such relief. Solle had created the misapprehension, a matter of significance in the earlier cases. Even if the mistake was characterised as one of law, the equitable decisions of *Bingham v Bingham* and *Lansdown v Lansdown* predated the mistake of law bar. The case was clearly within the type of private rights which the House of Lords had recognised as remediable in *Cooper v Phibbs*. Courts of equity would have been untroubled with concerns about types of mistake and the perceived effect upon consent, but they would have been concerned with bars to relief. It is in this context that Denning LJ's concern that the party seeking relief could not himself be at fault is to be understood by reference to the earlier equitable decisions.[248] The conduct of the party seeking relief could not offend conscience[249] nor could this party be negligent in the conduct of his own affairs.[250] On all of these fronts, Denning LJ's judgment was consistent with the earlier body of equitable cases, sparse as it was.

There were two major areas in which his judgment was not consistent with the earlier body of law. The first was in his implied acceptance of a doctrine of mistake at common law. It is true that courts of common law lacked the remedial flexibility of courts of equity, and it is also true that the courts of common law often refused to recognise a contract based on a misapprehension. The lack of recognition, however, arose for reasons other than a mistake which vitiated consent. It was misleading to think of two pre-fusion legal systems, each with its own doctrine of mistake. It is the case that some agreements founded upon a misapprehension were good neither at law nor in equity, but for different reasons. The second major area in which Denning LJ's decision was not consistent with the body of earlier equitable cases was his preoccupation with rescission, notably rescission on terms. It will be recalled that equity offered three forms of discretionary relief to a party who entered into a contract affected by a mistake. Most equitable intervention occurred to either rectify an agreement or to refuse specific performance, not to rescind a contract, for rescission was a powerful remedy to which courts of equity rarely had recourse. It is impossible to gauge from Denning LJ's reasons if he was aware of this. Denning LJ constructed his restatement without the aid of counsel. The real novelty of *Solle v Butcher* lay not in the enunciation of a doctrine of mistake in equity but in Denning LJ's attempt to explain its relationship to mistake at common law in an attempt to put the entire doctrine on a footing which would apply in contexts beyond the core jurisdiction of the old courts of equity.

The decision caused a certain amount of textbook rewriting and reflection. Appropriately enough, Pollock's treatise ended shortly before the decision, in 1946

[248] See ch 3. It does not appear to have been considered by Denning LJ that Butcher might have been barred from relief by reason of his delay in acting to rescind the contract.

[249] *Henkle v Royal Exchange Assurance Company* (1749) 1 Ves Sen 318; 27 ER 1055. See ch 3.

[250] *Duke of Beaufort v Neeld* [1844–45] 12 Cl and Finn 248; 8 ER 1399 at 286; 1415. See ch 3.

when Winfield published the twelfth and final edition.[251] As we have seen, new ideas are generally disseminated by new authors in a field rather than existing ones. In the mid-twentieth century the new authors on contract were Cheshire and Fifoot, who published *The Law of Contracts*[252] in 1945. While they said that they wrote to overcome problems presented to readers by Anson's *Principles of the English Law of Contract* and Pollock's *Principles of Contract*,[253] their first edition conceived of mistake in terms not dissimilar from Anson and Pollock. Contract, they wrote, was based on consent and required the concurrence of intention of two parties. In the immediate post-war world, Pothier was preferred over Savigny for this proposition.[254] Consent could be vitiated by certain factors, among which was mistake.[255] A mistake had the effect, 'generally', of rendering the contract void 'in the sense that it nullifies the consent of one or both of the parties and so, properly considered, prevents the formation of contract'.[256] Not every mistake would vitiate a contract. A familiar division of types of mistake was constructed: common mistake, mutual mistake or a cross-purposes mistake, and unilateral mistake. Confusion arose when these types of mistake were not properly distinguished from each other because the rules varied according to the different types of mistake. The authors proceeded, as the nineteenth-century writers had, to discuss the applicable rules, concerned with a failure of consent, to each of these types of mistake, using without distinction a mixture of legal and equitable cases to support these applicable rules. The importance of *Bell v Lever Brothers* lay in the restrictions it placed upon the doctrine of common mistake, which was now largely confined to those instances where the contract was concerned with an initial impossibility. The chapter ended with a brief section on equity which, despite its grand description of the 'effect of mistake in equity' was concerned only with the discretionary remedies of equity: refusal of specific performance for mistake in cases of a unilateral mistake or rectification where the written contract contained a mistaken expression. The authors noted that these remedies provided equity with an exclusive jurisdiction. In relation to the refusal of specific performance, courts were concerned not to enforce a contract where there was even a suspicion of sharp practice on the part of plaintiff. Because the court had a wide latitude in these cases, it was not useful to attempt to define the precise circumstances in which it would be exercised.

[251] PH Winfield, *Pollock's Principles of Contract*, 12th edn (London, Stevens and Sons, 1946).

[252] GC Cheshire and CHS Fifoot, *The Law of Contracts* (London, Butterworth & Co, 1945).

[253] They wrote that the very success of the former had 'in some measure impaired its utility' and that the mode of treatment 'may be thought out of focus with present needs' (ibid, iii); of the latter they wrote that it retained 'the inimitable imprint of its distinguished author' but did not profess to be comprehensive and thus could not be offered without support to the student (ibid).

[254] Cheshire and Fifoot (n 252) 19. The quotation was take from RJ Pothier, *A Treatise on the Law of Obligations or Contracts*, trs WD Evans (London, A Strahan, 1806), Pt I, s I, Art I.

[255] Two other categories existed: the second was misrepresentation, duress and undue influence; and the third was illegality of purpose. It was important, according to the authors, to keep these categories distinct: Cheshire and Fifoot (n 252) 136.

[256] ibid.

Cheshire and Fifoot described mistake as 'a perennial source of anxiety to writers on Contract',[257] and while their treatment of mistake was unchanged in the second edition of their work they expressed doubt as to the necessity of mistake in English law, noting that only in the case of a unilateral mistake was the law prepared to nullify a contract and this might better be done on the basis of fraud.[258] Denning LJ's decision in *Solle v Butcher*, however, caused them to recall this doubt and to rewrite their chapter on mistake in the third edition,[259] and then again in the fourth edition.[260] The authors retained the view that mistake affected the formation of a contract and they continued to divide their subject into the same three types of mistake. However, they now sub-divided each of these types into common law and equity: no longer were the equitable and the legal cases mixed together without consideration of their origins.[261] This had the effect of making the subject even more difficult because 'the presence or absence of consent . . . affords no sure guidance through the labyrinth of mistake'.[262] Absent consent, there was 'no single and reliable substitute'[263] principle by which to organise the cases. In their deconstruction of mistake, it does not seem to have occurred to the authors that the initial collection of these cases under this unhelpful 'principle' of mistake (as vitiating consent) had commenced in the hands of the treatise writers. Instead, the authors accused the judges of having failed to proceed upon a consistent and uniform principle in these cases:

> From time to time they have paid tribute to the classical hypothesis of consensus ad idem and proclaimed that if mistake prevents the meeting of the minds there can be on contract . . . But a perusal of the cases forces the reader to conclude that this tribute is little more than lip service. The equation of mistake with lack of consent has been maintained only fitfully and with obvious misgivings, and the judges have certainly refrained from drawing the logical conclusion that a contract must inevitably be held void if the minds of the parties are at variance upon its terms.[264]

In addition to this new criticism of the utility of consent, the authors now pointed out that it was essential to distinguish between the different attitudes of law and equity. Cheshire and Fifoot proceeded on the implied assumption that the common law had always recognised a doctrine of mistake and that equity had developed a concurrent jurisdiction to relieve a mistaken party in different types of transactions. The authors were firmly in favour of a further development of the equitable jurisdiction: 'the requirements of justice will, indeed, be better served if

[257] GC Cheshire and CHS Fifoot, *The Law of Contract*, 4th edn (London, Butterworth & Co, 1956).
[258] GC Cheshire and CHS Fifoot, *The Law of Contract*, 2nd edn (London, Butterworth & Co, 1940).
[259] GC Cheshire and CHS Fifoot, *The Law of Contract*, 3rd edn (London, Butterworth & Co, 1952).
[260] Cheshire and Fifoot (n 257).
[261] Two principal changes to the treatment of their subject in the fourth edition of their work was that they abandoned the rigid bifurcation of equity and common law in relation to each type of mistake and reduced their types to two: common mistake, and where an apparent agreement was vitiated by a mutual or unilateral mistake: ibid.
[262] Cheshire and Fifoot (n 259) 174.
[263] Cheshire and Fifoot (n 259).
[264] ibid, 173–74.

it [equity] is allowed to play an even larger part in the future development of this branch of the law'.[265] The particular advantages of equity were those identified by Denning LJ: equity did not impose the arbitrary all-or-nothing requirement of finding a contract void but would allow relief to be given on terms, and this allowed justice not only as between the parties to the original contract but also to any third parties. The authors were even more critical of the decision in *Bell v Lever Brothers*. Describing it as 'no authority for any general doctrine of common mistake'[266] they noted that the formulation by Lord Atkin that such mistake would only operate in circumstances where the thing without the quality was essentially different from the thing with the quality, it could not reasonably be denied that the test had been met in the case itself. The authors went beyond Denning LJ's criticisms of mistake at common law and noted that in the case of common mistake, it was not correct to say that the law even recognised such a mistake; it certainly did not apply it. It was only in equity that a party might obtain relief from such a mistake. *Solle v Butcher* was given a prominent role. The authors decided that, in the case of common and mutual mistake, relief was not obtained on the basis of a lack of consent but on the ground of impossibility or by resort to equitable principles.[267] This was a radical departure from the treatment of the subject by earlier writers. In the case of a unilateral mistake, the authors now observed that it appeared that the true basis of the rule in these cases was that an unfair advantage had been taken by one party of the ignorance of the other.[268] This observation was made at the outset of the topic, which was then largely considered in the same terms as it previously had been, but with the addition of a new section on the effect in equity. Here it was observed that equity would often provide relief for a unilateral mistake although law held the contract to be good. This was apparent from cases such as *Paget v Marshall*, which was relied upon without any of the subsequent criticisms of the decision. The authors adverted briefly to the fact that the grant of relief was made upon the basis that it was unconscientious for one party to take advantage of a mistake[269] and that, at times, parties were given an option of having the contract set aside or enforced in the sense intended by the other party.[270] The authors concluded with the firm view that the intervention of equity was to be welcomed into the 'varied and complicated problems raised by mistake',[271] and the common law approach was to be deplored: 'elasticity is here, at least, to be preferred to a barren certainty'.[272] Fortunately there were signs that this was now the judicial attitude, and 'the case of *Solle v Butcher* may perhaps be taken as indicating a change of view or at least of emphasis'.[273]

[265] ibid, 176.
[266] ibid, 180.
[267] ibid, 191.
[268] ibid, 192.
[269] ibid, 206.
[270] ibid, 207.
[271] ibid, 208.
[272] ibid, 209.
[273] ibid.

This hope was not to be realised. Denning LJ's decision, despite its early promise and optimistic reception, fell from favour. A part of the reason lies in the absence of an understanding of how mistake had reached the state it had in 1949. It was difficult to distinguish when a mistake operated at common law and when in equity. The categories of mistake were, unsurprisingly given their origins, artificial in conception and elusive in application. Judges remained reluctant to find a contract void. Doubt, some justified, crept into the interpretation of the accuracy of Denning LJ's judgment. Changes in the law surrounding misrepresentations allowed a court greater flexibility to rescind a contract for an innocent misrepresentation and to award damages for a negligent mis-statement. Ultimately, the enactment of the Misrepresentation Act 1967 meant that English courts could attach consequences to the actions of a particular party rather than indefinite concerns about the effect of mistake upon consent. There is an irony in the fact that, just as equitable mistake was 're-recognised' after the Second World War, the core jurisdiction of Chancery in relation to mistake, namely the conveyancing and settlements, had undergone substantive changes in law and in practice.

Conclusions

The immediate impact of the fusion of law and equity brought about by the Judicature Act 1873 upon mistake was minimal. The division of jurisdiction under the Act meant that the unique remedies of rectification and specific performance, so central to the development of equitable mistake, were assigned to the Chancery Division of the High Court. There, a specialised equity bench and bar carried on much as before, working within the same practices and applying the same principles. Certain developments can be seen within the equitable cases during this time: the realisation in *Tamplin v James* that all claims would need to be dealt with in a single action; the final rejection of *Woollam v Hearn*, and the ability to rectify and then order specific performance of a contract; the growing necessity for mistake to be bilateral; and an increasing rigidification of equitable relief for mistake. The impact of *Brownlie v Campbell*, interpreted to mean that an executed contract could only be set aside for fraud, is an important one. But beyond the comparison of the applicable principles at law and in equity to mistake cases, designed to demonstrate that a single result would occur through the application of different considerations, there was surprisingly little discussion of mistake in equity and at common law in courts. These comparative discussions were not entertained as a precursor to attempt to fashion a coherent post-fusion doctrine of mistake. An important underlying reason behind this lack of development is that the common law, with the exception of a mistake of identity, really had little to offer in the way of a doctrine of mistake. It is true that there were cases in which a contract formed under a misapprehension was not enforced, but it was too much to say that this lack of enforcement had arisen as a result of a failure of consent. On the whole, common law divisions of the High Court ignored mistake. On those few occasions, such as *Clark v Lindsay* or *Galloway v Galloway*, in which mistake did arise in the twentieth century, the judicial considerations of mistake were cursory and inconclusive.

Mistake as a legal response, apparently formulated as a doctrine, entered the common law at a time when the traditional jurisdiction of equity was diminished as a result of substantive developments in revenue and real property law. The doctrine of mistake which entered the common law came from the treatise writers. The real significance of *Bell v Lever Brothers* is that it was the authoritative and comprehensive introduction of a doctrine of mistake, explained as a defect of consent which rendered an apparent contract void, into the common law. While it is clear from their judgments that their Lordships saw themselves as applying an existing doctrine, it is equally clear from an examination of the history of this doctrine that, far from applying a doctrine, they were creating it. It was created in the image of the treatise writers, notably Pollock. The problem with this birth was that *Bell v Lever Brothers* both was an unsatisfactory precedent for this doctrine and also rendered largely ineffective when the majority refused to apply it to the facts before them. In short, Lord Atkin's doctrine was stillborn. An uncritical reliance upon treatise writers, notably Pollock, had produced an unworkable doctrine based upon unsatisfactory precedents.

Because mistake, a late entrant into English contract law, formed a sort of legal cul-de-sac, it was a little explored route. *Solle v Butcher* was an attempt both to solve the particular problem at hand and to rejuvenate a useful doctrine for resolving misapprehension cases without attributing fault as misrepresentations. Denning LJ attempted this on the basis of the earlier equitable cases, but his attempt was flawed. While his statement of law was accurate in some ways, it was inaccurate in others and largely ignored the history of these cases. While his acceptance of a mistake in equity produced the more satisfactory result of a voidable contract, rather than an absolute nullity, the basis upon which he achieved this was justifiably questioned over time. As English law expanded the relief available for misrepresentation, a legal consequence for mistake became far less necessary and was largely ignored in English contract law. Only a desperate litigant invoked mistake.

10

Summary and Conclusions

Summary

A SUMMARY OF HOW English contract law changed to admit a doctrine of contractual mistake is useful before considering the conclusions which arise from this study. Mistake is a factor which vitiates the consent necessary to form a binding contract. The doctrine is a difficult one in English law because it is hard to predict accurately which mistakes are sufficient to vitiate consent. This problem is compounded by the seemingly different effects a sufficient mistake may have: it may render the contract void, or voidable, or it may be a ground upon which specific performance may be refused. The difference between a void contract and a voidable contract, of enormous significance to a third party, is said to depend upon whether the mistake is at law or in equity, although the distinction between these two areas is blurred. A complicating problem posed by these difficulties is that the decided cases rarely support the apparently essential concept that mistake prevents consent.

The history of the doctrine provides an explanation for these difficulties. While the origins of mistake can be traced to seventeenth-century equity cases this is misleading because it overlooks the basis upon which these courts of equity intervened to give relief for mistake. Chancery was able to intervene because of its broader discovery procedures and its unique remedial powers. Equitable relief was premised upon the unwillingness of a court of equity to allow a party to obtain an advantage through a mistake and it was for reasons associated with this unwillingness that specific performance would be refused, or a mistaken recording rectified or in extreme cases for a contract to be rescinded and set aside so that no advantage could be taken at law. The exercise of these powers was discretionary, exercised in a fashion highly dependent upon the facts of a particular case and where the parties could be largely restored to their original positions. When equity intervened, it did not do so because the mistake had prevented the consent necessary to contract but because it offended conscience in the particular circumstances to allow a mistake to confer an advantage. As a reason for intervention, the concern closest to consent was that the contract did not accord with the intention of the parties.

In providing relief for mistake, the equitable jurisdiction complemented that of the common law, which did not accord a legal response to mistake until late in the nineteenth century. The common law did not generate a legal response to mistake because cases of misapprehension were dealt with by a variety of largely procedural mechanisms. Nineteenth-century changes in civil procedure and the administration of common law justice, driven by a desire to make the legal system more efficient, removed many of these mechanical responses. These procedural changes simultaneously worked to focus attention on the mistake. The result was a greater concern on the substantive law by which this problem could be resolved. It was during this time period, from the 1860s, that the first attempts were made to write up English contract law in a scientific, rational form. These treatise writers found an existing guide to their attempts in the writings of the civilians, notably Pothier and Savigny, and in Roman law.

Classical Roman law provided something of an intellectual storehouse of ideas for later jurists. This accumulation of jurisprudence was not, however, without problems when English judges and jurists sought to borrow concepts from it. The Romans had conceived of a law of contracts rather than contract, with the result that when English jurists began to analyse contract as consent, their considerations were narrowed to only the consensual contracts, notably *emptio venditio*, for considerations about mistake. English jurists, familiar with a case-based system, found the Roman categories of mistake attractive and English law adopted most of these categories. This adoption was not slavish and resulted in certain oddities: mistake of identity, which the common law recognised first, was the one most weakly developed in Roman law, and the Roman considerations of an *error in substantia* were not critically examined. Roman mistake presented certain challenges to English adoption. It took a largely subjective approach and it was usually unconcerned with third parties. It was also not as critically well developed as English lawyers assumed and Justinian's codification contained its own logical inconsistencies. Roman law was important, however, to English law, not only as a direct source of ideas but because of the influences it had upon eighteenth- and nineteenth-century civilian theorists who built upon the work of medieval scholars and the Spanish late scholastics. As Professor Gordley has demonstrated, under the latter group a synthesis was achieved between Greek philosophy and Roman law. This work was, in turn, borrowed by the natural lawyers. In this process, however, the law transmitted became separated from the philosophy which underpinned it. The moral virtues underpinning contract theory, that the will of the individual should be upheld, were removed. A will theory, without this philosophy, remained. While the late scholastics had conceived of a mistake of substance in the context that things had metaphysical substances or essences which defined the thing, the removal of Aristotelian concepts impeded the understanding of a mistake of substance. The demise of Aristotelian metaphysics began in the seventeenth century but the legal synthesis based upon Aristotle survived and flourished. With its central philosophical justification removed, the natural lawyers borrowed from this legal synthesis. Jurisprudential theory in English contractual mistake was most greatly influenced by the French theorist Pothier and the German theorist Savigny. Both these men had been influenced in the development of their conceptions of contract by the work of the natural lawyers.

Pothier was the foreign jurist to whom most English judges and jurists turned in framing their conceptions of mistake and this influence is apparent from the mid-nineteenth century. Pothier's influence on English contract law is a complex one. He was regarded by English lawyers as a systematic writer of great clarity and it was in his writings that English jurists sought and found a useful basis around which English contract law could be organised. When they borrowed his conception of consent, they borrowed with it his conceptions of consensual defects, notably mistake. That equity contained a legal response to mistake no doubt acted to confirm that English law recognised mistake as generating a legal response. Error, for Pothier, was an element which could disrupt or prevent this necessary consent and he formulated his concept of error with ideas drawn from the Roman law of sale. Following this Roman lead, Pothier conceived of error as different categories or types.

Pothier's conception of mistake presented certain problems to English lawyers. He had removed from the late scholastic conceptions the idea of the essence of an agreement, making it difficult to distinguish when a mistake was fundamental and when it was not. In addition, Pothier conceived of mistake in a subjective sense and this rested uneasily with the objective approach of English law. Finally, Pothier wrote that error annulled agreements, a result which was bound to provoke certain injustices within the English law of obligations. The attraction of Pothier lay in his structure, and he was first employed in attempts to systematise contract law in India, first by Henry Colebrooke in 1818 and then by William Macpherson in 1860. Somewhat surprisingly, neither work had much impact in England. It was in 1867 that Stephen Martin Leake cautiously began the evolutionary process of adopting Pothier's theory of mistake into English law. Leake's adoption was a critical one, for Leake had been a practising barrister and, while he found Pothier useful, he was aware of the civilian's limitations as an explanation of English contract law. Where Leake led, less critical writers followed, notably Judah Benjamin, Sir Frederick Pollock and Sir William Anson. Pothier's influence was more pronounced in Benjamin's 1868 *Treatise on the Law of Sale of Personal Property.*[1] It is unsurprising that the former Louisiana attorney turned to Pothier as a means of ordering and unifying English cases decided on disparate grounds. Benjamin's treatise was enormously influential and was, in turn, the impetus behind two momentous mistake cases, *Smith v Hughes* (1871)[2] and *Cundy v Lindsay* (1878).[3] Overall, however, the direct impact of Pothier was limited. Selective borrowings were made by treatise writers and these were blended, both by the writers and the judiciary, with common law concerns and approaches. Pothier's theories, however, stimulated the recognition of mistake as a matter which generated a legal response and that the reason for this response was a failure of the consent neces-

[1] JP Benjamin, *A Treatise on the Law of Sale of Personal Property: with References to the American Decisions and to the French Code and Civil Law* (London, Henry Sweet, 1868).

[2] (1871) LR 6 QB 597; 40 LJQB 221; 19 WR 1059.

[3] (1877–78) LR 3 App Cas 459; [1974–80] All ER Rep 1149, (1878) 42 JP 483; (1878) 14 Cox CC 93; (1878) 26 WR 406; (1878), 47 LJQB 481; (1878) 38 LT 573.

sary to contract. While English law was largely able to overcome the subjective approach employed by Pothier, his description that the effect of mistake was to nullify a contract, was to present continued difficulties within English law.

While Pothier's influence upon mistake in English law has long been apparent, Savigny's influence has been largely concealed. Pollock was attracted to the clarity and organisation of Savigny's *System des Heutigen römischen Rechts* and borrowed from it to form the basis for his scientific exposition of English contract law. Savigny saw contract as a union of wills with the object of determining legal relations. A contract arose from a manifestation of will regarded as a juridical act. Three elements were necessary for this juridicial act: the will itself; the manifestation of the will; and the concordance between the will and the manifestation of it. The existence of a number of factors, including mistake, could render doubtful the existence of the juridical act, for it disrupted the manifestation of the will. Not all mistakes had effect, for mistake was only relevant when it was a mistake in expression. The effect of such a mistake upon a contract was to render it void. Savigny's conception of mistake was objective, in contrast to Pothier's subjectivity. Pollock saw contract as a form of agreement that existed where two or more persons concurred in expressing a common intention so that the rights and duties of those persons were thereby determined. He initially accepted Savigny's will theory and with it large elements of Savigny's conception of mistake. It seems not to have occurred to Pollock that there was an irony in adopting a system which Savigny had seen as a cultural construct, a manifestation of *Volksgeist*. Mistake, wrote Pollock, did not of itself affect the validity of contracts; to affect a contract, the mistake must be such as to prevent any real agreement from being formed. Following Savigny's lead, Pollock stated that where a mistake had effect, the contract was void both at law and in equity. Pollock sought legitimacy for his adoptions by re-explaining English common law and equity cases to accord with his Savignian mistake theory. Savigny's influence on Pollock's treatise waned from the third edition as Pollock was attracted to American jurists. Pollock modified his conception of contract as consensus but, bizarrely, left his mistake chapter as a failure of consensus.

Anson wrote his *Principles of the English Law of Contract* in 1879 with an eye to Savigny's will theory, although Savigny's influence was not as pronounced upon his work as it had been upon Pollock's. Anson was not as keen as Pollock to amalgamate legal and equitable cases concerned with mistake and shied away from concluding that mistake rendered a contract void in equity. Anson refined his work to a greater extent than Pollock and, by 1891, Anson had limited the ambit of mistake in contract law to the point of non-existence. He also ceased to contrast mistake in equity with mistake at common law. Although Anson wrote on mistake with greater clarity than Pollock, his theory was as difficult to apply in practice as Pollock's. Mistake was recognised, but given a very narrow ambit. Mistake in equity was largely ignored. Pollock and Anson brought a system of organisation to English contract law using the work of civilian jurists, but it came at a cost.

While the writings of men such as Leake, Benjamin, Pollock and Anson indicated that the common law recognised a doctrine of mistake, the cases indicated something very different. A prominent quartet of nineteenth-century common law cases are used as a foundation for mistake at common law: *Couturier v Hastie* (1856),[4] *Raffles v Wichelhaus* (1864),[5] *Kennedy v The Panama Mail Co* (1867)[6] and *Smith v Hughes* (1871). An examination of these cases reveals a more complex picture, for none was decided on the basis of a doctrine of mistake and, considered in the context in which they were decided, they indicate an absence of such a doctrine within the common law. The last two cases illustrate the impact that the treatise writers were having upon legal conceptions and the changes that this was to work upon the way lawyers argued these cases and judges decided them. All four cases arose from common situations, only one was thought by contemporaries to be of any broader interest, and it was only the treatise writers' uses of these cases that prevented them from the obscurity they merited. *Couturier v Hastie* was a case determined largely by the way in which pleadings could then be framed. The House of Lords heard argument based on Pothier's *Contrat de Vente*, and it seems that a legal conception of mistake was viewed as having some relevance to the problem, but not so much that their Lordships thought it relevant to hear the respondent's counsel. *Raffles v Wichelhaus* was another case in which the court viewed the result as so obvious that it was not worth hearing opposing counsel's argument. The court gave judgment for the buyer, apparently on the basis that there had never been any agreement. *Kennedy v The Panama Mail Co* was of interest to contemporaries, but only because it arose in the broader context of the shareholder litigation brought about by corporate collapses. Considered in context, the decision of Blackburn J refutes the suggestion that the common law recognised that a mistake as to a quality could negate an apparent contract. Blackburn J stated that the common law position was that, absent a warranty as to a quality or a fraudulent representation that the quality existed, English law recognised the contract as good and *caveat emptor* applied. It is ironic that his consideration of the Roman *error in substantia* as a means of demonstrating that rescission was not available for an innocent misrepresentation unless there was a complete difference in the substance of the thing was utilised by later writers in such a fashion as to 'introduce' mistake of quality into English law. It was largely Pollock who, much to Anson's criticism, employed the case to support his civilian-inspired proposition that a fundamental error as to some quality of the subject matter avoided the contract. The last of the quartet, *Smith v Hughes*, reflects the work of Leake and Benjamin. This was a failed deception case which presented the issue of whether or not a contract could be rescinded where one party entertained a misapprehension not induced by the other. Both Blackburn and Hannen JJ were clearly swayed by the approach of Benjamin to mistake: their decisions indicate the impact of Benjamin's interpretation of *Raffles v Wichelhaus* and *Scott v Littledale*.[7] Implicitly recognising that a bilateral mistake could prevent the formation of a

[4] (1856) 5 HLC 673, 10 ER 1065.
[5] (1864) 2 H & C 906; 159 ER 375; 160 LJ Exch 160.
[6] (1867) LR 2 QB 580.
[7] (1858) 8 El & Bl 815; 120 ER 304.

contract, both judges considered that a unilateral mistake could avoid a contract if this mistake was known by the other party and went to the nature of the contract being formed. The oddity of this reception of civilian-inspired mistake into the common law is that Benjamin's reasoning was based on the common law concept of estoppel. A contract was formed because the mistaken party could be estopped from denying it. The case was, once again, seized upon by later treatise writers. It solved the difficult problem of whether mistake had to be bilateral or unilateral and solved the dilemma posed by the subjective and objective distinction. That it embodied a concern by the court to prevent unconscionability made it that much easier to reconcile with the equitable cases. It also effectively prevented much scope for a doctrine of mistake.

Taken together, this quartet of cases indicate the traditional approach of the common law to contracts in the nineteenth century. Courts were keen to ascertain whether or not the parties were agreed—were they '*ad idem*'? If they were, what were the terms of their agreement? If a particular thing was warranted (even on the basis of a misapprehension), the common law viewed the question as one of construction and not formation. Where there had been a fraudulent misrepresentation, liability followed the wrongdoing. In absence of warranty or misrepresentation, *caveat emptor* applied. What is notably absent from the reasoning in these cases is that a contract could be avoided for a mistake which prevented agreement. Courts of common law were aware that where a mistake existed in relation to a written agreement courts of equity might intervene to provide relief if it was thought merited on the particular facts of the case. Courts of common law had resisted the development of a related doctrine in common law by refusing to allow equitable defences of mistake even after the legislative grant of such power.

This ambiguous relationship which both recognised elements of mistake from the treatise writers and traditional common law elements was also present in the mistake of identity cases of which *Cundy v Lindsay* was the most prominent. It is clear from earlier nineteenth-century cases that the common law both did not recognise a doctrine of mistake and was of differing views as to whether a voidable contract existed where the rogue assumed the identity of another or whether no contract arose. Benjamin explained that the result in *Hardman v Booth*[8] as a case where it could equally be explained that the contract was void for mistake as to identity. The House of Lords in *Cundy v Lindsay* was concerned with the problems that arose from the criminal law—both in the effect that a conviction for false pretences had upon the process of contractual formation and the restorative provisions of the Larceny Act 1861. Their Lordships' judgment that there was no contract because there was no intent on the part of the owner to deal with the rogue was made following Benjamin's explanation of the critical case of *Hardman v Booth* as one of mistake, and conveniently solved the problems arising from the criminal law. Ironically, it was in these fraud cases that it can be said that English law recognised a form of mistake by the end of the nineteenth century.

[8] (1863) 1 H & C 803, SC 32 LJ Ex 105; 9 Jur (ns) 81; 11 WR 239; 7 LT 638.

Although treatise writers recognised a doctrine of mistake from the 1860s judicial acceptance of the doctrine took much longer. While it might have been possible to achieve a substantive fusion of law and equity regarding mistake following the Judicature Act 1873, certain factors militated against this occurrence. One of these was that, despite the efforts of the treatise writers, the common law did not recognise a coherent doctrine of mistake to which it accorded a principle reaction to instances of misapprehension. In addition, the disparate equitable and legal treatment of instances of misapprehension was maintained by other provisions of the Judicature Act 1873. Cases in which rectification and specific performance were sought were referred to the Chancery Division, where they were largely resolved in accordance with the equitable practices prevailing prior to fusion. These practices were not static and changes can be discerned. Increasingly after 1875 the Chancery Division required that its discretionary relief would not be granted unless the mistake was a bilateral one. This may have arisen as a result of the treatise writers, although it is clear that there were concerns about the possible injustice that would arise with regard to the non-mistaken party. The increasing requirement that the mistake should be bilateral was a part of the process during which equitable relief for mistake was increasingly rigidified. While the Chancery Division continued much the same practices towards equitable relief, courts of common law made some movement towards the development of a doctrine of mistake at common law. Only in the area of identity was there any acknowledgement by common law courts of such a doctrine, and from the end of the nineteenth century many of the cases in which these acknowledgements were made were cases in which the judges sought to deny the application of the doctrine in the particular case. Where other forms of mistake were considered, the judicial considerations were brief and too inadequate to form a doctrine of mistake at common law. An exception arose in 1930 in *Munro v Meyer*,[9] a decision almost immediately superseded by the decision in *Bell v Lever Brothers*.[10] The decision in this case must be examined in light of the unfortunate circumstances in which it was brought. Mistake was only pleaded in the alternative and limited to either a mistaken payment or a unilateral mistake. Counsel for Lever Brothers appear to have been in some confusion until late in the day as to how to make their mistake arguments, apparently convinced from the time of the trial that the facts alone were sufficiently compelling for judgment to be given in their favour. The confusion which surrounded the legal arguments in the case appear to have led the judiciary, notably Lord Atkin, to consult the treatises, in particular Pollock. The resulting decision implemented Pollock's doctrine, flaws and all, into English law. One of these weaknesses was that the doctrine was incredibly narrow in its application. A related weakness was that it was very difficult, in cases of a mistake as to quality, to ascertain when a quality was sufficiently fundamental as to constitute an operative mistake. One of the greatest weaknesses in Pollock's doctrine was that

[9] [1930] 2 KB 312.
[10] [1932] AC 161.

it sought to remove wherever possible the 'peculiar' equitable cases and to re-interpret equitable cases such as *Cooper v Phibbs*[11] as having the same result at law as in equity. It is in light of this that Lord Atkin's judgment must be read.

Bell v Lever Brothers was not well received by contemporary commentators, and few mistake cases arose in its aftermath. It was not until 1949 that the matter was addressed to any extent. While Denning LJ's decision in *Solle v Butcher*[12] that equity would rescind such a contract on terms was undoubtedly motivated by considerations that the common law relief was too narrowly granted, he was right in acknowledging that courts of equity would have intervened that in such circumstances. The unsatisfactory manner in which *Bell v Lever Brothers* was decided indicates that he was right to conclude that the House of Lords had not considered mistake in equity. Denning LJ's decision was to cause something of a rewrite in the treatises, but the paucity of later cases and the uncurious nature of most contract writers meant that little was revealed of the earlier practices.

Conclusions

While remembering Fifoot's admonition that legal history should be undertaken for its own sake and not to serve an ulterior purpose,[13] it is suggested that a number of conclusions can be drawn from this study. These conclusions are as to the nature of common law legal development, the nature of legal transplants in common law legal development, and a greater understanding of the difficulties in the modern doctrine of mistake in contract law.

Common Law Legal Development

English contract law in 1850 had no doctrine of mistake based on the concept that mistake was a factor that disrupted the will or consent of the contracting parties such that no contract arose. By 1950 it did have such a doctrine. What stimulated such a legal change? What does this legal change tell us about common law legal development in this area? The change was effected by the interaction of jurists, barristers and judges. The stimulus to this substantive change arose in the procedural reforms of the common law in the nineteenth century. Victorians sought to administer justice in a quicker and more efficient form to meet the demands of their era. An unintended consequence of these reforms was a new way of looking at contractual misapprehension cases. The reforms both inhibited the mechanisms by which such cases had been resolved and simultaneously created new procedures which exposed the presence of such misapprehensions. The law was

[11] (1867) [LR] 2 HL 149.
[12] [1950] 1 KB 671, [1949] 2 All ER 1107, 66 TLR (Pt 1) 448, [1949] EGD 346.
[13] CHS Fifoot, *Law and History in the Nineteenth Century* (London, Bernard Quaritch, 1956) 21.

forced to find new mechanisms to deal with these cases of misapprehension. Procedural changes created a demand for new expositions of law based on substantive principles rather than digests of cases. The treatise writers wrote to meet these needs. But they wrote for other reasons, as well. English lawyers were unsatisfied with the lack of coherence presented by the common law of contract in the early nineteenth century. As French and German legal developments grew in sophistication, envious eyes were directed from across the English Channel. Some English lawyers were also taken with the need to organise their law as a precursor to codifying it. Within the broader nineteenth-century intellectual world, there was a growing sophistication in presenting principles organised in logical systems. In short, there was a growing demand to present the law in an organised, coherent manner divided into logical principles which could be applied to predict the resolution of disputes. The principal treatise writers of the second half of the nineteenth century stepped forward to meet this demand, and Fry, Leake, Benjamin, Pollock and Anson produced treatises which had the effect of 'creating' a doctrine of mistake. In addition, a growing commercial and mercantile empire demanded a legal system which could adjudicate commercial disputes; men such as Colebrooke and Macpherson wrote to meet this demand. The common law has traditionally admitted a very small role for the developmental efforts of actors who are neither judges nor legislators, but it is clear that in this area legal change was brought about by jurists. Jurists, however, could not act unaided and their impact upon two barristers and the judges who heard their arguments was critical. Ultimately, it was the acceptance of these ideas within judicial decisions which led to the creation of mistake as a legal doctrine. This process took about 70 years from its enunciation in the treatises until its application in *Bell v Lever Brothers*.

This process of change indicates certain weaknesses within the manner of common law development. Lawyers argue cases to win them and the rational development of the law may be either irrelevant[14] or even undesirable. Necessitous counsel can make desperate arguments and in many mistake cases the existing state of the law was against them. Odd cases also drove counsel and judges to consult the new, organised treatises on contract and to borrow from them. In this process the role of judges in developing law was limited.[15] Judges in many of these mistake cases were clearly attempting to resolve the strange problem before them. The development of doctrine as a means of providing future guidance was often overlooked or impeded by the arguments put forward. When Lord Atkin attempted to develop such a means he was driven to consult the works of Pollock and Anson to form the basis of his decision. This action revealed a world outside the courts where a sort of law was effectively formed. The problem was that the conditions in which this 'law', juristic writings, occurred were limited. There were only a small number of jurists engaged in this activity, with a comparatively narrow scope of debate or discussion occurring within the English-speaking world on

[14] See the observations of the former Lord Justice of Appeal, Richard Buxton, in 'How the Common Law Gets Made: *Hedley Byrne* and Other Cautionary Tales' (2009) 125 *Law Quarterly Review* (LQR) 60.
[15] ibid.

mistake during the formulation of this doctrine. While it is clear from their treatises that they were engaged in a form of dialogue, it was not as detailed as one would have wanted. It is striking, for example, that in later years Pollock abandoned consent as a basis for contract but left his mistake chapter standing. Equally, Anson chose to limit the potential ambit for mistake to such a narrow extent that it practically ceased to exist—but he did not remove it. The opportunity for critical examination leading to change was small: Pollock, for example, continued to use *Kennedy*'s case as a basis upon which to found his mistake as to quality when the case was obviously decided in complete rejection of such a theory. Eventually, this basis was accepted in *Bell v Lever Brothers*, a result which did little to add to the understanding of the law.

The jurists both guided judges and also responded to decisions, seeking to distinguish and reconsider them to fit an existing theory of mistake. Their work was to prove attractive to lawyers and judges because of its apparently coherent whole, the ease of reference, and the time saved in consulting such a selection. A cycle of influence and support can be detected in these cases. From the outset of the introduction of Benjamin's treatise in 1868, a pattern can be detected. Portions of the treatise were employed as part of the reasons for judgment, as can be seen in *Smith v Hughes* and *Cundy v Lindsay*. The resulting decisions were in turn utilised by treatise writers as judicial support for the doctrine of mistake they sought to advance. The result is that the treatise writers have had a remarkably long-lived influence upon the development of mistake. It is surprising that the writings of nineteenth-century jurists, borrowed from already outdated civilian ideas, largely set the framework for how this area of law was both created and developed. Long after Pollock became an obscure name, noted for either his correspondence with Holmes or his history with Maitland, his mistake chapter continues to form the dominant basis for the English law of contractual mistake.

The intellectual substance of the doctrine of mistake created is a curious one. Much can be made of the civilian borrowings by the treatise writers and the supposed affinity of the common law with its civilian counterparts. However, the borrowings were not extensive and the means by which they were grafted to the common law altered the content of these borrowings. The treatise writers borrowed the will theories of civilians, adapting them to suit the less sophisticated approach of the common law that contracts were about agreements. With will theory came mistake, and here the treatise writers relied primarily upon Pothier and to a lesser extent Savigny, ignoring later civilians. The theory of mistake created from these civilian jurists was not true to their own models, partly because certain aspects of the civilian theory were not fully understood by the treatise writers and partly because these writers strove to adapt civilian conceptions to the existing common law. English cases had to be used to support these theories; in its simplest form, the writers 'borrowed' equity cases concerned with mistake and simply reinterpreted them to stand for the same proposition in common law. Pollock's treatment of *Cooper v Phibbs* is an outstanding example of this technique. In other instances, the treatise writers grafted their borrowed theory to existing common law conceptions. The objective nature of English law sat uneasily with mistake and the treatise writers resolved this uneasiness by considering a unilateral mistake in the context of the existing concept of estoppel. *Smith v Hughes* was decided on the basis that a mistaken party could be estopped from asserting his mistake. Another example can be seen in the attempts to consider a mistake as to subject matter as akin to the failure of an implied condition. The objective nature of the common law came to triumph over the subjective elements of Pothier's theory because the common law was reluctant to disrupt an apparent contract upon which others might have relied. English law came to see categories of mistake, in much the same fashion that the Romans had, but this accorded with the common law's case-based system of jurisprudence. All in all, the common law's adherence to older theories and explanations in the face of new ones is striking. New developments were related back, or secured, upon older conceptual moorings. Judges and jurists moved from the known to the unknown new, without ever completely abandoning the old concepts and practices. Mistake continues to rest uneasily with a system of warranties and *caveat emptor*, and this results in present conceptual uncertainties and practical difficulties.

The use made of civilian theory is interesting because of the limited extent to which it was used. Judges and jurists made different uses of this jurisprudence. English jurists borrowed elements of contractual structure and with it elements of a theory of mistake. English judges were far less willing to borrow from civilians, and this demonstrates a degree of confidence in their own legal system. Judges were clearly aware of civilian theory, both in its original form and in the use made of it by treatise writers, but there is little direct reliance upon it. Fry J's quotation from Pothier in *Smith v Wheatcroft*[16] and Blackburn J's comparison of the Roman *error in substantia* with the common law in *Kennedy*'s case[17] are striking because they are so rare. When judges did borrow they did so to further support a decision made in English law or to compare and contrast the English position with that of the civilians.

The doctrine of mistake casts an interesting light on the development of contract law after the fusion of law and equity. Before fusion, equity accorded a legal response to a mistake for reasons generally associated with conscience and not consent. At common law there was no legal response as such to mistake. Even after the mid-century reforms which allowed equitable defences, such as mistake, to be pleaded in common law actions, common law courts were reluctant to entertain these defences. Contract was a concurrent jurisdiction of equity and common law prior to fusion, and little thought was given as to how these different areas would be dealt with after fusion. While exclusive areas of equitable jurisdiction, such as trusts, were to maintain their separate equitable identities, aspects of contract were less easily identified as equitable or legal after fusion. Judges appear not to have been concerned with the lack of an integrated approach. The matter was consid-

[16] (1878) 9 ChD 223.
[17] (n 6).

ered as a procedural one: and it is in this context that in *Tamplin v James*[18] the Court of Appeal was quick to pronounce that if specific performance were refused, the same court must now consider the issue of damages. At times, judges decided whether a contract which would be set aside in equity for mistake was also void or non-existent at common law. The difficulty presented by such cases is that there was little explicit consideration of the reasons why the common law would not have enforced the contract for such reasons lay outside mistake.

Over time, the equitable approach to mistake became much more rigidified, and the flexible relief present in the nineteenth century faded away in all but the family settlement cases. Part of this process may be explained by the treatise writers, such as Pollock, who wrote that law and equity treated these cases in the same way. Another part of the process was the growing reluctance of courts to set aside an executed transaction unless fraud was present. The growing desire for principles appears to have also worked against the highly case-specific resolution that had existed in the old court of Chancery. When the procedural aspects of moving between two courts disappeared, this affected the way in which rescission for mistake was dealt with. In some ways it can be seen that the narrower common law approach came to change the equitable approach in these areas of contract. The basis of the earlier equitable cases came to be overlooked, as a failure of consent became the dominant prism through which this area was surveyed. The structure of the Judicature Act 1873 and the re-formation of practical divisions between the common law and equity bench and bar also had an effect. The traditional equitable response to mistake can still be seen in cases where rectification or specific performance were concerned, for these were matters explicitly assigned to the Chancery Division. Rescission for mistake was largely overlooked in this process, and in practice very few cases arose at common law where mistake was relevant because common law practice and understanding admitted few such instances. Common law practitioners may have had little practical understanding of mistake. The apparent confusion of the lawyers involved in the litigation in *Bell v Lever Brothers* is startling. As mistake came to be judicially acknowledged at common law, its scope in equity diminished due to changes in its core jurisdiction brought about the demise of the family settlement and the ascendancy of a new legislative form of property ownership and registration. As the core jurisdiction of equity receded, mistake emerged in common law. When it did, however, the understanding of the lawyers as to the earlier equitable cases had largely disappeared.

Finally, the development of mistake in English contract law displays a tension between precedent and principle. Precedents are established by cases decided on the basis of particular facts; principles are created, generally by jurists, at a more general and abstract level. The principles are used to unify the law, to give it coherence and to attempt to render the application of the law more certain. Precedent demands that earlier binding cases be followed. A large part of the problem that arose in mistake was that the principles were not supported by the precedents. A

[18] (1879, 1880) 15 Ch D 215.

disjunction between principles and cases was present from the outset of the development of this doctrine. At times, judges sought to apply the reasoning of the cases; at other times, they sought to reinterpret the cases to make them accord with the advanced principle. Neither process lent certainty to the common law development. Unusually, there was little questioning of the entire doctrine of mistake; in this regard, the work of the jurists was highly successful.

Transplants

Alan Watson's *Legal Transplants*[19] forms the starting point for discussion about the subject, although there are earlier antecedents.[20] Watson's thesis is a complex one, presented in a large body of writings.[21] It has engendered a furious discussion amongst lawyers, and the body of literature concerned with transplants and receptions is voluminous.[22] His thesis is that legal transplants, 'the moving of a rule or a system of law from one country to another, or from one people to another'[23] has been common throughout history and is the principal explanation behind the growth of law.[24] Watson was 'persuaded' by the pattern of 'continual massive borrowing and longevity of rules and institutions' to conclude that 'there was no simple relationship between a society and its law'.[25] Watson also argues that the mechanisms of legal change are controlled internally by legal professionals.[26] Watson observed that the actors in a borrowing system will consistently turn to one system, a 'donor' system of general high standing with easily accessible rules, rather than search systematically for the best rule.[27] In this sense, the lawmakers of

[19] A Watson, *Legal Transplants, An Approach to Comparative Law* (Edinburgh, Scottish Academic Press, 1974), republished as a second edition with the author's Afterword: *Legal Transplants: An Approach to Comparative Law*, 2nd edn (Athens, GA, University of Georgia Press, 1993). See, also, A Watson, 'Legal Transplants and Law Reform' (1976) 92 LQR 79, and 'Aspects of Reception of Law' (1996) 44 *American Journal of Comparative Law* (Am J Comp L) 335.

[20] The concept itself fits within a larger subject, the diffusion of law: see W Twining, 'Diffusion of Law: A Global Perspective' (2004) 49 *Journal of Legal Pluralism* 1. As to the earlier antecedents, see O Kahn-Freund, 'On Uses and Misues of Comparative Law' (1974) 37 *Modern Law Review*(MLR) 1.

[21] W Ewald, 'Comparative Jurisprudence (II): The Logic of Legal Transplants' (1995) 43 Am J Comp L 489, 489.

[22] See, eg, R Abel, 'Law as Lag: Inertia as a Social Theory of Law' (1982) 80 *Michigan Law Review* 785, and L Friedman, 'Book Review' (1979) 6 *British Journal of Law & Society* 127. Michele Graziadei outlines the challenge Watson's work presents to legal functionalism: 'The functionalist heritage' in P Legrand and R Munday (eds), *Comparative Legal Studies: Traditions and Transitions*, (Cambridge, Cambridge University Press, 2003). An overview of the topic is provided in M Graziadei, 'Comparative Law As the Study of Transplants and Receptions' in M Reimann and R Zimmerman (eds), *The Oxford Handbook of Comparative Law*, (Oxford, Oxford University Press, 2006). The term 'transplant' is not without problems. See E Örıcı, 'Law as Transposition' (2002) 52 *International and Comparative Law Quarterly* (ICLQ) 205, 207–12 as to possible terms for this process and their respective meanings.

[23] Watson, *Legal Transplants*, 1st edn (n 19) 21.

[24] ibid, 95–101.

[25] Watson, *Legal Transplants*, 2nd edn (n 19) 107.

[26] A Watson, *Failures of the Legal Imagination* (Edinburgh, Scottish Academic Press, 1988) chs 1 and 2.

[27] A Watson, 'Legal Change: Sources of Law and Legal Culture' in A Watson, *Legal Origins and Legal Change* (London and Rio Grande, The Hambledon Press, 1991) 95.

one society may share more in common with the lawmakers of another society than the law does with the particular political, economic or societal demands of the society from which it is said to emanate.[28] The existence of a legal professional elite who orchestrate this transplant process is central to Watson's theory. His theory is complemented by Sacco's theory of legal formants,[29] which accepts that most legal change occurs through borrowing and that change by genuine innovation is a much rarer phenomenon.[30] Sacco accords importance to legal scholars as creators of law. A legal scholar creates law 'without wishing to or realizing that he is doing it'.[31] While he aims to be a source of law he resists giving his work an ad hoc legitimacy and seeks legitimacy by reference to another source of law or by 'imagining' a general principle capable of numerous different applications. The scholar's power lies in his ability to persuade others with his writing and through his teaching. Sacco argues that the role of the scholar is a diminished one within the common law systems, notably in England.[32]

Watson's theories have engendered many different debates. Because most of the contributions to the advancing discussion of legal transplants have been concerned with theoretical constructions it is interesting to compare the results of this study of contractual mistake in English law to these debates. Three particular transplant debates are relevant here: first, the relationship between law and society;[33] second, whether legal transplants are even possible; and third, the convergence of European private law.

In relation to the first of these debates, Ewald sought to explain Watson's work in abstract terms and then to apply his claims about legal development to legal sociology.[34] A purpose behind this application was simultaneously to refute traditional mirror theories of legal sociology and to introduce a more nuanced and complex view of the relationship between law and society. Cotterrell has observed that Ewald's interpretation of Watson's approach misunderstands legal sociology.[35] Cotterrell argues that Watson insists that law forms a part of culture: 'law is part of the different cultures of lawmakers ("that elite group who in a particular society have their hands on the levers of legal change"), lawyers in general and "the

[28] ibid, 105.

[29] R Sacco, 'Legal Formants: A Dynamic Approach to Comparative Law (Installment I of II)' (1991) 39 Am J Comp L 1. The theory approaches law from the perspective that behind a single legal rule is a 'living law' which contains many different elements (statutory rules, the formulations of scholars, judicial decisions) and only by interpreting these legal formants, the reasons behind these elements, is one able to properly interpret the legal rule. These legal formants may not necessarily be in harmony. The number of legal formants and their comparative importance varies enormously between different legal systems. Law can be applied only when it is interpreted and all the factors which affect the convictions of the interpreter are sources of law.

[30] R Sacco, 'Legal Formants: A Dynamic Approach to Comparative Law (Installment II of II)' (1991) 39 Am J Comp L 343, 397.

[31] ibid, 348.

[32] ibid.

[33] Ewald, (n 15) discusses Watson's theories in relation to comparative law and the sociology of law.

[34] ibid, 491, 508–10.

[35] R Cotterrell, 'Is There a Logic of Legal Transplants?' in D Nelken and J Feest (eds) *Adapting Legal Cultures*, (Oxford/Portland, OR, Hart Publishing, 2001) 77.

population at large".'[36] Watson recognises the importance of the enormous power and autonomy of legal culture, the 'outlook, practices, knowledges and values of legal professionals or people performing specialised legal tasks'.[37] Cotterrell argues that while Watson, as interpreted by Ewald, 'misunderstands legal sociology while making its own fundamental sociological assumptions'[38], there is value in Watson's work as a contribution to understanding the framework within which transplants occur. Cotterrell notes that in the legal transplant discussion there is ambiguity as to what constitutes 'law': sometimes positive legal rules are emphasised, at other times broader but indeterminate ideas of legal culture.[39] Because of the indeterminate nature of legal culture, an entire range of views on the feasibility of legal transplants is encouraged and 'legal culture may be seen as a discourse with its own internal dynamics and structure, also having complex relations with other cultural components of the environment'.[40] The way in which law is conceptualised colours how the success of the borrowing is assessed. Where law is emphasised as an instrument of some sort, attention is focused upon law in action and in this instance a transplant will not be considered significant, or even to have occurred, unless it can be said to have had effects upon the relevant aspects of social life in the recipient society. Where law is seen as an expression of culture (as a matter of shared traditions, values or beliefs), either of lawyers or of society generally, a transplant will not be considered successful unless it is consistent with these cultural matters or reshapes them 'in conformity with the cultural presuppositions of the transplanted law'.[41] Because of the complexities of these matters, it is, Cotterrell argues, preferable to 'see law as always rooted in communities of various kinds' rather than seeing it in the more traditional concern of law's impact or lack of impact upon society.[42] Here, Cotterrell builds upon Watson's view of legal transplants, for Watson sees law as based within and shaped by legal professional communities:

> For Watson the professional community determines where new law is borrowed from, resists external pressures for change, determines its own criteria of legal excellence, or shields its law (by obfuscation, monopolisation of knowledge, or other means) from outside influence for a host of reasons internal to the community of lawmakers.[43]

Cotterrell suggests that, to the extent that this professional lawmaking elite exemplifies a type of traditional community, 'their legal influence may be especially to help to make legal doctrine itself orderly, secure and stable in terms of (professionally) familiar, established legal traditions'.[44]

[36] ibid, quoting Watson (n 27) 100.
[37] Cotterrell (n 35) 77.
[38] ibid.
[39] ibid, 78.
[40] ibid, 78.
[41] ibid, 79.
[42] ibid, 80.
[43] ibid, 80.
[44] ibid, 85.

The second transplant debate engendered by Watson's work is whether or not legal transplants are even possible. The principal protagonist in this debate is Pierre Legrand.[45] The essence of this challenge is that law cannot move from one society to another without changing content. At one level, because the recipient controls the outcome of the process triggered by a transplant, it is impossible to claim that the foreign model is actually working in its new setting. At a deeper level, Legrand regards Watson's views as representing 'a most impoverished explanation of interactions across legal systems—the result of a particularly crude apprehension of what law is and of what a rule is'.[46] The difficulty with Watson's conception, for Legrand, is that Watson views the law as an autonomous entity, separate from its historical, epistemological or cultural context. For Legrand, the meaning of the rule is an essential component of the rule, 'it partakes in the ruleness of the rule'.[47] Rules themselves necessarily incorporate cultural forms, and these cultural forms cannot be transferred from one system to another. Law cannot therefore be transferred from a donor system to a recipient system because it will not have the same content outside the donor system. For Legrand, 'the "transplant" does not happen: a key feature of the rule—its meaning—stays behind so that the rule that was "there", in fact, is not itself displaced over "here" '.[48] In this sense, legal transplants cannot occur. Because each language and legal system has its own meanings and outlook these will interfere with attempts to transfer the law and render a transfer from one system to another impossible. For Legrand, the attempt to argue that legal transplants occur is based upon a limited perspective on law, a perspective which is derived from attention to texts and the expense of the intangible context in which these texts operate. It is a 'bookish' stance indicative of a political decision to marginalise differences and champion sameness. Watson's reply is a reaffirmation that a transplanted rule is not the same in the recipient society as it was in the donor society and that the recipient receives the tangibles of a rule and not the intangible 'spirit' of a legal system.[49] Watson had earlier recognised that the particular culture to which a jurist belonged affected the understanding of the parameters of legal debate.[50] Allison[51] accepts that processes of transplantation have occurred in which legal ideas and theories have moved

[45] Legrand's principal contributions to this debate can be found in: P Legrand, 'The Impossibility of "Legal Transplants" ' (1997) 4 *Maastricht Journal of Comparative Law* 111, revised as 'What "Legal Transplants" ' in D Nelken and J Feest (eds), *Adapting Legal Cultures* (Oxford/Portland, OR, Hart Publishing, 2001); and P Legrand, 'The same and the different' in P Legrand and R Munday (eds), *Comparative Legal Studies: Traditions and Transitions*, (Cambridge, Cambridge University Press, 2003). Watson's reply to Legrand appears in A Watson, 'Legal Transplants and European Private Law' (2000) 4.4 *Electronic Journal of Comparative Law Ius Commune Lectures on European Private Law*, 2 at www.ejcl.org.

[46] Legrand, 'The Impossibility of "Legal Transplants" ' (n 45) 113.

[47] ibid, 114.

[48] Legrand, 'What "Legal Transplants" ' (n 45) 61.

[49] Watson (n 45).

[50] A Watson, 'From Legal Transplants to Legal Formants' (1995) 43 Am J Comp L 469, 470.

[51] JWF Allison, *A Continental Distinction in the Common Law, A Historical and Comparative Perspective on English Public Law* (Oxford, Clarendon Press, 1996) 12–16, 236.

from one legal system to another, but he is critical both of Watson's theory[52] and also the success of such processes. For Allison, transplants can occur, but rarely successfully, and he observes that Watson himself notes that where a rule is 'inimical' to the domestic context of the receiving system transplantation is less likely.[53]

The third debate engendered by Watson's work is on the question of whether European legal systems are converging, a debate of immense significance for the peoples and institutions of the European Community. Legrand maintains, consistently with his denial of legal transplants, that European legal systems are not converging.[54] If a body of law common to all member states emerged, it would only emerge by way 'of a compendium of enacted propositions'.[55] The reason for this is that while 'rules' may move from one member state to another, they move without their culture, without their historical experience and without the inevitable social component inherent in the rule. Because of the different legal *mentalités* within the European Union, notably between that of the common law states and that of the civil law states, the legal systems are not converging as the differences between these *mentalités* produce irreducible differences at an epistemological level. 'In the absence of shared epistemological premises, the common law and civil law worlds cannot, therefore, engage in an exchange that would lead one to an understanding of the other, if only a virtual understanding.'[56] In contrast to the 'legal transplant', which is either rejected by the recipient or successfully incorporated into its legal system, Teubner has introduced a different metaphor, the 'legal irritant'.[57] Teubner's thesis is that the conception of a legal transplant presents a false dichotomy of 'repulsion or interaction'.[58] Legal institutions are more organic than mechanical for Teubner and cannot be moved easily from one environment to another. A 'transplant' implies that when the foreign rule is implanted in the recipient system that it functions, if at all, as it did in the donor system. In reality, 'when a foreign rule is imposed on a domestic culture . . . something else is happening . . . it works as a fundamental irritation which triggers a whole series of new and unexpected events'.[59] The new rule irritates a co-evolutionary process of separate trajectories. The new rule irritates the binding arrangements of the recipient's legal system and social discourse and forces these arrangements to reconstruct internally their own rules and to reconstruct the alien rule itself. Legal

52 Allison remarks that 'Watson's theoretical argument . . . is flawed and his empirical work unconvincing': ibid, 14.

53 ibid.

54 P Legrand, 'European Legal Systems are not Converging' (1996) 45 ICLQ 52. See, also, P Legrand, 'Against a European Civil Code' (1997) 60 MLR 44. Other commentators have taken a different view as to the process of convergence. See, eg, B Markesinis, 'Learning from Europe and Learning in Europe' in B Markesinis (ed), *The Gradual Convergence: Foreign Ideas, Foreign Influences, and English Law on the Eve of the 21st Century* (Oxford, Clarendon, 1994).

55 Legrand, 'European Legal Systems are not Converging' (n 54) 53.

56 ibid, 76.

57 G Teubner, 'Legal Irritants: Good Faith in British Law or How Unifying Law Ends up in New Divergences' (1998) 61 MLR 11.

58 ibid, 12.

59 ibid, 12.

irritants are not domesticated, they are not transformed from the alien to the familiar nor are they adapted to the new cultural context. Instead, 'they will unleash an evolutionary dynamic in which the external rule's meaning will be reconstructed and the internal context will undergo fundamental change'.[60] The result is that the recipient's legal system is changed from what it was, although it is not the same as the donor's system, and in this way new divergences are created. Not only is the legal discourse changed but it is also changed in relation to the social discourse to which it is coupled.

The development of mistake in English contract law sheds some light into all three of these particular transplant debates. We begin with terminology. Although 'transplant' is the familiar term, it does not accurately describe what occurred. A 'transplant' implies that an entire organ is taken from one body and implanted within another. This is not what happened in English law. A more accurate description of what happened was that there was a process of copying: English jurists, and to a much lesser extent, English judges, selectively and partially copied ideas from civilian theorists.

In relation to the first debate, this study indicates that there is strength in Watson's theories, and Cotterrell's observations on these, about the role of a professional legal elite. Contractual mistake as a failure of consent arrived in English law as a result of the actions of this elite. Jurists borrowed mistake as a concept and, slowly, it received acceptance by judges who were persuaded, in the language of Sacco, to adopt this theory. In this process, the legal profession appears autonomous from the greater society which sustains it. While there was public interest in procedural reform, there seems to have been virtually no public concern about the substantive shape of mistake. A rare exception was the mercantile reaction to the result in *Kingsford v Merry*,[61] where there was opposition to finding a contract completely void to the detriment of the bona fide purchaser for value. This reaction was one resisted by the judiciary, and the case came to be used as a case of mistake which rendered the contract void.[62] The separation of a broader society from a contractual doctrine such as mistake was probably increased by the fact that the changes to the law were gradual, evolutionary and imperceptible even to the eyes of many professional lawyers. Mistake cases arise infrequently and this infrequency combined with judicial resolution were not factors which would cause the doctrine to reflect societal conditions. Most of these cases concerned businessmen, and businessmen, to the limited extent that their interests appeared in the legal literature, desired certainty from the law. The copying undertaken by the jurists was undertaken not only as a means of providing a veneer of legitimacy to the theories they were advancing but also because it was easier than devising their own theories. The influential role of the treatise writers in this area of law casts doubt upon Sacco's generalisation that the importance of legal scholarship is diminished in English common law.

[60] ibid, 12.
[61] 11 Exch 577; 156 ER 960.
[62] See ch 8.

In relation to the second debate, whether or not legal transplants can occur, this study indicates that ideas can be copied but the effect of the copying is not to recreate the conditions of the copied system in the copier system. Mistake in modern English contract law is different than it is in modern French or German law. A part of the reason lies in the fact that what the jurists copied were ideas which had not been implemented into actual law. Later French jurists built upon the work of Pothier, and German jurists upon Savigny; bizarrely, English writers almost entirely ignored these later developments. Even more bizarrely, English writers copied ideas from works that were outdated when they undertook their copying. The result was that the 'transplants' were fairly ancient organs when they were implanted; unable to bear the strains to which they were subjected. A related problem was that the effects of the new ideas which came into the common law were both distorted and tempered by other factors within the recipient. The process by which this occurred supports Legrand's observation that the use which the recipient makes of a transplant is significant. The existing common law was at best indifferent to a doctrine of mistake and at worst inimical to it. Both law and equity had devised systems of dealing with misapprehensions. As a generalisation, both bodies of law anticipated that parties themselves would provide for the consequences of a possible mistake. If a party did not so protect himself, law generally did not intervene. It might be that the contract was unenforceable on some other ground, but it generally resisted relief for mistake until into the twentieth century. Equity provided relief where the conscience of the parties would be affected, but even in the equitable courts there was a reluctance to intervene. The focus was upon the interpretation of the bargain rather than the conditions under which it had been entered. The common law sought to uphold bargains rather than to set them aside, unless fault could be attributed to one of the parties. In these circumstances the result was a voidable contract, a contract which could be avoided in certain circumstances at the option of the party not at fault. Because mistake was a concept which in many ways worked against the common law, the treatise writers gave their creation a restricted ambit of operation from the outset. The interaction with the existing system of law meant that the doctrine was not received in the same way in which it had been formulated. This process of interaction differs from Teubner's conception of a legal irritant because mistake did not unleash an evolutionary force within the common law. As we have seen, the acceptance of mistake was one in which the doctrine itself was recognised but then formulated in such narrow terms as to obviate its application in most instances. Coupled with a judicial reluctance to declare a contract void, it is unsurprising that in practical terms the doctrine is of little effect. Instead, English law preferred to set aside a contract where there had been fault, and a broad ambit was given to misrepresentation. In short, the common law has largely rejected mistake in substantive terms. Allison's conception of an unsuccessful cross-over from one legal system to another is the most applicable of these models. Transportation indicates a degree of success or perhaps some form of functionality; neither is present in relation to mistake. There was an acknowledgement that mistake formed a part of English contract law but there is little successful application of such a doctrine.

This examination of mistake in English contract law is something of a cautionary tale in the larger development of European private law. In so far as there appears to be a similarity of approach in recognising mistake as a vitiating factor in the common law and in the civilian law, this approach is more apparent than real. One must treat with a certain amount of scepticism claims of similarities. This study indicates, however, that English law has been, and is, receptive to new ideas. But it also indicates that care must be taken in how these ideas are received into the common law. There is only so much tinkering that can be done within an existing edifice and this has ramification for the reception of ideas and for the development of private law on a pan-European scale. The means by which mistake was copied by the treatise writers itself provides a model by which some of these problems can be overcome in any later transplants. Had the nineteenth-century treatise writers reflected not only on the material they copied but also on the underlying structure of their own legal system, many of the problems which arose in relation to mistake would have been averted. A significant impediment to the functioning of the doctrine has been that the principles enunciated are not really supported by the precedents produced.

Contractual Mistake in Modern Law

The twenty-first century opened with two significant mistake cases: *Great Peace Shipping Ltd v Tsavliris Salvage (International) Ltd*[63] and *Shogun Finance Ltd v Hudson.*[64] In applying different aspects of the doctrine of mistake to the cases before them, the Court of Appeal and then the House of Lords expressed dissatisfaction with the state of the law. In *Great Peace v Tsavliris*, the Court of Appeal was faced with the central yet enigmatic problem of mistake in contract, namely, the relationship between mistake in equity and mistake at common law. The consideration of the doctrine of mistake and the resolution of the problem need to be examined in light of the history of the doctrine to understand the nature of the confusion. It is suggested, with respect, that both might be have been different in light of this history, although the actual decision probably would have stood. The particular case was concerned with rescission, namely whether a contract to provide salvage-related services to a stricken vessel was either void at common law or voidable in equity because the parties mistakenly believed the two vessels to be closer than they were. It is unsurprising that such a difficult case arose in relation to rescission because, post fusion, this had been a difficult area. Lord Phillips MR gave the decision of the court and addressed four interrelated problems: first, what is the nature of the doctrine of mistake at common law?; second, was there an established doctrine of mistake in equity before *Bell* v *Lever Brothers*?; third, could

[63] [2002] EWCA Civ 1407, [2002] 3 WLR 1617.
[64] [2003] UKHL 62; [2004] 1 All ER 215.

such a doctrine stand with *Bell v Lever Brothers*?; and fourth, was the court bound to find that such a doctrine exists, having regard to *Solle v Butcher* and subsequent decisions? The central problem was the interrelationship between mistake in equity and mistake at common law. The relationship mattered because of the different results, void or voidable, that were said to attend these different forms of mistake. The great difficulties attendant in resolving these problems are eased when they are considered in light of the history of the doctrine.

Lord Phillips carefully examined the decisions of the Court of Appeal and the House of Lords in the case, reaching the conclusion that, although 'there was judicial dissent as to the result, there was general agreement as to the principles of law applicable'.[65] The reason for this agreement was that the judges had, to greater or lesser degrees, based their judgments on the principles to be found in a small number of contract treatises. Lord Phillips quoted Lord Atkin's judgment in *Bell v Lever Brothers* at length and included his observations that a mistake as to the quality of the subject matter of the contract would only affect mistake where it was both the mistake of both the parties and was 'as to the existence of some quality which makes the thing without the quality essentially different from the thing as it was believed to be'. The work of Pollock has disappeared in the twentieth century and with it the understanding that he had created this poorly defined and narrow test. Lord Phillips acknowledges that the precedents (*Couturier v Hastie*, *Kennedy*'s case and *Smith v Hughes*) employed by Lord Atkin to support this doctrine are slender. As Lord Phillips concluded, these authorities 'provided an insubstantial basis for his formulation of the test of common mistake in relation to the quality of the subject matter'.[66] Lord Phillips also observed that Lord Atkin himself thought that the true analysis of the cases lay elsewhere. Lord Atkin had undoubtedly relied upon these cases because these were the cases that Pollock himself had employed to define a fundamental error. Lord Atkin appeared not to have rejected the theory, although he clearly found disjunction between the ratio of the cases and the theory they were said to support; 70 years later the disjunction was still apparent. Lord Phillips characterised as an 'alternative basis' advanced by Lord Atkin to underline his mistake test that of an implied term which could also be applied to cases of frustration.[67] With respect, an examination of the development of the case indicates that Lord Atkin was actually rejecting this test because it did not advance the 'inquiry how to ascertain whether the contract does contain such a condition'.[68] In doing this, Lord Atkin was rejecting the argument advanced by Lever Brothers' counsel Sir John Simon. Although the report does not record a reference to Salmond and Winfield's treatise,[69] the argument was contained within that work. Salmond had written that

[65] [2002] EWCA Civ 1407, [2002] 3 WLR 1617 para 36.

[66] ibid, para 61.

[67] ibid, para 61.

[68] ibid, 225.

[69] The late Sir J Salmond and PH Winfield, *Principles of the Law of Contracts* (London, Sweet & Maxwell Ltd, 1927).

an *error in causa* (a misunderstanding which prevents the existence of any consensus *ad idem* and therefore of any contract) was immaterial and irrelevant to the validity of a contract except in two instances. One of these was where the fact erroneously believed to exist constituted an express or implied condition of the contract. If it did not exist then the contract was invalidated by the failure of the condition.[70] Lord Atkin rejected this argument. Salmond and Winfield gave no authorities by which to support the argument, which may have worked to diminish its attractiveness. It is Lord Atkin's rejection which prevented the later development of a link between mistake and frustration based on implied conditions; in making this rejection, he reached the conclusion that the device was artificial much more quickly than would occur in frustration.[71]

The influence of the treatises on Lord Atkin's decision are not apparent because he never mentioned them. Lord Phillips noted that Lord Atkin gave no examples of a case which was rendered void because of a mistake as to quality. The reason that Lord Atkin confined himself to narrow examples is because there were no cases at common law where mistake as to a quality, as such, had formed the basis of the decision that the contract was void. It was this very point which had disturbed Wright J in the High Court. Lord Phillips observed that *Bell v Lever Brothers* was difficult to reconcile with the earlier decision *Scott v Coulson.*[72] It is difficult to reconcile and it strengthens the argument that *Bell v Lever Brothers* was wrongly decided. It is no coincidence that Lord Warrington, who, as counsel in *Scott v Coulson*, represented the plaintiff in his suit to set aside the contract, was to dissent in *Bell v Lever Brothers. Scott v Coulson* was an equitable case in which the plaintiff sought rescission of the contract and not a declaration that the contract was void *ab initio.* Relief was granted because of the defendant purchaser's unconscionable conduct; knowing that the insured life, AT Death, was already dead, he allowed the sale to proceed. It is suggested, with respect, that what this difficulty indicates is that which has been obscured from modern eyes: the extent to which Lord Atkin was creating a doctrine of mistake based on the theories in the treatises.

Having concluded that the common law, in *Bell v Lever Brothers*, recognised that a common mistake as to a quality of the subject matter could render a contract void, Lord Phillips proceeded to consider whether there was an equitable power to set aside a contract binding in law on the ground of a common mistake. He considered this in light of Denning LJ's decision in *Solle v Butcher*, stating that either Denning LJ had purported to usurp the common law principle posited in *Bell v Lever Brothers* and replace it with a more flexible equitable principle or the equitable remedy of rescission he identified operated in instances where the contract was not void at law. Hitherto, Lord Phillips observed, the latter position had been accepted. The development of the doctrine suggests, with respect, that Denning LJ

[70] ibid, 191. The authors gave as an example a horse bought on the misapprehension it was sound, an example very close to one of Lord Atkin's: [1932] AC 161, 224.

[71] This did not occur until 1956: *Davis Contractors Ltd v Fareham Urban District Council* [1956] AC 696.

[72] [1903] 1 Ch 453; [1903] 2 Ch 249.

was actually attempting both these actions; the second was the means by which to reach the end posited by the first.

To determine whether there was an established doctrine of equity which allowed a contract to be set aside for mistake despite its validity at common law, Lord Phillips reviewed the work of contemporary writers[73] and the decision in *Cooper v Phibbs*.[74] Lord Phillips agreed with contemporary writers that the House of Lords in *Cooper v Phibbs* did not purport to lay down a broader doctrine of mistake in equity and, by implication, that there was no such equitable doctrine that allowed a contract to be set aside in equity where it was binding in law. It is suggested, with respect, that the contemporary search for a doctrine in equity is a modern question which would not have had relevance in the pre-fusion world. The modern approach is one which derives from the writings of the scientific treatises of the nineteenth century. The earlier approach was one in which elements of procedural and substantive law were integrated without resort to a doctrine as such. This study indicates that Chancery did not conceive of a doctrine as such; instead, it allowed equitable relief including rescission, if the circumstances of a particular case warranted such intervention. Chancery had been content to make decisions after a highly detailed factual examination; such orders were made more in accordance with the particular facts than with any doctrine as such. As we have seen, this relief was not granted on an arbitrary basis but in accordance with previous grants of relief. There was, however, no doctrine of mistake based on a failure of consensus. Equity intervened in these instances precisely because the agreement was binding at law: rescission was ordered to prevent one of the parties from obtaining an unconscientious advantage by reason of the mistake where the circumstances allowed the parties to be restored to their original positions. Rescission was unusual because it prevented a party from even the possibility of relief at law. The history of mistake makes clear that when Chancery had provided such relief the common law did not recognise mistake as a matter which would operate to render a contract void. The contract would, in all likelihood, be enforceable at common law, and it was for this reason that the parties sought equitable relief. Following fusion, when the treatise writers re-explained the basis for this equitable intervention in accordance with will theory and extended the doctrine more broadly; the effect of their actions was to create a doctrine which was not supported by precedent and which obscured the earlier practices.

The third problem addressed by the Court of Appeal in *Great Peace Shipping* was whether an equitable doctrine which permitted the rescission of a contract valid at law for mistake could stand with *Bell v Lever Brothers*. Lord Phillips observed that the arguments made before both the House of Lords and the Court of Appeal in the latter case did not distinguish between mistake in equity and mis-

[73] Notably R. Goff and G. Jones, *The Law of Restitution*, 5th edn (London, Sweet and Maxwell, 1998), and RP Meagher, WMC Gummow and JRF Lehane, *Equity Doctrines and Remedies*, 3rd edn (Sydney, Butterworths, 1992).

[74] Further assistance on the interpretation of this case was derived from P Matthews, 'A Note on *Cooper v Phibbs*' (1989) 105 LQR 599.

take at common law. There was no suggestion by Lever Brothers that a contract valid at law might be set aside in equity for mistake. Having heard these arguments, the majority did not recognise a distinction between mistake in equity and at common law. Lord Warrington's statement distinguishing the equitable practices was regarded as supporting the majority in this regard. The result was that:

> We do not find it conceivable that the House of Lords overlooked an equitable right in Lever Brothers to rescind the agreement, notwithstanding that the agreement was not void for mistake at common law. The jurisprudence established no such right. Lord Atkin's test for common mistake that avoided a contract, while narrow, broadly reflected the circumstances where equity had intervened to excuse performance of a contract assumed to be binding in law.[75]

It is suggested, with respect, that it was not only conceivable but that this is what occurred. As has been detailed in this study, the presentation of mistake by Lever Brothers was advanced as a desperate alternative, and their counsel did not consider the relevance of the equitable practices. The surviving records indicate that a certain confusion persisted until the end as to the nature of the mistake and why relief should be granted; this confusion was compounded by the nature of the pleadings and the conduct of the case. Lever Brothers' lawyers appear to have sought their guidance from the contract treatises of the day, and these did not distinguish between law and equity with regard to rescission. The distinction was further obscured because Lord Atkin formed his own decision with references to the treatises, notably Pollock's work, which sought to minimise the difference between law and equity. The reason that Lord Atkin found that common mistake avoided a contract in the same circumstances where equity had intervened was because that was the way Pollock had stated the circumstances. Lord Warrington's statement, taken in context, indicates that while equity might have set aside the termination contracts, it would not necessarily have viewed them as void at law.

The final problem addressed by the Court of Appeal in *Great Peace Shipping v Tsavliris* was the effect of *Solle v Butcher*. Because it had already been decided that *Cooper v Phibbs* either demonstrated or created an equitable jurisdiction to grant rescission and that, even if it did, the House of Lords in *Bell v Lever Brothers* delimited the earlier case by holding that it was void at common law, the only logical conclusion was that *Solle v Butcher* had been decided without the equitable basis Denning LJ claimed for it. The remaining rationale for his decision was, thus, that he sought to 'outflank' *Bell v Lever Brothers*. As the preceding chapter indicates, there was a policy motivation behind Denning LJ's judgment, although this is more understandable at a point at which the House of Lords could not reverse its own decision. The criticism which attended the decision in *Bell v Lever Brothers* and the paucity of cases after it was decided indicate that Denning LJ was not alone in his disapproval of the narrow, possibly non-existent, ambit accorded to mistake. If mistake was not operative in *Bell v Lever Brothers* case it was difficult to envisage circumstances in which it would operate. The underlying question to be

[75] [2002] EWCA Civ 1407, [2002] 3 WLR 1617, [2003] QB 679, 715–16, per Lord Phillips.

addressed is whether or not equity provided the jurisdiction which Denning LJ claimed for it. This question is complicated because, as we have seen, Denning LJ's account of the doctrine of mistake is both partial and only partly correct when viewed from a historical perspective. While the Rent Acts would have been curious creatures to a Court of Chancery, it is clear from their cases concerned with the Statute of Frauds that Chancery would not allow a statute to prevail over a mistake and allow an unconscientious result. Would Butcher's mistake have been the sort that equity would intervene in? Butcher's mistake was brought about by Solle's representations. While these may not have been actionable as misrepresentations, and a majority at the Court of Appeal would not have intervened on this basis, they would have been enough to cause a court to assist Butcher. Although Solle may not have been aware of the mistake when they contracted, a court would have sought to prevent him from an unjust benefit conferred solely by reason of a mistake created by his misrepresentation. The facts of the case are not dissimilar to those in *Paget v Marshall* or *Garrard v Frankel* or even *Cooper v Phibbs.* On balance, it is likely that a court of equity would have intervened to provide relief. If English law wishes to end the application of *Solle v Butcher* it must do so on the grounds of legal policy and not on precedent.

The question of why the doctrine in *Solle v Butcher* did not succeed in changing the conceptions of mistake awaits comprehensive treatment. The development of mistake points to a number of factors. Mistake in equity operated in particular contexts and generally in circumstances where the terms of the contract between the parties limited its potential role. Combined with this was the natural reluctance of courts to set aside apparent contracts in absence of fault. As Lord Phillips observed, the parameters of this jurisdiction were not fully developed by Denning LJ and this cannot have increased the confidence of counsel concerned to bring their case within it. English contract law contains a very broad doctrine of misrepresentation, a breadth which was increased by the development of negligent misstatement in *Hedley Byrne v Heller*[76] and further expanded with the enactment of the Misrepresentation Act 1967. The requirements of the Misrepresentation Act 1967 that the maker of a statement had reasonable grounds to believe that it was true up to the time of contracting meant that generally only a mistake created by a third party would fall within a doctrine of mistake.

This takes us to our second twenty-first-century case. In *Shogun Finance v Hudson* the House of Lords was faced with facts found more commonly in contract tutorials than appellate courts. The case concerned a hire purchase agreement entered into between the finance company and a rogue pretending to be Patel. The issue was whether the contract was void or voidable. While their Lordships were concerned to some extent with issues of statutory construction,[77] the appeal turned on the application of the mistake of identity cases to the case. It is not surprising given the contradictory state of the case law that such a simple

[76] [1964] AC 465.
[77] Hire Purchase Act 1964, s 27.

deception gave rise to five separate reasons for judgment and that their Lordships were divided as to the result. All expressed degrees of dissatisfaction with the state of the law.[78] The central difficulty was that their Lordships were faced with contradictory results in the decided cases. The application of a doctrine of mistake of identity, as established by *Cundy v Lindsay*, meant that the agreement was void; if, however, there was no mistake as to identity because the hire purchase firm meant to deal with the person present before the motor dealer, the contract was voidable for fraud because of *Phillips v Brooks.*[79] The legal problem was exacerbated because of the factual issue of whether or not the motor dealer acted as the agent for the finance company. The cases appeared to establish that the method by which the rogue perpetrated his deception could determine whether the agreement was void or voidable and, therefore, whether or not the third party defendant had title to the car or not. All their Lordships accepted that if the contract was negotiated at a distance, *Cundy v Lindsay* was applicable and the contract would be void. If, however, the contract was negotiated face to face, a presumption arose that Shogun intended to deal with the person before them and the contract was only voidable. It was on this point that their Lordships were divided; the majority applied *Cundy v Lindsay* and found the contract void, while the dissenting Law Lords would have overturned *Cundy v Lindsay*, and with it the newly named 'face-to-face presumption', and find the contract voidable for fraud. For Lord Nicholls and Lord Millett, neat distinctions in the case law were substantively artificial and illogical, and dangerous in practice. *Cundy v Lindsay* was 'the principal obstacle which has prevented the courts from rationalising this branch of the law',[80] and a case in which the reasoning was unsound because of its subjective approach to contractual formation.[81] Although textbook writers treated the case as one of unilateral mistake, this was not the basis upon which it was decided.[82] Lord Nicholls stated that 'if the law of contract is to be coherent and rescued from its present unsatisfactory and unprincipled state' it would be best to overrule *Cundy v Lindsay* and give preference to *Phillips v Brooks.* Their Lordships reached this decision largely by looking forward at the development of the law and by considering the legal policy as to which innocent party should more logically bear the risk of the fraud.

The history of the development of mistake of identity in English contract law largely supports the view of the dissenting Law Lords in their unease with *Cundy v Lindsay.* In deciding the case, their Lordships were faced with a number of contradictory cases which presented illogical distinctions which had arisen from the later contortions of judges and jurists who sought to explain the cases in such a way as to advance a coherent principle. The history of mistake of identity explains that there was no coherent principle which could be advanced on the basis of the

[78] Per Lord Nicholls, [2003] UKHL 62; [2004] 1 All ER 215, 219; by implication, per Lord Hobhouse, ibid, 233; per Lord Millett, ibid, 233–36; per Lord Phillips, ibid, 262; and per Lord Walker, 263.

[79] [1919] 2 KB 243.

[80] [2003] UKHL 62; [2004] 1 All ER 215, 242, per Lord Millett.

[81] ibid, 246, per Lord Millett.

[82] ibid.

cases. In the first half of the nineteenth century, courts regarded such contracts as voidable rather than void. This changed by the 1850s, and *Hardman v Booth*, with the Larceny Act 1861 in the background, was decided in accordance with the changed result that such contracts were void. The complications presented by the criminal law were a factor in *Cundy v Lindsay*, both in the relationship between the offence and the contract—the belief that if the rogue was convicted of obtaining goods by false pretences, then the contract could not be good—and in the concern about the ultimate ownership of the goods. The House of Lords in *Cundy v Lindsay* viewed the case as indistinguishable from *Hardman v Booth*, which Benjamin had explained in his treatise as a mistake of identity. Although the Law Lords in *Cundy v Lindsay* did not base their decision on a doctrine of mistake,[83] the influence is clearly there. This was, in turn, reincorporated by treatise writers as support for the doctrine they had earlier advanced. Changes within the criminal law, notably the passing of the Sale of Goods Act 1893 and the removal of an automatic revesting of property, led courts in later cases to different results. In *King's Norton Metal v Edridge* and *Phillips v Brooks* the courts correctly separated fraud and mistake. In short, the history of the development of this area of law indicates that *Cundy v Lindsay* is an unreliable precedent, designed to meet needs no longer pressing in English law. It also indicates that the decision that these sorts of cases were uniquely void for a mistake of identity was not of long standing in English law. The distinction between contracting at a distance by correspondence, in which the owner intended to deal with a particular person, and where the parties dealt with each other face to face was a distinction introduced to justify decisions made on other grounds. The distinction arose as a result of the inability of later courts to either overturn or distinguish *Cundy v Lindsay* on more satisfactory grounds. Oddly, the distinction overlooks the fact that the basis of *Cundy v Lindsay* lay in *Hardman v Booth*—which was a fraud practised face to face. The underlying question as to whether or not Pothier's considerations formed a part of English law is that they have formed a useful tool or a convenient rationalisation for English judges from *Boulton v Jones* onwards, but they have never formed the basis of any of these decisions.

A final remark: English contract law recognises a doctrine of mistake, constructed from various cases concerned with mistakes, but the form of the doctrine is full of its own mistakes. The recognition of the doctrine came about by mistake. The problem which remains is how to rectify this mistake.

[83] A point noted by Lord Millett, who observed it was textbook writers and not the Law Lords in the case who treated it as an example of a unilateral mistake: ibid, 242.

INDEX

Index